The Arts Good Study Guide

Ellie Chambers and Andrew Northedge

Details of this and other Open University publications can be obtained from the Student Registration and Enquiry Service, The Open University, PO Box 197, Milton Keynes MK7 6BJ, United Kingdom: tel. +44 (0)845 300 60 90, email general-enquiries@open.ac.uk

Alternatively, you may visit the Open University website at http://www.open.ac.uk where you can learn more about the wide range of courses and packs offered at all levels by The Open University.

To purchase a selection of Open University course materials visit http://www.ouw.co.uk, or contact Open University Worldwide, Walton Hall, Milton Keynes MK7 6AA, United Kingdom for a brochure. tel. +44 (0)1908 858793; fax +44 (0)1908 858787; email ouw-customer-services@open.ac.uk

The Open University
Walton Hall, Milton Keynes
MK7 6AA

First published 1997. Second edition 2008.

Edited and designed by The Open University.

Typeset in India by Alden Prepress Services, Chennai.

Printed and bound in Malta by Gutenberg Press Limited

ISBN 978 0 7492 1708 2

2.1

CONTENTS

Preface   vii

Acknowledgements   xii

PART 1 Studying intelligently

CHAPTER 1
Investing in yourself   3

1.1   Who this book is for   3
1.2   How this book works   4
1.3   Investing in your development   6
1.4   The challenge of studying   7
1.5   Becoming a skilful student   12
1.6   Thinking about how you learn   13
1.7   Being a reflective learner   14
1.8   Investing in Information Technology   16
1.9   Investing in your future   24
References   25

CHAPTER 2
Taking control of your studies   26

2.1   Taking responsibility for your own learning   26
2.2   Managing your work   29
2.3   Managing time   32
2.4   Managing your study circumstances   38
2.5   Managing your morale   41
2.6   Being a successful self-manager   44
References   45

CHAPTER 3
Understanding how you learn   46

3.1   Developing ideas about learning   46
3.2   What does learning mean?   48
3.3   Why do they write like that?   52
3.4   Reading, listening, speaking and writing   58
3.5   Becoming knowledgeable   65
Reference   66

PART 2 The essential skills

CHAPTER 4
Reading   69

4.1   Reading is easy, isn't it?   69
4.2   The experience of reading   69
4.3   Getting round obstacles   73
4.4   How quickly should you read?   82
4.5   Reading actively   86
4.6   Reading critically   90
4.7   Reading and learning   92
References   93

CHAPTER 5
Making notes   94

5.1   Thinking on paper   94
5.2   Capturing knowledge   95
5.3   Supporting your memory   106
5.4   Organising knowledge   111
5.5   Supporting creativity   115
5.6   Making notes strategically   117
Reference   118

CHAPTER 6
Learning through talk   119

6.1   Talk in higher learning   119
6.2   Learning through group discussion   120
6.3   Making a presentation   138
6.4   Group visits   144
6.5   Listening to talk   145
References   151

CHAPTER 7
Writing essays   152

7.1   Getting to grips with writing   152
7.2   What are you meant to write?   155
7.3   The significance of titles   159
7.4   Essay structure   160
7.5   Presenting an argument   163
7.6   Making your case convincing   171
7.7   'Proper' English   175
7.8   Writing style and audience   182

7.9   What is a good essay?   186
7.10 Review   188

CHAPTER 8
Managing the writing process   **190**
8.1   The challenge of writing   190
8.2   Stages in the writing process   191
8.3   Expressing ideas in writing   209
8.4   Making your essay flow   213
8.5   The experience of writing   217
8.6   Summaries   222
Reference   223

CHAPTER 9
Processes of study in the arts and humanities   **224**
9.1   The arts and humanities   224
9.2   Becoming familiar with the text   230
9.3   Approaching analysis   233
9.4   Interpreting meanings   239
9.5   Evaluation   247
9.6   Communicating your ideas   253
9.7   Beliefs and theories   259
References   262

CHAPTER 10
Online research and project work   **263**
10.1 A world of information at your fingertips   263
10.2 Finding information   264
10.3 Finding academic material   267
10.4 Misuse of online data   270
10.5 Using research in project work   272
10.6 Doing project work   278
References   283

CHAPTER 11
Preparing for examinations   **284**
11.1 The positive side of exams   284
11.2 Myths about exams   285
11.3 What to avoid   290
11.4 Revising for exams   293

11.5	Getting 'geared-up' just before the exam	301
11.6	Working out your tactics for the exam	304
11.7	Will you do yourself justice in the exam?	309

Postscript 310

Appendix 311

Index 315

PREFACE

This second edition of *The Arts Good Study Guide* is much more than an update of the original. The book has not only been rethought and rewritten in many places, but also supplemented. It includes new chapters, and parts of chapters, notably on computer-aided study. We have taken the opportunity not only to bring the book up to date, ten years on, but also to strengthen it and widen its relevance. It is, again, written in the belief that studying is one of the most interesting and satisfying things we can do – and that learning how to study well is among the most challenging.

Purposes

The Arts Good Study Guide retains its primary purpose as a guide for students of arts and humanities subjects (though not primarily for those studying fine or performance arts); for those who have a serious interest in the long-term development of their learning and study skills. It is not a source of quick fixes and instant remedies. It assumes a willingness to invest time in working on exercises and reflecting on them. It is a thoughtful, theoretically grounded exploration of the nature of studying. At the same time, it is a practical guide to reflective experimentation with study techniques, drawing as it does on many years of exploring these skills with students.

Changes

The first edition of *The Arts Good Study Guide* reached an audience far broader than the part-time, adult, distance-learning students for whom it was written. Consequently, this new edition has been recast to address the needs of *all students* aspiring to study beyond school level. It has also been restructured to reflect the sweeping changes in university study over the past decade. Thus it now has *four more chapters* than before, and is organised in *two parts*. However, the basic strategies for studying and the underlying assumptions about the nature of learning remain.

Part I: Studying intelligently
The first part of *The Arts Good Study Guide* addresses the broad strategic aspects of successful study and consists of three chapters. These chapters address one of the key changes of the past decade, the *relocation of study skills* from their former status on the periphery of higher education, as 'remedial' activities for beginners, to the *mainstream* under the new label 'learning skills'. Developing skills as a learner is now recognised as essential preparation for life in the twenty-first century. This is reflected in the title of Chapter 1, 'Investing in yourself'. These skills are not simply practical but are also *strategic*, requiring a capacity for self-management: hence Chapter 2, 'Taking control of your studies'. They are also *reflective* skills, which depend on self-knowledge, self-analysis and an understanding of the learning process: thus Chapter 3, 'Understanding how you learn'. This chapter includes an introduction to the principles of critical-analytical reading and writing,

reflecting growing recognition of the importance of supported entry into academic discourse for an increasingly diverse student body.

The other key change of recent times is the revolution in study practices brought about by *computing* and *the internet*. This is addressed right from the start of the book, in Chapter 1 Section 1.8: 'Investing in Information Technology'. Students are often aware of only a few of the many ways in which a computer can be used to support their studies; this section encourages exploration and experiment. Parts of the rest of the book have also been reworked to reflect changes to basic study activities brought about by word-processing, global access to online information, electronic information storage, and the like.

Part 2: The essential skills

The second part of the book gets down to the practical business of developing skills in the core activities of studying. As in the original edition, readers are asked to undertake genuine study activities, most of them based on a single text, '"On the Town": Women in Augustan England', by Joyce Ellis (1995). So the content of the original chapters generally remains, but 'Making notes' has been separated off from 'Reading' to give both processes wider relevance and to allow exploration of electronic note making. And the chapter formerly entitled 'Different ways of studying' has been recast as 'Learning through talk', including extensive new material on online group discussions and making presentations.

The two chapters on writing remain the longest and perhaps the most important, since acquisition of an academic writing voice and the abilities to assemble material and present it in the form of an argument are in many ways the culmination of the transition into competent academic practice. Retitled 'Writing essays' and 'Managing the writing process', they retain the same broad division into the 'what' and 'how' of academic writing. However, the first has been reorganised to make the treatment more transparent and accessible.

The chapter 'Processes of study in the arts and humanities' is reworked using a poem by Robert Frost as the basis of discussion. There follows a new chapter, 'Online research and project work' which introduces the basics of searching for pictures online. The final chapter, 'Preparing for examinations', is the least changed, though again there is reworking.

Notes

Level

We have assumed that many readers will be starting studies at post-school level. However, students in the later years of schooling may find the book useful preparation for the switch to higher level studies. Equally, students who have progressed beyond the entry stages of a degree will find much to reflect on.

Assumptions about computing

We have assumed that all readers will have at least some access to a computer and to the internet. Many will already be using a computer for routine study tasks, while others will be looking for advice on ways in which they might profitably switch to computer-based working.

Terms used

Because the original *Arts Good Study Guide* was used in schools, colleges and campus universities, we have dropped the use of specific Open University terminology and adopted more general terms. However, one or two are somewhat awkward. For example, we have largely avoided the term 'lecturer' on account of its narrow connotations, even though it is the typical descriptor of the post in higher education. And we have used 'tutor' mainly in the context of discussion groups because its usage varies between institutions. Instead, we have tended to use 'teacher' throughout.

Personal acknowledgements

The first edition of this book benefited enormously from the comments of Open University colleagues and students, and the same is true of the second edition. So it is important that we include here those who contributed originally as well as those who contributed to the new edition.

First edition

Many people contributed to the writing and production of the original book. As part of our preparation, we asked some students to volunteer their work. We are very grateful to them, and to their tutors. Grateful thanks also to Blanche Gaskell and Vina Quinn-Searle who, as student assessors, gave us their comments on draft chapters. Members of the OU Arts Faculty's A103 course team offered helpful advice or assistance: especially Cicely Havely (Chair), and also Colin Cunningham, Julie Dickens, Lorna Hardwick, Trevor Herbert, Liz Manning, Derek Matravers, Jim Moore, Nora Tomlinson, Linda Walsh, Nigel Warburton and Roberta Wood. So too did colleagues in the School (now Faculty) of Health and Social Care, host to the access course *Living Arts*: Martin Robb (Chair), Margaret Allott and Stella Warriker, with secretarial support from Val O'Connor. Other colleagues in the OU who gave us their time and ideas include: Tim Benton and Hilary Robertson (Arts Faculty); Ann Brechin and Tony Walton (School of Health and Social Care); Nicola Durbridge, Magnus John, Jan Rae, Mary Thorpe and Olwyn Wilson (Institute of Educational Technology); Giles Clark (Book Trade Department); Tony Coulson (Library); Simon Rae (Academic Computing Service). Thank you to Sîan Lewis, who designed the book. Thanks also to our friend Gill Parsons, then of North Hertfordshire College, for her help with Chapter 6.

Special thanks to Nora Tomlinson, who read every word and made many insightful, detailed suggestions for improvements; to Margaret Allott for her efficient organisation of the project and friendly support; and to Clive Baldwin for his skill and patience as editor of the book.

Second edition

For this new edition we are indebted to members of the OU Arts Faculty's AA100 Course Team for their comments on draft chapters, especially Richard Brown, Debbie Brunton, Jessica Davies, Anne Laurence, Charlotte Stevens, Carolyn Price; and to Carol Green and Yvette Purdy (Arts Course Management) for their unfailing helpfulness and support. Grateful thanks go to Gillian Farnen and Clare Spencer, OU Arts Associate Lecturers, for their careful reading and insightful comments on all the draft chapters. Our thanks too to colleagues in the OU Institute of Educational Technology who gave their support: Peter Knight, Wendy Morgan and John Pettit. And we are grateful to the book production team: Emma Wheeler (Media Project Manager), Richard Jones (Editorial Media Developer), Peter Heatherington (Graphics Media Developer), Hannah Parish (Media Assistant), Liam Baldwin (Visual Resources Officer), and Mahruk Bailey (Assistant Project Manager, OU Worldwide). Thanks also to Sheree Kaur, Sharon Monie, David Sheppard and Kristoff VanLeeuwen.

Particular thanks to our colleagues Jessica Davies, Trevor Herbert, Audrey Linkman, Simon Rae and Derek Sheills for their various contributions to the book (acknowledged in footnotes).

We are also grateful to those students who completed a questionnaire asking for their reflections on the learning process or who agreed to allow quotation from their online messages. (Note that the names which appear in the book are fictional). The students who contributed in one way or another are: Billy Anderson, Lorna Archibald, Shirley Bain, Gillian Brewin, Shona Brydson, Jacqui Campbell, Janice Clerk, Jo Chandler, Roseann Cooper, Lesley Dickinson, Ceri Edwards, Ceri Evans, Suzie Eaton, Carol Ferguson, Nicky Gane, Julie Gibbins, Gwyneth Girling, Simon Harris-Dack, Melanie Harvey, Hayley Hill, Gillian Howie, Patricia Jordan, Matthew Lane, Nicola Lloyd, Pauline Knox, Tracy Mogridge, Shirley Moody, Sophie Nichol, Charlotte Northedge, Laura Northedge, Shona Paterson, Tracy Reynolds, Angela Parker, Jan Reis, Janie Richter, Chris Robinson, Kelda Sinclair, Tina Smith, David Shortall, Diane Sloey, Peter Staffell, Ann-Marie Stewart, Deirdre Stewart, Mandy Sutch, Stella Taylor, Matthew Thompson, Jennie Tomlinson, Laura Ward, Ruth Webb, Gail White, Julie Williams, Pepe Wilson and Correne Witchard.

Finally, we are grateful for permission to use Joyce Ellis's article as a basis for study exercises in this and the original book.

The authors

Ellie Chambers is Professor of Humanities Higher Education in the OU Institute of Educational Technology; Andrew Northedge is Professor of Learning and Teaching in Higher Education in its Faculty of Health and Social Care. The book is based on their long experience of teaching, of researching into study processes and discussing them with students. Andrew Northedge first wrote *The Good Study Guide*, with students of the Social Sciences in mind. With his help, Ellie Chambers adapted the book for arts and humanities students; in this second edition, she has written chapters 9 and 10 in their entirety. Although we are joint authors, for convenience we use the singular, 'I', throughout the book.

Student voices

You will see quotations from students scattered about the book. These are largely taken from Open University internet chat areas, with the permission of the students. They are intended to offer informal reflection and light relief. They are simply dropped in where relevant and signalled by large quotation marks. The contributors are among those acknowledged above.

ACKNOWLEDGEMENTS

Grateful acknowledgement is made to the following sources for permission to reproduce material within this book.

Text

'Stopping by Woods on a Snowy Evening' from *The Poetry of Robert Frost* edited by Edward Connery Lathem, published by Jonathan Cape. Reprinted by permission of The Random House Group Ltd. and Henry Holt and Company.

Ellis, J. (1995) '"On the Town": Women in Augustan England', *History Today*, Vol. 45, no. 12, pp. 20–7, History Today Ltd.

Figures

Figure 1.2: 'Kolb's reflective learning cycle, adapted for study skills' [online] Smith, M. K. (2001) 'David A Kolb on experiential learning', the encyclopaedia of informal education, http://www.infed.org/b-explrn.htm (accessed 31 August 2007).

Figure 1.3: Making Sentences game [online], BBC Skillswise: Words, http://www.bbc.co.uk/skillswise/words/grammar/interestsentences/compoundsentences/ (accessed 31 August 2007).

Figure 4.1: Sample electronic 'concept card' [online], Pindersoft (2007), CardFile Pegasus, http://www.pindersoft.com/index.htm (accessed 31 August 2007).

Figure 10.4: An ordinary search [online], Google, http://www.google.co.uk (accessed 31 August 2007).

Figure 10.5: An advanced search [online], Google Scholar, http://scholar.google.com (accessed 31 August 2007).

Figure 10.6: Intute gateway [online], Intute: Arts and Humanities, http://www.inture.ac.uk/artsandhumanities (accessed 31 August 2007).

PART I
Studying intelligently

CHAPTER 1
Investing in yourself

Welcome to *The Arts Good Study Guide*. This is a book of advice, practical exercises and tips to help you develop your study skills and get the most you can from your studies: better results, a greater sense of personal achievement and more enjoyment.

1.1 Who this book is for

This book is designed for students of the arts and humanities. If you really enjoy reading novels, looking closely at paintings or listening to music, or if you are fascinated by a particular time and place (such as Classical Greece, Renaissance Italy, Victorian or Modern Britain) and you want to know more about how to study these subjects, then the book is for you.

You may be just starting out on higher level studies, or part way through a degree and looking to boost your performance. The book will be just as helpful whether you are studying:

- full time or part time
- on campus or by distance learning
- having recently left school, or after a long break away from study.

But why should you need a study skills book?

Activity 1.1 Why should you read this book?

Do any of the following thoughts hover in your mind?

Tick any boxes that apply.

1 With so much to study already, I doubt I can spare the time for a book like this. □

2 I'm not sure I need to bother with study skills. I have come through years of schooling. Why read about it now? □

3 I already have my own ways of studying and I don't enjoy being told what to do. □

4 I think I need a few hints and tips, not a whole book. □

5 I find it easier to get advice from people than from books. □

1 I doubt I can spare the time for a book like this ...
A fair point. This is a chunky book and there always seems to be more to study than there is time for. But you will certainly waste a lot of time if you don't study effectively. Reading this book will actually save time, by helping you make better use of it. You don't need to drop everything right now and read the book from cover to cover. Skills take time to develop. Just set yourself to read a chapter every three or four weeks, in amongst your other studies.

2   I'm not sure I need to bother with study skills ...

Perhaps you think study skills are for beginners, but studying never becomes easy. There are always new challenges and your skills can always be improved. Successful students recognise the importance of continuing to develop and refine their skills.

3   I already have my own ways of studying ...

A good thought. It is right to feel attached to your ways of doing things. But you don't need to commit yourself to remaining forever locked into the same practices. Why not try new approaches? This book will not tell you what to do. It will help you to review what you already do and weigh up alternative strategies. You remain in control.

4   I think I need a few hints and tips, not a whole book

Hints and tips are very helpful, and there are plenty in this book, but they are not enough. If you really want to get ahead in your studies, you need insight into the way your mind works together with flexible strategies for getting the most from all kinds of learning opportunities. To achieve this you need to invest small chunks of 'quality time' over a fairly long period. You will not understand your own learning overnight. That is where the book will help. It offers exercises and discussion within a coherent overall approach to thinking about study. The exercises will help you work out ways of meeting immediate challenges, but the understandings you develop will help you take control of your learning throughout your life.

5   I find it easier to get advice from people than from books

Advice from teachers and other students is excellent for building up your confidence and giving you new ideas to try out, but studying at a higher level is often a solitary business. Working on your own with a study skills book helps you build up your capacity for this independent learning.

Key points

Why read this book?

- It will help you make better use of your study time.
- It offers much more than handy hints and tips; it will help you to understand how you learn and build up your capacity for independent study.
- Whether you are an experienced student or a beginner, this book will build on your existing skills and insights.

1.2   How this book works

The book is in two parts. Part 1 considers studying as a whole and how to think your way into it. Part 2 focuses on how to develop your skills by engaging you in specific study tasks.

Part 1: Studying intelligently

To be a successful student you must constantly use your intelligence. You must approach your studies strategically and systematically. This first chapter of the book is about recognising the value of investing significant time and effort in developing your study skills, including use of a computer. Chapter 2 'Taking control of your studies' then discusses how to get yourself organised so that you can manage your studies effectively. Chapter 3 'Understanding how you learn' explores the nature of learning at university level, to help you better understand what it is you are trying to achieve.

Part 2: The essential skills

Your courses involve a lot of reading, discussion, and essay writing. Part 2 of the book – necessarily longer and more detailed – explores the essential skills you will need to study successfully in arts subjects. These skills include:

- Reading secondary sources (Chapter 4)
- Making notes to help you understand and remember (Chapter 5)
- Listening to lectures (Chapter 6)
- Talking in seminars, workshops and online (Chapter 6)
- Writing essays (Chapters 7 and 8)
- Understanding processes of study in the arts and humanities (Chapter 9)
- Researching online and for project work (Chapter 10)
- Preparing for exams (Chapter 11).

1.2.1 Ways of using the book

This is not a book to read from cover to cover in a single sweep. You should dip into it and select what you need. Begin it now, but keep coming back to it as your studies proceed. The book is designed to be used in a variety of ways.

- If you want to work seriously on developing skills in a particular study area, then set aside an hour or two to work carefully through a chapter, doing all the activities in full.
- If you want to review a particular skill area (say, note making or preparing an essay), skim through the relevant chapter to get a general overview from the headings and pick up ideas from the boxes and key points lists.
- If you need advice on a specific point, such as avoiding plagiarism or preparing slides for a presentation, look it up in the book's index and read just a paragraph or two.

The book is intended to be easy to use whichever way you choose, with a detailed contents list at the beginning, a comprehensive index at the end, and topic boxes, key points lists, and references throughout.

1.2.2 Making an investment in yourself

If you *only* 'dip in' for tips, however, you will miss the best of the book. Tips often sound like little more than common sense, whereas when we study the difficulty is putting principles into practice. By far the best way to learn study skills is to start from practice and then think about the principles. For this reason, the chapters in Part 2 are based on *real study tasks* and *detailed practical activities*. You are invited to immerse yourself in them, then reflect and consider what wider conclusions you can draw. This approach is relatively time consuming but it produces significant benefits. Think of it as an investment in yourself and in your future as an independent learner.

The activities in three of the chapters in Part 2 are based on a short article, "'On the Town': Women in Augustan England' by Joyce Ellis (1995), which you will find at the end of the book. You are invited to study this article in Chapter 4, to make notes on it in Chapter 5, and to read some short essays about it in Chapter 7. *To get the full benefit of these key chapters you will need to invest an hour or so in reading the article and doing the accompanying activities.*

Once you have invested time in getting to know the book, you will be able to keep returning to it over the years. Because of the study tasks you are engaged in, some ideas will make sense right away. Others will strike you more forcefully as you become a more accomplished student. And some are basic truths about learning that you may need to return to periodically throughout your studies to understand again at a new level.

> ### Key points
>
> - When you face an immediate study challenge skim through the book to find the advice you need. Use the book's index.
> - Invest an hour or so in yourself from time to time by working seriously on one of the chapters.
> - Keep referring to the book as you progress through your studies, using it as a 'companion' or guide.
> - Occasionally return to chapters you have read, to remind yourself of what you learned and to rethink your strategies.

1.3 Investing in your development

In the past, education was associated with childhood. Most people expected to leave studying behind them when they entered adult life. Now, however, in a rapidly changing world, none of us can afford to assume that we have finished with learning. Employers too must keep educating and training their workforces. We are all expected to be lifelong learners, continually adapting to change by acquiring new skills and new ways of thinking. A rather daunting prospect perhaps, but also exciting.

From this perspective, your present studies are just one phase within a lifelong project of maintaining your competence as an educated person in the twenty-first century. By taking a course you are investing time and money in your future. But it is important to get a good return; you cannot afford to stumble into your studies hoping for the best. You need a clear eye on *what* you are trying to achieve and *how*. In short, you need well-developed learning skills.

Box 1.1   Key skills

The UK government has, in collaboration with employers, identified certain 'key skills' that all of us are said to need:

1   Communication

2   Application of number

3   Information technology

4   Working with others

5   Problem solving

6   Improving own learning and performance

'Key skills are a range of essential skills that underpin success in education, employment, lifelong learning and personal development.' (Department for Education and Skills [DFES], 2004)

'In a world that requires people to respond to and anticipate change, these skills are essential to remaining employable.' (Qualifications and Curriculum Authority [QCA], 2000)

This book offers plenty of support with most of these skills.

Communication skills are addressed in Chapter 4, on reading, Chapter 5 on making notes, Chapter 6, on listening and discussing (which also contributes to *working with others*), and Chapters 7 and 8 on writing.

Information technology is specifically addressed in this chapter and in Chapter 10, but it crops up throughout the book.

Improving own learning, meanwhile, is what the whole book is about.

Key points

■   Invest in your study skills. In a world in which you need to keep learning throughout your life, developing your study skills is one of the most valuable investments you can make.

■   Invest time in your development. The time spent on this book will be as valuable to you as the time spent on your course work.

1.4   The challenge of studying

But why so much fuss about the skills involved in studying? Surely studying is a fairly straightforward activity – you read books, listen to lectures, attend seminars or talk online, and write essays. Where's the problem? Well, perhaps it's not so simple ...

Jan put her pen down with a sigh and looked at the clock again. It was now 8.17. She had started three-quarters of an hour ago and couldn't believe she was still only on page two.

Have to be up early tomorrow – can't afford to be too late tonight. Perhaps I'll make a cup of coffee and really concentrate until 9.30 when Don gets back. Oh, and then Phil's coming over for a drink. I've got that other really long chapter to read by Thursday too. And Wednesday night's out because of squash.

She looked at her note pad. The title of the article was written neatly across the top. The rest was blank. They'd said you should make notes as you read.

Right. 'Sum up the main points of the article'. But what are the main points ...? I can't even work out what it's saying half the time. It's really irritating the way they just assume you know things you've never even heard of. And I might get on faster if I didn't have to keep stopping to look up every second word. Who on earth is this written for? Not me, that's for sure. I really liked the look of this article – I thought it was going to be interesting ... I'd better just tidy up the table a bit I think.

There was a wail from upstairs. One of the children...

She made another cup of coffee and flopped into the chair again.

Only half an hour left now. Must concentrate. I'll go back to the top of the page – on second thoughts, I may as well start all over again and really try to get some notes down this time since I can't remember a word of it. Will I ever be able to remember anything I read? I wonder why Charlie keeps waking up like that. I hope there's nothing wrong with him ... Oh I'm so tired. This is so boring. Every sentence is a battle. It's too late to get anywhere with it now. I'll just put my feet up for a bit, watch the news ...

Meanwhile, in another room a few streets away ...

Nathan screwed up yet another sheet of paper and aimed it at the waste-paper basket. He stared blankly at his screen. What now? He had made half a dozen starts and hadn't once reached the end of the paragraph before crumpling up the printed page in disgust.

How can I be stuck when I've hardly started? How long is this whole thing going to take? 'Did eighteenth-century women migrate to towns mainly because of the attractions of the towns, or mainly to escape from life in the countryside?' How should I know? Even these historians don't seem to be able to make up their minds. What if I said it was a bit of both, probably. Or maybe I'll just take a few sentences from here and there and change the words around a bit – then at least they can't say I've got it wrong. But the tutor said write in your own words ...

As his mind wandered back to the tutorial he winced. Why hadn't he just kept quiet, like he'd meant to? He hadn't really understood what they were going on about – but the tutor seemed so keen for everyone to join in. By the time he'd wound himself up to say something things had moved on. He couldn't get a word in edgeways. But then the tutor had looked straight at him and he'd just blurted it out anyway. He'd actually been shaking and feeling hot as he spoke. Ridiculous at his age. They had pretended to 'use' what he'd said as they carried on the discussion, but he knew he'd made a complete fool of himself. How could he face going back?

Anyway, I didn't get much out of it – no notes. In fact I can hardly remember a thing that was said. I'll give it a miss next week. Or will the tutor be offended if I don't turn up? ... Oh well, must get back to this wretched essay. I just don't know where to start. Perhaps I'll rescue some of the bits I wrote before and try to sort of cobble them together. No. I can't bear to look at them again. Why am I doing this to myself?

Is studying really as bad as all that? Surely not. But sometimes things do look pretty bleak. Although Jan and Nathan are fictitious, their problems are real enough – and not just among new students or 'weak' students. They are general problems that all students face: problems of struggling to *understand*, of struggling to *write*, of *managing time*, of *completing a task*, and of keeping up *morale*.

- Jan has a problem with *making time* for study between the demands of child care, her social commitments and her leisure interests.
- Both Jan and Nathan have problems *using time* effectively.
- Both are confused about *what* exactly they should be doing and *how long* it should take.
- Both get *stuck* and cannot see a way forward.
- Jan is repeatedly *distracted* – by a child's needs, her own thoughts, by making coffee and tidying her desk, and most of all by the boredom she experiences while reading.
- Nathan is inhibited by the revulsion he feels when he reads his own words, and by his general *feelings of inadequacy* as a student. He seems to think of himself as a weak student and feels overawed by the tutor and the other students. He is approaching his essay so tentatively that he cannot take hold of the subject and express his thoughts. Instead, he sits, hypnotised by the title, casting around in desperation.
- Both have *lost* the surge of *enthusiasm* they felt at the start of their studies. They are in danger of giving up and wasting all their good intentions. They need some help!

However, they may be doing better than they think. Studying often feels like a struggle. In fact, it is in the process of struggling that important learning often happens. We have been spying on Jan and Nathan when they happened to be at an especially low ebb, but we can easily join them again when things are looking up.

Figure 1.1 Henry Pickering, *Lady Dixie*, *c*.1750–3, oil on canvas, 122 x 99cm (Castle Museum, City of Nottingham). Lady Dixie typifies the accomplished young woman of the period, dressed at enormous expense for public view. Photo courtesy of Nottingham City Museum and Galleries

Jan, Nathan and some fellow students have decided to make a trip to an art gallery. They are grouped round a picture (in fact the one in Figure 1.1, of Eleanor Francis Dixie). Jan is listening as Carol finishes speaking:

'... but surely the whole point is that she's supposed to be standing about like a clothes horse, dripping jewels.'

'Horse is about right', she adds.

'Yes', Nathan cut in, 'I bet she's there to show the world how wealthy and powerful her father is. He must have commissioned the portrait I suppose. And paid for it. I wonder if we could find out ...'

'Get him – "commissioned the portrait" indeed', said Jan with a grin.

'But it's true', Anna said to her. 'There's absolutely nothing in the background ...'

'Mmm, nothing to look at except that glorious frock', agreed Carol wistfully. 'It takes up over half the picture space.'

'And look at the colours in it!', said Philip.

'I see what you mean', Jan replied. 'But look at her eyes too. She seems to be staring straight at me – well, down on me really – the mouth, kind of quietly pleased with herself. Obviously a thoroughbred.'

'Isn't her left arm a bit out of proportion?' asked Hansa, suddenly.

'Elongated', mused Nathan. 'Elegant, trailing fingers ...'

'A glove I think. And those aren't rubber gloves she's dangling either – her hands have never been near the washing up' said Jan, to general laughter.

Later, as they stood at the bus stop, Jan said to Nathan 'Really nice people aren't they?'.

'Yes, they are. Quite a mixture too. At first I was terrified – I thought they were all real culture vultures. Didn't dare open my mouth.'

'Mmm. I never thought I'd be walking round a gallery talking about art. I didn't even think I'd make it through the first chapter of the book! I'd never have done it without Carol – in the end I rang her up and she helped sort me out.'

'And I never thought I'd be talking about commissioning portraits ... all that jargon', laughed Nathan. 'Now I keep coming out with it – "and on the one hand this, and on the other hand that". In fact the problem is how to stop myself.'

'Yes – well, you seem to pick it all up pretty easily.'

'Oh yeah? You should have seen me struggling with that first essay. Nearly drove myself mad – and the whole family. The writing's the hardest part even now. Still, I seem to be improving a bit. I don't like the look of that next piece of reading though, do you?'

'Oh, I don't know – it could be quite interesting. Look, here's my bus! See you next week Nathan. Bye.'

And so they disappear off into the sunset, and we see how wonderful studying can be after all.

Well, I just wanted to show that although studying is frustrating and tough sometimes, it is also very satisfying and rewarding – and can even be fun. Many students say that not only do they gain greater knowledge and understanding of the subjects they study, but also more *confidence*, *broader interests*, and more *purpose* in life; that it helps them to achieve more in areas of their lives not directly connected to study. This is another reason for reading about study skills and thinking seriously about *how* as well as what you are studying. If you develop a wide range of study techniques and strategies you will not only improve as a student, you will strengthen your capabilities all round.

1.5   Becoming a skilful student

No magic tricks, or quick fixes, will make you a skilful student overnight. Study skills improve gradually through picking up practical know-how, swapping ideas with other students, being creative in trying out new approaches and taking the time to think about how your studies are going.

1   Accumulating practical know-how

You pick up practical know-how from day-to-day study experience. For example, with more experience Nathan would have recognised the importance of filing, and would have kept important documents, such as notes for an assignment, together in a folder. Developing an effective filing system is not a difficult skill. It does not require great insight or hours of practice, just application and a little thought. Other kinds of practical know-how include knowing:

- where to get information about what your course expects from you (e.g. timetables, booklists and past exam papers)
- where to find instructions about what to do and when
- how much time to allow for different tasks (e.g. researching for an assignment, then planning and drafting it), and
- who to go to for help and support.

You accumulate this knowledge by reading information sheets, asking questions and working out your own solutions.

2   Mastering the core study tasks

As well as general know-how, you need to develop insights and techniques for tackling the core tasks that take up most of your study time. The chapters in Part 2 of this book offer practical examples and guidance to help you develop a broad repertoire of strategies and skills you will be able to apply to a wide range of study tasks.

3   Knowing how to keep your spirits up

There is nothing more damaging to your studies than low morale. You saw how little progress Jan and Nathan made when filled with doubt and despair – starting one thing, then another, frittering away time and achieving little. Managing your morale is a key topic of Chapter 2.

4   Taking control

To be successful as a student you must be determined to take control of your studies. It is easy to let a course just 'happen' to you – lurching along from one day to the next without an overall plan. Instead, you should strive to make the most of the time and money you are investing in the course. You can't afford to be half-hearted. Nobody will be impressed if you blame the course, or your circumstances; you have to take responsibility for your own learning. This too is a main theme of Chapter 2.

5   Becoming an independent learner

You also need to think hard about the big questions.

- What do you want to achieve from your studies?
- How much of yourself and your time are you prepared to invest?
- Where do your studies stand in relation to other priorities in your life?

The higher you go in the education system, the more accountable you are for your own progress. In school, teachers shouldered much of the responsibility for what you learned and how. At higher levels you have to decide your own priorities, set your own targets and work out your own strategies for achieving them. *You* decide what subjects you are interested in, what points of view you agree with, what evidence you accept and what opinions you will express.

It takes a while to adjust to this autonomy, especially if you are returning to study after a long break. Nevertheless, your target is to become an *independent* learner. Ultimately, you want to be able to find your own way around any subject you become interested in without the support of teachers. Then you are free to find out whatever you want to know. The purpose of this book is to support you in achieving that independence.

1.6   Thinking about how you learn

In order to set about your studies intelligently, you need some kind of notion of how you learn. This does not have to be complicated, just a workable, practical understanding – enough to enable you to make choices between different study strategies and to evaluate the outcomes of your choices.

1.6.1   Drawing insight from other people

You can develop a fuller understanding of your own learning by talking to other people about *their* experiences of learning. Talking with other students is a powerful way of 'thinking aloud'. You make sense collectively of the way the learning process seems to work. Teachers offer insights too, both in class or online, and through their comments on your assignments. And, of course, you can read what other people have to say about the learning process in books like this one.

See Chapter 3, Understanding how you learn

1.6.2   What kind of learner are you?

While there are general truths about learning that apply to everyone, it is also clear that people differ in the ways they learn. Since this book tends to focus on the general truths, you may want to look up other sources to explore your personal characteristics as a learner. Educational researchers have developed various schemes that distinguish between different types of learner. Here are some examples.

Serialist vs holist One scheme divides students into two categories: *serialists*, who tend to work in a sequential way through study tasks, starting at the beginning and proceeding step by step until they reach the end; and *holists,* who tend to approach a task as a whole and hop about from one part of it to another, trying all the time to keep the overall picture in view. For example, a serialist is said to be more likely to start a book on page one and read on to the end, while a holist might read the contents list and the conclusion, skim through some of the illustrations and then dip into selected sections to build up a picture of what it is about. Either strategy can work, but some people are said to have a clear preference for one or the other (Pask, 1988).

Controlled vs impulsive Some students work in a steady and systematic way. Others are inclined to put in bursts of intensive study, learning a lot quickly before shifting to something else. Again, both approaches work.

Deep learning vs surface learning Some students tend to search for the underlying meaning of a text as they read (deep learning), while others are more inclined to treat a text as information to be remembered (surface learning). Deep learning is seen as a much more appropriate strategy for most university-level study (Marton et al., 1997).

However, there is disagreement about how useful it is to make distinctions between learning styles, and about which distinctions are most meaningful. New classification schemes and new versions of old schemes continue to emerge. If you want to explore the topic of learning styles you can follow it up for yourself by searching the internet. Type 'learning styles' in the search box and you will find plenty.

Ultimately, you need to piece together your own picture of yourself as a learner, not rely on questionnaire scores. For this you need to become a practised observer of yourself. In effect you become your own psychologist, tracking how your mind works and comparing your experiences with those of other students and with what you read about learning. Then you can work out what kind of a learner you think you are and develop study strategies accordingly.

1.7   Being a reflective learner

But whatever kind of learner you think you are, to become an independent learner you need to be *reflective*. By reflecting on your study experiences you develop real insight into the ways you learn. Then gradually, as your insight grows, you become able to take control of your studies. The process of learning through reflection on experience is illustrated in Figure 1.2 (an adaptation of David Kolb's diagram of the experiential learning cycle). Whether or not you find diagrams helpful, this one aims to identify what it means to learn well.

1   Planning
You look ahead to the course work you have been set and the deadlines for completing it. You also think about what is going on in your life, the time available for study and any difficulties you have to circumnavigate. Then you think strategically about how to manage the work: Which parts of the work present the toughest challenge? Which parts are most important to complete? In what sequence will you tackle the various tasks? What targets will you set yourself? Will you try out any new ways of doing things?

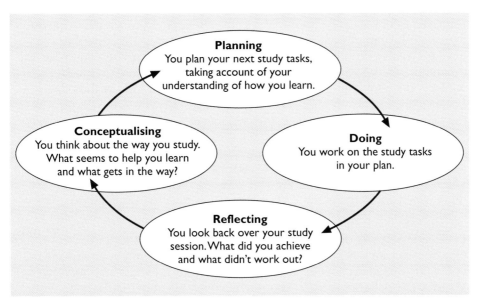

Figure 1.2 Kolb's reflective learning cycle, adapted for study skills (Source: Kolb, 1984)

Having thought about such questions, you then sketch out a plan in the form of a task list.

2 Doing
Then you work at your studies, following your plan as best you can.

3 Reflecting
At suitable moments, you pause to reflect on how your spell of study has gone. (This could be at the end of the day, the end of the week, or at a point during your studies when things have ground to a halt.) What have you achieved? You tick off items on your task list. What did you not complete? What events intervened? Which parts were hard going, and which parts did you enjoy? Did anything go differently from previous sessions? Perhaps make a few notes of your answers to these questions.

4 Conceptualising
Then you try to make sense of what you have observed. What seems to help you learn? – where did your strategy work best? What seems to interfere with your learning? Did you misjudge some of the tasks, or the time required? How does this all fit in with your ideas about the way you learn? What changes in your approach to study might help you to learn better?

See Chapter 3 Section 3.1, Developing ideas about learning

5 Continuing round the cycle
This brings you back to the planning process, as you look ahead to the next set of tasks. However, now, as a result of the reflective process, you have more insight than last time. You can make better plans, which you then test out further by 'doing', 'reflecting' and 'conceptualising'. As you continue your studies, circling round and round the reflective cycle, your understanding steadily deepens and you become more skilful.

In reality, of course, the process of reflective learning is much more messy than Kolb's diagram suggests. The four stages are not neatly separated off from each other. You might well 'reflect' on learning or revise your 'plan' in the middle of 'doing' some study, or you might 'make sense' in a new way whilst you are 'planning'. And mostly you are not aware of the four stages because this feels like a single, coherent process. However, the purpose of the diagram is not to propose a strict sequence of steps to carry out. Its value lies in helping you to think about the nature of reflective learning – what it involves and what it delivers. The essential point is to keep the ways you approach your studies under continual review. You think ahead about what you want to achieve and take note of what you actually achieve. And you think over your successes and your failures, so that you bring increasingly subtle insight to your studies.

6   Keeping a study diary

One way to take a reflective approach is to keep a diary of your studies. If you write a page each week about what you have achieved and how you feel about it, this will trigger ideas about why you study in particular ways. Use headings such as 'Main achievements', 'Main setbacks', 'Feelings about study', 'Lessons learned', 'Major tasks ahead', 'Ideas for tackling next tasks'. It can be an informal, loose-leaf diary – just sheets kept together in a folder – or perhaps an online diary or blog.

As you look back over your notes, you will see patterns in your experiences of study. These will help you to think strategically about whether you are achieving as much as you could. Even keeping a study diary for a fairly short spell will stimulate valuable reflective and strategic thinking. Some courses may ask you to keep a diary, but you don't have to wait to be asked.

1.8   Investing in Information Technology

Acquiring Information and Communications Technology (ICT) skills is another main plank of the Key Skills agenda devised by government and employers. One of the most important investments you will make is to develop these skills because studying has acquired a radically new flavour in the twenty-first century. The ICT revolution has transformed the ways in which ideas, information and texts of all kinds are recorded and communicated; and, in the process, it has brought far-reaching changes to university education.

But this does not mean an end to classrooms and libraries. Of course, many of the traditional elements of university education still offer excellent value. Books, articles and visual material in print remain most people's favourite way of grappling with new knowledge. Notes jotted on paper remain indispensable. However, computers and the internet have reconfigured the academic scene. Universities use websites to display information about their courses. Departments often post lecture notes, reading lists and assignments online. Students 'meet' in electronic classrooms, conferences and chat rooms, and submit word-processed work. University libraries present themselves as electronically organised information centres, with links to vast databases. And research without the internet is all but unthinkable. Even for ordinary, everyday study tasks a computer has become invaluable.

The ideal is to have a computer with an internet connection in your own home, available whenever you need it. Then you can get to know your software really well by playing around with it in spare moments. And an electronic filing system, full of your past work, becomes an ever more valuable resource supporting you throughout your studies. If you don't own a computer you may be able to hire one, with support from your university. Or you may be able to access one in a library, your university's computer centre, or at work. Make enquiries to find out what the options are.

> I couldn't afford to buy a computer so I hire. It's well worth it. I just love working on it, especially the internet. And it's great for essays. I look at what I've printed off and I think, "I wrote that".

A computer can help you with your studies in many different ways. Some are discussed here, and others elsewhere in the book.

- A computer can help you organise and keep track of your studies (Chapter 2 'Taking control of your studies')
- You can create good structured notes using your computer (Chapter 5 'Making notes').
- Your computer enables you to 'talk' to other students and your tutors online, whatever the time of day (Chapter 6 'Learning through talk').
- One of the most exciting facilities offered by computers is the ability to search on the internet (Chapter 10 'Online research and project work').

Key points

- Nowadays it is difficult to study effectively without access to a computer and the internet.
- If you don't own a computer, look for ways of getting regular access to one.

1.8.1 What equipment and skills do you need?

To use a computer for studying there are some basic things you need.

- **A computer** Preferably one not much more than three years old (technology moves on quickly). Cheap entry-level computers are usually fine for study purposes, unless you are told otherwise by your university. If a computer comes with a software 'bundle' make sure that it meets your needs (see Software, below).
- **A printer** Printers are generally cheap; it is the cost of replacing ink, or toner, that counts. Laser printers may be more expensive than ink-jets but for black and white printing they can work out cheaper per thousand pages.
- **An internet connection** To use the internet you need to have an account with an internet service provider (ISP). If you can already send emails and

view websites then you have an ISP. For advice on choosing an ISP ask at a computer shop or your university's computer centre, or ask someone you know who uses the internet. A broadband internet connection offers faster access speeds than a dial-up connection.

■ **Software** Check with your university to find out what software is required for your course; it may even be supplied. You will need a word-processor and possibly a presentation package, a spreadsheet and database. The most convenient way to buy these is as a software 'suite' (e.g. Microsoft Office); there are usually good discounts for students. If you are considering a cut-down package, seek advice at your university before buying as it may not cover all your needs.

Students have very different levels of ICT skills. Some have grown up using computers as part of their daily life, while others have picked up the bare minimum needed to get by or have even avoided computers altogether.

❝ I've used a computer at work but only as a glorified typewriter. ❞

Whatever level you start at it is well worth setting aside regular chunks of time to work on your skills. Developing ICT skills has a lot to do with confidence. Give yourself time to play with the software, exploring the 'tutorials' and 'How Tos' provided, and with the internet. Don't be shy about asking for help from friends, family, other students and your university advisers.

Getting started

If you are a complete beginner, it is best to get someone you know who is familiar with computers to show you the basics. It is much easier to learn 'hands on', by watching, imitating and experimenting; you will soon pick up the gist of it. You will need to know how to:

■ open your software and create a new document; label, save and file your documents

■ select text and move it around (using a mouse, the arrow keys, the 'return' key and scrollbars)

■ change the appearance of selected text using **bold**, *italic* (etc.) and different fonts

■ use an internet browser (such as Internet Explorer, Netscape, or Mozilla Firefox)

■ use a printer

■ send and receive email messages

■ look for information in your software's Help facility.

Once you can handle the basics you may be able to get along fine on your own, developing new skills as you need them using on-screen tutorials and manuals supplied with your computer and software. Alternatively, there are many guidebooks for beginners. An excellent way to get to know your software is to spend time playing around, trying things out and browsing the Help facility. (You will find that your computer can check your spelling and grammar for you, count up the number of words in your documents, and manage your footnotes and references.) If you have a study task to do and the computer can help, don't be put off because you find things tricky at first.

Communications

If your studies involve using email and online conferencing (see Chapter 6), you will need to invest time in learning:

- how to set up a connection to your university's internet server (following all supplied instructions carefully)
- how to use the appropriate communications software, taking advantage of any manuals, online 'tutorials' or campus workshops
- where to go for help when connections go wrong or you need advice on using the software.

With online communications there is always an intense burst of initial learning and perhaps some tension if you run into difficulties establishing internet connections. But when messages start to flow, it becomes easy.

> Work at your own speed and don't ever presume that someone else is right and you are wrong. Read the instructions (I printed out everything, this for me was a necessity) and if at first you don't succeed, then try again. What was initially daunting has now become second nature.

Taking precautions

A computer will occasionally behave oddly but the consequences are seldom disastrous; there is usually a way of rescuing the situation. So while there is no need to be anxious, you do need to take a few precautions.

- Develop the habit of regularly saving your work; as soon as you start a new document, give it a label and save it.
- Find out how to 'back up' the documents on your hard drive, then back them up regularly.
- Seek advice about virus protection from your university or your computer supplier.

Box 1.2   Should you be able to type?

Many people get by with two-finger typing. But you won't enjoy the full benefits of word-processing until you can make words appear on-screen at a reasonable speed. The good news is that your computer can help you. There are excellent typing tutor programs available (enquire through your university, or search online). A few weeks of regular 20-minute sessions will have you touch-typing faster than you can write.

Learning to touch-type does take a substantial time investment. There is no shortcut to avoiding an initial period of regular practice, which can be frustrating and tiring. However, with several years of study ahead, your investment will be repaid many times over.

See Chapter 10
Section 10.2, Finding
information

The wider value of ICT skills

The skills you develop will be of value far beyond your course, both at work and in your life generally. As we saw in Box 1.1, the UK government has placed IT skills at the heart of its Key Skills strategy, along with communication skills (for more information see the Qualification and Curriculum Authority's 'Key Skills' publications, QCA 2002a–d). The core elements are the abilities to:

- search for and select information
- explore, develop and exchange information
- derive new information
- present information, including text, images and numbers.

You can even acquire an ICT certificate as proof of your achievements: for instance, a European Computer Driving Licence (ECDL). This consists of seven modules: Concepts of Information Technology; Using the Computer and Managing Files; Word-processing; Spreadsheets; Databases; Presentation; Information and Communication. (For more information visit the ECDL website at www.ecdl.com/main/index.php.)

Key points

- **Use the Help facilities** When you run into difficulties check the software's own Help resources first. You will often be able to sort things out for yourself.
- **Ask others** If you are still stuck, ask for help from family, friends, other students or your university advisers.
- **Get a guidebook** Consider borrowing or buying a guidebook for your software package.
- **Keep exploring** Don't feel you have to learn everything at once. Set time aside occasionally to find out about a new feature of the software.
- **Watch the clock** A computer helps you do many things very efficiently but it also has a tendency to eat up time. Keep an eye on how long you spend on the computer, and maintain a balance with other study activities.
- **Don't strain yourself** Working long hours at a computer can cause serious strain to your eyes, hands, wrists, neck and back. Position your computer and chair properly (your university should be able to advise you on this) and take regular breaks away from the screen.
- **Learn to touch-type** This is a big investment of your time, but very worthwhile.

1.8.2   eLearning

We have seen that you can use a computer to enhance conventional text-based studies but computers can also be used to deliver the content of courses, bringing learning experiences and resources right to your desk from a website, a CD-ROM or DVD.

eLearning materials

Courses in the arts and humanities involve a wide range of primary source material, digitised versions of which are now available: eBooks, illustrations of art works and artefacts, objects and events on film, sound recordings, and so on. Some of these resources are extremely rare – you could never expect to get access to them in person – and others are from distant places or times. Collections of these materials are now available to everyone in online libraries and databases. Your university may provide links to databases via the internet, or offer its own selections. Some elearning material incorporates a range of high-quality resources designed to work together, for example video or audio material used alongside text resources – archive footage of an historical event or a scene from a play you are studying, or a music performance on CD alongside the score. Accessing and combining a range of resources of these kinds offers a rich learning experience.

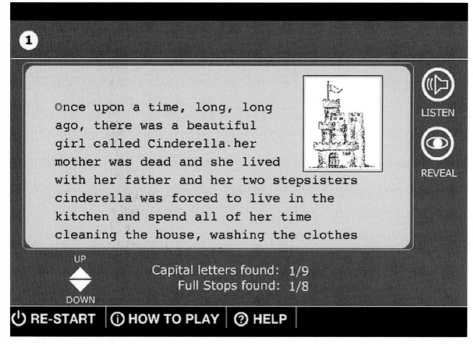

Figure 1.3 Learning about punctuation interactively (Source: BBC (2007), *Skillswise: Words* ('Making sentences' game), available at http://www.bbc.co.uk/skillswise/words/grammar/interestsentences/compoundsentences/, accessed 31 August 2007)

Sometimes electronic materials allow you to learn interactively. Instead of being exposed to things in a sequence devised by your teacher or a text's author, you make your own selection of learning activities and work at your own pace. English grammar, for instance, is notoriously difficult to learn from a teacher. It often sounds unnecessarily complicated when explained and can quickly become boring if not targeted specifically at your needs. It is also hard to tell whether you have understood the principles until you try them out. Software such as that shown in Figure 1.3 allows you to choose which particular aspect of writing skills to focus on. If you want to work on using capital letters and full stops, you read a few lines explaining the principles, then plunge in and try punctuating some sentences. In this test, you have to find nine capital letters and eight full stops by clicking where you think they should go (two examples have already been found in the sample shown in Figure 1.3).

Another way electronic materials can provide a unique learning experience is by 'modelling' a complex dynamic process, such as the growth of a city. You can watch the process as it evolves, stopping it to explore the details and replaying key moments. Or you can go back and rerun it, with changes to some of the conditions, to see how the process is affected.

eTuition

A growing number of courses provide all tuition online. You don't meet your teacher directly; instead you participate in online tutorials then email your assignments to your tutor. The tutor may set the class a task, which is to be completed by each student and subsequently discussed among the whole class prior to being submitted as part of an assignment. Or you may be asked to work with certain other students in online small-group learning, also on tasks that may be assessed. eTuition delivers many benefits, though not the same benefits as face-to-face tuition. There are matters you can explore in person which become tedious or confusing when pursued through written email messages or in conferences (for example, the process of a group deciding which topic to focus on and how to divide up the work among them). On the other hand, you have instant and ongoing access to friendly group support, without the expense and time involved in attending classroom-based tutorials.

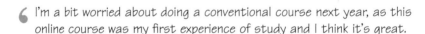

> I'm a bit worried about doing a conventional course next year, as this online course was my first experience of study and I think it's great.

Virtual learning environments

A virtual learning environment (VLE) gives you access to the university's services and resources, as well as to course materials, at the click of a button. Most universities now have a VLE, but they vary enormously. Figure 1.4 is an example of an Open University student homepage.

Key points

- eLearning has the potential to bring an immense wealth of resources right to your desktop.
- It also allows you to customise your study to match your interests and needs, working when you like and focusing on whatever you choose.
- In effect, your desktop travels with you wherever you have access to a computer and an internet connection.

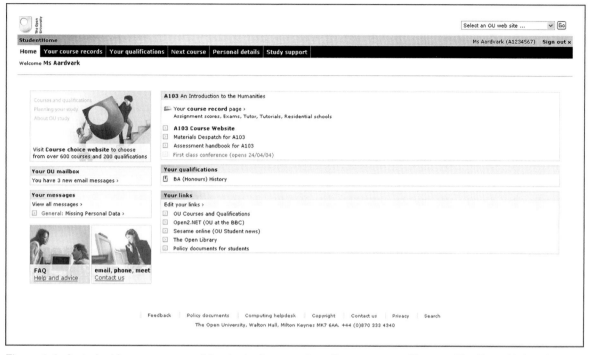

Figure 1.4 A student homepage, providing instant access to online resources (Source: The Open University (2007), 'StudentHome' (sample page), available at http://www.open.ac.uk/studenthome/experience/index.shtm, accessed 31 August 2007)

International access

Higher education has always transcended national boundaries through its international community of scholars. Now eLearning is taking internationalism to a new level as it enables students from different parts of the world to enrol on the same courses, and also allows students whose lives take them around the world to continue their studies regardless of where they happen to be.

You don't have to be an ICT expert to gain a tremendous amount from using a computer; whether for routine tasks such as word-processing assignments and filing documents, or for web searching, online conferencing and using interactive learning materials. A computer brings you learning opportunities undreamt of in previous generations, though it does not displace conventional university teaching and learning. There is, however, an initial hurdle to overcome – you have to be prepared to invest time and effort in familiarising yourself with the software and facilities relevant to your studies. In the first weeks the experience can be quite time consuming and irritating. But if you have the confidence to drive on through setbacks and a willingness to seek help when stuck, there does come a time when it all seems perfectly straightforward and natural. Using a computer then becomes seamlessly integrated into your experience of study.

1.9   Investing in your future

Understanding how you learn is a lifelong process. At every stage you can discover more. And it is not always a matter of learning something new. There are many basic truths you can revisit and understand again at a new level. Some sections of this book will be just as helpful if you return to them in future years, when you have much more experience of studying.

Key points

Study skills are not a set of 'tricks' that you learn once and apply forever. Becoming a skilled student involves:

- accumulating practical know-how about things you have to do as a student and how to do them
- mastering the essential skills in your area of study
- knowing how to keep your spirits up
- being determined to take control of your studies in a practical and realistic way
- becoming an independent learner by taking broad responsibility for your own studies and making your own judgements about your priorities and your progress
- taking a reflective approach to your studies, so that you learn from experience and continually refine your skills
- developing an understanding of what learning is and how it happens, so that you can plan and monitor your own learning.

Taking this approach, your study skills will continue to develop throughout your life.

Studying with full concentration and deep thought expands your mind. It enables you to participate in new realms of ideas. It extends your powers of expression and helps you engage with the world with new confidence. But none of this is guaranteed. If you cannot connect effectively with your studies, if your time dribbles away on patchy, half-focused activity, then studying leads to frustration, disappointment and low self-esteem. That is why developing your study skills is one of the best investments you can make in yourself. It is an investment which will bear fruit throughout your life, enabling you to keep abreast of things in a rapidly changing world. This book assumes that you are intelligent enough to give serious thought to why and how you study, and determined enough to invest significant time in improving your skills.

References

Department for Education and Skills (DFES) (2004) *What are Key Skills?*, available at www.dfes.gov.uk/keyskills/what.shtml (accessed 31 August 2007).

Ellis, J. (1995) '"On the Town": Women in Augustan England', *History Today*, vol. 45, no. 12, pp. 20–7.

Kolb, D.A. (1984) *Experiential Learning: Experience as the Source of Learning and Development*, Englewood Cliffs, NJ, Prentice Hall.

Marton, F., Hounsell, D. and Entwistle, N. (1997) *The Experience of Learning: Implications for Teaching and Studying in Higher Education (second edition)*, Edinburgh, Scottish Academic Press.

Pask, G. (1988) 'Learning strategies, teaching strategies, and conceptual or learning style' in Schmeck, R.R. (ed.) *Learning Strategies and Learning Styles*, New York, Plenum Press.

Qualifications and Curriculum Authority (QCA) (2000) *Key Skills Units: Levels 4 and 5*, London, Qualifications and Curriculum Authority.

Qualifications and Curriculum Authority (QCA) (2002a) *Key Skills: Information Technology: Level 1*, London, Qualifications and Curriculum Authority.

Qualifications and Curriculum Authority (QCA) (2002b) *Key Skills: Information Technology: Level 2*, London, Qualifications and Curriculum Authority.

Qualifications and Curriculum Authority (QCA) (2002c) *Key Skills: Information Technology: Level 3*, London, Qualifications and Curriculum Authority.

Qualifications and Curriculum Authority (QCA) (2002d) *Key Skills: Information Technology: Level 4*, QCA/99/455, London, Qualifications and Curriculum Authority.

CHAPTER 2
Taking control of your studies

Studying at higher levels is always tough. Yet you can make it one of the most satisfying experiences of your life by rising to the challenge and taking control of your studies. To do that you need to understand the nature of university study.

2.1   Taking responsibility for your own learning

University is a world of its own, with customs and values you encounter nowhere else, and extraordinary freedom to do, think and speak as you please. Faced for the first time with this openness it is natural to feel confused. Here is an account of two campus-based students. Jenny, a full-time student, is a recent school-leaver. Tracy is a mature student with a young family and a part-time job.

> Jenny looked around the coffee bar, soaking up the atmosphere. It was her first week at university. Round the other side of the table she could hear Tracy telling a friend that she was really determined to try for a good degree, in spite of her family and work commitments. She was saying that she'd worked out a plan for setting aside 25 hours a week for study and she was hoping this would be enough. Jenny listened sceptically. She was anticipating a far more intensive study routine. At the departmental freshers' talk she had been inspired to remodel herself as a serious student. She wasn't sure how, but she imagined herself working round the clock if necessary. Tracy, she guessed, was heading for disappointment.

Activity 2.1

This account is based on real people (though their names have been changed). Can you guess which of the two was the more successful in her studies?

Back to the story ...

> Three years on, Tracy achieved an excellent degree while Jenny's was a more modest achievement. As Jenny discovered during the semester when they were studying the same course, Tracy produced her work very consistently. She said she had only a few 'windows' between her shifts and looking after her children, so she had to be disciplined and use them to the full. In spite of crises when the children were ill or child-minding arrangements broke down, she had mostly been able to find 25 hours a week. Looking back, Jenny realised that Tracy had seemed as much on top of the work as any of them. By sticking to a well-defined and realistic plan, she had achieved what she intended. She also visibly enjoyed her studies.

Activity 2.2

As the account continues, think of some reasons why Jenny was less successful than Tracy. Jot them down.

Tracy said that studying in short bursts suited her, as she found it difficult to keep her mind focused intensively for more than a few hours at a time. However, Jenny, with no job or family commitments, aimed higher, vaguely committing herself to whole weeks of intensive study. Yet she found herself easily distracted. Stretches of a day would slip away and, feeling guilty, she blotted her studies out of her mind by reading a novel or sneaking off to play pool. She comforted herself with the thought of all the potentially virtuous days that lay ahead.

At school, Jenny's work had been timetabled. Teachers made sure she fitted all that was required into the school year. Now she was at sea. At university, time came in vast undifferentiated swathes. What to do with it all? With 112 hours in a week (allowing eight a night for sleeping) how many was it reasonable to spend on study? And working out what to do with the hours was just as hard. Take the booklists. How many books and articles should she try to read? It took her so long to read just a few pages, she felt defeated looking at the lists. And should she make notes as she read? If so, how long should that take?

She would sit in the library for hours, dipping into one book after another, stopping frequently to gaze around at other students – most of whom she didn't know – or out of the window. What was she trying to achieve? How would she know when she had achieved it? By comparison, she went to lectures gratefully. It was clear when they started and finished and what she was supposed to be doing. At the end, her lecture notes were scrappy, but at least she felt she had met a target.

Eventually, during her final year, Jenny discovered that she could learn a lot from close reading of just selected sections of text, and that making notes could sometimes be very satisfying while at other times it was not necessary. The trick was to take control, to decide what she wanted to find out and then work at it until she had absorbed enough to be going on with. It was a shame that she had not talked to Tracy about these matters in the first year. In the end, like most students, she stumbled her way towards an adequate strategy for coping with the work, but she could have got there much more quickly, learned a lot more and avoided a lot of anguish on the way.

I think that the most significant difference between Jenny and Tracy is that from the outset Tracy knew that she had to take responsibility for her studies. The teachers on her pre-degree access course had impressed this upon her and had emphasised the value of intensely focused, high-quality study, compared with bitty time-filling. Jenny, by contrast, just had good intentions. She thought big, but did not know how to deliver. Nobody had told her what university would be like and she had given little thought to how she would cope. Here are some aspects of university study that I think took her by surprise.

Independent study

Jenny expected to be learning mostly in a familiar group of students, as at school, with a teacher shepherding them along together. But, although she attended several lectures and seminars each week, she was surprised to have little personal contact with staff and little guidance; and she was often amongst students she knew only by sight. She had no idea that she would be spending so much time studying under her own steam. In short, Jenny had unrealistic expectations of study at university.

Absence of work schedules

Nor had it struck Jenny that organising her time was now her own responsibility. If little work was set, she generally did little. She did not think to follow Tracy's lead and write out a schedule of tasks for herself. She just hoped for the best. She assumed that success was mainly to do with how clever you were. She had yet to appreciate how central time management is to achievement in adult life.

Breadth of courses

She was also completely taken aback by the broad sweep of the courses, with more topics and set texts than it was possible to cover. She had expected to be told what to study when. And she assumed that teachers would help to pull the courses together from time to time to make sure everyone was keeping up. Instead, they just moved on to new topics. Some topics were not even covered in class. She had not realised she was expected to make decisions about where to focus her efforts and to work selectively.

Long time horizons

Jenny had never worked to assignment deadlines so many weeks ahead. She didn't think to plan her assignments across a semester, fitting them in alongside other study commitments. She assumed there would be time later. She felt she had enough to worry about with the reading and that, anyway, she would be better able to tackle the assignments later, when she had learned more. She did not realise that working on assignments would help her understand the reading, nor that spacing them out would help her build up her skills and confidence. She got into particular difficulties with the dissertation, the deadline for which lay almost a year ahead. In spite of secret hopes of carrying out an impressively penetrating study, she ended up cobbling the thing together in a last-minute panic and so learned little from the experience.

Responsibility for seeking help

Unfortunately, even when Jenny began to recognise that she was not coping, she didn't think of seeking support. She kept her feelings of inadequacy to herself and sank into a cycle of avoidance and denial. Although she knew about the counselling service and the study support unit, it never occurred to her that it was for people like her. She did not realise how common her experiences were, nor how quickly the support services could have helped her transform her studies. She didn't even talk things over with friends, such as Tracy.

In summary, Jenny was unprepared for taking responsibility for her own studies. For a long time she felt adrift, until eventually it dawned on her that *she* had to seize control.

Key points

It is vital to take responsibility for your own learning at university because:

- you spend a lot of time in private study
- you are responsible for your own day-to-day work schedule
- the scope of courses tends to be broad, touching on many more topics and texts than you can cover, so you have to decide where to focus your efforts
- you often have distant deadlines and have to work out your own strategy for meeting them
- you are expected to seek out support when you need it, not wait for it to come to you.

2.2 Managing your work

Taking responsibility involves managing your own progress through the coursework. You are studying for your own reasons and under your own particular circumstances, you have your own background in the subject, so it is up to you to work out where to make special investments of time and effort. You may have particular difficulties with parts of the subject, or with finding time, or accessing books, and it is for you to develop a strategy that addresses these challenges. That strategy might include seeking advice and support, but *you* remain the person in charge.

2.2.1 Sketching the big picture

To take control of your work, you need to begin with the big picture. What are the main components of the course? Are there key texts? Is the course divided into topics or themes? What work do you have to hand in – and when? Are there other assessed elements, such as an exam? All this information will be available on printed sheets or on a departmental website. Make sure you have tracked down the relevant sources; then take time to go through them carefully with highlighter pens or write down notes of the most important things you have to do.

Identify priorities Use different coloured highlighter pens, or double and treble underlining, or star ratings, to indicate the importance of different course components. What is absolutely essential? What is optional? What looks particularly challenging? What will need to be planned well in advance?

'Own' the course Take ownership of the course information by putting your markings all over it. It is easy to feel overwhelmed by 'official' documentation, so assert yourself. You are the one doing the course, so build up your *own* picture of the course.

Having reviewed the big picture, pick out some of the first tasks and begin to think about how to tackle them.

2.2.2   Breaking big tasks into smaller tasks

A key principle in keeping on top of your studies is to break big tasks into more manageable ones.

> ❛ I set myself just one or two small, manageable tasks. I find if I can achieve these it's so much better than setting myself a full working day and then not getting round to much at all. I often feel so virtuous at having achieved the little tasks that I go on and do more. I get a kick out of ticking things off my list. ❜

The trouble with big tasks is that their scope and shape are hard to take in. You can't see where to start, so, like Jenny, you keep putting things off. And if you do get started, it is very hard to tell how much progress you are making. Smaller tasks give you much more control.

Make tasks specific It helps to turn vague, abstract tasks, such as 'make progress with the article', into specific, concrete tasks, such as 'read the next eight pages'. You then know where to start and what to do. You can set yourself a time allowance and check your progress as you go. And when you complete the task, you can give yourself a pat on the back.

2.2.3   Making a To Do list

An excellent way to begin to engage with your work is to create a To Do list. This is a simple device, but very effective, particularly if you use a computer, which makes the list easy to update. The example in Figure 2.1 shows the tasks a student, Mel, planned to carry out arranged roughly in the order they would be tackled. Each item has some stars indicating its importance, and an estimate, in brackets, of the number of hours it might take. Notice that tasks 2 and 3 have been broken down into sub-tasks.

Activity 2.3

You may already have a To Do list. If not, make yourself one. List your study tasks for the week or two ahead using pen and paper, your computer or PDA (personal digital assistant). Use coloured paper if you have any, then the list will be easy to find amongst other papers.

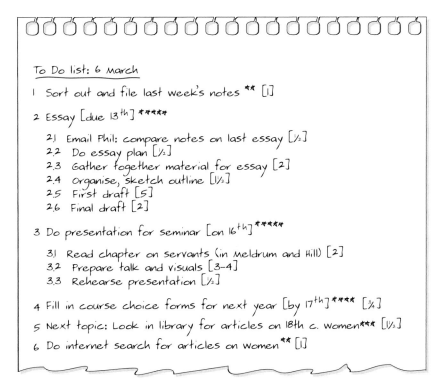

Figure 2.1   Example of a To Do list

If you use a word processor, number the items in your list. Try moving the items around: put the cursor on an item, hold down the Shift and Alt keys and use the arrow keys ↑↓. Try the right arrow for 'demoting' a task to a sub-task and the left arrow for 'promoting' it back. If these moves don't work with your word-processor, try the Help menu. When your list is done, save it and print it off.

Using your To Do list

As you complete the tasks, cross them off your list. When other tasks arise, write them in. If you made the list on your computer, go back to the saved list to delete completed tasks and add in the new ones; then rearrange the sequence as appropriate, save the updated version and print it off. In this way the uncompleted tasks will gradually move up your list. Nothing gets forgotten, and you don't have to keep writing out a new list.

A To Do list is a guide to action. It turns a shapeless mound of work into a sequence of tasks you can tackle. It tells you where to start and enables you to track your progress. You may find yourself working on tasks out of sequence, and that's fine. Your To Do list is a creative tool, not a straitjacket. With it in front of you, you can think intelligently about modifying your plans when things don't work out. You remain in control.

> ### Key points
>
> To manage your work effectively you need to:
>
> - review course information, marking up the important features, so that you can build up the 'big picture' of what you have to do
> - break big tasks into smaller, more manageable tasks
> - make a To Do list to help you steer your way through the work.

2.3   Managing time

Having got the work into perspective, you need to think about how to manage your time.

2.3.1   How much time should you spend on your studies?

The official view

University courses in the UK are measured in credits and each credit is notionally ten hours of study. So a 60 credit course, for example, is seen as involving around 600 hours of work. Spread over a 30-week year, this translates to twenty hours of study per week.

Most full-time students study 120 credits per year, which works out at around 40 hours a week – equivalent to a working week in many jobs. Meanwhile, a part-time student might study 60 credits per year, equating to a twenty-hour week. (This covers *everything*, including time spent getting things sorted out at the beginning of the course, searching the internet, managing your notes, talking with your teacher, preparing for exams, and so on.)

However, the link between credits and hours is intended only as a rule of thumb. The UK Quality Assurance Agency for Higher Education stresses that credit is awarded for achievement not for 'time served' (QAA, 2001).

The reality

But what about real life? Are you in a position to set aside the number of study hours implied? If you are not, don't just give up the idea of studying. A lot depends on the quality of your learning. If you are very focused, like Tracy, you can achieve a lot in fewer than the recommended hours. A part-time student with a full-time job will do very well to find twelve good hours a week for intensive study. But with other tasks squeezed into spare moments, that can be enough.

Be aware of the 'official' number of hours your course expects, but be realistic about the number of hours you can actually give to your studies. If you find yourself having to manage with less, be assured that plenty of other students are in the same position. In the end what counts is how well you use your study hours rather than the sheer number of them. As a major review of learning and teaching in North American universities observes:

> ... many of our students [are] trying to balance significant demands of families, jobs, and careers ... many of today's students seem unable

to devote sufficient time to their studies. Students need help balancing these demands, and [making] the most of the time that they have available ... There is no magic number of hours that students should study in order to maximise learning ... the amount of time isn't the issue. It's how that time is spent.

(Vorkink, 1995, p.70)

2.3.2   Creating time

How, then, do you find the hours you need? When studying comes into your life it generally means that something else has to go. However, it is important to strike a balance which allows you to carry on with the important things in your life, including relaxation and entertainment.

Effective studying requires a lot of time in reasonably good-sized chunks. You have to become an expert at creating usable time. One way to set about this is to draw up a study week chart (see Figure 2.2) showing time spent on your 'typical' week's activities and see where there is room for manoeuvre.

	Monday	Tuesday	Wednesday	Thursday	Friday	Saturday	Sunday
AM							
PM							
Eve							
Total							

Figure 2.2   Chart for working out time spent on a 'typical' week's activities

To find time for study in a busy life, you need to review the way in which your time is normally taken up. You may need to identify opportunities for making extra time – whether first thing in the morning, after putting children to bed, at weekends, during lunch hours or on journeys. Part-time students need to be especially resourceful about this.

Activity 2.4

Make yourself a study week chart like the one in Figure 2.2. Either draw it by hand or, better for future updates, use your computer – use a table-creating facility or a spreadsheet template (look in Help if you don't know how). Then, once you have saved the chart, you can keep making new copies whenever you want to revise the schedule. When you have created your chart, fill in the hours spent on your main non-study activities each day (work, home or family commitments, travel, leisure etc.).

How many study hours per week will you aim for? Write in a target number of study hours for each day in the 'Total hours' row, trying to make them add up to your target number of hours per week. Then start marking in possible study slots, to see if you can achieve your daily totals. What will you cut back on? Where might clashes arise? Can you achieve something close to your target number of study hours per week?

Don't be alarmed if you found this activity difficult. Life is messy. Indeed, having struggled to draw up a study week chart, life will intervene to make it hard to stick to. But sticking to it is not necessarily the point. Even if you constantly have to change your chart it is still worthwhile making it. Deciding to change it makes you think about your priorities. Planning helps you to think strategically instead of just drifting.

Key points

The first steps in managing study time are to:

- estimate how much time your course requires
- work out how you can release an adequate amount of study time within your 'typical' week.

2.3.3   Using time strategically

Having identified the time available for study, it is important to think strategically about how to use this precious time.

High- and low-quality study time

Not all your available time will be of the same quality. It will range between:

- *high-quality study time* – when you are alert, able to concentrate and can work undisturbed for a decent length of time
- *low-quality study time* – when you are tired, your concentration is poor, there are distractions around you, and you do not have long enough to get deeply involved.

> I'm an early bird. I think and write much better straight after I get up.

> My best time to study is in the morning after 11am, when the kids are at school.

> I concentrate best after 9 o'clock at night, when I've got everything from the day sorted out.

You need to manage your studies so that you use your best quality time for the tasks that most need it. When are your best times for study? When do you concentrate best? When do you have fewest distractions? When can you find decent chunks of time?

Activity 2.5

Take your chart and highlight your best quality study time. How much high-quality time do you have in a week? Is it enough? If not, are there ways you could reorganise your activities to give yourself more high-quality time. Could a friend or partner help by sharing some of your other responsibilities?

Now look at your To Do list. Which items do you think need the high-quality time? Which could you do in lower quality time?

Give your highest quality time to demanding tasks such as reading a difficult text or article, or drafting an essay. These are worth starting only when your mind is alert and you have a good stretch of time ahead of you.

There are plenty of other tasks, such as organising notes, reading through a draft essay, filling in forms or talking things over with another student, that can be squeezed into odd moments when you are less alert. Experiment to find out which times of day are best for different kinds of task.

Mapping the course weeks

Now you are ready to get down to specifics. What do you actually need to achieve within the time that is ahead of you? Again it is useful to start with the big picture. For how many weeks does the course last, and how can the coursework be mapped across them? What you need is a course calendar. If your course provides one, mark the key milestones, such as dates when assignments are due, then post it on a wall in a prominent place.

If your course does not supply a calendar, make your own. You could buy a year planner for your wall, or just find a calendar feature on your computer and use that. You can print off calendars for the next month or two and fill in the details by hand, or you can type in key course information before printing. If you like working on a computer, it is worth investing a little time exploring whatever calendar program or template you have; they can probably be used in a variety of ways.

Planning the week ahead

- Your course calendar provides an overall map of the course weeks.
- Your study week chart tells you where to find time in a typical week.
- Your To Do list shows you the tasks immediately ahead of you.

Now you need to work out how to fit the tasks into the actual weeks ahead of you in order to keep abreast of the targets on the calendar. Figure 2.3 shows a study plan for Mel, who is studying part-time and also has a part-time job (Monday–Thursday afternoons). She has a son who goes to playgroup each afternoon and spends Saturday mornings (sometimes longer) with grandparents. Mel likes to take him out and about on Sundays, while Wednesday, Friday and Saturday evenings are her times for exercise, relaxation and going out. She is trying to find about 14 hours for study each week. The week shown in Figure 2.3 covers items 2 and 4 in her To Do list.

	Monday	Tuesday	Wednesday	Thursday	Friday	Saturday	Sunday
AM	Study – 1 hr (email Phil; start essay plan)	Study – 1 hr (finish plan; start getting material)	Study – 1 hr (finish sketch)	Study – 1 hr (start first draft of essay)	Housework/ washing	Study – 3 hrs (second draft of essay; check over)	Free
PM	Work	Work	Work	Work	Study – 3 hrs (finish first draft)	Shopping etc.	Free
Eve	Evening class	Study – 2 hrs (get material; start outline sketch)	Go to the gym	Study – 2 hrs (first draft)	Free	Free	Study – 1 hr (course choice form; file notes)
Total (15)	1	3	1	3	3	3	1

Figure 2.3 Example of a completed study plan for 6–12 March

Activity 2.6

Sketch out a study plan by copying the tasks from your To Do list into your diary, or a fresh copy of the blank study week chart you made for Activity 2.4, or a printed-off calendar for the month ahead. Or you could do the whole thing on your computer or PDA using a calendar planning feature.

With your study plan and To Do list beside you, you have the means to stay in control of your coursework. When things go wrong, as they will, you can readjust intelligently. You can consult your study plan to see where there is room for manoeuvre in your schedule; and, if time is running out, your To Do list will tell you which activities to prioritise.

2.3.4   Using time well
It is one thing to plan your time strategically, and quite another to stick to your plans.

6 Why, oh why, when I find three hours of peace and quiet, and all I want to do is write my essay, do I suddenly become hungry? ... then I make that urgent phone call to a friend ... Then I remember some birthdays I mustn't forget ... Better put some washing in the machine too. ... Now what was that essay topic? 9

Box 2.1   Why is it so easy to be distracted when studying?

It is the feeling of drifting around in a meaningless way, with no end in sight, that makes us so ready to grasp at any distractions we can find. When you don't really understand the text you are reading and you are not sure what you are trying to achieve, you feel restless and uneasy. Distractions provide relief. They offer the chance to focus on familiar and meaningful aspects of your life and escape from the uncertainties of studying. Routine, orderly tasks are particularly appealing. You reassure yourself that you can control your domestic world, even if your studies feel chaotic. The urge to avoid uncertainty is very strong. That's why it is so important to set yourself specific study tasks – they help to give shape and meaning to your work.

Keeping up your concentration

Work out ways of keeping yourself actively engaged as you study.

- As you read (your own copies of articles and book chapters) mark important passages in the text. The choices you make about which words to highlight keep your mind busy so that reading feels less passive. It is not just the writer who is running this show; you are in there making judgements of the writer's words. Make notes in the margin too, when you agree or disagree. When you hit a difficult passage, try writing a short summary of it in your own words.

- Check your progress. Are you going to reach your target? Do you need to change strategy to finish in time? Set yourself an interim target to achieve before your next break.

- Sit somewhere else for a while. Switch to a task you find more interesting. Take a short break. Do something physically active.

- Focus on what you find interesting. Play to your strengths and approach your studies creatively. Don't let the course dominate you: stay in control.

Time vs task

Try to balance *time management* against *task management*. If you become too obsessed with *time* you tend to think in terms of 'hours put in' rather than what you have achieved, and you find yourself filling up the time with relatively unimportant tasks. To avoid this you need to set out with the goal of completing specific tasks (even if you don't always succeed). On the other hand, if you focus too much on completing a *task* you can let it drag on for too long, which may stop you attending to something else just as important. You need to switch your attention between task management and time management to achieve a balance.

Key points

In order to manage your time strategically, you should:
- mark up a course calendar to keep key targets clearly in view

- create a study plan for the week ahead by mapping your To Do list onto the study times you have identified in your study week chart
- identify your high-quality study times and use them for the tasks which require most concentration
- keep yourself actively engaged with the ideas in the course
- stay in control of your study strategy, switching tasks from time to time
- balance time management against task management.

2.4 Managing your study circumstances

Your studies will, inevitably, be affected by your circumstances. But whatever those circumstances are, there is a lot you can do to make the best of them.

2.4.1 Setting up a place to study

Activity 2.7

Where are you reading this book? Are you able to concentrate without disturbance?

- Are you comfortable? Have you enough space to work in?
- Do you have all the equipment you need close at hand?
- Do you have space to keep books and files?

Do your answers to these questions suggest that you should make changes to your study environment?

If you try to study at the kitchen table, with other people milling around and the TV on, the odds are stacked against you. To study you need to be able to concentrate intently. If you can set up a regular study area it helps get you into the habit of switching off from everything else. You may prefer different places for different activities – for reading, for jotting notes, for writing assignments. For some activities you need a surface on which to spread books and papers. For others you need access to a computer. You also need somewhere to store your files, if only a big box, and you need adequate light and heat. You may not be able to set up the ideal study environment, but you should try to get as close as you can. Concentrating on study is hard enough without struggling against your surroundings.

2.4.2 Equipping yourself

It is much easier to study efficiently if you have the right equipment:

- pens and highlighter pens
- A4 note-pads and printer paper
- paper clips and a stapler
- cardboard pocket files, filing boxes and sticky labels
- pads of coloured Post-it notes
- a box of index cards

Figure 2.4 A typical 'study kit'

- a good dictionary – unless you use online dictionaries
- shelf space for books and filing boxes.

As we saw in Chapter 1, you will also need access to a computer with an internet connection, a printer, and software.

See Chapter 1 Section 1.8.1, What equipment and skills do you need?

2.4.3 Maintaining a filing system

An important aspect of your study environment is entirely of your own making: the degree of confusion you allow to develop, as course paperwork accumulates – notes, handouts, printed material, completed assignments. If you never know where things are, your efficiency is significantly reduced. You find yourself deciding against using that excellent quotation for your essay because it would take you too long to find it; and, anyway, you doubt that you kept a note of the reference. In studying, much can be achieved simply by being able to organise material effectively. The sooner you start the better, because you can quickly become overwhelmed.

Treat your filing system as work in progress. Have to hand a good supply of wallet folders and labels, or spring-clip files and dividers. Keep adding new folders, or file sections, whenever you think you need them, and take the trouble to label them straight away. You can always stick on new labels as you work out better ways of organising the system. The time you spend on the upkeep of your filing will pay great dividends later. If you can find things quickly, your past work remains a permanent asset. In the end, what counts is not so much what you can remember as *what you can lay hands on when you need it.*

See Chapter 10 Section 10.2.2, Filing web addresses

2.4.4   Taking advantage of amenities

Studying is enough of a challenge to make it worth taking advantage of every support available to you; yet students often don't.

> In his first weeks at university Ryan felt overwhelmed by information, so he left all the leaflets and handouts in a pile to 'look at later'. Consequently, he remained unaware of the many services and amenities available to him. He missed the library tour and the introductory session at the computer centre. And he didn't think to explore the university website carefully. He just waited for the initial confusion to subside and hoped he would hear about things when he needed them. Generally he didn't. He simply missed out.

Don't let uncertainty and inertia prevent you from taking advantage of all that is on offer.

Websites

Your university's website is a good place to start. Set aside time to explore it thoroughly. There may be induction pages designed to introduce you to the university. And there may be a VLE that will point you to the services and facilities designed especially for students like you.

Be sure to visit your university library's website, to find out about access to online resources. Look for guidance on how to use the library system, for online introductory tours or workshops you can attend. It is vital to invest time familiarising yourself with the resources available to you and how to access them. Don't rely on picking up this knowledge as you go along.

Bookshops and libraries

Visit bookshops and libraries in your area to find out what they have on your subject. It can be rather daunting to walk into a large library or bookshop not knowing how to locate the section you need, especially if you are not sure what the section is called – but assistants will help if you take the plunge and ask them. You may be pleasantly surprised at how much relevant material is on hand. Or you may be disappointed and have to learn how to order books and articles through the library using the inter-library loan system, or join book-exchange schemes with other students.

2.4.5   Social arrangements

It is hard enough to make sense of subjects that are new to you without being constantly interrupted. Unless you can arrange to be left alone while you study, you are in for a very hard time. The people in your life may not realise just how hard you need to concentrate when you are studying. Or, in some cases, they may be quite dependent on your support and feel they have the right of instant access to you at all times. They may even secretly hope you will drop out, so that they can 'have you back'. These are issues that need to be talked about. Your studies are very important to you, and you may have to discuss the need for space in your life to pursue your goals. Alternatively, your family and friends may be delighted for you and keen to support your ambitions. Whatever the case, you must try to negotiate boundaries around your time, so that you can work undisturbed for fairly lengthy spells. You must make sure that those around you understand your study needs and know when to leave you alone.

Key points

To make the best of your study circumstances you need to:

- fix up a suitable place to study
- get supplies of basic equipment, so that you are not held up when you need things
- set up and maintain an effective filing system
- find out about all available services and facilities
- explore and learn to use the available routes to academic information
- make arrangements with family and friends to leave you in peace to study.

2.5 Managing your morale

Nothing drives learning forward more effectively than enthusiasm, and nothing damages progress more than low morale. Yet study is intrinsically unsettling and frequently affects your mood. You may be competent and confident in the rest of your life, but study sets you back in the role of beginner. You find yourself dependent on teachers whose approval makes your spirits rise and whose disapproval may hurt. You experience the excitement of new insights, but dislodge old, comfortable ways of thinking. 'Truths' you took to be obvious become uncertain, yet new half-formed knowledge slips frustratingly from your grasp. Often it seems you know less than you did – that your studies keep revealing new incompetence.

The uncertainties of the student role can bring big mood swings: from inspiration to despair, from pride in achievement to a collapse of confidence. It is important to be ready for these highs and lows, and to understand them, so that they don't blow you off course. Here is a list of common 'lows', to help you think about them and put them in perspective. A list of 'highs' follows, to help you seek out the uplifting side of study.

2.5.1 What lowers morale?
Initial shock

- **Disruption to your daily life** So much study to fit in, creating pressures on family commitments, social commitments and leisure interests.
- **Information overload** Too much to take in: timetables, tasks, deadlines, books to buy, new names and faces, places to find, course descriptions, regulations, special services, student societies.
- **Culture shock** New ways of talking and thinking, new ways of relating to tutors and other students, new environments, new assumptions about the world and what is important: a whole new identity as a student.

Personal pressures

- **Loss of confidence in your own abilities** Apparent lack of progress, and doubts that you will make it to the end of the course.
- **Lack of structure in your life** Feeling disorganised and not in control of events.
- **Alienation** Feeling set apart from university ideas, language, people, attitudes, ways of talking, ways of relating; doubting that you will ever 'belong'.
- **Dislocation** Feeling that your studies are distancing you from your family, friends and community.

> ❛ My family wanted to know, "What are you trying to prove?" I fought and fought. Now they don't bother me because they know I'm studying. ❜

Everyday crises

- **Feeling overwhelmed by the work** Too many challenging and complicated tasks and little idea where to start.
- **Struggling to make sense** Feeling adrift in a sea of meaninglessness.
- **Writing assignments** Not being able to get started, not finding the books you need, struggling to achieve a plan, feeling that you will never finish, hating what you have written, feeling inarticulate.
- **Bad days at the office** You leave your notes on the bus, the library is closed when you get there, your internet connection breaks down, your printer runs out of ink.
- **Disagreeable course elements** A tiresome book, an irritating lecturer, a dreary seminar group.
- **Disappointing results** A presentation goes badly, an assignment grade is worse than you expected, your tutor seems only to find fault.
- **Obsession with grades** Irrational concern over why you lost five marks on your last essay, or why your tutor made that criticism.
- **Mid-term blues** Your interest in the subject flags, you don't seem to be making progress, it is sunny outside and you can't remember why the course seemed a good idea.
- **Exam anxiety** The exam looms like a black cloud casting a shadow over your enjoyment of the course.

These are typical low points. If you experience them you are no different from countless others. The important thing is to know how to combat them.

2.5.2   What lifts morale?
Achievement

- **Completed tasks** You finish a difficult article, make good notes, submit your assignment; you feel capable and effective.
- **Good results** A better than expected assignment grade, nice things written on the essay.

Creating structure

- **Tidying up** You label some folders and get the growing pile of notes sorted out.
- **Admin** You complete the forms you were sent, choose your next courses, arrange to see your tutor, pay your rent.
- **Planning** You update your To Do list and plan the week ahead; you feel organised and on top of things.

Knowledge

- **Understanding** You get really interested in an article, have a flash of insight during a lecture, say something that everyone discusses in the seminar; you feel your mind shifting up a gear.
- **Using knowledge** You find yourself taking sides in a TV debate; you chat to someone and hear yourself bringing new knowledge into play; you find yourself approaching life differently.

Personal development

- **Expressing yourself** You speak in seminars or join in an online conference; your writing style opens out and you feel yourself putting thoughts into words fluently.
- **Accepting new challenges** You volunteer for a turn as discussion chair, choose the tough assignment option.
- **Self esteem** You notice how many things you have achieved which you once doubted you could do; you find yourself thinking, 'If they can do it, so can I.'

Belonging

- **Enjoying your student group** You look forward to contact with other students; they ask about your life, make you laugh, help when you need support and care whether you do well.
- **Feeling valued by your tutor** Your tutor shows interest in your assignments, asks your opinion in class, is sympathetic during a difficult patch, gives thoughtful advice when you ask.
- **Speaking your mind** You don't worry about saying what you think in class or online, you don't mind being out on a limb with your views; you enjoy the cut and thrust of debate.
- **Feeling comfortable as a student** You don't feel like an outsider in the university setting, you know where to find the resources you want; you feel you have a right to all the amenities.

Sharing

- **Peer support** You talk about study problems with other students and share tips for coping; you realise that your struggles are quite normal and that, with mutual support, everyone can make it in the end.
- **Staff support** You talk with your tutor about problems with your essay; you ask a counsellor about difficulty sleeping; you feel that university staff are on your side and want you to succeed.

■ **Home support** You talk with family and friends about your study experiences.

2.5.3   Managing your morale

Studying makes everyone feel inadequate at times. That is why talking with other students is so helpful, whether in person or online. It puts things in perspective and keeps your spirits up. What matters is not what you have failed to do, but the progress you have made. When your spirits sag remind yourself of your achievements. Focus on the parts of the course you enjoy. Remember, *it is your course.* Make sure you enjoy it and get what you want from it. If you don't enjoy the course you won't learn much and you may not even stay with it to the end. Thinking positively is not an indulgence, it is essential.

Key points

Here is what you should do when studying gets you down.

■ Focus on aspects of study that you enjoy and do well.

■ Make a list of what you have achieved. Forget the plans you didn't fulfil. Ignore the abilities and achievements of other students – it isn't a race.

■ Do some organising to show yourself that you are in charge. Tidy your workspace, set yourself some concrete tasks. Update your To Do list.

■ Talk to other students outside class. Talk to your tutor. Remind yourself that you are a normal person, experiencing normal challenges.

■ Remember that you are doing this for *you.*

2.6   Being a successful self-manager

To be a successful student you have to become your own manager, guiding yourself through your studies. These are the essentials.

Be active As a student, you are not a passenger. You are the driver. You have to take the initiative in finding out what needs to be done, drawing up plans and implementing them. You don't wait to be told.

Be strategic Assess your situation. What needs to be done? What difficulties present themselves? How can you best achieve your goals? Develop plans which take these factors into account, but modify them as appropriate. For example, when you recognise that your powers of concentration have dipped, take the strategic decision to switch to a less demanding task. Don't flounder around. Weigh things up and work out how to achieve the best you can under the circumstances.

Be systematic Take time to gather information and organise it. Maintain your filing system, work out detailed plans. For example, the study plan in Activity 2.6 required you to find out deadlines, create a To Do list and then map out your week's study. By developing such a plan systematically you will have a much clearer picture of what has to be achieved and of how to manage your progress flexibly and intelligently.

Be analytical Analyse complex issues into more manageable components. For example, in updating your To Do list, you break big tasks into sub-tasks. You then shift items up and down the list, thinking about the consequences of different sequences of tasks.

Be reflective Learn from experience (see Figure 1.2 'Kolb's reflective learning cycle'). Review your study activities regularly and consider whether your strategies are working well.

See Chapter 1 Section 1.7, Being a reflective learner

Give yourself incentives Remind yourself of your goals, long- and short-term, and keep track of your progress towards them. Set yourself targets and take satisfaction in your achievements.

Manage your morale Keep your spirits up by playing to your strengths and focusing on what you enjoy. Set yourself manageable tasks with clear outcomes. Keep your To Do list, your files and your workspace well organised, so that you feel on top of your studies. Keep in touch with other students. And keep reminding yourself that this is all for you.

Key points

The theme of this chapter is that to enjoy studying and achieve success you have to take control. To do this, you have to:

- take on responsibility for your own learning, no longer relying on being told what to study, when and how
- review the work set by the course and break it into sequences of specific, manageable tasks
- find ways of creating study time, then plan how to use it to best effect
- make efforts to create the best circumstances for study that you can
- work at keeping up your morale
- take an active and intelligent approach to managing yourself.

References

Quality Assurance Agency for Higher Education (QAA) (2001) *The Framework for Higher Education Qualifications in England, Wales and Northern Ireland,* available at: http://www.qaa.ac.uk/ academicinfrastructure/FHEQ/EWNI/default.asp (accessed 31 August 2007).

Vorkink, S. (1995) 'Time on Task' in Rickey Hatfield, S. (ed.) *The Seven Principles in Action*, Bolton, MA, Anker Publishing Company Inc, pp. 67–78.

CHAPTER 3
Understanding how you learn

Most of this book takes a practical approach to studying. It focuses on specific tasks explored through real examples. This chapter, however, is concerned with how you *make sense* of your experiences of learning so that you can *think* about the way you approach your studies. In other words, it is concerned with 'conceptualising' (see Chapter 1 Figure 1.2).

3.1 Developing ideas about learning

See Chapter 1 Section 1.7, Being a reflective learner

In order to think, you need ideas. You will develop many ideas about learning through your own experiences of studying. As you experiment with different ways of studying, you will form concepts such as 'studying actively' and 'using time effectively'. But you will acquire concepts about learning from other sources too. You will develop them as you talk with other students about their study experiences and as you pick up advice from teachers. Reading this chapter offers further help with conceptualising. It will help you to think about the steps you can take to make sure you learn well.

3.1.1 Different kinds of learning

We learn all the time. Daily experience continually shapes how we think and act. This learning is very visible in young children; however, in adult life we tend not to think of routine everyday adaptation to our surroundings as learning. Rather, we associate learning with those times when we have to make a conscious effort to accumulate new knowledge and skills – such as when starting a new job, finding our way around a strange town or learning to drive.

Practical learning A lot of this learning is achieved by doing – by trying things out, watching others, asking for advice, reflecting on experience, practising, and simply 'being there' as part of the action, so that we gradually become familiar with the surroundings and how to act within them.

Abstract learning However, you can't learn history, for example, simply by 'doing' in this sense. You can't 'do' the Middle Ages as direct experience; our knowledge of the past is the product of historians gathering information, interpreting and debating what it means, and writing accounts. It is a product of human enquiry, thought and debate. At bottom, its currency is abstract ideas. Much learning in the arts and humanities is like this.

So, how do we learn ideas? That is the subject of this chapter. My focus will be on the type of learning most associated with the word 'study' – the learning of *abstract knowledge*, achieved through reading, listening, discussing and writing.

A note on ideas and skills in the arts and humanities

But focusing on the learning of ideas, rather than the learning of *skills* in arts and humanities subjects – for example, the skills of analysing a poem, a painting or a piece of music – gives a false impression, because learning skills such as these goes hand in hand with learning ideas or concepts. For instance, in music, understanding the concept of 'concordant harmonies' involves listening to many different pieces of music – the actual *objects* of your study. To hear these harmonies you need to know how to listen carefully, and be able to pick out and analyse particular sequences of sound. These are some of the skills you learn as you study music.

In arts and humanities subjects you study many different kinds of object – written, aural and visual – such as: poems, novels and plays; musical performances and scores; paintings, sculpture, artefacts, buildings and their plans; philosophical treatises and writings; historical documents and records for particular periods and events. These objects of your study are called *primary sources.*

You also read a lot about these objects in textbooks, scholarly articles and teaching texts; you watch TV programmes, films and DVDs, and listen to radio talks about them. In such texts and programmes, scholars, critics and teachers analyse and interpret the meanings of the particular objects they choose to study. These academic accounts are called *secondary sources.*

In this book we are concerned with how to study secondary sources (except for Chapter 9). How to study the objects themselves is what your courses in the arts or humanities teach you.

Using this chapter

Read this chapter when you feel ready to think more about the learning process. It covers a lot of ground, so you may want to read a section at a time rather than tackle the whole thing in one go.

- Section 3.2 'What does learning mean?' explores the way that learning happens in the background while you are busy getting on with your study activities.

- Section 3.3 'Why do they write like that?' is about the very distinctive way academic subjects are discussed and written about. This will help you to follow arguments when you are reading and listening. It will also help you to write better essays. You may want to read this section, or read it again, when you have written an essay or two.

- Section 3.4 'Reading, listening, speaking and writing' looks in detail at the advantages and the challenges of studying in these different modes. It will help you to reflect on your experiences after you have been studying for a while.

3.2   What does learning mean?

As a student you spend hours learning a subject, but what is the nature of the learning you are trying to achieve and how do you make it happen?

Activity 3.1

Bring to mind some studying that you have done, and jot down a few thoughts in answer to these questions.

1   How do you know that you have learned something you have studied?

2   What is 'learning'?

3   What do you have to do to learn something?

These are difficult questions to answer. I put them to some students (two of them arts students) who were part-way through their degree studies to find out what conclusions they had drawn from their experience. In the following sections you can compare some of their answers with your own. It doesn't matter if your answers are different – just treat any differences as food for thought.

3.2.1   How do you know you have learned something?

Have you ever reached the end of a chapter and wondered whether any of it would still be in your head in a few days' time? Have you been asked about a lecture or talk you attended and found yourself unable to say anything much about it? I am sure most people would answer 'yes' to both questions. But do experiences such as these mean that you have learned nothing – that your time was wasted? Ought you to be able to give a detailed summary of what you have read or heard? The answer to both these questions is 'no'. Your mind does not work like a photocopier, making exact copies of what you read or hear to store as files in your head. The learning of ideas is a much more subtle process than that. Evidence of what you have learned does not emerge as a well-formed replica of what went into your head. It can show up unexpectedly and fragmentarily while you are working on other things. Here is how one student put it:

> When you are in lectures, or talking with mates, and some piece of information enters your head, then you know you've learnt it; also when you get interested and start analysing an idea in your head.

So, ideas and information you have learned begin to appear in your thoughts and words as you are listening and talking. They become part of your mental equipment. Also, when you find yourself interested in a new idea and turn it over in your mind, this too is evidence that the learning process is underway.

Another student had a similar view:

> I can tell I have learned something when I'm able to rephrase an argument in my own terms and link it to other arguments ... I also know when I have learned about a whole topic when I can organise an overall picture in my

head of how all the different points relate to each other. For example, I found it very satisfying to be able to piece together an overall picture of ... post-war European cinema, and the different movements in various countries.

So, being able to turn over new ideas in your head is another sign that you have begun to learn them: being able to put them into your own words and organise them, so that they fit together to create an overall picture.

As you learn new ideas you begin to be able to *use* them to say things of your own. A student noted that:

You know something must have begun to sink in when you eventually find the confidence to start thinking about your approach to the next essay – you begin to feel you might have the knowledge to hack it.

Interestingly, another observes that one sign of having learned a new idea is that you are able to carry on and learn more:

When you find you can understand new aspects of the subject, then you know you learned what you read before.

Knowledge does not sit like a rack of neatly organised CDs in your head which you can take out and play whenever you want. Instead, what you learn becomes embedded in the way that you think. It isn't easy to say 'look, this is what I have just learned', yet evidence of your learning constantly emerges.

Key points

Evidence of learning from study

Learning through study doesn't create a detailed record of knowledge in your head; rather, it develops the way you think. Indirect evidence of what you have learned will appear in a number of ways.

- New ideas and information pop up in your thoughts as you are talking to others, reading, listening and thinking.
- You find yourself becoming interested in a new idea and thinking it over.
- You can put an argument into your own words.
- You can create your own summary of a topic.
- You find yourself developing a point of view or coming to your own conclusions about an issue.
- You are able to think your way into an essay.
- You are able to move on and learn something else.

These are signs that learning has happened, but what exactly is 'learning'?

3.2.2   What is learning?

> I think learning is mainly understanding what you have read or heard. If you understand it, then it is easy to remember without actually having to memorise. The other main part of learning is being able to fit what you learn together with what you already know.

This student, then, suggests that there are two key aspects of learning:

- making an effort to understand as you read and listen
- connecting this understanding with what you know already.

Here is a student who takes a similar view:

> At one level learning is about taking in other people's ideas, and also, facts. At another level it's about analysing and working on these ideas and combining them with your own thoughts to create a viewpoint. For example, I took in ideas and data about people's perceptions of nature and reworked them to link with another topic, conservation, to produce new ideas. And I retained the original information in the process.

Although these students were studying different fields, both recognise that you have to take in new ideas and information and that you have to do some work to weave them together with what you already know. Another student points to a third aspect – being able to express new knowledge.

> Learning is gaining knowledge and the ability to express it in the way that is expected.

For knowledge to be useful, you have to be able to speak and write it. So, learning is not simply about getting ideas and information *into* your head, it is also about being able to *communicate* what is in your head to other people, and being able to do this in the accepted ways.

Key points

We have identified three aspects of learning through study.

- **Taking in new ideas** by making the effort to understand what you read and hear.
- **Working on new ideas** by fitting them together with what you already know.
- **Expressing new ideas** by using them to say things of your own.

What are the practical implications of this view of learning?

3.2.3   What do you have to do to learn something?

These aspects of learning are rather like stages in a dialogue that you have with the subject you are studying. You listen or read, you think, and you speak or write. In the process of participating in this dialogue, your mind adapts to the way the subject works. This adaptation is the essence of higher-level learning.

> I find learning normally just happens – I dive in, take bits at a time, write notes, and then maybe go over them another time – it's a gradual process. Writing essays is an important part of learning for my courses.

Notice that, although learning 'just happens' for this student, he actually takes a very active approach to it – diving in, taking a bit at a time, writing notes and going over things. So he is doing a lot, but it doesn't feel to him like 'learning' is a deliberate activity. It is more like finding out and thinking about things, and working out what he wants to say about them. And notice too that writing essays plays an important part. Making notes is a key way of working on new ideas. In the process of deciding what to note down you begin to take in the ideas you have heard or read. Then, as you start expressing new ideas in an assignment, you make the ideas your own. That is why written assignments, and especially essays, are a key part of learning.

Here is how another student said she learned:

> Most things I learn come originally from my reading, which I take notes from, and we sometimes discuss in seminars. Often the things I learn most about are essay topics, because the process of structuring and writing an essay helps me to understand the main points of the argument.

She too puts reading and note making at the heart of learning, but adds discussing in class. This is another way of pursuing your dialogue with the subject. Like the first student, she sees essay writing as central, but she emphasises the process of planning – the thinking required before writing.

These students do not see learning as being achieved by a single action. You work at it in stages and you approach it as an active effort to make sense of the subject, by organising your thoughts, working out what you want to understand and looking for answers.

> I have realised that in order to feel happy about understanding a topic in my head I have to organise it. I try to plot things out on paper as I learn them. I also plan essays quite thoroughly, as this helps me to learn my notes. My note taking has changed because I don't just write down everything I read now. I work out what I want to get from an article before I read it.

Key points

Studying is like having a dialogue with your subject. Your mind adapts to the way ideas are used within the subject – this adaptation is the 'learning'. So, learning involves:

- making an effort to understand as you read course texts and listen to lectures
- making notes selectively and creatively
- thinking about what you are learning and organising it in your head, on paper or onscreen
- listening closely to and joining in with discussions in class or online
- reworking your notes, especially in preparation for assignments
- treating writing as a key learning experience.

You might like to look back now to Activity 3.1 and the notes you made then. Would you give the same answers now? What do you think you have learned from this section of the chapter? Has your 'dialogue' with it altered the way you think about learning?

3.3   Why do they write like that?

Reading a study text is challenging. It isn't like reading a newspaper. You have to concentrate much harder. So why do they write in that difficult way? In this section we consider who 'they' are and explore the key features of academic writing.

Activity 3.2

What do you think makes academic writing challenging to read? Here is the opening sentence from Joyce Ellis's article, '"On the Town": Women in Augustan England' (extracts from the article are included in the Appendix).

> Modern demographic research suggests that in what is known as the 'long eighteenth century' the female population of England's larger towns expanded dramatically, producing what one demographer has called 'a remarkable predominance of women' in contrast with the more balanced or emphatically male-dominated populations of smaller settlements.

> (Ellis, 1995)

Do you find it easy to 'get into' this kind of writing? Jot down your thoughts about what makes this passage tougher to read than a newspaper article.

These are the challenges I picked out.

Unfamiliar wording 'Demographic research' may well be an unfamiliar notion, and we may not know quite what it refers to. In the main, though, it doesn't seem to me that the words themselves present the most difficult challenge in this passage. It is rather that this is a long, complex sentence which expresses a number of (albeit related) ideas.

Abstractness This sentence is about abstract ideas: demography, population expansion and the 'contrasting' (pre)dominance of female and male in different 'settlements' during a particular period in the past. There are no events to visualise in your mind. Instead, you have to hold in mind these abstract ideas, and so it is easy to lose the thread of what is being said.

Style The writing is very compact. A lot is squeezed into a few words, and there is no attempt to be 'chatty'. The main business is to lay the groundwork for an argument about women in eighteenth-century society and nothing interferes with that.

Assumptions Ellis assumes that readers know what is meant by 'the long eighteenth century'. She also assumes that we are interested in the demography of the period, and that we are aware of the importance of this subject for historians.

3.3.1 Accessing academic knowledge
The specialised use of words, the abstractness and the compactness of style in the passage in Activity 3.2 are typical of the language associated with academies (universities, colleges and research institutes). This is an example of 'academic discourse'.

Engaging with academic discourse
If you want to acquire academic knowledge you have to learn how to engage with academic discourse – a fairly lengthy process, but you certainly don't need to wait until you are fluent before you join in. The aim of this section of the chapter is to help you understand the way academic discourse works so that you can read and listen to it more easily.

Academic disciplines
Although Joyce Ellis's article was published in *History Today*, a popular history journal with a readership beyond the academy, she seems to assume her audience to be members of the academic community of historians or, more specifically, social historians of the eighteenth century.

Members of a discipline community 'meet' through debates in journals and at conferences. And when they speak or write in these debates they assume a certain amount of background knowledge amongst other members of the discipline. For example, they make reference to earlier debates which they assume discipline members will be familiar with and they try to anticipate objections that discipline members might make to their arguments. They are also aware of the research standards expected within the discipline. In effect, the discipline functions as a self-regulating community, with a common interest in maintaining high standards of research and debate.

Academic values

The members of an academic discipline are held together by the goals and values they share. These include commitment to:

- a perpetual search for better understanding within their subject area
- high-quality research
- open debate (in which all members have the right to participate)
- logical argument
- fairness and impartiality
- free exchange of information and ideas, in order to promote the advance of knowledge within the community (on the assumption that members will not take unfair advantage).

Individual members may disagree strongly with each other's ideas, but, through their commitment to these values, they can participate together in the community's core work of advancing knowledge. Recognising the importance of these values will help you to understand the way they write and speak.

Getting to know your discipline

The subjects you study may fall within a single discipline (such as art history or literature) or across several (e.g. cultural studies). In either case you will find that, alongside texts, ideas and information, you are learning about the history of your discipline(s). Gradually, as you build up a picture of influential past writers and key debates, you see why particular issues have come to be treated as important. This is extremely valuable because, as we have seen, what is said in academic discourse often takes such background knowledge for granted. Eventually, you find the meaning of articles in your discipline(s) much more transparent, because you know 'where they are coming from'. You discover that you are becoming a member of the community, able to join in debates and understand what is going on.

Key points

- Academic knowledge does not come in handy, off-the-shelf packages. You have to seek it out by engaging in academic discourse.
- It is easier to understand academic discourse if you are aware of the value placed on a perpetual search for knowledge through research, debate and logical reasoning.
- Understanding becomes easier as you get to know some of the background to your discipline(s) and become more aware of what is generally taken for granted.

3.3.2 Key features of academic discourse

We have talked of the values underpinning the search for knowledge and understanding within academic disciplines. Now we explore in more detail the way those values shape academic discourse. This will help you understand what is going on as you read and listen. It will also help you learn to write in the academic way, but bear in mind that it takes practice to become skilled in this way of writing. You will pick it up a little at a time as you continue your studies.

Here then are eight key features of academic discourse, which make it powerful but at the same time challenging to read and to write.

1   Debate

Debate lies at the heart of academic discourse. Discipline members advance knowledge as they take up different positions on an issue and try to refine or to defeat each other's case. Ideas emerge from these debates either strengthened or else damaged and in need of reworking. Any academic article you read is likely to have been written as an argument against someone else's position, in whole or in part. For example, we will see that Joyce Ellis takes issue with the view of women's attraction to the towns expressed by many writers and satirists of the period. She argues that there were good reasons for women's migration to the town, beyond the satirists belief that towns were 'meccas of unbridled consumption and frivolity to which women were irresistibly drawn'.

As a newcomer, it is easy to miss the point of something you have read because you are not aware of the debate it refers to. Learning about major debates in the history of your discipline is an important part of becoming competent in your subject. You also have to get into the mindset of valuing debate. In essays, for example, you are often expected to compare different points of view, and present each one fairly, before weighing them up against each other. And you write from the point of view that readers will be 'debating with you' as they read.

2   Scholarship

Academics are expected to maintain standards of scholarship by keeping abreast of debates within their discipline. You presume that writers will have researched recent publications relevant to their subject; that is, they will have conducted a 'literature search'. When Joyce Ellis refers to 'modern demographic research' you expect her to have read the relevant sources and to be able, if asked, to explain how she reached her conclusions. (In fact, had she been writing for a mainstream history journal she would almost certainly have done this in footnotes.)

Because academic arguments build on what has been written before, writers are expected to supply details of their sources. References are scattered throughout academic texts to indicate who contributed to the debate, and when – for example, '(Ellis, 1995)'. A list of references or a bibliography at the end of the text gives full details of all the references made within it. Learning to include references in your assignments is one of the most visible steps towards adopting an academic writing style.

See Chapter 8 Section 8.2.8, Reviewing, revising and polishing

See Chapter 7
Section 7.6.1,
Explaining and
illustrating an
argument

Free exchange of knowledge within a discipline rests on the assumption that members will play fair and give due credit when they use other people's ideas, arguments and research. Not to do so is seen as a major breach of faith. If you go further and pass off another person's work as your own, this is 'plagiarism' and it will seriously damage your reputation.

3   Argument

In academic discourse, what you say should unfold as logical argument. An argument starts from a clearly established issue for debate, then presents a sequence of points, each logically connected to what has gone before. This sequence is arranged so as to lead up to a conclusion. You have already seen the first manoeuvres in launching an argument in the earlier extract from Joyce Ellis's article. Activity 3.3 contains another example, from paragraph 3 of the article.

Activity 3.3

What women sought in the towns, the satirists argued, was freedom from male control. Such claims, however, reflected long-standing literary conventions and equally long-standing male anxieties rather than contemporary reality. It is much more plausible to argue that urban life attracted a disproportionate number of women not because they were trying to escape from or to subvert accepted gender roles but because 'correct' female behaviour was all too often dysfunctional in a rural setting.

(Ellis, 1995)

Can you see how Joyce Ellis sets up her argument? Look at each sentence in turn and jot down what you think it does.

- The extract begins with a short sentence. It puts one side of the argument, the satirists' view, in a nutshell (though she will go on to illustrate it).
- The second sentence presents, equally briefly and baldly, critique of the satirists' claims.
- The final, longer, sentence indicates Ellis's own 'much more plausible' position, in opposition to the satirists, and the direction her argument will take.
- Every word is part of the setting up of Ellis's argument, which she then goes on to develop in the rest of the article.

When you read Ellis's article in full for the activities in Chapter 4, you will see that everything in it has a direct bearing on what is said in the opening paragraphs. In an academic text you assume that every part contributes in some way to the author's argument. As you read you should be trying to pick out this argument. Similarly, when you write an essay you should plan it as an argument leading from the title to the conclusion. Anything which does not contribute to your argument you should leave out.

4   Criticism

In academic discourse, as well as presenting your own arguments you criticise other people's. In this context, to criticise means to discuss weak *and* strong aspects of an argument. Knowledge advances through examining arguments and claims carefully, and judging their strengths and weaknesses. And through creative criticism we try to clarify the objects that interest us and come to understand them better. In everyday life it may seem impolite or boring to keep picking holes in what someone says, but in academic discourse it is a duty. You are expected to be constantly on the look out.

5   Analysis

Simply, analysis means taking things apart to see what they are made of and how they work. Ellis offers some analysis of why women migrated to towns by illustrating the restrictions they experienced living in the countryside. In academic discourse, you analyse arguments to see how the logic flows from one step to the next. This is what you did in Activity 3.3, when you examined Ellis's opening argument by taking it apart sentence by sentence.

Analysis and criticism go together: *critical analysis*. When you are asked to critically analyse primary texts – a painting, the power struggles in a period of history or the way words are used in a poem – this too is very far from a destructive, or a reductive, activity. The critical-analytical approach is perhaps the most distinctive characteristic of academic discourse.

6   Evidence

You do not accept what you have read simply because it is written by a respectable person, or because it is written with style and conviction. You expect to be offered the evidence to back up the argument. It may be evidence which the writer has found from personal research, or evidence quoted from other sources. When Ellis, for example, refers to 'modern demographic research' she is referring to evidence from other sources (as she says in paragraph 2, to 'hours of rigorous, computer-aided academic research').

7   Objectivity

Arguments are expected to be presented objectively, or neutrally. They are judged on the quality of their logic, scholarship and evidence, not who they are presented by nor how enthusiastically, stylishly, or entertainingly. As a writer you set your own beliefs and feelings to one side and try to adopt an objective stance – detached and unemotional. Your views or interpretations must be backed by objective evidence, not just asserted; you leave readers to analyse, criticise and come to their own conclusions.

8   Precision

Finally, academic discourse strives to be precise. You try to say exactly what you mean to say, and no more. You avoid sweeping generalisations. You avoid overstating your case. You leave out whatever does not make a direct contribution to your argument. There are no frills – no pleasantries, diplomacy, or 'human interest' hooks. This is a task-oriented discourse, and that task is to seek greater knowledge and understanding. In an ideal world, all else is irrelevant.

Key points

Academic discourse is the tool-kit of the academic trade. The basic tools are:

- **Debate** Setting up ideas and viewpoints against each other in order to test them out.

- **Scholarship** Showing how an argument links to the literature of the discipline.

- **Argument** Presenting connected sequences of points that lead to conclusions.

- **Critical analysis** Taking an argument apart to evaluate its strengths and weaknesses.

- **Evidence** Presenting the evidence to back up or support an argument.

- **Objectivity** Writing in a detached, unemotional way, leaving the argument to stand on its own merits.

- **Precision** Saying exactly what needs to be said to present an argument.

You need to be aware of these tools at the outset, so that you have an idea of what you are aiming towards. Your skill in using them will develop as you continue your dialogue with the subject.

3.4   Reading, listening, speaking and writing

As we have seen, studying is like having a dialogue with your chosen subject. You take in new ideas and information, then you reply, putting the ideas and information to use. The four basic ways of engaging in this dialogue are reading, listening, speaking and writing.[1] Two use the written word and two the spoken word.

Table 3.1   Engaging with new ideas and information

	The written word	**The spoken word**
Take in	*Reading* books, articles, online	*Listening* Lectures, audio-visual media
Reply	*Writing* essays, reports, notes	*Speaking* seminars, tutorials, online conferences

Each mode of dialogue offers advantages and challenges. We explore these in the final section of the chapter.

---

[1] In a sense, we also engage in dialogue through 'viewing' audio-visual material. This is discussed in Chapter 6, Section 6.5.

3.4.1 Reading

A large amount of your study time is likely to be spent reading, whether it is onscreen or the printed page – though for most people print remains the best medium for concentrated reading.

Advantages of learning through reading

Accessibility The written word is immensely accessible. You don't have to seek out knowledgeable people and persuade them to speak their knowledge to you. Books and journal articles, printed or electronic, make knowledge available across boundaries of space and time. You can learn from writers from all over the world, past and present.

Flexibility You can carry printed texts around with you and work anywhere for a few minutes or several hours, at times of your own choosing. You can skim through pages to find what you want, then focus in detail on a single paragraph. And you can stop to make notes or mark the text, then pick up again exactly where you left off.

Control The text does not run ahead of your thoughts, as spoken words can easily do. The knowledge sits there on the page, waiting for you to grapple with it. You can pick over sentences, pondering their exact meaning, and you can revisit them as many times as you like.

Challenges of reading

In spite of its advantages, reading is a demanding activity. When you start on a text it can be hard to pick up the gist of what the author is saying. And even when you have got started, it takes concentration to keep the meaning flowing in your head.

See Chapter 4, Reading

Box 3.1   How reading works

As you read you strive to recreate in your mind the flow of meaning that was in the author's mind as she or he was writing. But words on a page do not 'speak' their meaning. You have to project meaning onto the words by a kind of guessing ahead. This means you need some notion already of what the words might mean. You also need to be able to maintain a fairly steady momentum, so that you have a flow of meaning in your head ready to project onto words as you arrive at them.

When you are reading well you don't notice yourself doing it. If you are reading a thriller and you are swept along by the plot, the flow of the narrative corresponds so smoothly with the words on the page that it feels as if the story is happening in your head. As you turn the page, you are ready with the words to complete the phrase you are reading. Indeed, when the words are not quite what you are expecting, you may not even notice; your mind just carries on in its own groove.

However, reading study texts is very different from reading a novel for recreation or a newspaper. Because you are unfamiliar with the subject

---

and the way of writing, it is much harder to project ahead what the words on the page may mean. And if they fail to match what you are expecting, you have to stop and take a rerun. Sometimes you just can't guess at all, and your reading grinds to a halt.

Activity 3.4

As you were reading Box 3.1, were you able to make the meaning 'happen' in your head? Did you have difficulty forming the ideas in your mind?

It is not surprising if you struggled to make sense of the box. Unfamiliar ideas are difficult to read about because you can't always put the words together to make sense of them, so then you can't guess ahead to the meaning of the next words.

Box 3.2   Frames of reference

If you found the second paragraph in Box 3.1 easier to read than the other paragraphs, that is probably because the familiar activity of reading a novel provides a frame of reference – you can imagine it. You know what to think about, and that supports you in guessing the meanings of the words.

Frames of reference are very important in making meaning. You need to be able to set your thoughts in context. When you say 'Like what? Give me an example' to someone, you are asking them to supply a frame of reference to help you follow their meaning. In abstract arguments the frame of reference can easily slip out of focus. One way of creating a frame of reference for yourself is to try to link what you are reading to your own life. This can help you to guess ahead and make the meaning happen.

These are some of the principal challenges of reading.

- **Getting started** Having a sense of what the text is about and what it is trying to say (establishing a frame of reference) so that you can get a flow of meaning going in your mind.
- **Keeping going** Sustaining the flow of meaning as you encounter unfamiliar words and ideas.
- **Coping with blocks** Developing strategies to kick-start your reading when the flow of meaning stalls.

3.4.2   Listening

There are various ways in which you can learn by listening – lectures, seminar discussions, the radio, TV or recorded material. What all these have in common is that the speaker drives the flow of meaning. You still have to work at making sense of what you hear, but you are carried along by the momentum of the speaker's words.

Advantages of learning by listening

Framing When people speak they usually recognise, at some level, the need to let listeners know what they are talking about. Good lecturers establish a clear frame of reference for what they are going to say.

> Last week I outlined the main features of the Beveridge Report and the circumstances under which the post-war Labour government set out to implement its recommendations. This week I'm going to look at how and why the initial principles were modified by both Labour and Conservative governments over the next thirty years.

> As you will remember, Beveridge had set out to slay the five giants: Want, Disease, Ignorance, Squalor and Idleness ...

Even if the speaker doesn't frame the topic as explicitly as this, there are usually indirect clues. Unlike reading, when you have to get a frame of reference up and running for yourself, when you listen the framing is done for you.

Pacing The speaker drives the meaning forward. You don't have to work at sustaining the momentum. Even when you hear unfamiliar words and ideas that don't make much sense, you can carry on listening, pick up clues and tune into the meaning once again.

Multi-channel communication Speakers invest words with meaning through the way they are spoken and through facial expressions, hand gestures and body posture. They may use visual aids such as slides, or handouts showing the structure of the ideas they are presenting. Consequently, the flow of meaning is supported by much more than just spoken words.

Hearing an expert Hearing the language and ideas of the discipline spoken by an expert gives you first-hand experience of how the discipline's ideas are used to make sense of the world. You hear how arguments are linked to the big debates, how criticism works, how evidence is presented, how conclusions are drawn. The speaker 'models' the way the academic discourse is spoken, giving you valuable support in developing your own ability to speak it.

Box 3.3   Taking in new ideas by listening

You know the old conundrum about which came first, the chicken or the egg? Working with new ideas involves a similar puzzle. We have seen that members of an academic discipline share many assumptions about the questions they are setting out to answer. When you try to join in a discussion, it can be hard to make sense of what is being talked about because you don't know what the underlying assumptions are. The only way you can begin to grasp these assumptions is through participating in discussions within the discipline. But participating is what you are having difficulty with because you don't share the assumptions. So which comes first?

To get into a new topic you have to circle around for a while, picking up the gist as best you can, until ideas and underlying assumptions start to come together for you. The problem is particularly acute when you are reading because you are on your own, whereas when you hear someone speak you get a sense of how the meaning is intended to flow. Even if you don't understand fully, you pick up clues about the kind of ideas in play, where the argument starts from, how it draws on evidence and where it ends up. These clues give you much more to work with next time you are reading and thinking about the topic on your own.

Ironically, when new ideas eventually 'click', it is hard to remember what was so difficult. Because the ideas and your assumptions now fit together, the meaning seems obvious.

Challenges of listening

See Chapter 6 Section 6.5, Listening to talk

Of course, the advantages just outlined depend on a reasonably good speaker, and lecturers can be rather variable. But even with a good speaker, listening is demanding.

- **Keeping pace** A speaker has to guess the pace at which 'average' audience members are able to absorb the flow of ideas – too fast and listeners are left floundering, too slow and attention wanders. The speaker's guess may not be right for you.

- **Maintaining concentration** Even when the pace is manageable, it is easy to lose the thread after a period of close concentration. You may become distracted because you are learning a lot, which is making you think, and the next thing you notice you have lost track.

- **Making notes** It is hard to stay in touch with a speaker's line of argument and make high-quality notes at the same time.

- **Summarising and recalling** Even when you follow a talk closely, it is difficult to pull together everything you have heard. Since the speaker is in control, you have to go with the flow and it can be hard to keep the 'big picture' in mind.

We have looked at reading and listening, the 'taking in' modes of learning. Now we turn to speaking and writing, the 'expressive' modes through which you learn to put new ideas to use. This is where you gain control over your new knowledge.

3.4.3 Speaking

See Chapter 6 Section 6.2.6, Online group work

Opportunities to learn through speaking generally arise in group work of some kind: seminars, tutorials, workshops and team projects (though you can of course also learn from informal chats outside the classroom). Later in the book (Chapter 6) another kind of speaking is discussed – speaking in online conferences – which is, in fact, writing. But this is a hybrid form, a kind of speaking-writing.

Advantages of learning through speaking

Spontaneity By joining in with a discussion you experience new ideas in action. This helps you gain hands-on knowledge of how to develop arguments. You don't have time to stop and worry about what to say. You seize the moment and make sense as best you can. Whereas reading and writing give a sense of dealing with ideas at arms length, in discussion you are in there amongst them.

Momentum In the flow of a discussion the supports for making meaning are all around you. No staring blankly at page. You simply ride on the framing and momentum generated by the group.

Dialogue In a discussion you participate in a two-way exchange. Questions can be asked and answered, understandings can be shared. As you explain a point to someone else, you find you understand it better yourself. Much of your student experience is one-way; either you are taking in arguments from a writer or speaker, or you are delivering your arguments in an assignment. In dialogue you can share in shaping an argument and experience being part of a community of thinkers, making meaning together.

Instant feedback Discussion helps you learn how to use the language of your subject. You try out ways of saying things and find out instantly whether you have been understood. This live practice is also very helpful in improving your fluency in writing.

Social context Discussion helps you to feel that you are part of the discipline community and this in turn helps you develop an 'academic voice'. Over a sequence of discussions you gradually find yourself using a more critical-analytical voice. This helps you when it comes to writing essays.

Challenges of speaking

- **Awkwardness** Classroom discussion may sometimes be strained and intimidating, with awkward silences and nobody venturing to say much. If you are new to the subject matter the risk of appearing foolish can loom large.

See Chapter 6, Learning through talk

- **Finding an opening** In a large class, and within an evolving debate, it can be difficult to find the right moment to join in – unless the teacher breaks the class into small student groups.

- **Keeping track** The focus of discussion shifts (a little or a lot) with each new speaker, so it can be difficult to keep track of the subject of discussion. This can also make it hard to work out what to say.

3.4.4 Writing

Writing enables precise expression and detailed criticism. You can move words around or substitute other words to see if an idea can be expressed more clearly and accurately. You can come back to the idea as many times as you like, and, because it is fixed on the page, you can build on it. You can create a sequence of clearly connected points – a precisely stated argument – and offer it to others for criticism. This is why academic knowledge is strongly associated with the written word. It is also why writing is a key mode of learning. It draws your attention to the structure of arguments, to the assembling of illustration and evidence, and to coherent presentation.

Essay-assignments offer the most compelling opportunity to learn through writing. For many students this is the most demanding of study activities but, as the students in Section 3.2 of this chapter observed, it also leads to the most profound learning. If you are tempted to think of assignments primarily as a means of achieving grades, don't. They play a key role in your learning.

Advantages of learning through writing

Putting knowledge to use Writing gives you the incentive to pull together the knowledge and understanding you have gained through studying and to work out how to put it to use. This helps you to make the knowledge your own, so that it becomes part of your thinking.

Taking control Whereas it can be difficult to organise a coherent argument when you speak, you can build arguments carefully in writing. You can sketch out plans and alter what you have written to make your argument more convincing. It is your best opportunity to learn how to argue effectively.

Using your own words You can use the language of the discipline to say things in ways that make sense to you. This is vital to becoming a competent user of the ideas and arguments of your subject.

Expert feedback Assignments provide your best opportunity to receive coaching in how to present arguments using the language of the discipline. Your relationship with your tutor through your writing plays a key part in developing your identity as a member of the academic discipline.

Box 3.4   Developing a discipline identity

Who are you speaking as when you write? What is your relationship to the knowledge you are presenting? Is it in any sense your knowledge, or are you just going through the motions? To argue convincingly you need to develop a sense of identity as a member of the academic community which discusses this knowledge. Though initially you are an apprentice member, you still share ownership of the community's knowledge. Developing this sense of identity as a student of your subject is part of finding an academic 'voice'.

In a sense, your student years are a period of apprenticeship to your subject discipline. As you learn the language and culture of your discipline you gradually secure a more established identity, which allows you to participate with increasing effectiveness.

Challenges of writing

Because writing advances your learning significantly it calls on all your resources.

See Chapter 7, Writing essays, and Chapter 8, Managing the writing process

- **Deciding what to say** Working out the assignment task and making a selection from the many sources and issues you could discuss.

- **Presenting an argument** Working out an argument, and how to illustrate, support and present it.

- **Speaking to your reader** Writing in a way that makes sense to someone else; creating a flow of meaning and keeping the reader in touch with it.
- **Keeping up morale** Surviving the long slog and the crises of writing.

Here now is a summary of the advantages and the challenges posed by the four modes of discourse we have discussed in this chapter.

Table 3.2   Advantages and challenges of different modes of discourse

	Advantages	**Challenges**
Reading	You can search, focus, analyse, revisit, make detailed notes and reflect	Getting to grips with the meaning, keeping it flowing, coping with blocks
Listening	Meaning is framed and driven along for you, and you hear the discourse as spoken by an expert	Maintaining concentration, thinking while listening, trying to summarise and recall
Speaking	You can ride on the framing and momentum generated by others and develop your verbal skills	Feeling confused and exposed, expressing unfamiliar ideas, competing for 'air time', losing the thread
Writing	You can put ideas to use, learn to argue using the language of the discipline, and develop your voice and identity	Deciding what to say, structuring an argument, supporting it, creating a flow, finding a voice

3.5   Becoming knowledgeable

In this chapter we have seen that learning at higher levels is primarily about understanding ideas. You make these ideas your own by engaging in debates through reading, listening, speaking and writing. You also learn the skills of academic discourse, which enable you to construct powerful arguments backed by scholarship and evidence. The outcome of all this is considerably more valuable than a 'pile of information' in your head. You become an actively knowledgeable person – able to follow what experts are talking about, able to question what you read, able to ask probing questions and criticise arguments, and able to find things out and present arguments of your own.

If this sounds rather overwhelming as you embark on studying, remember the people you met in earlier chapters, such as Jan, Nathan, Jenny and Ryan. Everyone struggles to begin with. We all doubt our abilities and determination. Becoming highly educated is a long route with many twists and turns, but it is also a very interesting journey, full of insights and moments of achievement. You don't have to spend every minute thinking about the big issues discussed in this chapter; just get stuck into next week's work and enjoy it. What you have read here is for those moments when you are puzzled about why you are not making progress or when you want to understand more about what it is you are striving to achieve.

I hope that the ideas in this chapter have provided a helpful background for the more practically-focused chapters in Part 2 of the book. And I hope that Part 1, by taking a broad view of the study enterprise will, as its title claims, help you to study intelligently.

Reference

Ellis, J. (1995) '"On the Town": Women in Augustan England', *History Today*, vol. 45, no. 12, pp. 20–7.

PART 2
The essential skills

CHAPTER 4
Reading

4.1   Reading is easy, isn't it?

On any ordinary day, without even noticing, you read shop signs, newspaper headlines, TV listings, a magazine, or a story. So why would a message like this one appear in an online student chat room in the early weeks of a course?

> ❝ Is there any one out there feeling overwhelmed by the reading, or is it just me? Starting to think about giving up – bit pathetic I know, but just wondering if any of it is going in! Feeling bogged down – not sure whether to keep going, or try to recap or what. Any suggestions gratefully received. ❞

Clearly, reading for higher level study is quite different from everyday reading. The most obvious differences are:

- **Quantity** As a student you can find yourself reading for many more hours a week than you usually do.
- **Challenge** Instead of the ideas slipping easily into your mind, as when you read a newspaper or magazine, you find yourself having to concentrate to grasp them.

But there are more subtle differences too:

- **Purpose** Instead of reading to pick up information, or to be entertained, when studying your aim is to introduce yourself to *new ideas* and *ways of thinking* that will enable you to understand aspects of the world differently.
- **Active engagement** Studying involves actively working with new ideas, not just racing through the words. You have to look for the *meaning* as you read, asking yourself '*what is the author trying to say?*'

Research into how students read (for example, Entwistle, 1997, p. 19) has shown that to be successful you need to understand these more hidden aspects of the reading process.

4.2   The experience of reading

The best way to develop your understanding of the reading process is to follow the principles of the Kolb learning cycle, by *doing* some reading and then *reflecting* on your experience. So, Activity 4.1 asks you to read an extract from the article by Joyce Ellis (1995) '"On the Town": Women in Augustan England' which appeared in *History Today* and is reproduced in the Appendix. To keep the task manageable I have reduced the length of the article and, for ease of reference, paragraph numbers have been added.

See Chapter 1 Section 1.7, Being a reflective learner

It is important that you read the article now as a lot of discussion in this and later chapters will assume that you have read it.

Box 4.1   Making copies of Joyce Ellis's article

You will find Ellis's article at the end of the book. Since you will be coming back to it several times to work on it in different ways, it could end up looking a mess. A better option is to photocopy the article, print off a few copies and work on them freely.

Activity 4.1

Read the article "'On the Town': Women in Augustan England', making a note of the time you start reading it.

When you've finished reading, calculate the time you spent on it; then write down briefly your thoughts about the following questions. Don't be tempted to skip this exercise; it will help you reflect on your reading.

1   Did you enjoy reading the article? How did you go about it?

2   Did you experience any difficulties as you read?

3   How long did it take you?

4   Where and at what time of day did you do the reading?

5   In a sentence, what is the article about? (Don't look back – just work from memory.)

6   What two or three points have stuck in your mind? Do you think you will be able to remember what is in the article in a few weeks' time?

7   Did you mark parts of it as you read (underlining or using a highlighting pen), or make any notes?

Here are the responses of two students: Philip and Hansa. At the time of reading they were, no doubt like you, busy with coursework too. Compare your notes with theirs and think about any differences that emerge.

1   Did you enjoy reading the article? How did you go about it?

Philip: It was interesting, but a bit of a struggle to finish. I read it straight through, but stopping and starting – and flagging a bit sometimes.

Hansa: Yes I did enjoy it, mainly because I am very interested in the role of women through history. It gave practical reasons for women's attitudes. I read it through once – quite quickly – and then again going over the bits I found difficult.

2   Did you experience any difficulties as you read?

Philip: I had to read some sentences over and over because they're long and needed to be unpacked to get the sense of what the author was saying. You had to pay attention to the punctuation to make sense of it – for example, para. 10, 'Moreover, whereas in earlier periods ... coffee houses' and the whole of para. 12.

Hansa: I didn't understand some words – 'Augustan' [in the title], 'demographic' [para. 1], 'dysfunctional' [para. 3], 'an assize' [para. 10]. I found it quite long.

The students agree that the article is quite demanding and that parts of it were difficult to follow.

3   How long did it take you?

Philip: Just over half an hour.

Hansa: About 20 minutes.

This reading was not part of the students' coursework so they had little incentive to spend a lot of time on it. In later answers they indicate that they would have spent more time re-reading the article if they needed to remember what was in it.

4   Where and at what time of day did you do the reading?

Philip: At home at my desk, beginning 8.20 pm Thursday.

Hansa: Sunday 11.00 in the morning. It was a nice day so I sat outside.

The students found the opportunity to do the reading at very different times of day and in different surroundings. Clearly there is no 'correct' time or place for reading. It depends on you and the patterns of your life.

5   In a sentence, what is the article about?

Philip: It's about the expectations of women in the eighteenth century.

Hansa: Why women migrated to the towns in the eighteenth century.

Hansa's answer shows a sense of the main theme of the article, but I think Philip's is a bit too general and vague to be very helpful.

6   What two or three points have stuck in your mind? Do you think you will be able to remember what is in the article in a few weeks' time?

Philip: The strength of opinion at the time against women moving into towns. I'll remember some of it I think.

Hansa: How isolated women could be in the countryside by lack of transport and bad weather. Needing a bone-setter! The references to literature, for example Jane Austen. I'll remember the general information but probably not the names of people who are quoted.

Some of the points that have stuck in mind are more central to the article than others. I doubt, for example, whether Hansa would need to remember the literary references or the names of those who are quoted.

7   Did you mark parts of it as you read (underlining or using a highlighter pen) or make notes?

Philip: Yes, I underlined a few bits.

Hansa: No.

It appears that neither student was working very actively while reading. But it would be a mistake to draw firm conclusions from just these brief notes. In Chapter 7 you can read extracts from essays these students wrote about the article and consider whether the impressions we have gleaned here are reflected in the quality of their writing.

How did your answers compare with those of Philip and Hansa? Did reading their responses cast light on your own approach to reading the article?

Here's what I thought. I had mixed feelings as I started reading. The mention of 'demographic research' in the very first sentence put me off a bit – the title 'On the Town' sounded a lot more fun than that. I found the first sentence quite difficult to read and had to go back over parts of it. It is written in a complicated way: 'Modern demographic research suggests ... , producing ... in contrast with ...' I felt the writing was holding me very much at arm's length.

The first sentence of paragraph 2 struck me as off-putting in a different way. It seems to be written as if we are all 'in the know', or should be. If in fact you don't know anything about this standard cliché, where does that leave you? (Perhaps on the outside, feeling pretty stupid?) However, I was reassured by the next sentence; 'underhand stratagems' sounded much more interesting and I set off again in a happier frame of mind. Generally, I thought the author expected me to have a wide vocabulary so that I could take in my stride expressions like 'meccas of unbridled consumption and frivolity to which women were irresistably drawn'.

Then, I went on to find the last half of paragraph 3 and paragraph 4 difficult to grasp – full of abstract ideas and complex sentences. At this point I was feeling rather frustrated by my slow progress. Instead of stopping to make full sense of it all, I decided simply to underline certain words ('dysfunctional', and in paragraph 4 the phrases 'conventional expectations', 'contemporary norms' and 'an ideal') so that I could come back to them later. Then I highlighted paragraph 5 in the margin, in which Ellis describes an historical change that had a big effect on these women's roles in the countryside.

From paragraph 6 I began to enjoy myself. I found it all quite easy and engaging reading. I was struck by how the writing flowed, with one part of the discussion seeming to lead naturally to the next, carrying me along with it. And I began to realise that, generally, Ellis would make a point (for example about the difficulty of travelling around in the countryside), then spend quite a lot of time explaining and illustrating it. I particularly enjoyed some of these illustrations. To think that carriages would turn over and women break their bones simply visiting neighbours! And imagine being house-bound for four months. Although 'antique' writing can be difficult, I found the quotations Ellis used quite readable. And I found myself thinking about how very different life is for women who live in the countryside now.

Also, it was intriguing to read about the views of visitors to England: it had never occurred to me that women went window-shopping in the eighteenth century. I didn't bother trying to remember people's names. But I did try to underline the *main points* Ellis was making as I went along, so that they would stand out. That way, I could keep these points separate in my mind from all the illustrations of them. It was only mildly disappointing to discover that these weren't 'naughty town-women' after all.

So, looking back, my difficulties were mainly at the start, in paragraphs 1–4. After that I found the article so interesting that, in the end, I felt it was worth going back to the difficult bits and spending some time getting to grips with them. What about you? How did you get on with the opening paragraphs? Some of the sentences are dense, and complex in structure – they are not at all easy to read and understand. And, generally, how did you cope with the level of the vocabulary?

Key points

Reading for study purposes is a demanding activity. You will learn best if you:

- take an interest in what the text is about
- make a determined effort to understand the main arguments
- work actively on the text as you read.

4.3   Getting round obstacles

Philip, Hansa and I experienced various difficulties as we read the Ellis article. Perhaps you did too. If so, how did you respond? Was your progress held up, or did you manage to keep going? With a lot of reading to do, it is important to find ways round the obstacles you encounter.

4.3.1   Unfamiliar words

Hansa didn't know the words 'Augustan' and 'demographic'. The term 'dysfunctional' is not common in everyday speech either. Were there words you are not familiar with? If so, what did you do about them?

Should you stop reading to look words up?

It depends. Obviously, it slows you down a lot if you have to keep stopping, and sometimes you lose your grasp on the gist of the article in the meantime. You have to decide whether a word seems important. Does it keep coming up? Is not knowing the exact meaning interfering with your understanding of the text enough to make it worth stopping to find out? Hansa could have picked up what demographic meant from the context, well enough to be going on with at least – after all, we get to know the meaning of most words as we experience the way they are used. And when she was next using her computer she could have looked up 'dysfunctional' and 'Augustan' in an online dictionary and found useful clarification of their meanings (such a search is described in Chapter 10).

Sometimes it is not one particular word that is difficult, but a string of them. For example, when I read 'It is much more plausible to argue ... rural setting' (para. 3), I had to slow down. Having taken in the meaning, it seemed to me that 'dysfunctional' was the main word I needed to pay attention to and that's why I underlined it.

See Chapter 10 Section 10.2, Finding information

Box 4.2   Frustration with specialist terms

It is easy to feel put off by unfamiliar terms, or by words used in unfamiliar ways. You feel excluded from those 'in the know' and it's annoying having to struggle to squeeze meaning out of every sentence. But specialist language is not used deliberately to annoy. Developing new ideas and fitting new terms to them is part of the process of creating knowledge. In the end, you have to accept that grappling with specialist terms is a part of learning in your discipline.

Indeed, specialists develop their own 'language'. We accept this quite readily in the case of technical or scientific language. But it is true even in subjects we tend to think of as involving our feelings and personal responses, such as music, literature and art. This language gives specialists extra power to explore the objects they study in a systematic and detailed way. It ranges from the precise, technical terms used when we analyse or take apart a piece of music to see how it works (*chord, melody, harmony,* for instance), to style and period labels (such as *Augustan, Renaissance*), and the language of theory in literature or history. If everyone uses this specialist language when they discuss a poem or write about a painting then we can be sure that we are all paying attention to the same things in it (this 'rhyme', that 'figure'). And because it is a language we *share*, it is easier for us to understand what each other means to say. It helps us see whether we agree or disagree with someone else's interpretation of the poem or painting, and just what it is we disagree about. And it helps us explore the reasons for our disagreement.

Dictionaries

One way to tackle the challenge of unfamiliar words is to have a good general dictionary, and to keep it right beside you when you are working. This is an *essential* resource when you are studying arts and humanities subjects. You could use a traditional printed dictionary, an online dictionary, or both. A printed dictionary is easy to keep by you wherever you happen to be reading; you might use *The Concise Oxford English Dictionary* or, if you can afford it, the two-volume *Shorter Oxford English Dictionary*. An online dictionary has the advantage when you want to look something up quickly while you are using the computer.

See Chapter 10 Section 10.2, Finding information

But don't expect too much from a general dictionary. Some specialist terms may not appear in it, and words that do may not be defined in exactly the way they are used in your subject. So you may also want to use a *specialist* dictionary or companion for the subject you are studying. These dictionaries are rather difficult and technical though, and you will perhaps get a better insight into the meanings of key terms in your subject from textbooks and the other secondary sources you study.

Concept cards

Another way to tackle unfamiliar terms is to start a concept card system, using index cards. When you meet a word or phrase that seems important, take a new card and write it at the top, followed by any useful information you have found and any questions you want the answers to. File the cards alphabetically, and add new clues to the term's meaning as you go along from seeing it used in different contexts.

Or, using your computer, you could search online for index card software; just type 'index card' into the Search box. The example in Figure 4.1 is from PS CardFile Pegasus.

Of course, making concept cards is time consuming. You need to weigh up how much benefit you are getting and how much time is worth investing in it.

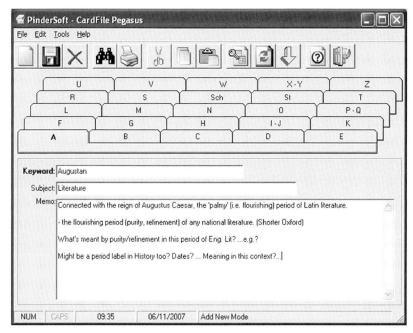

Figure 4.1 Sample electronic 'concept card' (Source: Pindersoft (2007), CardFile Pegasus (software), available at http://www.pindersoft.com/index.htm, accessed 31 August 2007)

4.3.2 Coping with difficult reading

Philip and Hansa said they found some sections of Ellis's article difficult, not just individual words. What should you do when you can't make sense of what you read?

Paraphrasing

Take the first sentence in the article. When you are faced with this kind of complex sentence it is a good idea to break it down – make several sentences of it. So you might have 'Modern demographic research suggests that .../This produced .../That contrasts with ...' Then you have to fill in the gaps. As you do that, keep it simple. The new sentences might go:

> Modern demographic research suggests that many women migrated to the larger towns.

> This produced towns with far more women than men living in them.

> That contrasts with smaller towns, where either the sexes were more
> balanced or there were many more men.

When you need to paraphrase like this you can try doing it in your head. But
sometimes you will have to write things down to make sense of them, even
though that slows you down.

You can often put off looking up various words and terms by paraphrasing as
you go along, aiming just to get the gist of things. Usually, it is better to read
through to the end of a text and get a sense of what the whole thing is about
before worrying too much about the difficult parts. I have dwelt on some
opening sentences here because it is rather depressing if you can't make
much sense right at the start.

Spotting the underlying 'question'

Another way of coping with difficult reading is to ask yourself what the
underlying problems or questions are that the article is aiming to explore and
'answer'. A key to being able to follow the article – and also a key to finding it
interesting – is to understand what problems the text is trying to solve. So let's
try to see what the underlying questions are in the Ellis article.

Activity 4.2

Read through from the middle of paragraph 3 again (from 'What women
sought in the towns, the satirists argued ...') to the end of paragraph 5.

Then home in on the last sentence in paragraph 3 ('It is much more plausible
to argue ... rural setting'): try to restructure this sentence and put it into your
own words – as I did earlier with the first sentence in the article.

Now write down what you think Ellis's underlying questions are: what
questions is this text addressing?

First, the final sentence in paragraph 3. When I tried to paraphrase this what
struck me was that Ellis begins by telling us what this 'more plausible
argument' *is not*. So I put that part to one side and started with the rest of the
sentence. This is what I came up with:

> It is likely that so many of these women were attracted to the town
> because they could no longer fulfil their 'proper' function in the
> countryside – not because they objected to the very idea of there
> being 'correct' behaviour and roles for women.

So, reading this sentence in the light of the surrounding text, what questions
is Ellis addressing? I think the broad question is quite a simple one: 'Why did
these women migrate to the larger towns?' But there is a more subtle and
difficult question too: 'Was it because they wanted to escape from or reject
women's conventional roles – or was it because these roles had become
much less satisfying to play in country settings than in towns?' In other words,
was going to towns a way of rebelling against their roles or a way of getting a
lot more fun and satisfaction out of them?

This is the crux of the matter I think. Once you recognise it, you can see what Ellis is trying to do in the article. You can see that she is presenting an *argument* about this question, not just a descriptive account of what life was like in country and town. You can try to follow her argument as you read – picking out the *main points* she makes – and see whether you find it convincing. This makes things much more interesting.

Creating an interest

So, as you start out on a text you hope that the writer is going to pose one or two interesting questions that will give you something to think about and enable you to search for meaning as you read. But you may have to keep your wits about you to spot them, as we have just seen. Or you may be unlucky. The writer may fail altogether to get across what questions she or he is setting out to explore. In that case you will have to try to set some questions for yourself.

Box 4.3   Setting your own questions

Questions make reading interesting. Unless you are reading with a question or two in the back of your mind ('Why did higher ranking women no longer have a satisfying role to play in the countryside?', 'What effects did this have on them?') you cannot *engage* with the words on the page.

When you can't get involved in the text you are reading it tends to be either because you cannot see what question is being addressed or because you cannot see the *point* of the question being addressed – why it is an important question, what hangs on it. You may need to stop reading closely, and skim right through an article; or with a book, look at the preface and the conclusion, or skim a few chapters – anything that helps you see *what* questions the text is addressing and *why they matter.*

You were asked to read 'On the Town' out of the blue. Normally, though, you would be studying this kind of text as part of a course, and reading it in that context. It will be linked to other coursework you are doing; other texts, seminar discussions, an assignment. This context usually gives you clues to the questions the text explores and to its meanings. But, even so, if it simply does not stimulate your interest then you have to shift your strategy and work out a way to *create* an interest for yourself.

To develop an interest in a subject, you can try to:

■ link what you are reading to questions you are already interested in
■ work out why other people have found the topic interesting – what questions they were concerned about, and why
■ make connections between the subject matter and your own experience.

On the last point, we could compare our experiences of travelling or living in the countryside with Lady Jane Coke's. Hansa, for example, found the 'practical reasons' given for the women's attitudes particularly appealing.

More broadly, in arts and humanities subjects we can often become personally involved in our studies, by responding to a poem or a piece of music emotionally and in our imaginations.

Getting through and moving on

If none of this works, then find a strategy for 'getting through' the reading as best you can. For example, search for information on a particular aspect of the topic or focus on material you will need for your next assignment. In other words, if you can't find an intrinsic purpose for reading the text, then create one by actively seeking something out. Then just move on. You are not achieving anything if (like Jan in Chapter 1) you spend hours messing about with something that is not engaging your thoughts. Often when you come across something you don't understand you can *keep moving on*, and still get a lot out of a text. The difficult parts may make more sense when you come back to them another time, or from a different angle. Don't let the tough parts get you down.

You don't have to understand *fully* to benefit from reading when you study, but you do have to constantly keep weighing up:

- why you are reading a particular text
- what you need to get out of it, and
- whether you are making enough progress to justify the time it is taking.

Finally, notice that Philip, Hansa and I approached the job of reading the article differently. Hansa read through quickly once, then again more slowly trying to sort out her difficulties. Philip worked his way through from start to finish, re-reading parts of it and trying to work out everything as he went along. I started off by doing that, but then I became frustrated because I was not making enough progress and didn't feel engaged in my reading. I made the decision to speed up and come back to the difficult parts later. In other words, I *changed the way* I was reading in response to how I was feeling about it rather than just giving up.

But all of us were successful, in that we got to the end of the article and found it interesting. There is no 'right' way to read. The important thing is to be *flexible*; to be able to judge how well you are progressing, and how you are feeling, and adjust your approach accordingly.

Key points

- When you find parts of an academic text difficult, it is generally best to read through to the end and come back to the hard parts later.
- You can often get the gist of complicated sentences by restructuring them for yourself and putting them into your own words.
- Identifying the underlying question(s) the text is addressing makes the argument easier to follow and also makes an article more interesting to read.

- Adjust your approach according to how you are feeling as you read. If you feel frustrated because you are not making progress or finding things interesting, try speeding up.

- Do not expect to understand everything fully on first reading. Get through the reading as best you can, and move on.

4.3.3   The academic style

Sometimes it is not the difficulty of a text that bothers us; rather, we are thoroughly put off by the whole *way* in which it is written. What we read in everyday life usually starts from a well-defined point of view. A newspaper editorial might try to persuade you to see an event in a particular light, or a magazine article offer a straightforward solution to a problem. You can agree or disagree, take it or leave it. But academic writers are generally much less committed to reaching speedy conclusions. Instead of making a direct attack on a particular question or problem, you may find they start by raising broad, abstract issues (such as demography). And it is not always easy to discover just what issues or questions *are* being addressed; you may feel that the author is taking you all round the houses instead of coming straight out with a view. The text may be littered with qualifications ('in some cases', 'in part', 'to an extent'), and conditional phrases such as 'it might be said that ...' or 'it could be argued ...'. Eventually, the author may offer a conclusion couched in very guarded language: 'It would therefore seem that ...', or 'The evidence tends to suggest that ...'. Why is this?

Box 4.4   Academic writing

Academic writers use cautious, considered language in an effort to be as exact as they can in their analysis and argument. They try to say only what they mean and what they think can be justified. In academic writing language is used precisely, so that closely related arguments can be prised apart and analysed in detail. Learning how to read, think and write in this way is a central part of learning at degree level.

This is not to say that the academic use of language is better than more conversational forms. It is different; it has different aims and purposes. It is a particular use of language that aims to be precise and objective.

For example, take this sentence in paragraph 7 of the Ellis article: 'The education given to men from the social elite was almost expressly designed for a rural setting'. *Almost* expressly? Ellis is acknowledging that there were other sides to these men's education. What exactly they were is not important here so she doesn't go into them, but she does not want to give us a false impression either. You may have noticed that she is always careful to balance the picture she presents of women's life in the countryside with that of men's. In the passage just before this, about Lady Jane Coke getting marooned, she adds, 'Of course, to some extent, her husband was marooned too ...'. She does not want to exaggerate the woman's predicament by simply paying no

See Chapter 3 Section 3.3, Why do they write like that?

attention at all to the man's. She wants to build up a strong case. So she doesn't leave herself open to the counter-argument that men might have suffered just as much in the countryside: she says they didn't.

This reminds us that Ellis is presenting an *argument* here, not telling a story, and that she wants her argument to be convincing. That means you have to pay close attention to it, and think about what she says. In the end, you are not likely to be convinced if she exaggerates one side of the case or just ignores whatever doesn't happen to suit her argument. Comparing her account of the subject with those given by other historians helps you make this kind of judgement.

Besides striving to be precise and accurate, academic writers tend to use a cool, *passive* voice. The passive voice emphasises the thing being discussed, not the person doing the discussing. When Ellis concludes 'The steady migration of women into towns was the logical consequence of conventional perceptions of femininity' (rather than 'I think women moved into towns because ...'), she is drawing your attention to her *argument* rather than to herself as the thinker of it. And we never discover what she personally feels about these 'conventional perceptions of femininity'.

In this kind of writing it is not supposed to matter who is doing the enquiring or what state of mind they are in. Only what is directly relevant to Ellis's enquiry is included in her account of it. And that account consists of analysis, argument and description presented in a calm, detached manner. This is because Ellis, as an academic, is aiming her words at an *academic audience*. She is assuming that you are a cool, detached and very critical reader. She takes for granted that you will be interested in the strength of her arguments, not in her as a person. But it would be wrong to think that the detached stance and rather distant tone of much of this writing means that academics don't care about their subjects, or don't have strong views about anything – far from it. And I do not mean to say that all academic writing is done well either. Some of it is *too* 'remote' and some far too stodgy, in my opinion.

But does this mean that you have to use the passive voice in your essays? Academic uses of language change over time as much as any other, and the tendency in the academy has been towards less formality. Nowadays universities often have no objection to students using the first person 'I' in essays and other writing; your university will offer you guidance about what exactly is expected of you. What really matters is whether you argue a case, and the kind of argument you put together. We return to these issues again and again in Chapters 7 and 8.

Key points

- An academic text is not a narrative, however instructive. It is an *argument*, written to be convincing.
- To be convincing, academic writers try to write in a precise and balanced way.

- They tend to write in a detached, dispassionate way, often using the passive voice, to emphasise what it is they are writing *about*.

- In order to be precise, they use a specialist language: when you enter a new subject area you have to learn its specialist language.

- The point is to understand that much of the academic writing you will read in articles and books follows certain accepted 'rules', or conventions, and why. Then you are less likely to be irritated or put off by the way the texts you study are written, although it can take a bit of getting used to.

4.3.4   Disagreeing with the author

You can feel very frustrated if you do not agree with the point of view of the writer of an article. For example, you might wonder why Ellis doesn't explore or present any evidence for the argument that town life attracted women because they *were* 'trying to escape from or subvert accepted gender roles'. You might think she dismisses this argument out of hand, by ridiculing the satirists who promoted it. Perhaps you don't see why this is a less plausible argument at all. So you may feel increasingly impatient as you work through her version of things – like having a conversation with a very talkative person who goes on and on without giving you the chance to speak. It can sometimes feel oppressive if you disagree at a fundamental level and want to raise objections. It may be hard to keep driving yourself on through the text.

Of course, we are all entitled to our own views. However, if you want to access a body of knowledge, you have to be ready to enter into the ways of thinking in that discipline. To benefit from reading texts you have to be prepared to get alongside the writers and think their thoughts *with* them. You have to be ready to try out the writers' points of view in order to understand what they are saying (see Box 3.1 'How reading works'). *Then* you can pause to reflect and react.

Sometimes ideas seem unappealing or implausible when you first meet them, but if you were only to read what you already agreed with you wouldn't learn very much. Part of the skill of studying is learning to cope with not feeling happy about what an author is saying and *distancing yourself* from your hostile feelings, so that you can read on. Eventually, you may decide that the author has a point, or not, but first you must give yourself the chance to find out exactly what she or he is saying. To participate in academic debate you have to be able to think on all sides of an argument. For this, you need to use your feelings constructively.

See Chapter 3 Section 3.4.1, Reading

When you disagree with a text, write down your criticisms and counter-arguments point by point – in the margins or as notes – instead of just fuming. You can learn a lot by reacting against what you read because it often helps you sort out your own ideas.

4.3.5   Reading environment

Were you held back at all in your reading by where you were doing it? Were you reading in an armchair, sitting at a desk, like Philip, in the garden, like

Hansa, or on the train? Any of these *could* be a good place, but did it actually work for you?

Wherever you were doing the reading, did you feel able to maintain your concentration for a good long spell? Did you have all the materials you needed to hand, such as pen, paper and dictionary? Did you need a surface to write on as you read? Do you read best in a regular spot, or do you like to keep moving to different places?

Don't just take your reading environment for granted. Think about all these things, and whether you are giving yourself a reasonable chance of success. You may not be able to arrange a 'perfect' environment, but there are often significant things you can do to improve the one you have.

Key points

To get through large amounts of reading you have to be ready to cope with obstacles. You need:

- strategies for coping with difficult words and with passages you can't at first understand
- patience with the academic style of writing
- an ability to detach yourself from disagreement with the author's views
- a well set-up reading environment.

4.4   How quickly should you read?

How long did it take you to read the Ellis article? Did you read it quickly enough, or perhaps too quickly? Reading speed is a persistent worry when you study. There always seems to be much more to read than you have time for, so you feel a tremendous pressure to read faster. But then, if you go too fast, you don't learn much. So what is the 'right' speed? The answer is – it depends on what you are trying to achieve.

4.4.1   Skimming

It is surprising how much you can pick up if you skim quickly through a few pages.

Box 4.5   Skimming first sentences

You can get a rough idea of what a piece is about by skimming through the first sentence or so of each paragraph, picking out a key phrase. Doing this for the first four paragraphs of the Ellis article, I came up with: female population of towns expanded; women's enthusiasm for urban life; not only women preferred urban life; higher-ranking women's lives confined in the countryside.

This gives me a sense of what this section of text is about, but it does not convey Ellis's argument. It certainly doesn't save me the job of reading the article properly. However, skimming in this way is useful.

It helps me decide whether I want to go on and read the article properly.

It puts me in a frame of mind to understand the article.

It reminds me afterwards what the article was about.

There will be many times in your studies when you need to look through texts quickly, scanning lots of pages to get the gist of the issues or to find specific information. It is very useful when you pick a book off a shelf, for example, to be able to review it quickly so that you can decide whether or not to read it. You just skim through the contents list, glance at details about the author, look for familiar names in the reference list, scan the preface and dip into a chapter or two.

Similarly, when you are about to start reading an article or a book, you can prepare your mind by skimming through chapter headings, contents lists, introductions, summaries and conclusions. This helps you construct a framework within which to make sense of what you read. It also helps you think strategically about how to tackle the reading: whether to read the whole thing or just sections of it, how long to allow yourself, and whether to make notes. Rather than simply wading in, you prepare yourself so that you can work intelligently on the text.

However, it is important to be clear that this rapid *scanning* of texts *is not reading*. Skimming can tell you about a text, but you will not learn what is in it.

4.4.2   Reading to learn

In order to learn you need to *follow the argument* as you read. With an important text, *you should slow right down* and take it bit by bit. This intensive kind of reading is at the opposite end of the scale from skim reading. It plays an important part in getting you to the heart of the subject. Here is a student describing how she tackled a particularly challenging chapter.

> I found the reading very hard. Twice I sat down, got through a few lines and threw the towel in. Then I set myself an hour to read with highlighter, notebook and pen. I read a few lines, wrote on my notepad and in the margin what it meant to me, in plain English, and highlighted what I thought were important phrases. Then I moved on to the next few lines. I even ended up with small diagrams of how some things impacted on others ... It took me over an hour to read the six pages, but when I look at them now I just read my own words and the bits I highlighted. ... I find when I look at my notes that I can recall parts of it quite easily, and it made the whole complex discussion far more understandable. It takes time to go through so carefully, and you do need peace and patience, but it is worth it ...

See Chapter 3
Section 3.2, What
does learning mean?

When you are studying, the underlying purpose of reading is to *develop your thoughts* – to weave new ideas into the understanding you already have and to develop new points of view. If you try to bypass this thinking, you are not really *learning* as you read.

4.4.3   Choosing a reading speed

As a student you cannot afford to read at whatever speed just comes naturally. If you are trying to keep abreast of a course you have to push yourself. However, reading speeds range from a lightning skim through a whole book to intense concentration on a difficult paragraph. You need to become skilled at working at speeds right across the range. How quickly you need to read will depend on:

- what you already know about the subject
- how difficult the text is, and
- how thoroughly you need to understand it.

If, like Hansa, you spent 20 minutes on the article, you may have picked up as much as you wanted. On the other hand, if you stopped to think you could easily have spent more than Philip's half hour or so. If you read the article carefully more than once you could have spent an hour, and if you were also making notes perhaps you might spend an hour and a half.

Because of my special interest in the article for the purposes of this book, I have spent several hours on it. The longer I worked on it the more interesting I found it, and the more clearly I grasped the issues it deals with. This shows that there is no 'correct' amount of time to spend. It depends what you are trying to achieve. But you may find the target study rates in Table 4.1 helpful as a rule-of-thumb.

Table 4.1   Study rates

Text type	Words per minute	Pages per hour
Easy; familiar subject matter	100 or more	12 or more
Moderate; fairly familiar subject that you want to follow reasonably closely	70	8
Difficult; unfamiliar subject matter that you want to understand in depth	40 or fewer	5 or fewer

I call these 'study rates' because they include some time for thinking and working things out as you go, and for a fair amount of re-reading. (If they were simply 'reading speeds' they would be very slow, perhaps unless English is not your first language.) These rates give you study times for the Ellis article (about 1500 words) of around 15, 25 and 40 minutes, respectively. You can apply these rates to any secondary source material you are setting out to study. (Remember, when you read primary texts – poems, novels, historical documents, philosophical writings, etc. – you do not read them for the same purposes or in the same ways.)

If you adopt this strategy it will help you *assess in advance* the time you need to spend on reading tasks. This will help you *distribute* and *use* your study time more effectively. You may not be able to make your assessment very accurately, but some fairly reasonable idea is better than none.

Box 4.6 Time investment

In choosing to study, you have decided to invest time in developing your intellectual powers. Sometimes you will get a good return by investing in a very detailed reading of a short section of important text. At other times you will get a good return by dipping into several texts and skim reading in order to broaden your ideas. You have to weigh up the tasks ahead of you and then distribute your time in a way that gives you a good overall return. A key test is to ask yourself, 'Is this making me think?' If the answer is 'No', then your investment is being wasted. You need to switch to another activity.

4.4.4 Time chunks

Apart from sheer reading speed, there is the question of how to parcel out your study time. For a two-page read you would probably assume a single study session, but a chapter of a book might be spread over several sessions depending on the content and on your own time constraints.

> Hi, can anyone advise on how much to read at once? ... I've just spent 3 hours reading 2 chapter sections – made notes, read some bits twice, did the exercises ... then just sat thinking about what I've read. Started reading next section ... couldn't get into it, so have come away but feel guilty as I still have a couple of hours free. I don't think I can absorb any more today, but I'm worried my pace may be too slow for the course.

This is a message from a student to her online tutorial group in the second week of a course. Three hours is a substantial chunk of serious reading and it seems that she has taken in as much as she can for the time being. She might as well stop worrying and switch to some other task, such as planning an assignment or sorting out her notes. Or she could take a complete break and come back to the chapter later in the day. I would guess that this student's studies were going well – firstly, because she is actively engaging with the study materials, and secondly, because she is thinking about her study strategy and her use of time.

It is important to recognise that your span of concentration is limited. You can't study and learn intensively hour after hour, so it is better to divide your reading time into several shorter sessions than a few longer ones. However, if your reading sessions are *too* short, you don't get properly into the frame of thinking required by the text before breaking off again. You might find an hour or two a reasonable span for a reading session after a day of work. Or after half an hour of intense concentration you may need to take a short break, or switch to another task.

Reading habits are very personal; take time to reflect on your own. Practise setting targets of various numbers of pages to see what works best for you within the contours of your life.

Key points

There is no ideal reading speed. Skill in reading slowly is just as important as skill in reading quickly. To manage your reading, distribute and use your time effectively, you need to:

- pitch your reading *speed* according to your purpose and the degree of challenge presented by the text
- set yourself *targets* (number of pages per session)
- *monitor* your progress and keep adjusting your strategy.

4.5   Reading actively

To be able to *make* sense of what you are reading, you need to read actively. One method that can help is to use a pen or pencil.

4.5.1   Underlining and highlighting

Activity 4.3

Did you underline or highlight any words as you read the Ellis article? If not, go back over it quickly and mark the important words. Try not to mark too many words; pick out just enough so that you still get the main points if you read *only* those words.

I chose to underline rather than highlight. You can see my underlining for paragraph 3 in Figure 4.2. Does it look anything like yours? Why do you think I used double underlining in several places?

There is no one 'correct' way to underline or highlight. You may have had excellent reasons for marking quite different words. It depends what your mind focuses on as you read.

The words I underlined in the first line simply remind me what the first part of the paragraph is about. I thought it was important, too, to identify the idea of 'Country versus Town', a main theme of the article. The // mark shows me that there is a change of direction at that point – from men's attitudes to country life to women's. In the next sentence I made the word 'women' stand out to remind me that they are the main focus of the article. I also double underlined parts of the final sentence because this is where Ellis tells us what direction *her* argument is going to take (i.e. what questions the article is addressing).

Then I put the satirists' views, which Ellis does not agree with, in brackets, to separate them from the argument in the rest of the article (though in fact she returns to them in the last two paragraphs). The words underlined within these brackets remind me whose views they are and summarise what the

Of course it was <u>not only women</u> who expressed a <u>preference for urban life:</u> many men would have agreed with e.g. the north-eastern landowner who contemptuously refused his mother's pleas for his return from London in 1720 with the rhetorical question 'Surely you don't think me such a fool as to prefer the charms of a stupid. dull, (country) life to the pleasures of the (Town?) // But these pleasures were thought to be especially attractive to <u>women,</u> (not simply because women were by nature self-indulgent and superficial (!) but because urban life allowed them to gain the upper hand in the age-old struggle to escape their natural subordination. What women sought in towns, <u>the satirists argued,</u> was <u>freedom from male control.</u> Such claims, however, reflected long-standing literary conventions and equally long-standing male anxieties rather than contemporary reality.) It is <u>much more plausible to argue</u> that urban life attracted a disproportionate number of women (not because they were trying to escape from or to subvert accepted gender roles but) <u>because 'correct' female behaviour was all too often</u> (dysfunctional) in a rural setting.

Figure 4.2 Sample marked-up text

satirists thought. The words bracketed in the final sentence again refer to the satirists' views, not Ellis's. In fact I inserted these brackets and underlined Ellis's own case during the first reading. I also put question marks against the term 'dysfunctional' then, because it is clearly important to know exactly what it means. Sometimes I circle terms like this as a reminder to think about them again, or look them up later. And I put in the exclamation marks simply to express my feelings – these are *my* markings and I can say what I like. I often make a few remarks of my own in the margins of a text.

As regards the article as a whole, I made most marks in the first five paragraphs and the last. Otherwise, I tended to underline a phrase here and there to remind myself of the *main points* being made, and picked out some of the illustrations that follow as 'evidence in support'. For instance, 'well-born women were much less mobile' (in paragraph 6), and 'Montagu's bone-setter', 'Coke marooned'.

Now when I look at the paragraph, its meaning seems to come out to meet me halfway. The thinking I did while reading is visible to me in the underlining, and I quickly connect back to those thoughts when I read the underlined words. If that doesn't work, I can go back to the original words.

I often use underlining rather than highlighting because of its flexibility. I can accurately target specific words, double or treble underline, put an asterisk in the margin to emphasise an important point, put numbers against points, or write brief notes. If a text is particularly important, or I'm gathering material for writing purposes, then I might go through again with a highlighter, picking out a few key passages. But we all work differently. Some people prefer to highlight rather than underline because they feel it looks better and has a less intrusive effect. Experiment with different approaches to find out what works for you.

Too much underlining and highlighting

The challenge, especially when you are new to a subject, is to avoid underlining or highlighting too much.

> Will I be able to find what I'm looking for in a sea of yellow!? Hmm ... perhaps a change of colour is in order. Or will I then just have a multicoloured mess?

If you make too many markings, you defeat your purpose; nothing stands out. Worse, you may be using highlighting unthinkingly – *instead* of concentrating on what you read. The trick is to highlight or underline sparingly. See how few words you can mark and still be able to find the markings helpful. Aim to pick out key words, not whole sentences. Don't worry about capturing 'everything' – you can always go back to the original words if you need to.

Some passages of text need more marking up than others. I ended up with a heavily marked first page followed by a couple of pages with very few markings at all. Sometimes underlining slows you down, or makes reading boring. How much you need to do depends on the type of text you are reading and why you are reading it. You have to work all this out by trial and error. Experiment with different amounts of marking, then go back later and weigh up what seems to have worked best. Reflect on your experience.

4.5.2   Notes in the margins

> I regularly notice that I've just read something and not a single thing has entered my head. The only option is to re-read it and make small notes in the margins.

It is easy, with underlining or highlighting, to find that you have switched onto autopilot without noticing. The process becomes too passive and you follow the flow of the text without asking enough questions. Writing comments or questions in the margins is a way of keeping yourself more actively engaged.

But some people do not want to write in books or think it is wrong.

> In new books I underline anything important in pencil lightly so then if I'm not going to need the book any more I can sell it on.

> [I feel guilty] about 'defacing' nice new books. To get around it I use yellow stickies, with a phrase hanging off the edge of the page ... This works like a bookmark, but also points me to the important sections.

Obviously, you have to take into account whether you own the text you are studying – if not, you should not be writing in it at all. But if so, do you intend to keep it? If a book is important, why not assume you will keep it? Then you can think of writing in it as an investment. You invest significant time and mental energy in studying the book in any case; if writing in it means you can quickly reconnect with the ideas and information you have studied, that investment is greatly enhanced. The marked-up book becomes an item in your personal system of knowledge. Part of this system is in your head and part on your bookshelf. Within the overall cost of studying, creating your own personalised versions of significant books can represent excellent value.

Key points

Underlining or highlighting words as you read is a powerful study technique:

- it focuses your *attention* on the text
- it forces you to *think* about what the key concepts and issues are
- it leaves a *record* on the page of the meaning you found in the words as you read them.

When you return to a marked text you can quickly tune back in to those earlier thoughts – especially if you have written occasional comments and questions in the margins.

4.5.3   When you get stuck

I talked earlier about sometimes needing to create your own questions as you try to engage and grapple with difficult text (Box 4.3, 'Setting your own questions'). Reading for study purposes is an argumentative dialogue in your head. So asking yourself questions about what you are reading is also a way of keeping your mind active as you read. But even the most active and creative reader will sometimes get stuck. When this happens, don't sit staring at the page going over and over the same sentences. Find a way of tackling the problem.

Reading requires you to 'project' meaning onto the words on the page. When you are stuck it means that you have lost track of the argument and can no longer see what meaning to project. So, you have to find ways to reconstruct the argument in your mind. One way is to *cast around for clues* by looking elsewhere in the text.

See Chapter 3, Box 3.1, How Reading works

You might look *back* to the earlier parts:

- check the title and the introduction to remind yourself what the writer set out to discuss
- re-read some of what you have already covered to firm up the arguments, including any notes you have made in the margins.

Or you might look *ahead*:

- skim a few pages to see what is coming up
- turn to the conclusion to see where the argument eventually leads.

Another tactic is to use your pen:

- write down the main issues you think the text is addressing
- try to summarise what you have read so far, particularly the part just before you got stuck

- paraphrase difficult sentences
- underline words that seem important in the section you don't understand and try to explore their meanings.

Whether or not what you write is 'correct', the process of writing notes helps you get into the text. It makes you take hold of ideas and put them in your own terms. It helps you force meanings on to the subject matter.

If you are still stuck you might contact other students by phone, email or internet chat room. But if none of this helps, just skip ahead and try to pick up the thread somewhere else in the text; or leave it altogether and start on a different piece of work. It may all seem clearer another day. In any case, there is no point in sitting achieving nothing.

Key points

When you are stuck, attack the problem:
- look for clues in earlier or later parts of the text
- make detailed notes on the bit you are stuck on and on the preceding section
- cast around for ideas from other sources.

4.6   Reading critically

As well as making sense of what you read, you have to think about whether or not you are convinced by the arguments presented. At degree level, you don't simply accept what you read – you read critically, weighing up the strengths and weaknesses of the case the author makes. This means asking another set of questions.

4.6.1   Critical questions
How much trust can I put in this text?
You would generally assume that the set texts for your course are trustworthy. But when you find a text through your own research you need to run a few checks to assess the soundness of its content.

See Chapter 10 Section 10.3.3, Evaluating text-based websites and materials

Who is the publisher? If an article is published in an academic journal you can assume that its quality has been vetted by the journal's editors, and other academics as independent referees. Also if a book is published by a major academic publishing house, you can regard it as 'respectable'. And if it's a book from an academic series, you would expect the series editor to have vetted the quality. However, in other cases you would need to make further enquiries.

Who is the author? Does the author have a post in a university or another body that would give you confidence in the quality of her or his scholarship? Joyce Ellis is a university lecturer and researcher, with a long publication record, so we have every reason to suppose that her work is academically respectable. After all, she would not want to put her reputation and employment at risk.

In what context was the text published?

This amounts to asking *when* it was written and for what *audience*. Academic texts are written to make a contribution to the debates going on within the field. To understand where an author is coming from and why arguments are being presented in a particular way, you need to be able to place the text in context. Ellis's article, written for social historians and those from beyond the academy who have an interest in such topics, was published in the UK in 1995, so we might expect it to be a bit dated. Since then, at least four related books have been published: two on single women and two on servants during this period. If Ellis were writing the article now she might, for example, want to take account of recent research into the growing number of female servants who were attracted to the towns, and reflect on their possible effect on the gender imbalance she notes. If this were your field, you would need to be aware of these later publications and how their findings might affect the state of our current knowledge.

Is the argument well structured?

This question is not so much about whether an author's argument is right; rather it asks whether, as a line of argument, it is consistent and hangs together. For example, broadly Ellis is arguing from certain available demographic facts that a) there was a gender imbalance in the populations of towns in this period and b) what the reasons were for that imbalance, drawing on other types of evidence too. I can't see anything wrong with this procedure. Also, everything she includes in the article contributes to her twin arguments about women's lives in country and town; and she refers to events in an earlier period (paragraphs 4–5) to help explain the women's predicament at the time. It seems to me that it all hangs together.

See Chapter 3
Section 3.3.2, Key
features of academic
discourse

Having said that, we need to be aware that our demographic knowledge of the eighteenth century may be altered by future research findings, which might of course change the nature of argument a), and other kinds of evidence about women's motives may be unearthed or promoted which undermine Ellis's argument b). This is to say that an argument can be internally coherent but what it is founded on may be faulty, or an interpretation of events may come to be revised in the light of further or different evidence.

What evidence is offered?

Ellis offers plenty of evidence for the claims she makes about women's lives in country and town, from literature and from contemporary letters and illustrations. I have the impression that this is just a sample of a wide range of relevant evidence she had reviewed. Because of her academic standing, I would tend to assume that the evidence is reliable and her interpretations sound. However, if I were studying the subject thoroughly, I could go back to the evidence she draws on from both primary and secondary sources to verify her findings for myself.

Is there an alternative school of thought?

I am not an historian, but I guess there might be. If I were studying this topic seriously I would search for an article which tackled Ellis's topic from another perspective. When you encounter new ideas, it is useful to get more that one perspective on them so that you can weigh up one against the other.

Are the conclusions justified?

In general, I was reasonably convinced by the conclusions Ellis draws. But, again, if I were studying the subject seriously I might find that wider reading and further thought would raise a few questions in my mind.

4.6.2 Thinking for yourself

These are the kinds of question you need to ask in order to read critically. As a higher-level student, it is assumed that you will think for yourself and question what you read and hear – so you need to weigh up ideas and arguments as you read them. According to Marton and Säljö (1997, p. 49), research shows that successful students read as if they are constantly asking themselves such questions as: 'How do the various parts of the text relate to each other? Is the argument consistent or are there any logical gaps? How does this relate to what I already know?'

Critical reading lies at the heart of good learning. A questioning approach will help you become a more effective and enthusiastic student.

Key points

At higher levels of study you are expected to read critically; you don't simply accept what you read. Ask yourself the following questions:

- Can I trust what I am being told here?
- In what context was this published?
- Is the argument logical and coherent?
- What evidence is offered?
- What do other authors argue?
- Are the conclusions justified?

4.7 Reading and learning

Reading is a core activity in most courses of study. The purpose of it is to enable you to *learn*. But learning is not a passive process; you don't just let ideas wash over you. You have to *make sense* of them as you read and then *use* them to *think* with.

Key points

Reading for study purposes is not merely a matter of passing your eyes over hundreds of words. It is a set of practices which enable you to engage with the ideas in a text, including:

- setting reading targets
- underlining or highlighting and making notes as you read
- asking questions to make yourself think about what you read

---

- stopping to look ahead or look back when you lose the thread
- reading critically
- monitoring your progress from time to time, and
- changing tack when things are not going well.

You need to experiment with different ways of doing things, in order to develop a robust and flexible style of reading.

Some students contend with physical difficulties when reading. Others may be partially sighted, or have dyslexia. Some face the challenge of studying in a second language or in a different dialect from the one they speak in everyday life. If you are one of these students you may well be able to get help from your university. Contact the support services without delay – such arrangements often take time to set up.

References

Ellis, J. (1995) '"On the Town": Women in Augustan England', *History Today*, vol. 45, no. 12, pp. 20–7.

Entwistle, N. (1997) 'Contrasting perspectives on learning' in Marton, F., Hounsell D. and Entwistle, N. (eds) *The Experience of Learning: Implications for Teaching and Studying in Higher Education* (second edition), Edinburgh, Scottish Academic Press Limited.

Marton, F. and Säljö, R. (1997) 'Approaches to learning' in Marton, F., Hounsell, D. and Entwistle, N. (eds.) *The Experience of Learning: Implications for Teaching and Studying in Higher Education* (second edition), Edinburgh, Scottish Academic Press Limited.

CHAPTER 5
Making notes

5.1   Thinking on paper

Making notes is a significant study activity. It helps you engage purposefully and creatively with the many challenges of learning – keeping your mind active and bridging the gap between your own thoughts and the subject matter of your course. One of the clearest signs of becoming a capable student is having a range of flexible and effective note-making strategies.

When you make notes, you are operating on the borders between the indistinct inner world of your mind and the outer world with its bustling trade in ideas and information.

- As new ideas pass *into* your mind, making notes helps you translate and organise them so that they mesh with your current thought processes.
- As you prepare to put ideas *out* into the external world, making notes helps you get your thoughts into sufficient order to be shared with others.

Ideas frequently arise out of dialogue with others; note making is essentially a dialogue with yourself. As you make informal jottings you often find yourself expressing thoughts you had not been aware of. In effect, you 'discover' your own ideas through the unassuming activity of writing untidy scribbles.

Note making is 'thinking on paper' or 'thinking onscreen'. It ought to be a satisfying process of engaging with a topic and creating meaning for yourself. If you find it a chore, you should reflect on whether you are doing it right. Note making is *not* note *taking*, in the sense of passively writing down an accurate record of what is said or written. It is much more constructive and personal than that.

Note making is valuable in a variety of contexts and for various purposes. This chapter divides these into 'capturing knowledge', 'organising knowledge', 'supporting creativity' and 'making notes strategically'. Most space is given to the first of these, but the other three are equally important. There is also a section on 'supporting your memory' through the way you make notes.

Box 5.1   Recommended preparation

To get the full benefit from reading this chapter, you should first have worked through Chapter 4 Section 4.2 'The experience of reading'. This guides you through reading the article by Joyce Ellis reproduced in the Appendix. Having read the article you will gain much more from the examples in this chapter because you will know what is being summarised and be better able to reflect on your own note-making strategies.

5.2   Capturing knowledge

As you work to stay abreast of the relentless flow of knowledge and tasks presented by a course, it seems that ideas and information are only fleetingly in your grasp before you have to let go and turn your attention to something else. This is unnerving. You don't know whether to consolidate what you have already covered, or to keep driving onward. You wonder how much you are actually learning.

- Will the lecture you are struggling to understand evaporate from your mind over the coming days?
- Will the time you are investing in reading a book be wasted?

In one sense the answer to these questions is 'No'. As new ideas pass through your mind, your thoughts influence and reshape them. So, even if you can't remember the specifics, a trace is left. When you are asked questions later, your answers are influenced by such traces. This is seldom enough, though. You want to feel that you have captured at least some of the knowledge and brought it under your control. For this you need notes.

5.2.1   Notes from reading

In Chapter 4 we looked at ways of highlighting text and making notes in margins. Sometimes these markings are sufficient because you have understood the subject well enough. At other times you need to make additional notes to help pull your thoughts together and clarify them; for example, if it is a key text or one that you will not be keeping, or when you are getting ideas together for an essay.

There are many ways to make notes, ranging from a few jotted lines to elaborate diagrams. To explore these we will look at some examples. But first try making a few notes of your own.

Activity 5.1

From your reading of the Ellis article, how much of it do you think you will be able to remember in the future? What notes would you need in order to 'capture' the essence of it, so that it doesn't slip away from you?

If you didn't make notes as you read Ellis's article, go back to it now and make about half a page of notes.

How did you set about making the notes?

The type of notes you need depends on:

- the kind of text you are reading
- what you want to use the notes for
- the amount of time you think it is reasonable to invest
- how your mind works.

In other words, note making is very focused learning activity, directed towards specific study goals.

A summary card

If you want very brief notes, you could restrict yourself to an index card. Just go back through your highlighted or underlined text, looking out for anything you marked extra heavily, then pull out a selection of the points that seem most important. A card like the one in Figure 5.1 might provide all the notes you need.

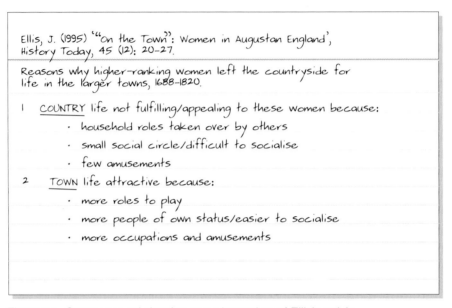

Ellis, J. (1995) '"On the Town": Women in Augustan England', History Today, 45 (12): 20-27.

Reasons why higher-ranking women left the countryside for life in the larger towns, 1688-1820.

1   COUNTRY life not fulfilling/appealing to these women because:
    · household roles taken over by others
    · small social circle/difficult to socialise
    · few amusements
2   TOWN life attractive because:
    · more roles to play
    · more people of own status/easier to socialise
    · more occupations and amusements

Figure 5.1 Summary card showing some key points of Ellis's article

Headings The top lines (correct details of the reference, including page numbers) are always *essential*. This is the very least you should note down, and keep in an index box or a computer file so that you can easily find the article again if you need to.

The second heading is also helpful in reminding us of the topic Ellis explores.

Layout Beyond that, I decided to bring out the 'country versus town' theme by using these as subheadings, each identified with a number. Notice the way I've used spacing and indented bulleted points so that it is easy to make sense of the notes when I return to them. My notes and their layout do not directly reflect the structure of the article. I have *re-organised* the main points into a pattern that makes sense to me – and one I'll probably be able to remember. (For this reason, it doesn't matter if your notes look different from mine; there are many ways to summarise the article.)

Outline notes

I will admit that I didn't arrive at the summary card in Figure 5.1 straight from reading Ellis's article. I began by making notes using the outlining facility on my word processor (in Microsoft Word this is the 'Outline' view). You can see the beginnings of these notes in Figure 5.2.

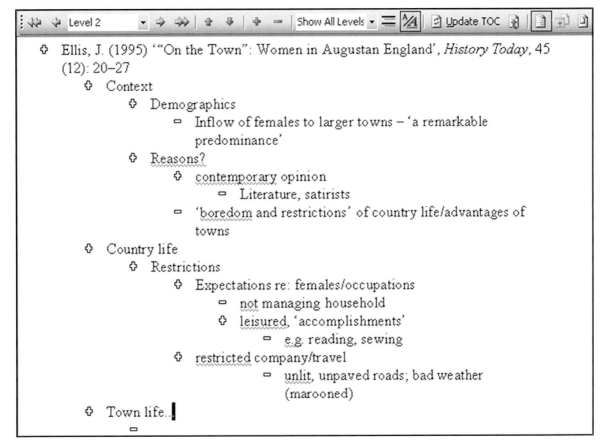

Figure 5.2 Some notes made in Microsoft Office Word's 'Outline' view

Outliners are superb tools for studying and for writing because they help you to organise content hierarchically. The title of my notes is at level 1, with key themes on the right ('Context', 'Country life', 'Town life') at level 2. Then my notes are arranged into main points (level 3), subpoints (level 4), and so on. Using an outliner it is very easy to move text around, promoting it to the left, demoting it to the right, or moving sections up or down the page. (In MS Word click on the button at the start of a line of text then drag it to where you want it, or use the buttons on the Outline view toolbar.)

I selected the View menu on my word processor and then clicked 'Outline'. Then I went back over the points I had underlined in Ellis's article. If a point still seemed important I typed it into my notes. I used the different levels to try to show the relationships between the points. However I didn't spend a lot of time thinking about this. I just put things wherever they seemed to fit, because as I worked I might see other, better, ways of structuring things and grouping points together, and I could easily move my points around accordingly. I was paying close attention to Ellis's article, but I was *organising* the material so that it made sense to *me*. Doing this helped me to understand better what it was she was saying.

See Chapter 4 Section 4.5.1, Underlining and highlighting

Notice that when I reproduced Ellis's very words in my notes I *always* used quotation marks. If you don't do this, it is very easy to plagiarise unknowingly. (Look up 'plagiarism' in the index and read the pages you are directed to; this is discussed in particular in Chapter 7 Section 7.6.1.)

Most word processors have an outlining facility. If you have never used an outliner it is well worth trying one out. Use your word processor's Help menu to find out how to do it, printing out the relevant pages to keep beside you at first. You will soon get the hang of it. (Alternatively, you could try out a specialised outliner program; you will easily find one if you do a web search for 'outliner'.) I find my outliner indispensable. One of the great advantages of making electronic notes is that it is very easy to file them on your computer and find them again quickly. You can also run searches for particular names or words, so when you are looking in your notes for a quotation to use in an essay you can locate it in moments.

A comprehensive overview

On the other hand, you may prefer to write notes by hand. You might, for example, try to capture the bones of Ellis's article on one page, as in Figure 5.3, laying the whole thing out so that you can take it in at a single sweep. You will seldom want to invest time in making such a detailed summary, but I offer this example to show how, in principle, you can extract the entire skeleton of an argument in a way that lets you see its structure and follow the logical links.

Activity 5.2

Read carefully through the notes I have made in Figure 5.3.

You will see that I have placed the points in clusters under headings as before, and picked out key words. I also use abbreviations a lot and some symbols in place of words. You can make notes that will be meaningful to you in all kinds of creative ways.

Notice that I quote from Ellis's article in the Conclusion section of the notes and so I include quotation marks. I also add a paragraph reference each time so that I can find the quotations again quite easily.

Abbreviations and symbols

Were you able to make sense of my abbreviations and symbols?

- I often abbreviated words (e.g. population, literature, references, especially, professionals, social, difficult, circulating) – and would have done more of this if these really were notes for me.
- I often left words out, and sometimes used a dash instead.
- I used an arrow ($\rightarrow$) to mean 'leads to'.
- I used > to mean 'became', and ∵ to mean 'because'.
- I didn't bother with full stops.

Some of these are standard abbreviations and others I made up. They all helped me to write quickly without losing track of the meaning. It is

Ellis, J. (1995) '"On the Town": Women in Augustan England', HISTORY TODAY, 45 (12): 20–27.

Reasons why higher-ranking women left the countryside for life in the larger towns, 1688–1820.

1 CONTEXT
Female pop. of larger towns expanded ∴ net INFLOW of women (see demographic research)
Why so keen on urban life? (see Lit. refs., e.g. Etherege; 'satirists' views)

2 ELLIS'S GENERAL ARGUMENT
Women esp. attracted to town because:
a) ROLE EXPECTED IN COUNTRY RESTRICTED & DIFFICULT – i.e. 'dysfunctional' (para. 3) viz., education for:
- household management   > done by profs.
- display: 'decorative', 'accomplished';   – but CAN'T fulfil role (see 3. below) reflecting men's status (para. 4)
b) TOWN ATTRACTIVE (see 4 below)

3 COUNTRY
a) small, scattered soc. circle   – only 'correct' to mix with social equals (unlike men)
b) travelling diffic. for women   – need carriage; poor roads & bad weather → accidents (e.g. 'bone-setter' Coke marooned 4 months)
c) few amusements (unlike men)   – read, sew, write letters, walk = BORING, unfulfilling

4 TOWN
a) new roles   – e.g. organising balls, theatre, concerts
b) easier to socialise ∴
- more of 'correct' people in compact area
- more mobile, safely (i.e. pavements; lighting; transport easy)
c) more amusements   – e.g. balls etc.; pastry shops, circ.library, shops – see German visitor

5 CONCLUSION
Women NOT attracted to towns ∴ wanted to 'escape from or subvert accepted gender roles' (para. 3) NOR ∴ seeking freedom to indulge naughty desires (i.e. satirists' view).
WERE attracted ∴ of MISMATCH between 'conventional perceptions of...correct female behaviour' and 'the reality of rural life' (last para)

Figure 5.3 Comprehensive notes on Ellis's article

important to develop your own system of abbreviations and symbols – this makes your notes both quicker to write and quicker to read.

Writing for yourself

By combining abbreviated writing with effective layout you can capture a lot of information very economically. Your compressed notes work for *you* because the ideas have already passed through your mind, so you don't need to explain them to yourself. You write just enough to reawaken the understanding you achieved as you were reading.

Box 5.2   Getting to the bare bones of an argument

Any text has a few central ideas running through it. However, if the writer stated these baldly, in the fewest possible words, you wouldn't be able to understand them or see their significance. A writer has to put 'flesh' on the bare bones, giving examples and talking you through the ideas so that you can see how they work.

Once you have understood the ideas, you don't need all the flesh any more. But you do need to hold the skeleton structure of the argument in your mind. Making notes is a way of helping you uncover this structure, so that you end up with your own version of the author's argument set out in a way that makes sense to you.

How much detail should you include?

Although there is a lot of information in Figure 5.3, I also left out a lot. So what did I choose to include? I began by writing full details of author, date, title, journal and page numbers at the top of the page – as we saw, vital information that will enable me to find the article again if I need to and perhaps even quote from it.

From Ellis's article I included the main points of the argument, following her structure, to make it clear to myself – except in the Conclusion. I decided to include the satirists' views there, so that their ideas would not get mixed up in my attempt to explore Ellis's own line of argument. And in these, more detailed, notes I have used a more elaborate hierarchy: from numbers, to letters, to bullet points.

On the right-hand side of the page I have summarised the examples Ellis offers to illustrate and support her main points. I do not go into the details of the illustrations and evidence, or her references to literature early on, but simply note them as reminders. And, given the emphasis of the argument (as expressed in my title), I don't explore Ellis's discussion of men's life in the countryside but, again, simply note it. Neither do I go into the details of the demographic research she outlines at the start; if I ever needed to grasp these points properly, I would revisit the article.

Working on a different article I might include the names of researchers and writers, Acts of Parliament, theories – basically the things I most expect to want to use again in the future.

> **Box 5.3   Health warning: making very detailed notes can damage your morale**
>
> The notes in Figure 5.3 may be more than you need. You don't want to slow yourself down too much by making notes, or undermine your interest in the subject. If making detailed notes makes you feel more confident in your grasp of the subject, then fine. But don't let note making become a burden.
>
> On the other hand, you may want to make quite detailed notes when you are:
>
> - studying a key text that is complex and difficult
> - preparing set reading for a seminar
> - getting ready to make a presentation
> - preparing to write an essay
> - revising for an exam.

Why make separate notes?

If you have already highlighted or underlined a text, why would you bother making separate notes? First, it helps you to see exactly what the text is about, so that it is then much easier to work the ideas into an essay or a presentation. Second, note making forces you to *think* as you decide what to write down and how to organise it on the page. Regardless of whether your notes are 'good', the act of writing them takes you much further into the meaning of the text. And thirdly, without notes, no matter how good your memory, ideas will gradually drift away from you.

So, although note making is demanding and time consuming, it is an investment which adds much to the value of reading. When a text is thought provoking and full of ideas that you can use in future assignments, the investment pays handsomely.

> ❝ I write the next essay topic on a sheet. Then, when I find a point I think is relevant, I write it on to the sheet, and include the reference so I can find it again. Post-it notes can be handy too. And I use index cards for key points. It doesn't seem a lot of work because it pays off when it comes to the essay. I know I've already got enough info to get started. ❞

There are many ways you might make notes on Ellis's article, and I expect your notes were different from my examples. It is very useful to experiment with different styles. Your notes on an important and challenging text you have read in depth will be quite different from the single line you might write on an article you happen to dip into. What you need is a *range* of note-making styles from which you can select according to the circumstances.

Key points

- Making separate notes is an additional investment which can add a lot to the value of reading a text. However, it is not necessary for everything you read.
- There are many ways of making notes, according to the nature of the text and your reasons for studying it.
- Notes should never simply be an abbreviated copy of the original text; they should be an attempt to pick out the bones of the argument.

5.2.2   Lecture notes

When you make notes while reading, the book just sits there – you are in control. But making lecture notes is much more challenging because you have to listen and write at the same time. Lectures can also vary quite a lot, so you have to be able to adjust your strategy according to the context.

Context

The kind of notes you need will depend on several factors.

- Is the lecture your only source of information on the topic? Do you risk losing important ideas and information if you don't write things down? Or are there texts on the topic? In this case your notes can be less detailed and more reflective.
- In your subject do you have to remember a lot of detailed information? Or is it more a matter of understanding theories and analyses; or of following arguments and understanding how ideas work?
- Does your lecturer use a slide presentation to show the structure and main points of the lecture? Are there handouts which provide a framework for your notes? Does your lecturer post an outline on the internet?
- Do you expect to use your notes towards writing an essay, to guide further reading, or in revising for an exam in a few months' time?

You may find out some of these things after a lecture has started, so note making is an unpredictable activity. You need to be well organised in advance, ready to swing into action with a technique to suit the situation.

But sometimes you may be advised *not* to make notes in a lecture because the lecturer wants you to listen actively or even take part in the session. In any case, you should never let note making replace the job of listening to the lecturer's argument unfold.

Cornell notes

One widely used approach to note making is the Cornell system developed by Walter Pauk (2001, pp. 236–46). It involves dividing a single sheet of note paper into four sections, as shown in Figure 5.4.

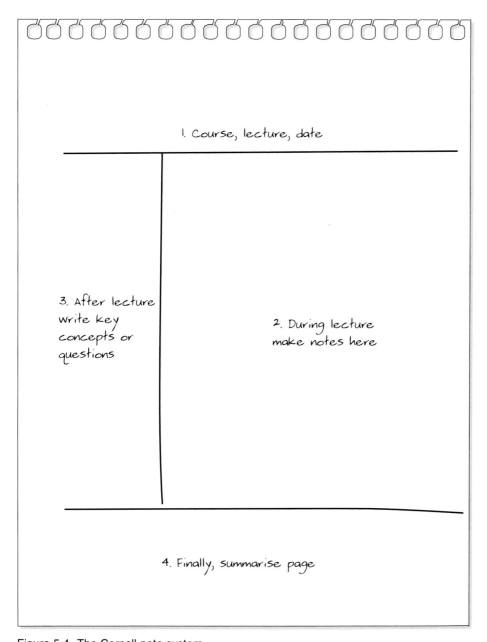

Figure 5.4 The Cornell note system

To use the Cornell system:

1 Fill in the top part (section 1) before the lecture.

2 Make notes in the main area (section 2) during the lecture.

3 Soon after the lecture, while it is fresh in your mind, read through your notes picking out key concepts and write them in the left margin (section 3). Better still, write down questions to which your notes provide answers. Working out the questions helps you to think about the meaning of your notes.

4   Cover up section 2 and test yourself by looking at the cues in section 3 and saying out loud whatever you can remember. As you work down the page, uncover the notes in section 2 to see what you remembered and what you forgot. Vocalising the ideas helps you into the language and thinking of the subject. You start to take ownership of new knowledge by making yourself a speaker of it. You also remember better.

5   Finally, reflect on the contents of the page, asking yourself such questions as: How does this fit with what I already know? How can I apply it? How significant is it? Then, in section 4, write a brief summary in your own words. This helps you to think about what it all means.

Making lecture notes in this way is much more than capturing a record on paper. You become actively engaged with the lecture and internalise what you hear. A systematic approach like this helps you to cope with the unpredictability of lectures by providing an off-the-peg strategy for taking control.

The Cornell system is not the only way to make lecture notes. For example, some people prefer to make notes in the form of 'mind maps': putting the topic of the lecture in the centre of the page, with sub-topics branching out (see section 5.4.2). However, the Cornell system provides a useful starting point if you are new to making lecture notes.

Tips on making lecture notes
What to avoid

■ Don't try to make verbatim notes, copying down the lecturer's every word – this is actually note taking. If you do, you won't be able to listen properly. You need to be thinking as you make notes.

■ Don't produce reams of notes because this just creates a reading burden later on. The lecturer will speak several thousand words. You want at most a few hundred.

■ Don't use a cassette recorder, and certainly not without the lecturer's permission. (But if you have special needs owing to visual impairment or dyslexia, for example, you may need to seek permission.) Normally, this is an inefficient use of your time because to extract the main points you will have to listen to the whole lecture again and then make notes. You may as well make the notes the first time around.

Listen out for the structure of the lecture

■ A lecturer usually has a few main points to get across. The rest is explanation and illustration, much of which you don't need to record.

■ Listen out for phrases such as 'The main issues are ...', 'Another important factor is ...', or 'So why is this?' These signal that key points are about to be made. Take note of pauses, changes in tone of voice and body language indicating that points are about to be summarised or new themes begun. And pay particular attention at the beginning and end of the lecture when clues to structure are most likely to be given.

■ Include examples given by the lecturer in your notes, not just concepts or facts. Examples are very helpful in reminding you what the ideas in the lecture are about.

Use the lecturer's words

- Although you are trying to pick out just the key points from what the lecturer says, don't try to translate into your own words. You haven't the time and it will interfere with your listening. In any case, one of the key benefits of a lecture is to hear how the specialist discourse of the subject is spoken. By selecting from the lecturer's own words, you will be better able to follow the flow of ideas and pick up the way the knowledge is put to work.

Make notes meaningful

- Don't note down single words; they are not enough. You have to be able to make sense of the notes when your mind has moved on to other things. The meaning of words arises from the context in which they are used.
- It generally helps to write fragments of sentences, leaving gaps that your mind can easily fill in later when you read the notes.

Abbreviate

- Avoid writing things out in full; use your own abbreviations.

Organise your points on the page

- Don't be stingy with paper. Spread your notes across the page and use lines, arrows, brackets, boxes, and so on to emphasise divisions and links in the material. A general principle is to set things out hierarchically with main headings on the left and sub-points indented, as shown in Figure 5.3.
- Work out a way to add comments and questions so that you can distinguish these from your main notes, for example by putting them in square brackets.

Take advantage of handouts

- If your lecturer provides you with a handout before a lecture, you can write your own notes directly onto it. This becomes more like a commentary than a basic record of the lecture.
- If you get a handout at the end of the lecture, it may be worth transcribing key points from your own notes onto it so that you can build on the lecturer's way of structuring the main ideas and information.
- If your lecturer doesn't provide handouts but puts notes up on a screen or whiteboard, then take advantage of this when structuring your notes.

Keep an open mind

- If you find yourself disagreeing with what the lecturer says, then write down your objections and queries, but don't let this interfere with making notes of the lecturer's arguments. Try to be open minded; you may see things differently as you get further into the subject.

See Chapter 4, Section 4.3.4, Disagreeing with the author

Tidy up afterwards

- It is tempting to put your notes away straight after a lecture, thinking you will return to them another day. However that day seldom comes, and it is extremely valuable to spend a few minutes tidying up the notes while the lecture is still fresh in your mind. You will be able to fill in blank spaces and make illegible words legible. If you don't do it then, your notes may be unintelligible later when your thoughts have moved on.

Note making strategy

Reflect regularly on whether you are getting what you need from your lecture notes. Ask other students what they do. Think of making notes as one element within your overall study strategy. As the Cornell system emphasises, the way you make notes is tied in with:

- preparing yourself before a lecture (by reading and annotating set texts and by reviewing your notes from the previous lecture)
- focusing your attention during the lecture
- consolidating your learning after the lecture (by tidying up, reviewing and summarising your notes).

You need to approach lectures armed with more than just good intentions. You need a clear sense of purpose and a workable technique – that is the value of starting with a systematic approach like the Cornell system. As you get to know the subject and exchange ideas with other students you can go on to develop an approach of your own.

Key points

- Aim to make lecture notes concise and organised.
- Try to map the main points; don't try to record everything.
- Use the space on the page or any handouts to structure your notes.

5.3   Supporting your memory

Making notes from reading and from lectures is a way of supporting your memory. But how important *is* memory when you study? Were you trying to remember particular things as you read Ellis's article? If so, what?

5.3.1   What should you be able to remember?

Activity 5.3

Which of the following points from Ellis's article do you think it would be useful to remember?

	Yes	No
1 The female populations of the larger towns expanded dramatically during 1680–1820 because of a net inflow of female migrants.		
2 Women could use sedan chairs in towns.		
3 The roles expected of higher-ranking eighteenth-century women living in the countryside were restricted and difficult to carry out.		
4 Sophie von La Roche was a German visitor to England in the 1780s.		

5   In the larger towns, new more fulfilling roles were available to higher-ranking women.

6   Etherge's *The Man of Mode* (1676) was referred to.

7   Women were by nature self-indulgent and superficial, and wanted freedom from male control.

It would be foolish to say that anything is definitely not worth remembering, but some things are more important than others and you can't remember everything. My answers to Activity 5.3 are:

'Yes' to questions 1, 3, 5, and 7 (with qualification).

'No' to questions 2, 4 and 6.

Although points 1, 3, 5 and 7 are worth remembering, they are not points you would actually set out to memorise. You will just 'know' them if you have made sense of the article as you read it. The act of understanding puts thoughts in your head which then become part of what you are generally aware of. Memory is not a particularly helpful concept here; *understanding* is much more significant. In particular, we are not meant to understand point 7 as 'true'; this is, of course, the satirists' view of contemporary higher-ranking women.

On the other hand, it would not be particularly useful to remember points 2, 4 and 6. Point 2 is just one example of the conveniences of the town that Ellis refers to, and is not even among the most important of them. Neither would it be helpful to remember the names of the people mentioned in Points 4 and 6, again simply illustrative of Ellis's themes.

Box 5.4   Facts, names and figures

Should you try to remember facts, names and figures? It depends on your purposes. Often the answer is 'No' because you only need to get the gist of the argument. But if you do think particular details would be useful to hang on to, write them down in your notes. Don't try to memorise them.

Having said that, if you study subjects such as law, languages or history, you do have to do quite a lot of memorising: the details of cases, vocabulary, the dates of events. In history, for example, it helps if you try to remember an event and its date together, as one 'item', from the start – always saying to yourself 'the battle of Trafalgar in 1805' or 'the Great Reform Act of 1832', for instance. Once you have a few dates for the period lodged in your mind they serve as landmarks. You can then position other events in relation to them, in the context of the overall 'story' you are telling yourself. That way you can keep the memorising you need to do within reasonable bounds. But even here, it is more important to understand the whole picture, to get an idea of sequences of events and to appreciate their meaning and significance. This is what is needed in essays and exams. It is also easier to remember particular dates, actors and events within a meaningful framework.

It is *not* the purpose of reading to be able to store the whole text in your mind. Even authors, on re-reading their own texts, come across ideas they had forgotten they'd had. If authors are not able to recall in detail everything they have written, why should you want to? What you want is to be able to *think* with the ideas that the author has presented.

You know you have retained some of what you have studied when you can re-read a piece more easily the second time around, or more easily read another text on the same subject. You will also find that ideas you have encountered begin to appear in your conversation and your writing. This shows that your mind is gradually accommodating to new ways of thinking.

In other words, a lot of learning is not directly to do with *memory* as conventionally understood – being able to produce rapid answers to quiz-type questions, for example – but rather with getting new ideas embedded into your thought processes. However, to the extent that memory plays a part it is worth recognising some of its key features.

5.3.2   How memory works

In most courses there will be *some* things you need to commit to memory. So how can you use your memory to best advantage? A good place to begin is by exploring your memory's powers.

Activity 5.4

Find a clock or watch that displays seconds. Spend one minute trying to memorise the items listed below. Then get a piece of paper and without looking back at this page write down as many of the items as you can remember.

lemon tart	sweet corn	sparkling water	ham
Beverages	corn flakes	*Desserts*	yoghurt
apple juice	*Starters*	leg of lamb	steak
cheese	<u>Dinner</u>	*Side dishes*	broccoli
cucumber	beer	rice	<u>Supper</u>

How well did you do? There are twenty items. Did you remember eight or more? If so, you did well. Seven items from a list is as many as most people can remember unless there is some kind of pattern to latch onto. Did you use any kind of strategy? You'd be exceptional if you did, in such a short time and with little to help you.

Activity 5.5

Now try a test that offers more support. Here are another twenty items, this time organised in a menu format (and a traditionally British menu at that). Again, give yourself one minute to memorise them, then see how many you can write down.

Breakfast	Lunch	
muesli	*Main course*	*Dessert*
grapefruit juice	lamb chop	ice cream
bacon	roast beef	apple pie
eggs		
tomato	*Vegetables*	*Drinks*
	potatoes	mineral water
	carrots	wine
	spinach	

Did you do better? You should have been able to remember more items this time because there are four important principles working in your favour: grouping, nesting, visual structure and links to existing knowledge. These are ways that your mind copes with large amounts of information, by organising and structuring it. Structured information is more easily remembered.

Structuring information

Grouping

In Activity 5.4 the items are presented as four lists, but there is nothing meaningful about the grouping. Although some items are underlined or italicised, you had very little time to work out how to make use of these features. To your mind, this was not much different from one long list.

In Activity 5.5 the items are laid out as groups under two main headings (Breakfast and Lunch), and the four italicised words are subheadings that have a meaningful relationship to other words. Now you have just six headings to remember along with whatever sticks in your memory from the lists. Information is much more memorable when it is grouped meaningfully.

Nesting

Another feature of Activity 5.5 is that some groups of items are 'nested' within other groups. There is a broad division into Breakfast and Lunch. Then nested within Lunch are subgroups: Main course, Vegetables, Dessert, and Drinks. Nesting is a powerful principle. It is the essence of what an outliner does. Look at Figure 5.2 with its main categories, sub-categories and sub-sub-categories. Instead of knowledge being a formless mass, you can organise it into categories within other categories. In this way your mind can store and then access enormous amounts of information. You can use this principle to great effect in revising for an exam.

Visual structure

The use of grouping and nesting in Activity 5.5 is emphasised by the way in which the words are laid out on the page. Also the underlining and italicisation highlight the principles underlying the structure. Indeed the headings no longer seem like words to be memorised. Instead of being part of the problem, they become part of the solution.

Linking to existing knowledge

Finally, Activity 5.5 takes advantage of knowledge about meals and food common in Britain. The Breakfast items are often seen together and the Lunch items are grouped as you might see them on a menu. When you read the items in Activity 5.4 you couldn't predict what might come next, but in Activity 5.5, if you are British, the items are quite predictable. This allows your mind to group them into well-established categories and you will be able to find them again. Because the knowledge in your mind is already elaborately structured, new information can be organised to take advantage of this structuring.

Other memory techniques

Two of the most commonly used techniques are visualisation and mnemonics. You can explore memory techniques by searching the internet – perhaps start with 'mnemonics' as a search term.

Visualisation Imagine a scene, then place the items you have to remember into that scene. You might have done this with the food items in Activity 5.5 by visualising a plate with meat and vegetables on it, or visualising a table with the breakfast items sitting there. To remember the items, you bring the picture back to mind and 'see' what is there. Our minds are good at storing images of complex visual scenes. Finding ways to organise information visually, particularly if you can make use of scenes and actions, adds greatly to the power of your memory.

Mnemonics Make up a nonsense phrase or a rhyme to help you remember something that has no obvious meaning you can latch onto. For example, I was taught 'Richard of York gave battle in vain' as a mnemonic for remembering that red, orange, yellow, green, blue, indigo and violet are the colours of the rainbow. To remember the major elements of music, 'rhythm means hitting the tin drum' unpacks as: rhythm, melody, harmony, texture, timbre, dynamics. And 'In fourteen hundred and ninety two/Columbus sailed the ocean blue' is a well-known rhyme that reminds us of the date. Mnemonic techniques have a very long history stemming from the days when knowledge was held in people's minds and transmitted orally. You can have some fun making up your own.

But memory 'tricks' are generally useful only when information is fundamentally lacking in meaning, or for special circumstances such as last-minute preparations for an exam. Rather than put your energies into creating *artificial* meanings and structures, it is generally much more valuable to develop *real understanding* and genuine long-term structuring of knowledge in your mind.

5.3.3   Worries about memory

Age and memory

Older students often worry that their memory might let them down. In terms of raw speed and 'processing power', everyone's memory does gradually decline. However, in practical terms, this is balanced out by the fact that you accumulate better organising structures in your mind for 'filing' information and ideas. As you get older, you will have a much more effective memory for certain things because you can make better sense of them, and you have developed a more sophisticated mental organisation. As long as you keep *using* your mind to *think* about and *organise* new information, your studies are unlikely to be affected by declining memory until very late in life.

Putting memory in its place

Perhaps you worry that your memory may let you down in your studies, but memory is less important than you might think. As you progress to higher levels of study, the focus is increasingly on understanding and putting ideas to use. In most higher-level courses there is little need to spend time 'memorising' in the sense of learning lists of words by rote. Instead, you can concentrate on the much more interesting challenge of learning to think in new ways.

Key points

- Pure memory plays a relatively small role in higher-level studies; it is what you understand that counts.
- If you need to remember things, write them down in your notes.
- You can help your memory by applying the principles of grouping, nesting, visual structuring and linking to existing knowledge when you are making notes.
- When you have a specific need to remember information, there are various techniques you can call on, such as visualisation, mnemonic phrases or rhymes, and word associations.
- Don't worry about the effect of age on your memory; greater knowledge and efficiency generally outweigh any physical changes.

5.4 Organising knowledge

As we have just seen, a way of making new knowledge memorable is to impose some structure on it. You might do this as you go along, making notes that summarise readings and lectures. You can do it as you gather together material for an essay or prepare for an exam. Or you might do it periodically just to clear your head and feel more on top of things. When you have been reading books or listening to lectures and are feeling swamped by new ideas and information, it can be helpful and morale-boosting to do some reviewing and organising.

5.4.1 Pulling your knowledge together

There are various ways in which you can set about organising knowledge. One simple but powerful technique is to draw a grid or table and arrange ideas and information in the cells under different headings. Figure 5.5 is the grid I used (in Chapter 3) to organise my thoughts about how we learn through reading, writing, listening and speaking.

Written word		Spoken word	
Reading		Listening	
Advantages	Challenges	Advantages	Challenges
Writing		Speaking	
Advantages	Challenges	Advantages	Challenges

Figure 5.5   Example empty grid ready for ideas

Making this grid encouraged me to think *analytically* by reflecting on the key differences between learning through the spoken and the written word. It also made me realise that while learning is most obviously done through reading and listening, I must also think about what to put in the 'Writing' and 'Speaking' boxes. As I wrote in these ideas, I found myself questioning whether they were really different from what I had written in the boxes above, and if so, how? The grid headings also reminded me to pay attention to both the advantages and challenges of all four modes of learning.

In other words, the grid encouraged me to think *systematically* by helping me dig out and examine ideas that I had not formulated properly. And setting ideas alongside each other helped me to examine their coherence. I played around with what was already in my mind, getting things clearer and more organised, and eventually this stimulated me to do some more reading to develop my analysis. So working with a grid helped pull together my existing knowledge and ideas, and primed me to move forward again.

You can make similar use of grids to pull together knowledge and ideas from your course. For example, if you are studying post-war European cinema you could create a grid that shows the different movements in various countries between certain dates, along with notable examples of the films produced and the studios/directors involved. This might yield a satisfying, and memorable, skeleton overview of the subject. The study of history is most obviously time-based, and here a grid might show important events during a period, which is perhaps divided into decades, along with the major actors and also the implications or ramifications of those events. Another kind of grid, or a timeline, might represent events in one country or part of the world over the period compared to events in another or others.

Grids such as these are especially easy to use if you are working on a computer, taking advantage of your word-processor's table-creating facility. In Microsoft Office Word, you just click on 'Table' and drag out a table with the number of columns and rows you want. Having created a grid and given headings to the columns and rows, you can either work with it onscreen or print it off and write on it by hand. Alternatively, you can simply create columns with headings:

> I have four columns headed Key themes, Key words, Key writers, Key examples. As I work through a topic I add things to the lists, so that at the end I have organised information to hold on to.

5.4.2 Making connections

A grid offers the power of schematic structure. However there are other ways to organise knowledge that encourage you to make creative links between ideas. Mind mapping is one such technique. Figure 5.6 shows a comprehensive mind map for Joyce Ellis's article.

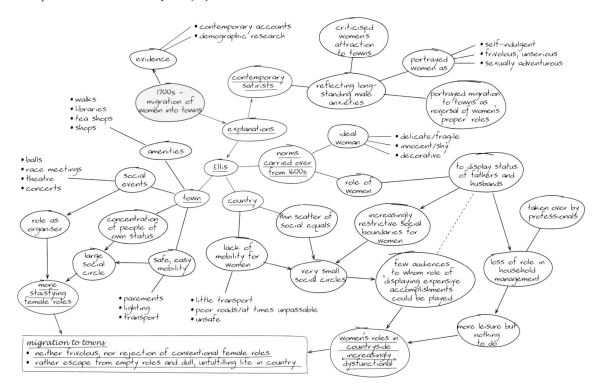

Figure 5.6 A mind map for Ellis's article

Activity 5.6

Take a few minutes to explore the diagram. Start with the shaded bubble and follow the arrow to 'explanations'. Then you have a choice between tracing Ellis's own argument first (to 'town', or 'country', or 'norms', and beyond), or the contemporary satirists' views. And so on.

Consider whether the diagram 'works' for you. Look back at Figures 5.1, 5.2 and 5.3 and compare them with this Figure (5.6). Which summary method do you think is most helpful?

You will have seen that the shaded bubble states the topic. Then the bubbles circled in red around it contain main themes, each linked to the topic by an arrow. In turn, each main theme has more detailed notes linked to it. Notice that some of these notes link to further notes of their own: for example, 'to display status of fathers and husbands', at the right of the diagram, leads to 'increasingly restrictive social boundaries …' and 'loss of role in household management'. You can mark as many connections between elements of a diagram as you find useful. Ultimately, Ellis's conclusions appear in red, at the foot of the mind map.

Perhaps this diagram looked rather complicated and daunting at first sight. It is as comprehensive as I could make it. It's unlikely that you would want to go into this kind of detail very often – though you might want to if you were writing an essay based on an article you found difficult to understand, for example. As to which method of note making works best, I can't answer that for you; as we saw, it will depend on how your mind works, what you want to do with your notes, and how much time you are prepared to invest in making them.

I made the mind map in Figure 5.6 by going through my underlining of Ellis's article, picking out what seemed important and fitting it into the diagram where it made sense to me. I did it with pen and paper, but I could have used my computer. You can use the drawing feature of your word processor or obtain mind mapping software. To get an idea of what is available search for 'mind mapping' on the internet.

Creating a diagram is an additional time investment, but visualisation can help a lot in clarifying your thoughts. It is worth playing around with techniques such as mind mapping to find out whether the gain in understanding and remembering is worth the time and effort. Some people use detailed mind maps mainly when revising for exams. They encourage you to *group* things together and to make *links*, both of which help to structure your memory.

> I find doing mind maps for revision really helps. It gives you confidence that you do actually remember something.

Key points

- Grids and mind maps enable you to bring together and summarise a lot of information so that you can get a structured overview of it.
- Setting out ideas or information in a grid helps you to organise your knowledge and encourages systematic analysis of similarities and differences.
- Making a mind map lets you work more creatively and helps you to see how different aspects of a topic link together.

5.5 Supporting creativity

We have explored how valuable notes can be for capturing and organising knowledge, but they are equally valuable for helping you work up ideas for a *presentation* or an *essay*.

5.5.1 Capturing thoughts

Notes help you to capture your ideas as they float by, whether you are doing course work, reading a newspaper or sitting on the train. At the time, your thoughts may seem obvious and not particularly important, yet these scraps may be the seeds of your creativity. Ideas don't conveniently flow into your mind the moment you sit down to write. You have to trap them as they come to you. Keep a note-pad or a wad of Post-it notes handy. If you are working at your computer, you could create a document called 'Essay Notes' and work in outline view. Then, when a thought strikes, type in a new line. You can move things around later to get your ideas straight. Or you could use electronic 'stickies' to keep track of ideas (see Figure 5.7); search for 'stickies' on the internet.

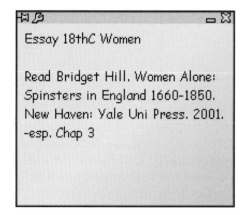

Figure 5.7 An electronic 'sticky'

> ❝ I use virtual "stickies". They are incredibly useful, just like real Post-its, you can have them 'on top' or hidden, and are dead easy to use. I use mine for referencing websites – when I visit a website, I just put the address, the data, and the date I accessed it on a sticky, then when I write the essay I've got the reference info all to hand. It's free too! ❞

> ❝ These things are great. I have sent one to 'sleep' so it will appear in the middle of March to remind me to start work on the project. ❞

5.5.2 Shaping ideas

When you have written down lots of scraps of ideas, you can gather them together and start organising them to make an effective line of argument. Begin with the most promising ideas and set aside those you have lost interest in. Then try different ways of grouping and sequencing them to make the logic flow.

You can do these informal jottings on the back of the proverbial envelope, or you could sketch out a mind map. Alternatively, this is where your outliner comes into its own. Having typed in various ideas you can rearrange them effortlessly. Expanding and collapsing an outline allows you to examine the flow of your argument at different levels of detail. Figure 5.8 shows the same outline as Figure 5.2 but with only two heading levels showing. You can switch back and forth between the big picture and fine detail whenever you want to check on how things are shaping up.

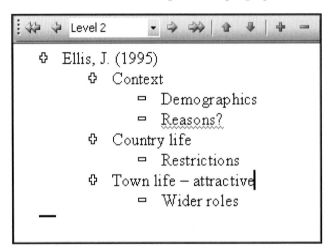

Figure 5.8   Microsoft Office Word's 'Outline' view showing two levels of heading

5.5.3   Sketching what you might say

See Chapter 8, Managing the writing process

Another kind of creative note making is sketching out possible sentences and paragraphs for your essay. Many of your jottings will be thrown away, but the point is that by working first in note form you create an informal space where you can let your mind 'speak' without the pressure of having to get it right.

Key points

Your notepad is a private, low-key space where the pressure is off and you can be creative. Here you can:

- capture thoughts as they pass
- shape ideas into convincing arguments
- sketch out ways of putting arguments into words.

5.6   Making notes strategically

Note making is not a single skill but a range of activities whose common feature is that you *write for yourself*, rather than for an audience, so that you don't have to worry about explaining yourself. Making good notes involves:

- **Taking an active, enquiring approach to study** Asking yourself questions such as: 'What is this about?', 'What do I want to remember?' and 'What do I want to say?', and writing down the answers.

- **Flexibility** Making sketched notes or detailed notes according to circumstances and need. Ask yourself: 'How will it help me if I make notes of this?', 'What will I use the notes for? Are they just to help me focus or will I use them in my written work?', and 'Do I need detailed notes or just an outline?'

- **Reflection** Looking at your notes and asking yourself: 'Are they doing the job I want?' and 'Could I be using my time more effectively?'

How many notes do you need?

> I seem to be writing so many notes. Reading, highlighting, then making own notes. Am I doing too much? My time is limited. Can someone reassure please?

> That sounds pretty much like me. I've been writing notes, highlighting, and typing up the key points. I'm hoping that as we get more confident we'll know what notes we should be aiming to have.

Making notes can help your studies in many different ways, but it is not plain sailing. If you make too many then studying becomes tedious. You have to weigh up *when* to make notes, what *kind* of notes to make, and what level of *detail* suits your needs.

What will you do with your notes?

The time you invest in making notes is wasted if you don't also invest in maintaining an effective *filing* system. But having stored your notes, will you use them? Will you sit down one day and read carefully through them all? If your notes are lengthy, unstructured and disorganised, you probably won't ever make use of them. Going back over old notes is seldom as urgent or appealing as moving on to something new, except perhaps when you are looking for material for an essay or pulling together ideas for an exam. But it doesn't really matter if you go back to your notes only occasionally. The process of writing them is valuable in itself.

See Chapter 2 Section 2.4.3, Maintaining a filing system

Key points

Benefits of note making

- Note making keeps you *actively focused* on studying.

- It is good for your *morale* because it's a creative task with a visible product; you can see that you have been studying.

- It makes you look for *meaning* in what you read and hear; and it helps to translate that meaning into your own words, turning knowledge 'out there' into your knowledge.
- Notes serve as an *extension of your memory*; they give you access to a far wider range of knowledge than memory alone can provide.
- Working in note form helps make *writing* a creative activity.
- Making notes that *pull together* the course is a key part of preparing for an exam.

Note-making strategy

- You need to find the right balance; don't turn studying into a chore. Note making should be a focused and creative process, done for a purpose, which makes study more satisfying.
- If your notes are to be useful in future, you need to make them succinct, intelligible, well organised and effectively filed.
- Experiment with different ways of making notes and reflect on their effectiveness so that you develop a repertoire of robust, flexible techniques.

Reference

Pauk, W. (2001) *How to Study in College*, Boston, Houghton Mifflin Company.

CHAPTER 6
Learning through talk

6.1 Talk in higher learning

From birth most people learn about life through speaking and by hearing other people talk, so talking and listening seem natural ways of learning. Certainly talk is a main means of learning in school. However, at higher levels of study the emphasis shifts to reading and writing – although talk retains a significant role, with lectures, seminars, tutorials, presentations, workshops and field trips featuring prominently in the curriculum of most courses.

But it is important to qualify this. Talk does not play a prominent role in everyone's life. If you experience communication difficulties you will be highly skilled in using alternatives to speech and listening. Also, distance education offers the possibility of gaining a degree without direct use of the spoken word. So, although this chapter explores the benefits of learning through talk and from hearing talk, we should bear in mind that these benefits can accrue in other ways than through speech, with online dialogues and conferences (or forums) a prime example.

6.1.1 The dynamics of dialogue

Talk has the capacity to sweep your thoughts along. Compared to words sitting on the page for you to invest with meaning, the dynamics of speech can be very compelling. And talking also offers you opportunities to try out ideas for yourself in discussion with others. Instead of composing carefully written sentences, you pitch in and try to explain your thoughts as they come to you. You take part in intensive, disciplined discussions in which your ideas are put to use. Being able to grasp the significance of what others are saying and make a well-argued contribution of your own is part of what it means to be knowledgeable in your subject.

See Chapter 3 Section 3.4.3, Speaking

Section 6.2 of this chapter explores the many facets of learning through *group discussion*. Section 6.3 discusses how to make effective seminar *presentation*s, and Section 6.4 learning through *visits*. Finally, Section 6.5 looks at various ways of learning by *listening* and *viewing*.

Key points

- Although university learning emphasises the written word, talk and discussion have traditionally played an important role.
- The dynamism and fluidity of talk are very helpful in grappling with the meanings of new theories and concepts.
- Moreover, being able to 'speak' your knowledge is an important skill in itself.

6.2   Learning through group discussion

Discussion groups of various kinds are a common feature of degree-level courses. Indeed, in many courses attendance at group sessions is compulsory and in some your participation is assessed. The key feature of this form of study is that it allows *dialogue*. Most of your study time is spent in one-way communication – either you are at the receiving end or you are writing to an absent reader. By contrast, in a discussion ideas can be traded back and forth between teacher and students and amongst students themselves. These sessions go by a variety of names and the nature of the dialogue can vary enormously, but all are intended to be *interactive*.

6.2.1   Different types of learning group

The terms *seminar*, *tutorial*, *discussion group*, *class* and *workshop* are all used to refer to sessions involving a tutor and a group of students. However, different institutions, and sometimes different subject areas, use the terms differently. For our purposes it is not important which term is used. The significant factor is that you are expected to learn through group interaction. I will mainly use the general term *discussion group*, but the issues I discuss will be relevant to your own group learning situations whatever they are called. I will also use the term *tutor* for the group leader.

Whatever the label, there are several factors that give a discussion group its character.

Group size A discussion group can involve very variable numbers of students. In small groups (around eight to ten students, say), all group members can participate. They can say what they think, interrupt each other, and still expect to reach a workable consensus on the issues. In medium-sized groups (about ten to twenty students), although everyone should be able to speak fairly regularly, there is more need for turn-taking and waiting for appropriate opportunities to speak. Some form of 'chairing' is required, whether by the tutor or one or more students, to manage the discussion. In larger groups a number of students can contribute but some, necessarily, are mainly listeners (however, these groups may be divided into small groups for part of the time.)

Degree of tutor control In some groups the tutor controls all that happens: setting the agenda, doing most of the talking, directing questions to individual students and commenting on their answers. At the other end of the spectrum, students take turns to lead sessions, with all group members contributing freely and commenting on each other's contributions; meanwhile, the tutor stays in the background. Between these two extremes lie many options in which control is shared between the tutor and the students to differing degrees.

Structured or open-ended Some group sessions are run to carefully structured plans – for example, with pre-designed tasks and students breaking into smaller groups, then reporting back according to prescribed guidelines. Others simply start with a broad topic and pursue whatever themes and issues arise. Again, there are many points between these poles.

Theoretical focus or 'practical' Some groups address tough theoretical issues to help students engage with textual analysis (for example, literary, art-historical or music criticism). Others may encourage students to focus on the world around them, using real-life case-study material (aspects of philosophy, law and religious studies, for instance).

Topic-centred or student-centred In some groups the agenda is driven by the current course topic and the concepts and theories associated with it. In others, students are encouraged to bring their own course-related concerns to the group for discussion – perhaps a problem with a forthcoming assignment, or concerns about coping with workload or exam preparation.

Whatever the label used for group sessions, what they offer will depend on your tutor's approach and on the culture and traditions of your subject, your department and your university. The only reliable way to find out about them is to attend.

Key points

- Discussion-based learning sessions are given various names including *seminars*, *tutorials*, *group discussions*, *classes* and *workshops*.
- The dynamics of the discussion are significantly affected by the size of the discussion group, from full participation by all in small groups to occasional participation by many in large groups.
- The character of a group is also affected by the degree of control the tutor exerts, the extent to which sessions are structured, the balance between theory and practice, and the degree of emphasis on student needs as opposed to the topic.

6.2.2   How groups help you learn

Group discussion is an unpredictable process and it is not easy to pin down exactly what you learn from it. After a group session you may have few notes and only a hazy memory of what has been talked about. Yet important learning processes can be stimulated within the flow of a discussion.

Activity 6.1

What benefits do *you* think students can gain from group discussion? Jot down your thoughts.

Here are my conclusions.

Ideas at your level

In group sessions you can steer the discussion to a level that suits you. If concepts are very abstract, or theories obscure, you can try to get the group to apply them to examples you understand. If you are confused you can ask for clarification. Meanwhile, your tutor can listen out for where difficulties seem to be arising and try to explain matters in ways that make more sense to you.

Collective thinking

In a discussion you take your understanding forward alongside other students. As one student tries to express a thought, another may contribute from a slightly different angle, while a third then tries to clarify what is being said. The group progresses by pooling its thinking resources. Within the shared understanding generated by the group, you find yourself able to use ideas that you cannot yet grasp independently. When you are reading, writing or thinking on your own it is easy to get stuck. Discussion is a way of playing flexibly with language and ideas, negotiating meanings in a supportive environment.

Making connections and recognising implications

Discussion helps you to explore how ideas link to each other. As a result of listening to other people, you suddenly see that a concept has wider meanings than you had realised and a whole lot of implications. You begin to appreciate your new knowledge as not just a set of separate items, but as a body of interconnected ideas you can work with.

Applying ideas

Many theories and concepts that you think you understand turn out to be more fuzzy and ambiguous than you realised when you try to apply them to examples – whether to a new poem or document, or a real-world religious practice. Other students' approximations or guesses help you towards making your own.

Practising skills

Group sessions also provide an environment in which you can develop skills. You might be provided with problems to work on, documents to analyse and draw conclusions from, creative writing exercises, or a sample essay to mark and discuss. This type of session is often described as a 'workshop'. It is an opportunity for a tutor to provide feedback and support – coaching you in the skills you need in your discipline.

Learning the language of the subject

Meanwhile, as you participate in discussions, a subtle form of learning goes on in the background. Gradually, you become more comfortable and confident with the language of your discipline. Specialist terms start to become meaningful. They begin to slip unnoticed into your vocabulary.

Picking up academic ways of thinking and arguing

Also going on behind the scenes is a general shift in your approach to your field of study. Discussion helps to initiate you into the culture and ways of thinking of experts in your discipline. You begin to understand how arguments and evidence are judged. You get a feel for how the debates work – how to position yourself and how to present an argument. And as you share in discussion you begin to develop an identity as a member of your discipline community. You begin to get the feeling that 'this is the way *I* talk – this is *my* field of knowledge. I belong.'

Boosting morale

Learning with a group helps keep your spirits up. You make friends and feel valued within the group. Soon you find out that everyone is experiencing the same kinds of difficulty as you, and you can exchange ideas and study tips. Knowing that other people are working alongside you, the subject matter seems more accessible and more interesting.

Key points

- Discussion is a communal mode of learning which allows you to share the burden of understanding new ideas.
- Discussion helps to develop your thinking as you follow the cut and thrust of argument and try out your grasp of theories and concepts.
- Meanwhile, you pick up the language of your subject and come to understand the culture and values of those who study your field.
- Group study lifts your morale as you discover that you are not alone in your struggles and share ideas and study tips with other students.

6.2.3 The variability of group work

Group discussions vary enormously from one group to another and from session to session. Energy surges; then slumps. Deadlock is followed by rapid progress. Students get irritated with each other, and then come to terms. Even for tutors this variation is baffling.

> What's puzzling is that sometimes it seems to go pretty well, then the next time it falls flat and I can't really tell why.

However, some of the variability is perhaps not so surprising.

Different kinds of student

If a group of students is knowledgeable, enthusiastic about the subject and eager to enter into debate, a very different discussion develops from when they are unprepared, uninspired and reluctant to join in. A lot depends on how experienced they are, both in discussion environments and in life. Mature students are often noticeably readier to speak than people recently out of school.

Social and cultural diversity

Social and cultural backgrounds are also important. Some students feel disadvantaged by their schooling. Some are used to a co-operative classroom culture, while others assume competition and point scoring. Some are from cultures which expect vigorous, egalitarian participation in group work; others are used to deference towards seniority and particularly towards a teacher. And some have different expectations of participation for men and for women.

Different tutoring styles

Tutors also differ in their styles of teaching. Some like to keep discussion under tight control while others prefer to guide students in exploring ideas for themselves.

> ❛ Yeah, he won't tell you the answer, he makes you think for yourself, but he sort of prompts you along the lines. ❜

Some tutors like to make sure that students understand the subject 'correctly'. Others try to steer students towards arriving at their own judgements.

> They don't say you're wrong, but they can sort of work it round so that you realise that you were wrong.

> (Anderson, 1997, pp. 185–98)

Changes over time

The nature of discussion changes markedly as you progress through your studies. You begin in groups where people are relatively nervous, unprepared and unsure of what is expected. But gradually everyone becomes familiar with group working and more confident in their subject knowledge. Discussions become less awkward, better informed and more challenging.

Box 6.1   Collective progress

The combination of *regular discussions* and *private reading* and study is immensely powerful. A group that meets over a period of time gradually develops a *shared understanding* of the subject matter. The discussion doesn't go back to first principles each time. It builds on the achievements of previous meetings. As your own thoughts become more developed through working on the course, so the shared understanding among the group also becomes more sophisticated – and the collective frames of reference that the group constructs during discussions become more powerful. The result is that you are able to take part in discussions that come increasingly close to the level of the ideas you are reading in texts.

Group discussions depend on 'group chemistry'. Particular combinations of people, circumstances and events produce very different kinds of group experience. Sometimes group work is the highlight of a course, leading to profound learning, personal commitment to the subject and valuable friendships. In other cases it plods along at a more mundane level or even becomes quite uncomfortable.

Key points

- Groups vary enormously depending on the subject you are studying, the kinds of students on your course and the expectations and experience they bring.
- Group work is also much affected by the personal style of your tutor.
- Group study changes as you progress through your courses and you and your peers become more knowledgeable and confident.

6.2.4   The experience of group learning

Being in a discussion group can produce strong feelings. You may find yourself stimulated, amused and appreciated, or intimidated, bored and alienated.

Good experiences

Here is a collection of the kinds of thing students say about discussion groups they enjoy.

> The discussions are really interesting. You don't think of it as study – you know like, "work". ... Sitting there hearing such important ideas going back and forth, I kind of feel proud to be a student.

> It's such a relief to find that everyone else has the same struggles with the books and essays. You feel you've got friends to ask if you're in difficulties. Some of them are very interesting people, who cope with so much in their lives.

> The tutor's always ready to talk about things and never patronises us. It makes the subject come to life to be able to discuss with someone who knows so much.

> Now and then you get a flash of insight and wish you'd known all this years ago.

> It's great to be able to ask questions and get things sorted out, instead of just reading all the time. You suddenly get the point of the concepts and theories. You feel that you're getting closer to the heart of the subject.

When discussion groups go well they help you to understand your subject in depth and keep you motivated and working hard. Take full advantage while you can.

Difficult experiences

If your experiences in discussion groups are less happy, you need to think what to do about it.

Activity 6.2

Read the three fictional scenarios below and write down what you think the problems are in each case. Say what, if anything, you think the student could do about them.

1 **Ryan**

> I wish I knew what they're talking about. I sometimes think I get it, but then it goes again. And sometimes I really want to speak, but when I try other people are talking or the topic changes. Or my mind goes blank, I say something useless and the others just carry on. Better keep my head down. I'll make notes. Maybe I'll be able to make some sense of it all when I read them later.

2 **Angie**

Shouldn't I just say what I think? I thought Ella took us off the point, but should I have said so? And if Kelly goes on about her kids any more I'm going to scream. Why doesn't the tutor shut her up and get us back to the topic? I didn't finish all the reading and didn't know all the answers, so perhaps I'm meant to keep quiet. Or do we get marks for the number of times we speak and what we say?

3 **Caitlin**

We never seem to get to the heart of anything. People just say what comes into their heads, pretending they know about things when they obviously haven't understood the reading. And a couple of them are creepy – they really suck up to the tutor. University seems like a smug little world to me. I don't feel I'm learning a thing.

Each of these scenarios presents some important issues that can arise in discussion groups. There are many ways you might have responded to them. I hope my comments make some useful connections.

1 **Not understanding; difficulty joining in**

(Ryan: I wish I knew what they're talking about.)

Not understanding is always unsettling. But Ryan's course *should* be presenting him with lots of new ideas and terms, and he is bound to feel out of his depth sometimes. Most of the other students probably feel confused at times too. He needs to join in the discussion, which would help him tease out some of his difficulties. And when he doesn't understand he could ask someone to talk him through an example to illustrate what they mean. If he still doesn't get it, he can ask again. After all, it is his education. In any case, clarifying things can be just as helpful for the other students. It is much better to err in the direction of over-clarification than to have people sitting about in a fog of confusion.

When there is competition for speaking time it is always difficult to know when and how to join in. Instead of trying to say something ambitious straight off, Ryan should make a simple point or two or ask a simple question. Also, he needs to get to know the group – make friendly relationships – and establish a sense of identity within it. Otherwise, he will feel exposed and vulnerable when he tries to join in. And that makes you underestimate yourself and overestimate everyone else.

Finally, Ryan shouldn't worry about making notes during the session. Anything important ought to be available from course texts and handouts. Nor should he pin his hopes on working out the meaning of his notes afterwards. If they don't make sense as he writes them, they certainly won't later. He could jot down a few reminders, but it is far more important to stay actively in touch with what is being said in the discussion.

2 **Uncertainty about rules; frustration with other students**

(Angie: Shouldn't I just say what I think?)

It is often not clear what is allowed or expected in discussion sessions, and it seems brash to jump in without knowing. Some groups do talk about expectations and rules in the first meeting. But if nothing has been said Angie should ask, particularly if she thinks there may be an element of assessment involved. In that case, you should definitely make sure you understand what is at stake.

Angie *should* say what she thinks. If only the most knowledgeable students speak then most of the group will be left behind. Also the tutor will get the wrong impression about the level at which to pitch things. If Angie has done at least *some* of the relevant reading, she should dive in – few will have completed it all. But if she hasn't done *any* of the reading then she should keep quiet. It is not fair to use precious discussion time making up for what some students have failed to do in preparation. Pretending you have done the reading or trying to change the topic to something you know about undermines everyone's progress.

As regards her frustration with others in the group, if Angie doesn't see the relevance of Ella's point she could say, 'I'm not sure how that ties in, Ella. Could you explain?' – not in a critical tone, but assuming that for Ella there was a link. It is very helpful to the group as a whole if a member tries to pull the threads of discussion together and keep it focused. On the other hand, it certainly can be tedious when some students regularly insist on sharing the details of their lives with the group. But maybe Kelly, as a mature student, is worried that the younger ones are better educated – perhaps she is unconsciously shifting attention to what she sees as her strengths, her life experience. Of course, it is the tutor's role to 'shut her up', but he may be wary of upsetting Kelly by seeming not to value her experience. Or maybe he just feels grateful when anyone speaks. Angie is right in wanting to stay on topic and resist the commandeering of sessions by a few students. She might talk to the tutor out of class about her concerns.

3   Frustration with the group process; alienation

(Caitlin: We never seem to get to the heart of anything.)

Good discussion is elusive. Some classes don't go particularly well. However, there are usually things that can be done. When discussion keeps drifting around and students are 'busking' it usually means there is a lot of uncertainty, nervousness and lack of focus. Again, it would be perfectly reasonable for Caitlin to mention to the tutor that she is finding the discussions disappointing. Perhaps the group could focus on something more concrete, example primary sources or case studies for instance.

But why does Caitlin express such hostility? Perhaps she is reacting to the inequalities of the student–tutor relationship. Students sometimes play at being deferential, eager and grateful, and Caitlin looks down on those who accept such roles. Perhaps she thinks of university as a 'smug little world' because she senses the protected nature of the tutor's role – the power the tutor has over the student's immediate prospects, the potential for extolling the virtues of rigour and criticism while being in a position to crush dissent and reward compliance. I think it would help if Caitlin could create a more significant role for herself, by volunteering for something or taking a lead in discussions. This would get her involved intellectually, rather than sitting on the sidelines feeling detached and critical.

Key points

- How well you learn from group discussion is strongly affected by your feelings about the experience of being in the group.
- Group learning can be a very enjoyable, rewarding and supportive experience which builds up your confidence and maintains your morale.
- It can also be confusing, frustrating and alienating, so it is important to be able to reflect on your reactions to group sessions and think strategically about how to achieve productive relationships within the group.

6.2.5   Making groups go well
Students' expectations
Within a group the role of the tutor is not so much to 'teach' in the sense of telling students things (books and lectures do this). Instead, they set up topics and activities that will help the group to learn, and support the students as they work through them. Here is what students have said about tutoring and group work; the quotations that follow are taken from interviews with them (Anderson, 1997, pp. 184–98).

Students tend to like a tutor who is able to empathise with their concerns and offer support.

> Having an encouraging tutor helps, rather than someone who is obviously very clever, but so clever that they can't see your problem, because they understand it. It's nice having someone that can see why you've got a problem.

It is particularly important that the tutor knows how to create an unthreatening atmosphere within the group.

> I find that tutorials are at their best when there is a very, very informal nature about the class ... if you can open up, right, ask questions without fears of being stupid.

But students also expect to be challenged, by being given work to do and new ideas to think about.

> I dislike tutorials where we haven't been ... told 'Right, prepare something' ... if you're not given any kind of instructions to go and do some reading beforehand, then people have much the same view ... the sort of layman's view of the subject, and there's no discussion at all.

Neither do they expect discussion to be simply an exchange of 'opinions'. They expect the tutor to take a lead in shaping it – pulling out points, pushing people to think further, gathering together the threads of discussion. Of course, it's quite difficult for a tutor to play this role without sometimes intervening too much. And it is hard to strike a balance between open, creative participation and focused, rigorous analysis, particularly as students' preferences differ.

 I want it to be always very focused ... They are a waste of time if you just sit there and everyone just talks about what they feel like talking about.

I don't like when tutors focus all the time because I think that's wrong.

Clearly, it is difficult for a tutor to try to accommodate *all* the students' needs and preferences. Some of the responsibility for this has to be shared within the group.

Generally, students expect an open, democratic atmosphere within which all group members participate constructively and considerately. They disapprove of group members who fail to prepare adequately and hold the group back, and they disapprove even more strongly of group members who dominate, taking up an unfair share of the group's time (Anderson, 1997).

Ground rules

Students working alongside their peers, then, must have their channels open to those other people. An aim of discussion groups is to develop what have been called the *communicative virtues*:

- *tolerating* other people's points of view
- *respecting* the differences between people
- being *willing to listen* to others, in the spirit that one might be wrong
- being *patient* and *self-restrained* so that others may have a turn to speak.

So tutors will be paying attention to *how* the members of the group work together as well as what they say.

In order to make sure that all members of the group share their expectations of the discussions, groups sometimes begin by exploring what everyone hopes to achieve from them and what ground rules might be established. These are 'rules' that all members agree to abide by in the interests of the group as a whole. Here are some typical ground rules:

- listen attentively to others
- ask others for information
- give examples
- give reactions to the contributions of others
- encourage others to take part.

(Source: Forster, 1995, p. 16)

> ## Key points
>
> - The success of group learning depends both on the skills of the tutor and on willing, constructive participation by students.
> - Students generally want an informal, open, democratic atmosphere, but they also expect the tutor to play an active role in shaping discussion and drawing out the important points.
> - Students expect each other to abide by procedural rules, whether they are implicit or have been drawn up as 'ground rules'.

6.2.6   Online group work

Many of the issues we have been discussing apply also to students and tutors 'talking' online. I remarked in Chapter 3 that although you contribute to an online discussion in writing, this is in fact a hybrid form of communication – a kind of speaking-writing. Here is an example of what I mean.

Sophie: Hi – Still on the 2nd paragraph with ideas floating around now. Essay writing is a skill we acquire at school. Perhaps in a couple of essays it will become like riding a bike – you never really forget! For now I think I've got the stabilisers on!

Gita: Hi all – I really hope that I have answered the question because I was absolutely hopeless at writing essays in school. So I am on the tricycle never mind the bike with the stabilisers!

Leah: Well I sent my essay in. I found it hard as I'm not good with big words to describe things. So mine is written with basic words.

Aisha: Leah I think having no big words, just your own, makes it clearer that you have understood the thing you are writing about without using technical jargon or trying to spout from dictionaries ... As this is my first essay in 30 years, I keep looking at the question to make sure I'm not veering off course. Think it's going to take a lot of practice.

Cerys: Hi all – Getting my head around essays is hard for me. To keep myself focused I
– write out the question in a bold pen on A4 paper and then put it on the wall in front of me.
– put key points on a mind map (I'm not good at these but every bit helps)
– spread out the key headings on another A4 piece of paper on which I add my notes.
After this I rub my eyes a lot and get a drink.

Liam: Hi Guys – When you are writing an essay that has 'discuss' in the title, what do you do if you cannot find a good argument for AND against. For example, in the essay we're doing I can find loads of arguments that agree with the statement, but none that positively disagree. How can I say this in the essay?

This dialogue was extracted from an online conference in which students were 'talking' together by leaving messages in a common area.

Online conferencing

There are various types of conferencing system (also referred to as forums); these students were using 'Moodle', as is the group shown in Figure 6.1.

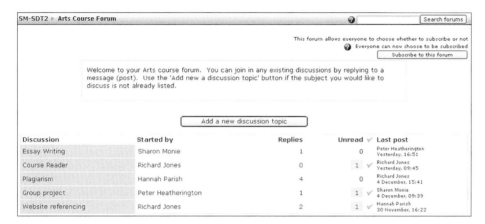

Figure 6.1   A short segment from an online conference

Essentially, a conference is a string of messages. On the right-hand side of Figure 6.1, in the 'Last Post' column, you can see that messages were posted by conference members at various times over several days. This is asynchronous conferencing, with each person participating at the time they choose from wherever they happen to be. It is like a slow-moving conversation you can join at any time, dropping in for say twenty minutes to read the latest messages and leave your own. The 'Discussion' column lists the different subjects being talked about: you can see who started each discussion and how many replies they have had. There have been four messages on the topic of plagiarism and a new topic has been opened concerning the Course Reader. This is typical; different themes are being pursued alongside each other within the conference.

This kind of conference can be especially valuable for students in distance education, part-time students who perhaps work unsocial hours, people who have difficulties with speech or mobility, those who are shy and find it very hard to participate in company with others, and all the night owls among us. Indeed, it may be the only way that some students can participate in group discussions while studying. And it offers certain advantages too. Having read a message, you can think and follow it up before 'speaking'; conferencing enables more considered responses than face-to-face discussion. Also, unlike those discussions, it is not ephemeral; all the messages sent to a conference are archived. That means they are always available – you can read some of them again and think hard about them weeks later, and even revisit the discussion as a whole when revising for an exam, for example.

Although conferencing works through reading text rather than listening to speech, it can have the flavour of a conversation amongst friends; the same sense of a spontaneous sharing of ideas and experiences, and of human contact. A short visit can spark new ideas, making you feel less isolated and more confident.

> ❝ I love this conference. If it wasn't available I wouldn't be enjoying the course as much. It's great to know that everyone is feeling the same – nervous, uncertain, etc. The tips and advice are great. Knowing that someone out there will have a few ideas for you to try whenever you get stuck, or give you a boost whenever it's all getting too much, is brilliant. ❞

At the same time, you are constantly *writing*; conferencing offers you plenty of practice at articulating your ideas.

However, online conferencing does not have to take place over several days. In 'chat rooms' you can have free-flowing, real-time dialogue, with people dropping in and out. A live web-chat is said to be *synchronous*, because everyone is online at the same time. If more than three or four people are participating, live chat tends to be frenetic and chaotic, but fun. An hour can be exhausting as you try to type fast enough to keep up with the flow. You have little time to compose messages carefully because the topic keeps moving on as new messages arrive. Chat rooms are more interactive than asynchronous conferencing forums and the spontaneity makes them feel sociable, but the quality of the content is more variable, and you may see only the messages that arrive while you are online.

Your course may provide facilities for online conferencing. Alternatively you could look for links to student chat rooms or message boards on your university website. Or you might link up with students of all subjects and all ages from around the world by visiting student conferences via portals such as Yahoo (www.yahoo.co.uk) or Microsoft Network (www.MSN.co.uk).

Tutorials online

See Chapter 1 Section 1.8.2, eLearning

If one member of a conference is the teacher, dialogue can be structured in the form of a tutorial. The tutor posts a message which poses a question or suggests an activity, and says how long the tutorial will run (for example, a week). Students then visit the conference to make their responses to the question or activity, and talk to each other about their work. From time to time the tutor revisits to correspond with the students, to summarise, and perhaps to move the discussion along with new questions. Students visit several times to see how the discussion develops, and at the end of the week the teacher draws the discussion to a close.

> ❝ The tutorial tasks made me think more about the texts I had been studying. So did the comments other students wrote. I found this a good way to be involved in group study. ❞

Group projects online

A conference environment can also be used for group project work. If the project is well structured and students participate wholeheartedly, online teamwork can be a very rewarding experience.

See Chapter 10, Online research and project work

> Hello All. I think it's brilliant that the project has got us all 'chatting' and having read the other team's report – I am equally impressed and think they have done a great job. This project has achieved a lot. I hope it continues into our next courses. It doesn't matter how skilled you are at computing – once you get over the fear of 'I can't' anything is possible!

The pitfalls of online conferencing

The conferencing environment can be intimidating at first; it looks complicated and formal until you get used to it. There are no signals as to what is supposed to be going on and no visual clues as to what other participants are thinking, so it is quite a challenge to leave your first message, to be read by strangers. Who are they? What do they think of your messages, and of you? Even when you become acclimatised to online conferencing, the experience can sometimes disappoint.

- Conferences are not always lively – they depend on active, motivated participants.
- Conferences are not always friendly – people can misread each other quite easily and fall out rapidly in the exchange of a few heated messages.
- Conferences can become confusing and tedious if they are not well focused and well managed.
- Conferences can be overwhelming if they are so active that there are always dozens of new messages to read every time you visit.
- Conferences can also be addictive, distracting you from other study activities.

Used well, however, they can be very supportive of your studies.

Making online conferencing work

Online conferences have the potential to be open, democratic and friendly environments. However, as in any social forum, some rules and conventions are required.

Box 6.2   Netiquette

The good manners of conferencing and chatting on the internet are known as 'netiquette'. An online conference is a kind of virtual social space, communally shared by a group of people. Unlike most social spaces it is unaffected by people's physical attributes (their appearance, manner, gestures, or accent). However, like any other social space, it has to develop its own culture so that people can understand each other and get along together (see Alexander, 2000). That involves some rules, for instance about how to address people and what kind of language is acceptable.

Conferencing is a team effort. Members have to be ready to contribute and support each other.

> The more you put into conferencing, the more you get out. One of the most important things is to answer someone when they speak, even if just to agree or disagree. Help bring other people into the conversation just by giving them a mention ... If no reply appears, you're worried that your original message was inappropriate! You find yourself logging on constantly to see if anyone has answered or even acknowledged that you are there.

Although online conferencing allows you to make considered contributions to discussion, it generally works best when everyone feels relaxed about what they say in messages – not worrying too much about spelling and grammar or getting their thoughts completely worked out before they write. Since you are communicating through the formal, structured medium of writing rather than the fluid medium of speech, there is a danger of losing the humanity and sociability of face-to-face conversation. It is best to be natural in your messages, getting them off before the thought evaporates rather than waiting until you have something 'significant' to say. Conferences become involving when everyone lets their personality show.

Key points

- Online conferencing is a way of making study more sociable. As in face-to face discussion sessions, it can give you the stimulation and support of sharing ideas and study experiences with like-minded students.
- It may be an integral part of your course, particularly if you are studying by distance education; or it may be an option you can explore for yourself by checking out the websites of your course, your university, the student union or the wider web.

6.2.7   Rising to the challenge of group learning

We have seen what the group can do, but what can *you* do to get the most from discussion groups?

Belonging

Your first priority is to feel part of the group. If you are to contribute effectively you need to think of yourself as a group member who has a useful contribution to make. In short, you need an 'identity' in the group. People have to know a bit about you and you need to know something about them. So at the start of the sessions don't sit in silence waiting for the tutor; and if you are online, use the 'chat' facilities. Talk to one or two other students about themselves: their lives, their plans, why they are taking the course, how they are feeling about things at the moment. Usually, they will ask you similar questions. This will make them feel more at home, so they will feel kindly disposed towards you. Don't worry about seeming pushy. People may appear reserved, but it is usually just nervousness and most people find it a relief to start talking. Over a few sessions you will be able to talk to most people if not the whole group. This will make you feel a lot less exposed when you contribute to discussion.

Be sure to position yourself physically within the group. Don't sit where you can't be seen. If your chair is on the edge of things, or facing slightly away, push it right in. It is harder to feel part of a group if you are physically on the fringes. And if people can't see you when you speak they feel less sympathy with what you say. You may find yourself in a downward spiral – you feel left out so you join in less; as others do join in and feel more comfortable, you feel even more left out.

Preparing

With the exception of the very first meeting, you can't expect simply to turn up to group sessions and sit there waiting to be taught. Discussion is an activity that helps develop learning you have already begun on your own. Setting aside time for *preparatory work* is *essential* to the group learning process. A reasonable rule of thumb is to spend two hours preparing for each one-hour group session. (This may include reading that you are doing for other aspects of your course too.) You may not always be able to complete the set work as thoroughly as you would like but you need to make a decent attempt. Otherwise, you hold the group back and let yourself down.

If, in a crisis, you have to skip the preparation it is still worth attending the session so that you don't lose touch with the group. But let your tutor know, so that allowances can be made in class. If the crisis continues talk to your tutor about how best to manage the situation. Even doing a modest amount of preparatory work is a lot better than nothing; but the general rule is *always prepare*.

Listening

It is important to stay closely in touch with the discussion as it proceeds, otherwise you will become confused and feel left out. But, as we saw in Ryan's case, listening can be difficult. When you are new to a subject and unfamiliar words are in use it is easy to lose the thread – especially with the focus continually shifting as different members of the group contribute. Don't just hope for the best. Nip confusion in the bud by asking for clarification. Ask for an example to make things less abstract. Don't be anxious that you are the only one confused. Other students probably feel just the same.

Speaking

Don't hang back thinking that other students are cleverer, more articulate and more knowledgeable than you. Remind yourself that they are probably thinking exactly the same about *you*. Throw caution to the wind and join in. It is not worth worrying about what others think of you because they are far less concerned about the quality of what you say than what *they* say and what you think of *them*. Don't let yourself be intimidated. It is just as much your discussion, intended to help *you* learn.

Box 6.3   Saying the simple thing

You may feel that you ought to wait until you have something important to say before taking up the group's time by speaking. Don't; it is far better to set your sights lower. Ask the simple question, make the obvious point, offer the straightforward example. What seems ordinary to you is often more interesting to other people. And, in any case, to have a good discussion the group does not require 'brilliant' interventions. It just needs everyone's mind focused on the main theme and a steady flow of contributions.

If you don't always speak a lot, don't worry. You can get plenty from a debate by listening hard and 'participating' silently, agreeing or disagreeing in your mind. And it certainly is not true that those who speak the most always know the most. As long as you try to join in some of the time it doesn't matter if you find yourself cast in a relatively minor role.

Helping the group process

Try to encourage other group members to participate, particularly those who haven't spoken much. Ask for their views and take an interest in what they say. Ask follow-up questions to give them the confidence that they made a point worth exploring. Refer to other students' contributions when you make your own. Try to summarise group members' points of view from time to time. Don't treat 'winning the argument' as your primary aim; use the group as a way to explore a range of different arguments. There are plenty of other opportunities for you to think about your own views; while you are in the group, value the diversity of viewpoints it enables you to explore. Doing these things will take some of the heat off your tutor, who, as we saw, has a difficult role to play and a crowded agenda.

Box 6.4   Philosophising

Group discussion is especially important for students of philosophy because philosophising is something you *do*, in dialogue with others. Usually, philosophical discussions involve close attention to particular ideas that the group needs to get clear about. In the process, what people say is scrutinised in detail: statements are taken apart, questions are raised, objections and counter-arguments are put forward. So you have to be very careful about what you say and how you justify it – indeed, that is a main *point* of learning to philosophise.

At first, this kind of discussion can be daunting. Some people in the group may seem to see it as a game, in which the 'winner' is the person who scores the most points in argument. If the topic is something you feel deeply about (an ethical issue such as abortion, for example) and your ideas are getting the treatment, you may feel that it is also *you*, as a person, who is being probed, criticised and found wanting. Try not to. And don't be reduced to silence by others in the group who may be aggressive or appear very confident. Remember that you are not actually in a competition with anyone: the purpose of the discussion is to help you learn how to argue a case well or, if you are sincere, to try to get at the truth of something. Unless you keep contributing you will not learn.

Arriving late, leaving early

Arrive in good time for group sessions. It disrupts the flow if there are frequent breaks for recapping. However if you are unable to arrive in time for the beginning of a session, or have to leave before the end (fairly common for part-time students), don't feel you have to miss the whole thing. Just let your tutor know about your difficulty and arrive or leave discreetly when you have to.

Key points

- Make an effort to talk to group members before and after meetings. It will make a big difference to your confidence to speak within the group.
- Do the best you can to complete the relevant reading or other preparation before group meetings. But if you haven't been able to manage it, tell the tutor. Don't skip the session.
- If you feel confused then say so. Don't get left out of things.
- Don't wait for inspiration before you speak. Just jump in, ask the simple question, give the obvious example.
- Don't be anxious about the quality of your contributions. Other people are concerned about what they say rather than what you say.
- Share responsibility for keeping the group going. Help to make the group enjoyable for other students – you'll enjoy it more too.

Group learning can be one of the most stimulating and supportive elements of your course but it can also be frustrating and tedious. It is worth reflecting on the group process so that you understand what works and what doesn't. That way you can play your part in making the experience as productive as possible.

6.2.8   Self-help groups

If you want more group study opportunities than your course provides, find some like-minded students and set up a study group of your own. Just arrange a place and time to meet and work out how you are going to manage the meetings. You will need a clear agenda and a group leader for each meeting, otherwise the group will drift into disorder and lose heart. Generally, someone has to take the initiative in deciding when and where to meet, what to discuss and how to proceed. If you can work all this out then you may find your self-help group just as useful as tutor-led sessions. Your tutor may even help you set up the group if you ask.

> **Key point**
>
> ■ A self-help group can be excellent, but it needs organising. Decide right at the start how you will share out leadership tasks.

6.3 Making a presentation

Many courses require students to make presentations to a group. You might be asked to do this on your own or in partnership with others. Presentations are often weekly events with a different student, or team, taking a turn each week. You might be asked to present a summary of an article or a book, or to research a topic for yourself. A presentation is generally expected to take ten to fifteen minutes at the start of a session, followed by discussion. In principle it is a very straightforward task. However, delivering your own ideas and words to an audience for the first time can be frightening, so it is worth exploring the basic principles.

6.3.1 Speaking to an audience
Why presentations?
A series of presentations by group members is an excellent way to 'democratise' the group learning experience. Instead of your tutor retaining all responsibility for knowledge, the whole group shares the work of connecting its discussions to the ideas and literature in the field. In the process, you develop skills that will be valuable in your future studies and in the wider world:

■ researching a topic and extracting key points relevant to a particular purpose

■ planning a short presentation and preparing any accompanying visuals

■ delivering a presentation to an audience.

What is a good presentation?
What are you trying to achieve with your presentation? What will make it go well?

> **Activity 6.3**
>
> Think back to a lecture or talk that you enjoyed. Then think of a lecture or talk you didn't enjoy.
>
> 1 Jot down a few notes about what you liked about the enjoyable lecture or talk, then a few notes about what you didn't like about the other.
>
> 2 Now draw a line down the middle of a piece of paper to make two columns. Put the headings 'Good Talk' and 'Bad Talk' at the top of the columns. Using the notes you have already written and anything else that comes to mind, make a list of the features of 'good' and 'bad' talks. For each item in the 'Good' column try to think of its opposite and write it in the 'Bad' column, and vice-versa.

This is a reflective exercise. You have used your own experiences to tell yourself what works well in talks and what doesn't. As you read through the discussion that follows, see how well it corresponds to your own reflections. I am sure you will have identified some points I haven't included, but it will be interesting to see whether we have agreed on the basics.

See Chapter 1 Section 1.7, Being a reflective learner

Pitfalls of giving presentations

Let's begin by looking at some of the things that can go wrong. There are several points you can easily misjudge when you make a presentation.

- Because you are nervous and hoping to impress you try to make *far too many points* in the time you have available.

- You think of your presentation as being addressed to your tutor, instead of the other students, so you pitch it at *too high a level*.

- Because you have been absorbed in pulling apart and thinking about the issues raised by your topic, you forget that the rest of the group has no idea what the issues are and you *fail to start from first principles* when you explain them.

- Similarly, because you have been reading intensively about your topic you become very familiar with *specialist terms* which mean nothing to other students, and you *forget to explain their meaning*.

- Because you are aware of the time constraints you *speak much too quickly*.

- Because you are nervous you *speak too quietly* and you *don't look at your audience* to check that points have been understood before moving on.

- For safety's sake you decide to *read* your presentation from a prepared script, so you can't 'connect' with your audience, and the presentation is dull and uninvolving.

Basic rules of presenting

- Keep it *simple*. Don't pack your talk with ideas or information.

- Make it as *clear* as you can. Explain everything as though to a beginner. Give examples. Remember that clarity is much more important than quantity or 'cleverness'.

- *Don't read* it – talk to your audience.

- *Don't rush* it. Take your time. Cut material rather than rush.

- *Use visuals* or *sound* when appropriate.

- Keep reminding yourself that the other students are not concerned with how clever *you* are but with how well *they* can understand what you say.

6.3.2 Preparing your presentation
Things to find out

- Are you supplied with any guidelines on making presentations?

- How long is the presentation meant to last?

- How long should you spend researching and preparing? Is the presentation meant to be the equivalent of an essay or should it be prepared quite quickly?
- Will you use visual aids, such as a flip-chart, an overhead projector and transparencies, or a slideshow on a digital projector? How do you get transparencies made? If slides, do you bring the presentation with you on a disk?
- Are you expected to produce a handout?
- How will discussion be handled after the presentation? Are you expected to stay at the front and answer questions? Will you, another student, or the tutor be expected to chair the discussion? Or do you just rejoin the group?
- Is the presentation assessed? If so, how are marks awarded?

Researching

Don't get carried away trying to cover a wide range of sources. Just cover the basic ones and use your time instead to make good notes. Then make notes from your notes, so that you end up with summary 'prompts' on cards. Focus on the parts you understand best; the better you understand your material the clearer your talk will be. The group discussion afterwards may help you sort out some of the less well understood issues.

Planning

Broadly the same principles apply as when you write an essay. You work up an outline, but instead of writing it out as an essay you speak it. Your notes will be quite similar to an essay outline, but shorter and more direct and punchy. As with an essay you need: a *title*; *an introduction* in which you set the context for your presentation, so that the audience knows what you are talking about and why; a sequence of *main points* supported by illustrations and examples; and *a conclusion*, in which you remind the audience of your title and say how you have addressed it.

The most important thing is to *avoid being too ambitious*. In fifteen minutes or so you can only make a few main points. If you prepare a lot more, you will end up gabbling and no one will understand a word of it. For example, if you are introducing a book chapter indicate in a few words what is special about the book (why it's worth having a presentation on it), what the central question is that the chapter deals with and how it approaches that question.

Nobody ever complains about presentations being too easy to understand. Use examples where you can to show what you are getting at. Work up a visual representation of your argument if it will make things clearer.

Preparing slides or transparencies
Using presentation software

Whether you make transparencies for use with an overhead projector or prepare a digital slideshow, the best way to prepare slides is to use presentation software (such as Microsoft PowerPoint) because it has many useful features that will help you design a good presentation. If you haven't used such software before, this is an excellent opportunity to learn which will be useful to you in many situations during your course and beyond. The software enables you to insert charts and pictures and usually has a facility for printing handouts (see Figure 6.2).

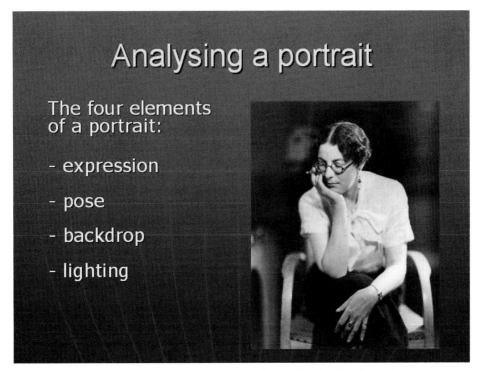

Figure 6.2   A slide created with Microsoft PowerPoint. For details of the photograph shown here, see Chapter 10, Figure 10.7

Presentation software can be confusing when you first try it out, so it is worth looking for some support:

- Your university computing centre may offer training.
- Your software probably includes 'wizards', which take you step by step through preparing a presentation.
- Tutorials may be supplied with your software.
- You could get hold of one of the excellent 'teach yourself' software manuals.

After a session to learn the basics, you'll be away.

Design
Take time over the design of your slides or transparencies.

- Use layout to show the structure of your argument.
- Use a large font size for the basic text (for example 20 point), and even larger for headings. And use plain fonts rather than fancy.
- Have one main theme per slide (think of a slide as being like a paragraph in an essay). Have two or three sub-points per slide (five maximum).

- Three slides may be all you need (plus a title slide and a concluding slide) depending on how much you have put on each and how easy they are to read.

When you have completed the slides, switch to slideshow mode and talk yourself through your points using only the slides as triggers. As you come to words on the slides that don't seem quite right, make adjustments; polish your work.

Spending time on the design of your slides is *not* time wasted. By thinking about exactly how to present your message you get it clear in your mind. This will help you to deliver a good presentation. But more than that, you will have learned a lot about the strategic skills of preparing a talk.

6.3.3   Practising
Rehearsing the talk
When everything is ready give yourself a full rehearsal.

- Speak your presentation out loud, timing yourself to see how long it takes.
- Speak loudly and clearly, at a measured pace.
- Speak from prompt cards (skeleton notes), or your slides. If you try to speak from detailed notes you risk losing contact with your audience because it is difficult to keep switching attention between the two. That is why slides are excellent – you can read your notes from the screen along with your audience, staying in touch with them throughout.
- Jot down a schedule showing the time by which you need to have completed each section of notes or each slide.

Then, you need to put any slides into the appropriate format for the presentation.

Beginning and ending
Having worked out what you are going to say, think about how you will get yourself started. It isn't good to launch straight into a presentation. You need to capture your audience's attention and establish a rapport with them. Will everyone in the group know you? In any case, begin with one or two informal remarks just to get your voice working and your audience listening. Establish eye contact with a few people in the audience. All this only takes a minute but it makes a big difference. Then don't forget to explain the *context* for your talk before getting on to your main points.

Think also about your closing words. A talk ends rather lamely if you just reach the end and stop. You need to think of a way to signal that you have finished and then either stay where you are for questions or go and sit down. It can be as simple as 'OK, that's it – now you can ask me questions'. This makes you sound confident.

6.3.4   On the day
Relax yourself Before your talk, try to spend a few minutes alone practising getting tuned up for speaking. You need some adrenalin flowing, but also a calm feeling that you are in control – that you have done the best you can to prepare, so you have no need to worry. Professional speakers often get their

voices working by humming loudly with the mouth shut then wide open, or singing a simple song loudly and clearly. Then take deep breaths, feel yourself slowing down, and compose yourself so that you can speak at a sure, steady pace.

Get set up Get to your session ahead of time. Check any equipment you will be using – switch it on and off. Try out your first slide or transparency and practise moving from one slide to the next. Find a chair if you want to sit – although unless yours is a very small group you will probably need to stand. Move furniture to make the space around you 'your space'. Make yourself feel that you belong there.

The delivery Remember, don't rush. Take the time you need to settle into your stride. Then go steadily through your talk, taking your audience with you. As you speak, glance around the audience. Look closely at one or two people from time to time to make sure they are still following you. If they aren't, change your tone, throw in another example, or ask a question – whatever it takes to get their attention back.

Keep an eye on the time. Stick to a measured pace so that people have time to connect fully with your line of argument. But be careful not to dwell on your opening so long that you run out of time before you get to the main points. If you see yourself dropping behind, speed up. You can build up to a fairly fast pace towards the end if the audience is with you. If necessary, skip points to make sure you finish on time. But don't forget to deliver your conclusion, however rushed the ending. Don't let the talk just fizzle out.

The discussion afterwards Don't become defensive during the discussion that follows. Accept criticism with good grace and show an interest in alternative points of view. Take the attitude – 'I did this to help the group. I've done the best I could. Now it's up to all of us to work with the topic and see what we can make of it.'

Keep a sense of proportion Keep in mind that a presentation is not a major event. You are simply serving a routine function for the group by kicking off a discussion. For everyone else it is just another session. All they are concerned about is whether they can understand what you say.

6.3.5   Group presentations

If you are asked to give a group presentation, rather than doing it solo, the same general principles apply but you share out the work. This can be an advantage in reducing pressure and allowing you to develop your presentation skills while supported by your team mates. However it can also create difficulties.

- It may not be easy to divide up the research activities or see how to coordinate them. The planning stages must be organised carefully.
- Disputes can easily arise, with team members working to different agendas and some, perhaps, feeling they have put in more work than others.

- Time has to be allowed for working out how to collate what different team members have found, for deciding what gets left out and for pulling together a coherent presentation.
- You may be less in control of what is on any slides you are presenting.
- If you are assessed as a team, there can be a sense of injustice in being awarded a communal mark for effort or for contributions of very different quality. However, often you are asked also to submit your notes or a written, reflective piece after the event, which is assessed separately and individually. The ultimate score – for presentation plus written work – may therefore be different for each team member.

Bearing all these possibilities in mind, it is clearly important to take team management seriously. You could try to establish ground rules within the team before starting the work. On the other hand, with a willing, cheerful team, the whole experience can be very rewarding.

Key points

- When you make a presentation, keep it simple and make it as clear as you can.
- Use examples to give your audience something to anchor their thoughts.
- Be sure to communicate with your audience.
- Take your time.
- Practise going through your talk and any slides beforehand.
- On the day, get there ahead of time: make yourself comfortable and check any equipment, exercise your voice, and practise relaxing.
- Remember: your audience doesn't care how brilliant you are – they just want to be able to follow what you say.

6.4   Group visits

As a student of the arts you are very fortunate in having a range of primary source materials available to you that are:

- all around you (houses, churches, stately homes, castles, law courts, religious services and festivals)
- specially collected together (in archives or online, in libraries, art galleries and museums)
- presented by others (poetry readings, plays, concerts).

You can also make use of secondary sources: for example, by finding historical background information or analyses of specific paintings on a gallery's website, or by using the structured worksheets or handouts that many galleries and museums offer.

Perhaps visiting these places and events is something you do quite regularly, along with other students or with friends, just because you enjoy it. Whether or not, such visits are an important part of your studies. Think back to Jan,

Nathan and their fellow students in Chapter 1, on a visit to a gallery. I didn't send them there just to show that they had fun on their outing and got to know each other better, though these certainly are among the benefits. Other valuable outcomes of group visits can include:

- *seeing things you might not notice otherwise*: your levels of consciousness and sensitivity are raised by discussion and new insights and ideas are sparked off
- *becoming more aware of your own ideas and tastes* as you experience the reactions of other people
- *becoming more curious and inspired to examine objects carefully*, fuelled by the energy and enthusiasm of the group
- *greater interest in your studies* by being able to discuss your ideas with people who share your enthusiasms.

The students also had the chance to see the paintings they were studying 'for real'. They could see the actual scale of a painting, rather than having to visualise it from the dimensions provided in a text, and they could appreciate its colours – which are often distorted in reproductions – and its texture. The original work *appeared* different and, consequently, the students saw and responded to it differently.

Likewise, consider the effects of seeing, walking around and discussing a large, public building compared to studying its structure and decoration in printed plans and illustrations. If you are studying Victorian architecture for instance, you will not have to go very far in Britain to find examples of 'typical' buildings, from town halls to terraced houses. Perhaps you live in a Victorian house: in the context of your course, you may come to look at something as familiar as your own home with different eyes. You can also take 'virtual tours' of buildings online.

So it is not just the 'going and seeing' that matters, but also the *purposes* behind the visit. When you make a visit as part of your studies, you are looking out for particular features and ideas you have been studying, thinking about and discussing them, rather than wandering around vaguely gazing at everything. This is true of a visit to a theatre or concert hall too. In your course you may have come to interpret the meanings of a play or piece of music in particular ways. Exposure to a performance which presents you with another person's interpretation can be very illuminating, and sometimes even unsettling. Perhaps you had never imagined it could be seen or heard in that way and, as a result, you will never understand it in quite the same way again. If you can't get out and about, recorded programmes do a very good job of providing similar 'experiences', as we shall see in Section 6.5.2 below.

6.5 Listening to talk

Listening plays a prominent part in many university courses. Mostly it takes the form of listening to 'live' talk but, increasingly, courses make use of recorded talk and talk accompanied by visual images. We will look first at learning from live talk.

See Chapter 3
Section 3.4.2,
Listening

6.5.1   Listening to lectures

Lectures have traditionally been the primary mode of teaching in higher education. However, doubt has frequently been cast on whether they are effective. So what can you expect to learn from them?

What lectures offer

Critics say that lectures simply 'present' knowledge instead of encouraging you to *think*: that listening is a passive and tedious mode of learning. They also claim that students can't concentrate for more than about twenty minutes and that after a lecture they can recall only a small proportion of what was said. Yet lectures continue to be a key method of teaching. And students themselves are not generally so critical of them (Beard and Hartley, 1984). They regard 'good' lectures as offering good value. So what can we conclude?

It is true that lectures are *not* a good method of delivering a lot of detailed information. Essential information is better presented in print because you can study it when you are ready to take it in and return to it as needed. But lectures do have an important part to play.

> ### Box 6.5   Lectures and learning
>
> Where lectures come into their own is in helping you to understand how the ideas in the subject work. The lecturer projects meaning into the words for you, adding emphasis by tone of voice, gesture and facial expression, so the ideas you are grappling with in the course are presented to you much more forcefully. But this is *not a passive* experience. *You have to make the effort to follow the argument.* However, you do it with the support of the lecturer, who can talk you through from the beginning to the end. Even if you don't understand it all you can still pick up the gist of how the debate is carried on.

This makes lectures an excellent counterpart to reading. When you are reading you can stop and think over difficult points so that you really get to grips with the details of the argument. But when you are listening you can take in the broad sweep of it and get a feel for what the subject is all about. With an unfamiliar subject, *both* approaches are useful. Listening takes you forward into new territory; reading lets you get your bearings and take time to map out the ground around you.

So, rather than depositing information in your head, the effect of a good lecture is to stir up your *thinking* on a subject and pose new *questions*. Well-delivered lectures help you to get inside the various discourses of your field of study. Their purpose is *not* to ensure that the lecturer's notes end up being your notes. What lectures offer is live discourse – words that engage directly with the thoughts in your mind.

Reading around lectures

See Chapter 3
Section 3.4.1,
Reading

The popular image of lectures is of students sitting in rows being *told* things. But this is highly misleading. The lecture itself is only the public part of a larger learning process. There is an equally important private component –

the reading you do before and after the lecture. Your course reading lists should show what readings go with the lectures. If you are not sure, ask.

As with group discussion, allow two hours of reading for each hour of lecture (see Section 6.2.7, 'Preparing'). Reading beforehand primes you for the lecture so that it doesn't just wash over you, and reading afterwards consolidates what you have learned during the lecture. Without the reading, the flow of ideas in the lecture is too much for you to take in and most of it floats away from you as you leave the lecture theatre. *If you don't do at least some reading around your lectures you miss most of the benefit.*

Learning in lectures

Lectures present you with three challenging tasks simultaneously.

- You have to *listen* to the lecturer's line of argument.
- You have to *think* about it and make connections with what you already know.
- You will want to *make notes* of some kind.

In practice you have to keep switching your focus between these three tasks. In an odd way the struggle to cope with this mental juggling act is helpful. By putting you under pressure, lectures force you to make leaps and take short-cuts. You have to seize the initiative and make what sense you can quickly, because the scraps you jot down are all you will take away with you at the end. You have to learn to think on your feet.

Making notes

Since your notes are made in time 'stolen' from listening and thinking, your note-making strategy matters a lot. You have to weigh up speed against quality and this means you have to think about your broad objectives. Why are you attending the lecture – how does it fit into your study of the topic? Why are you making notes? How will you use them?

See Chapter 5
Section 5.2.2,
Lecture notes

Then you need to develop a note-making strategy that meets your objectives.

Key points

The strength of lectures lies not in feeding you with information, but in:

- engaging your mind with the debates going on in the subject
- showing you how the explanations work, and
- letting you hear how the language of the subject is used.

To get the benefit from lectures you need to:

- make a decent effort to read some of the prescribed texts before and after lectures, and
- develop a note-making strategy that suits the subject matter, the circumstances and you.

6.5.2   Learning through sound and vision
What can you learn?

Most of us learn a great deal from broadcast material, radio and TV, and from digital media. However, when you watch a programme on religious practices or a historical reconstruction, you learn in a very different way from listening to lectures or reading books on these topics. (For convenience, I shall use the term 'audio' for all sound media and 'video' for all moving images plus sound.)

Box 6.6   Learning from video

With a book or a lecture you follow a sequence of words and try to make connections between them and what you already know. However, with video you see pictures and hear sounds that give the sense of actually 'being there'. You don't have to struggle to hold your focus on the subject matter. All your basic processes of experiencing the world are brought into play. Any accompanying sound recording, which explains and discusses what you see, seems to be simply elaborating on 'the truth' presented by the images. You tend to forget that this too is a version of things – that the programme maker is presenting an interpretation, a kind of argument. You need to approach what you see and hear analytically and critically, just as you do when reading an article or book.

If you have seen TV programmes on architecture you will know how well the camera can explore the façade of a building, zooming in on the smallest decorative features and showing you them in detail. The camera can also give you the 'experience' of being inside the building, as it moves around and through the rooms, revealing the ways in which the spaces work and how they relate to one another. These *spaces and relationships* are very hard to imagine just from looking at plans and photographs of a building. It is this sense of being able to explore the world directly – the dynamic, multi-layered quality of video – that can make a special contribution to your learning.

Video is also very valuable for showing *performance* in the arts, especially of music and drama. Recorded concerts and plays may be the only way some students can experience 'live' performance – although obviously this is not the same as direct experience in a concert hall or theatre. Video is also the only way in which many of us can 'see' objects and places that are far *removed in space or time* – works of art in galleries all over the world, buildings and their locations, the design of an ancient city. Furthermore, if you were studying the Parthenon in Athens for instance, you would be able to see it not only as it is now, from a number of different angles, but also with superimposed computer-generated images of the original structure and decoration, while a spoken commentary explains what you are looking at.

Dramatisations can provide *case-study* material, in a subject such as law for example. Here, some 'experience' of court procedure may be helpful, or a demonstration of an interview between client and solicitor can be used as the basis for classroom analysis and discussion. And *reconstructions* of historical events – especially battles it seems – abound. With such exciting possibilities available to us it is a wonder that video is still often seen as an adjunct to study at higher levels. However, in spite of all this promise, and much investment in multimedia teaching, print remains the most popular teaching and learning medium. Why?

It is almost as if the very power of video creates a problem. With your eyes and ears busy taking in richly textured images, information and arguments, you are fully absorbed, particularly if the subject matter is unfamiliar. Independent thinking and note making are difficult. It is easy to feel that the argument is running ahead of you, out of your control, so that you can't quite be sure what you are learning or what you make of it. The knowledge has a 'fluid' quality which is an advantage when the subject is a complicated process, but it means that the details soon begin to fade from your memory. You really need something written down as well – printed programme notes, or your own notes captured mainly immediately after viewing – to help 'fix' the knowledge in a more simplified, encapsulated form. Then you can look back over the experience and reflect on it.

Audio

Of all academic disciplines, the arts and humanities have taken most naturally to audio – indeed, some people complain that they have colonised the radio. Whole channels are devoted to music, plays are broadcast regularly, there are reviews of current art exhibitions, theatre and books, and talks of all kinds – from philosophical discussion and aural history programmes to chat about the latest novels. Daily, there is a feast of experience to be had.

In education, radio has made *discussion* and *analysis* its own. Audio talks share many of the characteristics of lectures, and fulfil similar functions: for example, enabling you to hear the academic discourse as spoken by experts – who, in this context, may indeed be world-renowned figures in their field. The difficulties involved in simultaneous listening, thinking and note-making are similar too. If anything, though, radio speakers are under even greater pressure than lecturers to pack a lot into a short time, and also to make their talks or discussion high-powered and impressive. Without the social context of the lecture and the presence of the speaker you may find it more difficult to follow the arguments they present. Again, you should make a point of reading any programme notes beforehand and, afterwards, try to write a summary of the main points that emerged.

Box 6.7   Learning from audio

When you are listening to debates between experts it is a positive advantage that audio is a less intense medium than video – that less is happening simultaneously. It is much easier to concentrate on an argument when you do not have to attend to visual images at the same time, and it is easier to sit with a pad in hand and make notes. A philosophical debate, for instance, can be very arresting when you have nothing but the spoken words to focus on. There are other ways of making a virtue of the absence of 'interfering' visual images too. Poetry readings can play directly on your imagination, as can serialised or recorded novels and plays. And music performances can be distilled down to the pure sounds. In fact, audio encourages you to give your whole attention to just what the speaker or performer intends.

Other benefits flow from the fact that audio recordings are relatively cheap and technically uncomplicated to make. In the context of distance education, audio is often used to broadcast magazine-style programmes which keep you up to date with new developments in your subject and course, or in touch with the thoughts and feelings of teachers and other students. You can get people into a studio one day and have the recording ready the next. This gives audio an immediacy and raw authenticity which glossier video productions lack. If you are a home-based student you tend to miss out on a lot of very useful background know-how about your course, which full-time students pick up on the grapevine in between lectures or in the bar. Audio recordings of this less formal kind can help fill that gap. For students who cannot attend group meetings they can also help to create a sense of 'belonging' to a lively academic community.

Case studies

See Chapter 1 Section 1.8.2, eLearning

Sound and vision make an undoubted impact when used to present case-study material, particularly in combination with activities that allow you to interact with them. This works particularly well when the material is developed for use on a computer, where interactivity can be structured in.

Learning from sound and vision

See Chapter 5 Section 5.4.1, Pulling your knowledge together

The skills you need for learning from video and audio can be quite varied. Generally it is worth asking yourself:

- Are you stopping often enough to make notes? Is it best to go right through the programme once then go through it again making notes?
- How many times is it worth rerunning a resource? The material will often be very rich and will repay being visited several times. But of course you need to balance this against other things you could spend time on. The pay-off for allocating time to revisit audiovisual material is that you will remember it well because of the power of the images.
- How does your next essay link to the audio or visual material? How can you make notes that will help you to extract what you need as you review it? Would it help to draw a grid or table to help analyse what you are looking at and listening to?

Key points

- Sound and vision are excellent for presenting the world in all its richness and dynamism, so they work well for case studies and for small, intensive bursts of study.
- But they are not always easy media to follow for sustained study. They tend to leave inadequate space for thinking and writing unless activities are built in.

- You need to work out your study strategies as you discover what is involved.

Studying through the spoken rather than the printed word can be a very lively and natural-seeming way to learn; however, it is also unpredictable and challenging. The dynamism of talk can make new ideas come alive, but you need to be flexible and strategic in working out how to get the most from it.

References

Alexander, G. (2000) *Extract from a Communications Guide, prepared by Gary Alexander for use on various Open University courses,* http://sustainability.open.ac.uk/gary/papers/netique.htm (accessed 31 August 2007).

Anderson, C. (1997) 'Enabling and shaping understanding through tutorials', in Marton, F., Hounsell, D. and Entwistle, N. (eds) *The Experience of Learning: Implications for Teaching and Studying in Higher Education* (second edition), Edinburgh, Scottish Academic Press.

Beard, R. and Hartley, J. (1984) *Teaching and Learning in Higher Education* (fourth edition), London, Harper and Row.

Forster, F. (1995) 'Tutorials in Arts and Social Sciences', in Forster, F., Hounsell, D. and Thompson, S. (eds) *Tutoring and Demonstrating: A Handbook*, Edinburgh, University of Edinburgh Centre for Teaching, Learning and Assessment.

CHAPTER 7
Writing essays

7.1 Getting to grips with writing

Of all aspects of studying, writing is the most challenging. But it is also the most rewarding. This is not a coincidence.

7.1.1 The importance of writing

Writing is not simply a chore you endure for the purposes of assessment. It is an *essential* part of the learning process. When you explain your ideas to others in writing you can't make the mental leaps you do when you are in conversation or mulling something over in your mind. You have to work out carefully exactly what you think about a subject. And you come to understand it for *yourself* in the process of explaining it to others. When you look back over a course you will find that the topics you have written about are the ones you understand and remember best.

Deepening your learning

See Chapter 3
Section 3.4.3,
Speaking

So, one reason why assignment writing is especially demanding is that it forces you into a deep and powerful kind of learning. In earlier chapters I have talked about how you absorb ideas from books and lectures. However, until you are able to *use* the ideas to say things for yourself, you have not really *learned* them. Ideas only become a properly functioning part of your thought processes when you can call on them in expressing yourself to other people. One way of doing this is through discussing new ideas with others. But the most effective way is to argue a case in writing.

Developing your writing skills

Writing assignments significantly develops your powers of self-expression, and being able to write clearly and persuasively is an extremely valuable social skill. You may eventually discover that the most significant thing you have gained from your studies is the ability to write much more effectively. This is as likely whether you start with a relatively weak writing style or with a well-developed one. Wherever you start from, there is valuable progress to be made.

Doing yourself justice

In many higher-level courses, most assessment is of your written work. Consequently, your results are affected throughout your studies by your ability to write the kinds of assignment required. So, investing time in developing your writing skills is critically important. You may find that it pays to spend a little less time on mainstream coursework in order to allow more time for developing writing skills; otherwise you risk getting less credit for your learning than you deserve.

> **Key points**
>
> Writing is a major part of studying for three reasons.
>
> - It deepens your *learning* of the subject you are studying.
> - It strengthens your powers of *self-expression*.
> - It is the major medium through which your progress is *assessed*.

7.1.2 Different kinds of writing

In the arts and humanities there are various kinds of writing you might do – mostly academic, but some creative and some more professionally orientated. The more *academic* type of writing focuses on ideas, theoretical perspectives, research, and textual analysis (using 'text' in the broadest sense, to include visual text and performance). This involves the skills of developing a clear and forceful line of argument. Different disciplines and fields have their own styles and emphases, but they share what we can call a *critical-analytical* mode of writing. In such courses the essay is the most common form of writing, in coursework and exams. Although there is growing emphasis on other forms of assessment, the essay retains its central role. Styles of essay vary to some extent between subject areas, but basic techniques can be applied, with a bit of adjustment, in most subjects. So, although developing an effective essay-writing style is a fairly long learning process, you can continue working on it from course to course throughout your studies.

See Chapter 3 Section 3.3, Why do they write like that?

Creative writing (or activity) draws on your own ideas and resources to a greater extent, although knowledge and understanding of the 'traditions' of writing, art or performance is almost always required. The more *professionally* oriented types of writing emphasise your ability to understand real-life situations, pick out salient features, and write about the issues they raise along with possible courses of action. They include, for example, reports, book reviews, problem analysis, case studies, and reflective accounts of work experience. These more practical modes of writing tend to address the needs of particular areas of professional training, such as journalism or law, and may involve links to specific work situations.

This chapter focuses on *essays*, the pre-eminent academic type of writing. Because developing writing skills tends to be a long haul, before going any further you may want to find out what kinds of writing your course involves. However, the various modes of writing are not utterly different and many higher-level courses do require essays at some stage. So, in any case, working on your essay-writing skills may be a good investment. If in doubt, ask your university department for advice.

7.1.3 Essay writing
What is an essay?
Originally, the meaning of the word 'essay' was a try or an attempt, but it now has the general meaning of *a short piece of writing on a set topic*.

- An essay begins with a *title* which sets out the issues to be addressed.
- It takes the form of an *argument* which leads the reader from the title at the beginning to a conclusion at the end.

The challenge of essay writing

The nature of this challenge depends, to an extent, on your cultural background and personal language history. Essays can be a big leap from the language environment of everyday life. If you have had little contact with the kind of formal, controlled language used in essays, you may need to spend more time on your writing skills. Don't hold back, thinking that you have more important priorities to attend to in your studies; your writing may be the most important. Everyone can develop serviceable essay-writing techniques eventually, but how long it takes will depend on where you are starting from. If you have further to travel, you need to invest more time.

Writing is not an extra you can tack on to the end of your other study activities. It requires serious effort and plenty of time. Because writing is challenging it's always tempting to put it off until the very last minute, but this is a big mistake. You risk missing out on learning the course content in depth and developing your writing potential to the full.

Getting help

In developing your writing it is extremely helpful to have support from *teachers*. Your tutors will be able to give you feedback on your assignment work, and your *university support services* may offer general help with essay writing skills.

It is also an excellent idea to swap essay plans and marked essays with other students, and share writing strategies and tips. This is *not* cheating – as long as you write your own essays of course. By comparing your approach and performance with others you can gain valuable insight into your own writing. Letting people see your work is daunting at first, but once you have broken down the barriers other students can give you new ideas and very helpful feedback.

Developing your essay-writing skills

To develop your essay-writing skills you need to address two basic questions.

1   What is a good essay?

2   How can I go about producing one?

We will consider the first question in this chapter and the second in Chapter 8. Much of the discussion in this chapter is based on short sample essays presented in Section 7.2. You will need to work on this section first to get the full force of the rest of the chapter.

Key points

- This chapter focuses on *essay* writing.
- Developing your essay writing can be a significant challenge if you are unfamiliar with more formal ways of writing. Make sure you give it the time it requires.
- Don't keep worries to yourself. Seek help from your tutors and from other students.

7.2   What are you meant to write?

A perplexing thing about essay writing is that it can be difficult to get a clear idea of what is wanted. Writing seems to be treated as a private activity. You know what *your* essays look like and what your teachers say about them, but you have very little idea what *other students'* essays are like and what comments they receive back. You might be told that your essays ought to be more structured, or less subjective, but you don't really know what a more structured or more objective essay would look like. This can be worrying.

As we saw, one of the best ways to find out about what is expected in essays is to see what other students write. This is not so that you can *copy* someone else's style; it is to broaden your vision of the possible ways you might approach an essay. In this chapter we explore two short essays about the Ellis article first discussed in Chapters 4 and 5. The writers were mature students taking an access course (you met them in Chapter 4). This is the task they were set.

> Write a short essay (of no more than 500 words) on the following:

> Did higher-ranking women in the eighteenth century migrate to towns mainly because of the attractions of the towns, or mainly to escape from life in the countryside? Discuss in the light of Joyce Ellis's article.

The word limit of 500 words is unusually low, simply to keep this chapter manageable. A target of somewhere between 1,000 to 2,000 words would be more usual – allowing more space for you to develop your ideas, illustrate them and provide evidence in support of them. Nevertheless, these short pieces help to reveal the central principles of essay writing.

Box 7.1   Recommended preparation

It is best to read the rest of this chapter after you have worked on Chapter 4 Section 4.2, which guides you through reading Joyce Ellis's article. You will also find it useful to have at least glanced at the notes made on the article in Chapter 5 Section 5.2.1. Knowing what the article is about will enable you to understand the writing challenge the students faced and judge how well they succeeded. It will also help a lot when following my discussion of their essays throughout this chapter.

Making copies of the essays

Although the essays by Philip and Hansa are printed here in the chapter it will be easier to work with photocopies since you will be 'marking' and improving them. Make several copies so that you can write on them freely.

Activity 7.1

Read the essays by Philip and Hansa on the pages that follow (or your copies of them).

1 As you read:
- mark any places where you find it hard to get the point
- jot any questions in the margins, along with other points that come to you
- write in alterations you think could usefully be made.

2 When you have finished reading both essays, take a sheet of paper and write the headings 'Strengths' and 'Weaknesses'. Note down the best and the weakest things about Philip's essay, and then do the same for Hansa's.

3 Try to weigh up the quality of the two essays.
- Do you think one of the essays is better than the other?
- Are they good in different ways?
- Overall, do you think that they are good essays?
- Are you judging mainly in terms of the ideas in the essays, or on how the essays are written?

4 Imagine you are Philip's teacher. Write a few sentences to him to help with his future writing.

5 Finally, look back over:
- our lists of strengths and weaknesses
- your conclusions about the overall quality of the essays
- your advice to Philip.

Can you draw any general conclusions about the qualities a good essay should have? Jot down your thoughts.

Before you begin, read Box 7.2 below.

Box 7.2 Developing your judgement of writing

Activity 7.1 is demanding and it will take you some time. You may not want to do all of it right now, but at least do Task 1. However, the whole exercise is *worth doing*. It is time well invested because you need to develop your ability to judge what works well in writing and what doesn't. You won't become a good writer by learning formal rules. Instead, you have to become a *reasonably good judge* of pieces of writing, including your own. 'Marking' other people's work is an excellent way of deepening your understanding of what you are aiming for in your own writing.

Here are the two essays I received. Philip's came with a note. Part of it reads: 'Writing this is a learning experience because I am starting late in life to going back to be re-educated. But I feel more than willing to attempt the challenge ...'

PHILIP'S ESSAY

On the Town. 'Woman in Augustan England' 1680–1820

Joyce Ellis presents to us a portrayal of woman living around the eighteenth century. The women who lived a fairly comfortable style of life belonged to a class of society where the father or husband would be a land-owner, these males were orientated to country life and all it entailed so they expected their wifes or daughters to fit in to a standard of life they felt gave a certain status to the country way of life. These were under-privileged women as the boredom of country life could become frustrating to them, does it not make you see a resemblance to the modern day young woman, she can combine marriage, raising children, and holding on to a career as well.

With society becoming more wealthy it was possible for the fathers and husbands to provide an even better standard of life for their wifes and daughters, more servants could be provided to do the work and this left the woman more time than ever to develop the social skills of the era, but this in turn led to extreme frustration among woman of that class. The country was no place now to exercise these new skills they had been taught, for one thing females outnumbered males at that time, also few chances arose to meet and mingle with crowds of people, but most importantly the demands of propriety meant that their conduct should be impeccable at all times any error would be seen in such a limited environment so therefore woman began to long for the urban or city way of living, if even for a short period so that they could deploy the art of socialising and mingling with a greater amount of society.

Towns offered woman a great variation of respectable ways in which to carry out the social skills, indeed many women have gone down in history as being great experts as organizers of social events thus enhancing their husbands standing. In a town or city, women could meet with many more of the female sex than they did in the country, they could exchange views and learn new ideas from each other, also they could meet with more of the male population as the citys had theatres concert halls, and many places where both sexes could mingle together respectably. In many ways going into urban life from the countryside was beneficial to woman of the upperclass.

This transition was not without a certain amount of jibes from the male population against the women of that time, who looked on them as being inferior in many ways, and considered those who chose to get away from boredom of the country as being improper in outlook.

Nevertheless woman, whether wealthy or poor need the stimulus of company and the need to escape from routine and boredom and so will continue to seek for the things that will be in their favour.

(483 words)

HANSA'S ESSAY

Did higher ranking eighteenth century women migrate to towns mainly because of the attractions of the towns, or mainly to escape from life in the countryside?

Eighteenth century society expected women to have accomplishments such as the ability to embroider, play the piano and sing. They were supposed to be fragile, delicate and innocent; they were taught at smart boarding schools or by private tutors, social skills to fit them for the role expected of them at the time, as 'embodiments of their husbands' and fathers' status'.

Life in the country during this period of history offered little scope for the indulgence of these skills owing to the sparcity of the population and the difficulty of transport, as women from the higher ranks were constrained to mix only with their own kind.

Thus the lives of these well born ladies were immensely boring. It was not considered fitting that a woman should take any part in the management of a country estate, or in the country pursuits of riding, hunting or fishing as enjoyed by the men and she was therefore reduced to spend her time reading or writing letters. However, in an urban environment, it was acceptable that women could socialise on a much wider scale and even organise and plan social events, an added dimension to their very constrained lives. Because of this, and because an urban environment offered women so much more scope, not only to display their accomplishments but also to induge their own desire for sociability, amusement and companions', the female population of England's towns expanded dramatically.

In view of the somewhat prescribed role forced upon women in the eighteenth century by the male dominated society which formulated social mores, it was inevitable that women would be attracted to the towns where the skills that society required of them could be more widely indulged and more fully displayed. In the towns there were more people of the same rank, so that women could socialise on a wider scale, and as there was public transport they had greater mobility. They therefore fled from the country in order to escape the restrictions and consequent boredom placed upon them by the very limited pastimes that a high ranking women in the eighteeenth century was permitted to indulge.

In effect, I think that the high ranking women of the eighteeenth century were neither mainly attracted to the towns, or escaping from the countryside, what they were seeking to do was to fulfil the very limited role with which society had burdened them as fully as was possible.

(426 words)

In what follows I discuss the points that struck me as I read the two essays. I expect that you will have picked out many of the same points. There is no great mystery about what is good writing and what is not. Good writing is easy to read and makes sense. Poor writing is unclear and confusing; it keeps making you stop to try to work out what is being said and where the argument is going.

7.3   The significance of titles

Which essay did you find easier to read? For me it was Hansa's. As I read Philip's essay I was uncertain about where his argument was leading me. He makes some interesting points, but there is no real sense of direction. On the other hand, Hansa's essay flows as an argument.

The first thing I noticed about Philip's essay is that although it begins with a title it is *not* the one he was given. This immediately creates two problems.

1   If I were Philip's tutor I would find it difficult to weigh up his essay against the challenge he was actually set.
2   The title he has made up is not a good one, so it weakens his essay from the outset.

Philip's title doesn't pose a *question* for him to answer. So I began reading without any sense of what he was aiming to discuss. He has given himself a broad theme, but no *purpose*. An essay never asks you to just 'write what you know about the topic' – it always requires you to present an *argument* of some kind. Often (as in this case) the purpose is to answer a question. Other essay titles may ask you to discuss a particular point of view, or compare and contrast two points of view. But however the title is worded, it is always meant to pose a 'problem' which your essay should then set out to argue about and (to some extent) 'solve'.

Philip neither starts with a problem to solve nor finishes with a solution, so there is a rather aimless feel to the essay. It isn't going anywhere in particular. This makes reading it a lot harder. Since, as reader, you have to *project* meaning into the written words, if you are not sure where the words are leading it is much more difficult to follow. A good essay is never just a string of sentences. It is a journey from the question in the title to the answer in your conclusion.

Box 7.3   Openings

There is a lot to be said for brisk, direct opening sentences in an essay. You need to set the reader's thoughts off in the right direction, so there is no virtue in a lot of formal throat-clearing. For example, it is *not* a good idea to fill the opening paragraph with dictionary definitions of some key words in the title. The first sentences should grab your reader's attention. They should be related to the essay question and should be doing important work for your argument. But they don't have to be fancy.

It is often said that in an Introduction you should say what you are going to do in the essay – then do it in the 'middle' part of the essay, and in the conclusion say what you have done. But this kind of writing to a 'formula' is tedious to do and pretty dull to read.

I think Philip's lack of clear purpose is the biggest weakness of his essay. We see it at the end of the first paragraph, where he throws in a comment about modern young women. The comment doesn't make a lot of sense to me, but in any case it has little to do with the topic. *Everything* you write in an essay should contribute in some way to answering the question in the title. This is the great value of having a problem to solve – it gives you a way of deciding what to include and what to leave out. It also helps you to organise what you put in, so that it builds up towards your conclusion. Because Philip does not have a clear purpose, he drops in stray points that don't lead anywhere. And in his last paragraph he is left making vague remarks about women in general – needing company and seeking things 'in their favour'. (Couldn't this be said about men too?) So the essay fizzles out, without doing justice either to the themes of Ellis's article or to Philip's own ideas. All of this is quite understandable in a first essay. But it points up the crucial importance of recognising that an essay is meant to be an *argument*.

You will have noticed that Hansa's essay starts with the title she was given. Also, at the end she tries to answer the question. So straight away Hansa's essay has some important strengths compared to Philip's. As well as finding her essay easier to read, I also found it more *satisfying* because she focuses on the question and comes to a conclusion about it. From the start she gets stuck into the argument, making a purposeful attack on the question in her opening sentences. And, while she covers a lot of the same ground as Philip, she develops a stronger line of argument overall – although not always as clearly as she might I think.

Key points

- An essay should take the form of an *argument*.
- This argument should start from the problem posed by the *question* or *title* of the essay, and it should lead your reader through to a *conclusion* set out in the final paragraph.

This is not easy to achieve, but it is what you should aim for.

7.4   Essay structure

In spite of getting off on the wrong foot by not sticking to the title, Philip's essay contains a lot that is relevant – as we can see if we pull it apart. Here is the basic content and structure of his essay set out in note form. (The question marks indicate points I would want to query.) Quickly check my notes against his essay to see if you agree that I have captured the gist of what he says.

Paragraph 1: Introduction – social context

1 Ellis – a portrait of C18 women whose fathers/husbands were of land-owning class.

2 Men were country-oriented → expected wife/daughters to fit into high-status rural life-style.

3 Women were under-privileged [?], owing to the boredom of country life.

4 *Contrast* with modern woman – who can combine marriage, children & career.

Paragraph 2: Tedium of country life

1 Increasing wealth → rising standard of life → more servants → women more time for skills → extreme frustration.

2 In country, women couldn't exercise skills
   – females outnumbered males [?]; few opportunities to meet.

3 Strict rules of social propriety, very visible → conduct impeccable at all times.

4 Longed for urban life – even for short spells – to be able to socialise.

Paragraph 3: Attractions of town

1 Towns → variety of respectable social options, including active role in organising.

2 More women to meet – exchange views – learn new ideas.

3 More meetings w. men – theatre, concerts – both sexes could mix respectably.

4 In many ways beneficial to women.

Paragraph 4: Contemporary explanations of women's migration to towns

1 Male jibes at women's migration to towns.

2 Viewed women as inferior in many ways.

3 Saw escape from boredom of country as 'improper'.

Paragraph 5: Conclusion – Women's need for company and amusement

1 Women need company and escape from boredom.

2 → will continue to seek things in their favour.

Setting out the content of the essay like this shows us a number of things. We can see straight away that Philip's essay has a structure. Each paragraph deals with a new aspect of the topic and the sequence of paragraphs shows a clear line of development. In the first paragraph Philip sets up the general background; he then explores the repellent side of country life, followed by the attractive side of town life; then he notes contemporary attitudes to the women's migration to towns; and in his final paragraph he draws a general conclusion. This is an excellent outline plan for a short essay. He hasn't entirely carried it off, but there is nothing wrong with the basic structure.

Similarly, Hansa's essay has a structure. To help us uncover it we can again set out what she says in note form. Again, check the notes below against her essay to see whether you think they are a fair summary.

Paragraph 1: Introduction – Role of women in C18 upper-class society

1   C18 soc. – expected women to have accomplishments (piano, etc.).
2   Image of women as fragile, etc.
3   Trained for role as 'embodiments' of male status.

Paragraph 2: Restrictions of rural life

1   Country life → little scope to display skills:

    – sparse population at higher social levels; travel difficult; tight social boundaries.

Paragraph 3: Tedium of rural life – attractions of town

1   Refined ladies' boring life – denied role as estate managers – excluded from country pastimes → reduced to letter writing, reading.
2   But in town, wider social opportunities:

    – role in social planning; opportunity to display accomplishments; enjoy socialising.
3   Offered women much more scope for display of accomplishments – desire for sociability/ amusement → rapid expansion of female urban population.

Paragraph 4: Women's need to be in towns to play out the role prescribed for them

1   Male-dominated society → women highly prescribed and restricted role → social skills required of them could only be satisfactorily enacted and displayed in town – where more people of same rank, good transport.
2   Women fled country to escape v. tight restrictions (→ boredom).

Paragraph 5: Conclusion

   Women not so much attracted to town – or escaping from countryside – as mainly trying to fulfil their very restricted social role as fully as possible.

The structure of Hansa's essay is fairly similar to Philip's. However, you may have noticed that the subject of her second paragraph spills over into paragraph 3. This immediately suggests an improvement – the first part of paragraph 3 could be put back to the end of paragraph 2 (from 'Thus the lives … writing letters.'). Then she will have a paragraph on the country followed by one on the town, which will help her reader to follow this shift of focus as her argument moves forward.

> **Key points**
>
> - An essay needs to be *structured*.
> - Part of this involves organising the points you want to make into *groups*, and giving a *paragraph* to each group.
> - Part of it is arranging the paragraphs into a meaningful *sequence*, leading towards your conclusion.

7.5   Presenting an argument

Philip clearly has a sense that he is meant to be arguing a case. Perhaps the best bit of argument comes at the start of paragraph 2. If you look at my notes you will see that I have used arrows to show how the argument works. He says that increasing wealth led to a rising standard of living, which meant that more servants were employed, which led to women having more time to polish up their social skills – but that this 'in turn' led to frustration, because country life no longer gave women enough opportunities to exercise their skills. This is very purposeful writing. He drives us forward through the logic of his argument.

As paragraph 2 continues, Philip tells us why women didn't have the opportunity to exercise their social skills in the country, saying first that women outnumbered men (though I'm not sure where he got that from) and then that few chances arose for mingling. At this point the logic is still clear – we have just been given two reasons *why* opportunities to exercise social skills were limited. But he then moves on to the oppressiveness of the rules of 'propriety'. It isn't obvious whether that still has to do with the exercise of social skills. Perhaps it is added simply as another source of the 'frustration' Philip mentioned earlier, but if so the connection is not made. It reads as an item in a list of points, not as part of a clear sequence. This lessens the impact of the earlier build up of the argument. That's a pity, because the last point is about these women longing for city life where they could exercise their skills, which would have followed on very nicely from the points about not being able to do so in the country. We end the paragraph with the sense that there were 'a bunch of reasons' why women were fed up with country life, instead of a sharp focus on the irony of having increasingly sophisticated skills but dwindling opportunities to use them.

Now that we have made an alteration to the structure of Hansa's essay we can see the stages of her argument more clearly:

- The role of well-to-do women
- Country life
- Town life
- The futility of trying to play the 'society woman' role in the country
- Conclusion.

7.5.1 Linking points together

Let's see how Hansa puts her argument together. Notice that she introduces the country life stage of the argument by referring *back* to 'these skills'; that is, the skills she has referred to in her opening paragraph. The new paragraph 3, on town life, begins with 'However, … '. That suggests a *contrast* between this and what she has just been discussing (country life). And when she begins the fourth paragraph with 'In view of the somewhat prescribed role … ' she is again referring *back* to the earlier stage when she discussed that role. 'In effect …' signals her conclusion. So we have a connected 'line' of argument here – a thread of meaning running through the essay that the reader can follow.

Looking at the flow of Philip's argument as a whole, we can see that it gets off to a weak start – without a title that gives a clear framework and purpose, and with a rather bland opening sentence. After this opening, the first two proper points in paragraph 1 (see my notes) actually do a good job of getting things going. Unfortunately, point 3 does not follow on particularly well and point 4 is simply a distraction. Yet broadly, once he gets going, you can see that in the first two paragraphs Philip is telling a 'story' about how and why women's roles in the countryside changed over time, and what this meant to them.

At the end of the second paragraph Philip concludes 'so therefore woman began to long for the urban or city way of living … '. This *leads* us into the next paragraph, and to the topic of women's roles in the town. He begins the fourth paragraph with 'This transition … ' which connects *back* directly to what he has said in the last sentence of paragraph 3. And by using the linking word 'Nevertheless' at the start of the last paragraph, Philip shows he knows he should be making a connection there too, even if he hasn't quite worked out how to pull the whole thing together at the end. So he has a good general sense of the need to connect each stage of his argument into a flowing sequence.

But although Philip links up the *stages* of the argument well, he doesn't always organise the points he wants to make *within* each stage into a meaningful sequence. As we saw, in the second paragraph he doesn't manage to weave the idea of the demands of propriety into the flow of his otherwise purposeful writing. Here is how the main points about women's role and their life in the countryside might be re-organised into a connected, logical sequence.

1 [Points about rising standard of living etc., which Philip handles well] → *these* women lost their household function.

2 *As a result*, they had more time to develop accomplishments and fulfil a 'decorative' role.

3 *But* the demands of propriety meant they could mix only with their own kind (unlike their menfolk).

4 *This* particular *population* was sparse. Lack of transport and bad weather prevented *these* women from mixing socially and *so* fulfilling their role in rural society.

5 *Instead* they were restricted to pastimes such as needlework, letter writing, reading and walking, in and around their homes.

Here a clear *line of argument* is being developed, connected up, within the stage of the argument that deals with life in the countryside.

Key points

- You have to *develop* an argument *in stages* towards your conclusion.
- That means you have to *link* each stage to the next, so that the reader can follow the *direction* your argument is taking.
- And, *within* each stage of the argument, you need to organise your *main points* into a satisfactory *sequence*.

7.5.2 Arguing to a conclusion

If we ignore the bits of his essay where Philip strays off the subject, how well does his argument work? Does he make a good case? Well, I think even Philip was feeling a bit doubtful about this since by the end he seems to be running out of steam. He obviously hasn't realised that his closing sentences need to pull together what he has said earlier, and present an *answer to the question* in the title (as given). Rather, he seems to be casting about for something grand-sounding to finish off with, so he makes the general point about women's needs.

Box 7.4 Conclusions

Your essay should end with a concluding section which sweeps briefly back over the arguments you have presented and pulls them together. This overview should show how the discussion in your essay has answered the question set. A conclusion doesn't have to be particularly grand. It just needs to give a clear sense of your having made a worthwhile response to the challenge in the title.

Your *primary purpose* in an essay is to arrive, in the final paragraphs, at an answer to the question. (Not all titles take the form of a question, but always there is some issue to be resolved.) The answer doesn't have to be a 'yes' or a 'no'. It can be a 'maybe', 'it depends', or 'partly yes and partly no'. The key thing is to show that your essay has addressed the specific challenge you were set.

Yet, as we saw, there is some quite vigorous argument earlier in the essay. So what does it all add up to? The gist of Philip's argument seems to be this:

- Men of the land-owning class enjoyed country life and expected their women folk to 'fit in'.
- But women found country life stultifying and frustrating.
- Town life offered them many more opportunities [so they migrated there, though Philip doesn't actually say so].

- The men mocked them for migrating, or criticised their impropriety.
- But women will do what they need to.

In the end, he presents the women's migration as a straightforward clash of interests between them and their menfolk. The upshot is that women refused to bow to pressure or criticism from men and looked to their own needs, as women in general will. This is a weak conclusion because it relies on a notion of 'what women in general will tend to do'. None of the rest of the essay presents any arguments about what women in general do, so we have no reason to agree. (After all, thinking about different times and different societies, there are many examples of women having felt themselves morally or practically prevented from seeking what was 'in their favour'.) Ellis is trying to explain why these women, bound into a particular society at a particular time, not only longed for town life but actually migrated to towns in large numbers. This calls for a more robust explanation than 'what women in general tend to do'.

Overall, then, Philip's argument is pitched in the right general area, but it doesn't really get to the heart of things. Nevertheless, I think it is a good attempt by someone who is new both to reading this kind of article and writing essays.

Turning to Hansa's essay, in the fourth paragraph we see her 'bringing together' what she has said in the first three – about the role of women, about country and about town life. This is a very good move. She is setting herself up ready to draw her conclusion. She wants to argue that women's attitudes to country life and town life arose directly out of their very restricted role as status symbols for their menfolk. We can summarise what she says as follows:

1   women were *attracted by* the towns (because they could fulfil their role better there);

2   women were *escaping from* the countryside (because they could not fulfil their role there).

So, at this stage, Hansa's answer to the essay question is 'a bit of both'. But then in her conclusion she seems to contradict that, by saying they were 'in effect' doing *neither*. What they were doing, she says, was *mainly* trying to fulfil the role that society had 'burdened' them with. (Notice that this 'mainly' *is* what the essay question asks her to reach a conclusion about.)

Hansa is saying that the important issue here is what was expected of women at that time – the *role* that was available to them. This is what really explains why the women migrated to towns. It was not essentially a matter of 'escaping' from the countryside because it was dull and soggy, nor of being 'attracted' to the town because it was more fun. The deeper and more important reason for women's migration was so that they could live more meaningfully *as the women they were expected to be*. This brings us much closer to the heart of the arguments in Ellis's article than Philip's account does. However, Hansa hasn't made her case very obvious. We have had to dig a bit to find it. When I first read her conclusion it took me by surprise; it seemed contradictory. Indeed, I think there is something missing from her essay.

7.5.3   A frame of reference

Hansa, like Philip, starts her essay by talking about the role of well-to-do women at the time. And also like him, she doesn't give us any idea *why* she does that. When you read the essay title it does not have any obvious connection to women's roles. So we are left a bit bemused. We can follow what Hansa is saying, but we don't really know what the *point* of it is.

If we compare this with Ellis herself, she begins (as we saw in Chapter 4) by talking about a 'dramatic' migration of women to the larger towns during the period. Clearly, a social change on that sort of scale needs explaining. In other words, she begins by showing why the whole issue *matters*. Having established that, she presents an argument about why the women migrated. She says she wants to disagree with the satirists of the time who presented these women as seeking 'freedom from male control'; in her third paragraph she tells us she is going to argue *against* the satirists' views. She also outlines what it is she is going to say. So, by then, we can see both *what* she proposes to do and *why*. In short, she has set up a 'frame of reference' within which we can understand the purpose of her argument. (Bear in mind how important frames of reference are for readers: Chapter 3, Box 3.2.)

This framework is missing in Hansa's and Philip's essays. If Hansa gave us some idea of the scale of the migration, and a few pointers to the debate she is engaging with, we would be able to follow her argument through to its conclusion more easily. For example, she might add something like this to the end of her first paragraph:

> They were also expected to live for long spells in their family homes in the countryside. When these women began to migrate to towns in large numbers, satirists of the period presented this as a wilful desire for 'freedom from male control' and a chance to enjoy frivolous pastimes.

There are many different ways of doing this kind of frame-setting. The point is that nowhere in her first paragraph does Hansa make a link to the title of the essay (and hence to the conclusion she is leading towards). She has her argument in her head, but she doesn't remember to set up a frame of reference within which her argument will make sense to her readers.

Key points

You have to remember that your readers need some kind of frame of reference for your argument. You need to find a way of presenting a context for your argument at the start, so that you set your readers' thoughts going in the right direction. They need some sense of:

- the background against which you are arguing, and
- *why* it is worth paying attention to what you are saying.

7.5.4   Introducing your own ideas

At the end of paragraph 2, Philip makes his point about the busy lives of modern young women. (Presumably he means to draw a contrast, rather than suggest a 'resemblance'.) Why did I suggest that this is not a good idea? Doesn't it show initiative to bring in a few ideas of your own? Is essay writing meant to be just repeating back what you have read in books and articles?

This is a tricky issue. Certainly you are meant to think as you write – to say things as you have worked them out for yourself. It would be very dreary indeed simply to repeat back what you have read, and you wouldn't learn much. On the other hand, your thinking is meant to be based on the ideas and information you have been reading about in your studies. The essay is an exercise in 'engaging with' these arguments and ideas, and trying to put them to use. This helps you to learn in depth. It is also an exercise in being disciplined in your writing – saying exactly what you intend to say, and only what you can justify saying. It is not an open invitation to write down your thoughts to see what your tutor makes of them.

> ### Box 7.5   Display your knowledge of the course
>
> The main substance of an essay should come directly from your studies. Construct your arguments using what you have read and heard within the course (unless you are instructed to do otherwise). Don't be tempted to bring in lots of extraneous knowledge. It is very hard for tutors to judge material they are unfamiliar with. And they are usually working with a marking guide based on what is taught within the course.

I can see three problems with Philip's attempt to introduce the comparison with modern women.

- If he is going to bring in something from beyond the Ellis article he needs to *justify* it. He can't just drop in a remark in passing and expect his reader to accept it without question.

- Because Philip's observation is not drawn from what he has read in Ellis's article, it opens up a whole new area – it *raises questions* about what kinds of generalisations can be made about women now, what kinds of comparisons can reasonably be drawn between then and now, and what kinds of evidence might be relevant to making this case. He simply does not have the space to tackle all this.

- In any case, it is beside the point; it is *irrelevant* to an argument about the reasons why higher-ranking eighteenth-century women migrated to towns.

> ❝ I find you have to relate everything back to the course work – it's what you get out of the books that counts. ❞

You are not forbidden from introducing ideas of your own into an essay, but you have to do it cautiously, and always take the time to back up your case so that your reader doesn't just dismiss it out of hand. Your reader is only interested in well thought-out arguments based on good authority or good evidence, not just anything you happen to want to say. Generally, as a newcomer to a subject, it is best to concentrate on trying to do an intelligent job of working with the arguments and information you have been reading or learning about in books and articles, lectures and seminars. Your own originality of thought has plenty of opportunity to shine through.

This even applies to the terms you use. For example, Philip says in paragraph 1, 'These were under-privileged women ... '. 'Under-privileged' is not a term Ellis uses, and it sounds pretty odd given that she is talking about wealthy society women. Privilege was what they *did* have. 'Socially cut-off', 'under-stimulated', or 'under-employed' are all terms that might more accurately be used. But basically it is wisest to stay close to the terms that authors use. After all, what grounds has Philip for placing these women in a particular category other than what he has learned from Ellis? She will have chosen her terms carefully, based on her own detailed knowledge of the subject and on the terms in use amongst other experts. Writing essays is also learning to use the language of the writers in the field you are studying.

Key points

- Dropping thoughts of your own into your essay, in passing, tends to raise lots of complicated questions that you cannot deal with.

- If you include points that distract your reader from the main flow of your argument, this diminishes its impact.

- Any ideas you do bring in need to be explained and justified.

- If you focus on working with the terms and ideas you have been studying, your own thoughts and interpretations will work their way in anyway. You don't need to make a special effort to bring in extra ideas of your own.

7.5.5 Making judgements

The essay title, then, invites the writer to engage in the debate between Ellis and the satirists. This involves coming to some kind of *judgement* between the arguments on the two sides. As we saw, Philip does not really commit himself. Insofar as he makes judgements, they are about the parallels between the situation of these eighteenth-century women and women now, and between eighteenth-century women's actions and those of women in general. I found these views both irrelevant and inappropriate.

Box 7.6   Making 'good judgements'

We make judgements about what we read all the time. Indeed, we read other people's writing *in order* to think through our ideas more thoroughly and to extend them. Unless we have some ideas of our own we can't make sense of what we read. And our ideas 'inform' our judgements.

> However, when you present your judgements in an essay they have to be *relevant* to the question you are discussing, and *appropriate* in terms of the sources of information and authoritative debate available to you. You must try not to make assumptions as you develop your argument. Ask yourself 'what if my reader disagrees with me?'

Hansa, on the other hand, does commit herself. In taking Ellis's line against that of the satirists, she brings her own judgement to bear. But does she manage to present her judgements 'relevantly' and 'appropriately'? In the first three paragraphs she very properly keeps her judgements to herself and sticks to outlining the women's general circumstances, and the opportunities available to them in country and town respectively. But then in paragraph 4 the gloves come off:

> In view of the somewhat prescribed role forced upon women in the eighteenth century by the <u>male dominated</u> society which <u>formulated social mores ...</u> (underlining added)

Hansa is saying that this society was dominated by men; that men made the social 'rules' and, presumably, 'forced' them upon women. Relationships between men and women at the time are certainly *relevant* to the essay question. But is it *appropriate* for Hansa to make such a statement as if it is based on her own knowledge of the facts – when actually, if she got it from anywhere, we know that it was from Ellis? At least, she should refer to the source of her information, saying perhaps, 'As we see from Ellis's article, this was a male dominated society ... '.

However, she would have difficulty doing that because Ellis does not say this explicitly anywhere. Ellis does not use the term 'male dominated', nor does she explore the question of where the rules of correct female behaviour 'came from'. So Hansa is not making a statement based on fact here. This is a judgement, based on her interpretation of Ellis.

What Hansa says, then, is inappropriate for two reasons:

1   because she writes *as if* she herself has knowledge that she does not have;
2   because she presents what is a *judgement* as though it were fact.

In effect, what she presents us with are her own *assumptions* about how eighteenth-century society worked.

Hansa's personal judgement comes through again right at the end of the essay when she talks about women being 'burdened' by their role. Again, she presents this as if it is obvious and well established that 'society' placed a heavy and oppressive load on these women. (I dare say some of their servants would not have found their way of life such a burden.) So, again, this 'pronouncement' jars. It feels as though we are being dragooned into seeing things from Hansa's point of view without having been given good reason to.

So although Hansa has brought in her own judgements in a way that is relevant, she has not quite handled them appropriately. But then in a first essay it is quite an achievement to have to engaged so well with Ellis's arguments. I doubt if it will take Hansa long to develop the ability to present her case more convincingly.

Key points

In the concluding paragraph of your essay you should give a direct *answer* to the *essay question* you have been asked (or a solution to the problem posed in the title). It does not have to be grand, but there should be a sense of having reached an ending.

The *judgements* you make should be:

- *relevant* and *appropriate* to the question you are discussing
- *justified* by the case you have argued in the main body of the essay.

7.6   Making your case convincing

One of the best ways of putting together a convincing argument is to make direct use of your source material – in this case, Ellis's article. Neither Hansa nor Philip does quite enough of it. Hansa does some in her opening paragraph, when she refers to the particular accomplishments women acquired – playing the piano, singing, embroidering – and, in the last sentence, quotes from Ellis briefly. In her second paragraph she also identifies the different pastimes men and women had in the countryside. (Philip does none of these things in his opening paragraphs.) They both need to make the Ellis article a more tangible presence in their essay because Ellis is both the *source of the information* they present and the *authority* for their arguments.

In making a convincing case, there are two basic tools available to you. First, *explain* fully what you mean to say, using ideas and illustration drawn from *authorities* on the subject. Second, provide *evidence* to support your case. Each requires a certain amount of know-how to be used effectively.

7.6.1   Explaining and illustrating an argument

The things you write about can seem perfectly obvious to *you* but be utterly obscure to a reader. Indeed, if you come back after several months to something you have written yourself, you can often find your *own words* mystifying. It is important to remind yourself that your reader cannot see into your mind. *Your points often need more explanation than you think.* It is always a good policy to take the time to spell things out clearly.

> I try to be clear and develop points. I don't assume that my reader knows what the topic is about. Explain, explain, explain.

> I just assumed I was being clear, but when I got my essay back (and had forgotten some of the topic) I couldn't follow some of my own points!

Illustrating your argument

When you present an argument you are often using words and ideas that are open to a range of interpretations. *Illustrating* a point you are trying to explain is giving an *example* that makes your meaning clear and helps to fix what you are saying more precisely in your reader's mind. So, when Ellis says that men actively enjoyed their life in the countryside she illustrates this claim by giving specific examples of the pleasures they enjoyed; riding, hunting, fishing and shooting. In turn, Hansa refers to these pastimes in her essay. This helps us imagine just how the men spent their time and so appreciate the point she makes. Hansa might have illustrated the attractions of the towns by mentioning some of the detail Ellis provides; rather than referring vaguely to 'social events', she could have made specific mention of the theatres and concert halls (as Philip does). This would help us to 'see' why women were attracted to the towns, and would not take up many more of her 500 words. In short, explanations and illustrations help your reader to see the force of your argument. They also demonstrate to your tutor that you understand what you are writing about.

Providing evidence in support of your argument

When Ellis describes Lady Jane Coke's fate, stranded in her house for four months during the winter of 1748–9, she is illustrating her point about the tedium of women's lives in the countryside in a particularly vivid way that sticks in our minds. However, at the same time as illustrating this point the example *also* offers evidence in support of her claim that these women's lives were tedious. In other words, she is backing up her argument. The quotation she uses ('continual rains') suggests that the information is drawn from an account given by someone who was actually there – possibly from Lady Coke herself, in a diary or letter. So this is 'first-hand' evidence. (We return to the question of evidence in 9.6.2.)

'Illustrating' your point is sometimes confused with giving 'evidence' in support of it. You need to keep these processes separate in your mind. But if you *can* find some section of text that does both jobs at once, it is very economical (taking up fewer of the words available to you). So this would be a good example to use in the essay.

Quoting

At some points you may want to use an author's exact words, to quote the author, in order to convey the precise point he or she makes or to provide evidence that indeed such a thing was said – as Hansa does at the end of her first paragraph. You will have noticed that in doing this she used *quotation marks*.

To take another example, you might write:

> In Ellis's view it was 'vital that [these women] conformed to contemporary norms which had shifted ... towards an ideal of delicate, innocent and essentially decorative womanhood'.

Notice that I have inserted the words 'these women' here, to allow the sentence to read correctly. To signal that this is *my* addition, I have put these words in square brackets. I have also left out a few words that I didn't need, but, by using three dots (an ellipsis), I have again signalled the change to the original text.

This exactness in the use of other people's words is extremely important. When you quote an author, it is vital that you reproduce the passage *completely accurately,* giving clear signals when you have made any changes. In most essays you shouldn't need to quote from secondary sources all that often, since the essential point is to learn to write in your own words. But when you do quote you *must* be accurate.

When you quote you should also include, at that point in your essay, a *reference* to the work you are quoting from and the page number for the quotation. Referencing is discussed in Chapter 8.

See Chapter 8 Section 8.2.8, Reviewing, revising and polishing

> ### Key point
>
> - Whenever you quote an author's words you *must* show that this is what you are doing by using quotation marks.
> - Everything between quotation marks, including punctuation, should be *exactly* as in the original text. If you deliberately add or omit something, you should signal the changes with square brackets or with ellipses.

Avoiding plagiarism

Still on the subject of working with other people's ideas, note that the emphasis has to be on working *with* other people's ideas rather than reproducing their words. If you copy your essay material directly from an article, without using quotation marks and without acknowledging your source, you will be accused by your tutor of *plagiarism*: that is, in effect, stealing other people's ideas. This also applies if you reproduce an author's argument (perhaps paraphrasing it) and fail to acknowledge that you have done so and where you have drawn the ideas from. In the world of writing, plagiarism is *a serious offence.* Furthermore, a well-referenced essay actually gets you credit rather than making your work look derivative.

It is also possible to be guilty of plagiarism without even being aware of it. As you are reading an article you might jot down passages from it in note form and, later on, working through your notes for an essay, simply forget where you got these passages from and assume that they are *your* words. You can avoid such 'accidental plagiarism' by getting into the habit of including a reference to your source as a *heading* in your notes, and using quotation marks *whenever* you write down another person's words. But this also underlines the importance of the point made in Chapter 5 about making the effort to translate what you read into *your own words* as you make notes.

This is all the more important now that we have the resources of the internet available to us. These days, cutting and pasting from a website into your notes is one of the most common causes of unintended plagiarism. The note-making skills discussed in Chapter 5 should be applied to internet sources in just the same way as other source material. On the other hand, you have no doubt read stories in the newspapers about students raiding websites for material to use in essays, and even buying essays written by other people.

See Chapter 10 Section 10.4.3, Plagiarising assignments

This behaviour is certainly not accidental, and when discovered (as it often is) it is always heavily penalised.

> **Key point**
>
> Reproducing an author's words without using quotation marks and referencing your source is *plagiarism*. So is unacknowledged paraphrasing of an author's argument. Plagiarism is *cheating*. It will be taken very seriously by your university; if you plagiarise you will be penalised.

7.6.2 Providing evidence

To be convincing, you need to support your arguments with evidence. But what exactly *counts* as evidence? 'Telling stories' drawn from your own or a friend's experience does *not* count as convincing evidence. Your essay will be seen as subjective: that is, slanted in line with your personal experience, opinions or beliefs. There are exceptions to this however. Sometimes you may be asked to draw on your own experience – in film studies, on your personal response to particular scenes for example. But on occasions like these your tutor is asking for something a lot more considered and reflective than mere reaction, opinion or anecdote. And in most cases you will need to draw your evidence from elsewhere.

For instance, we saw that it would have been helpful for Hansa to be able to rely on Ellis's authority when mounting her argument about male domination. Had Ellis in fact argued this explicitly, she could have used Ellis's terms and also quoted her words. In this way Hansa could both have *explained* herself clearly and offered *evidence* in support of her argument.

At present, Philip's and Hansa's arguments appear to arise too directly out of their own 'knowledge' and this is unlikely to be convincing to their readers. It is a vital part of writing skill in the humanities to be able to weave quotations and other references into your essays, so that you convey a sense of direct engagement with the texts you have been studying. Ellis herself does this in her article, when she draws on the findings of demographic research carried out by other academics. She has also researched primary sources such as contemporary diaries, letters and plays – and, as we saw, she quotes directly from some of them. In principle, we could check these sources for ourselves.

So, you are often drawing your evidence from information contained in the *same* texts from which you draw your basic arguments and ideas – as in the case of Ellis's article. Nevertheless, you need to get into the habit of referring to the *specific* evidence on which you are basing the points you make (Etherege's play, or Sophie von La Roche's observations), even though it has been done in the article. The fact that the author of the article has already drawn conclusions is not going to convince the reader that *you* understand how the evidence works. You have to *show* that you do.

Exploring the strengths and weaknesses of Philip's and Hansa's essays has revealed how important it is for an essay to have an *argument* which *answers the question* in the title. This is important because working out your argument tests your *understanding* of the ideas and information you have been studying. And developing it into a *well-organised* and *convincing* argument helps you to take control of your new knowledge and learn how to use it for yourself.

Key points

- An essay should have an argument running through it, from the title to the conclusion.

- In the conclusion of your essay, show that you have answered the question asked in the title. (If the title doesn't contain a question, make it clear that you have completed whatever task it sets.)

- In presenting your argument, take the time to explain to your reader what you mean. Use examples to illustrate your point.

- Don't expect your reader to take your word for things. Back up your points with evidence, or by referring to the views of other writers on the subject.

- Make use of your new knowledge by bringing in concepts and material from the course.

- Give your essay structure by organising it into a sequence of paragraphs with a logical flow.

- Always use quotation marks when you reproduce an author's words, and provide a reference for your source material (see Chapter 8).

7.7 'Proper' English

Now we will look at the *way* Philip and Hansa wrote and presented their essays. Another difference you may have noticed between them is that Philip's written English is less polished than Hansa's. It is often difficult to read because he doesn't use enough punctuation to help us make sense of his words, and because of certain mistakes he makes. I found Hansa's essay easier to read. Her writing is more technically correct and more assured than Philip's. But I think that sometimes it is too formal and elaborate.

Activity 7.2

Go back to Philip's and Hansa's essays, and the notes you made about them. Look at the way they *express* their ideas. Did you pick out any mistakes in their sentences, punctuation or spelling? How important do you think it is to spell words correctly?

7.7.1 Sentences

We can see that Philip knows what a sentence is because he writes some perfectly good ones. For example:

> In many ways going into urban life from the countryside was beneficial to woman of the upperclass.

This sentence begins with a capital letter and ends with a full stop. It has a subject (urban life) and a main verb (was). As any sentence is, it is a self-contained unit of meaning. It makes sense read out on its own. The only thing wrong with it is that 'upper class' should be two words rather than one, and Philip should refer to women not 'woman'.

But what about this sentence? (Read it out loud.)

> With society becoming more wealthy it was possible for the fathers and husbands to provide an even better standard of life for their wifes and daughters, more servants could be provided to do the work and this left the woman more time than ever to develop the social skills of the era, but this in turn led to extreme frustration among woman of that class.

It sounds long and rambling. But in fact all it needs is two full stops and a couple of minor corrections (to 'wifes' and 'woman') to turn it into three pretty sound sentences.

> With society becoming more wealthy it was possible for the fathers and husbands to provide an even better standard of life for their wives and daughters. More servants could be provided to do the work and this left the women more time than ever to develop the social skills of the era. But this in turn led to extreme frustration among women of that class.

Box 7.7   Writing sentences

A sentence starts with a capital letter and ends with a full stop, question mark or exclamation mark. It is a self-contained unit of meaning. Every sentence needs a *verb* – a 'doing' word – and (almost) every sentence needs a *subject* – a person who, or thing that, is 'doing'. *She popped the question* is a sentence. 'She' is the subject (because she was 'doing' the popping) and 'popped' is the verb (because that is what she was doing). If you are not sure whether you have written a sentence, a simple test is to ask 'Does it have a subject and a verb?' ('it' is the subject of that sentence and 'does have' is the verb).

It is quite possible to use grammar effectively without knowing the rules in a formal way. Many people can hear whether a string of words is a sentence or not because it 'sounds' complete when it is; they don't have to stop and think about whether it contains a subject and a verb. If you find it *isn't* obvious to you, even when you read your work out loud, get some advice (see the paragraph below for suggestions). You will find it difficult to develop your writing style until you have a reasonable feel for what a sentence is.

At first sight it looks as if writing in sentences may be a big problem for Philip. He *does* have a sense of where a break is needed, but he tends to use commas where he needs full stops. The sentences are there; he just hasn't *marked* them as sentences. I doubt if he needs to worry too much about this. With prompting from a tutor and plenty of practice – and especially through reading his essays out loud – his sensitivity to sentences will develop spontaneously. But, if you need to, you will find websites that offer support with sentence structure (search for 'English' and 'grammar'); your own university may provide one. Also, your word processor's grammar checking facility should give you some support. It won't be infallible but it can be useful to have the prompt, to help you double-check what you have written. Make sure you know how the grammar checker works (look under Help if necessary), and when you see a mistake picked out, take the time to find out what might be wrong. That way you will gradually build up your ability to get things right without needing help. Alternatively, buy a book on grammar or ask your local library for information about classes – your local college will probably run short courses on grammar and writing.

Hansa's writing is much more assured. But, as I said, some sentences strike me as over-formal and elaborate. Take this one, for example:

> Because of this, and because an urban environment offered women so much more scope, not only to display their accomplishments but also to indulge their own desire for sociability, amusement and companions', the female population of England's towns expanded dramatically.

Too many points that are important in their own right are squashed into this one sentence. Its construction is complicated: 'Because A … , and because B … , not only C … but also D, E and F, the female population … '. It would read more easily if she removed the central part of the sentence – 'not only to display … amusement and companions'. (And, incidentally, she doesn't want the apostrophe after the 's' in 'companions'.) There would still be more than enough to take in. Also, more emphasis would be placed on the last part of the sentence, which is actually the *main point* of it. As things stand, we arrive at 'the female population … ' over-burdened and out of breath, as it were.

In sentences such as this, Hansa's meaning is so condensed that it gets lost. She is trying to say too much. If she wrote more directly, in simpler sentences, her meaning would be clearer and she could give more emphasis to the points that are most important. A simple sentence contains one idea; if your sentences contain more than one idea, consider splitting them into two or more.

7.7.2 Punctuation

Some of the sentences we have looked at are harder to understand than they might be because they are not very well punctuated. Punctuation is the system of signals you give to your reader to show how the grammar of the sentence is supposed to work; punctuation marks are the 'stops' in a sentence that divide it up into parts. They make it easier to follow the meaning of the words. For instance, it is easier to read this sentence of Philip's if we put a comma after 'wealthy':

> With society becoming more wealthy, it was possible for the fathers and husbands to provide an even better standard of life for their wives and daughters.

Box 7.8 Punctuation marks

The basics of punctuation are the capital letter at the start of a sentence and the full stop at the end. You use commas to mark off any sub-parts of the sentence. Other punctuation marks include:

semicolon ;	marks a pause which has more emphasis than a comma but less than a full stop; also often used to divide up items in a list
colon :	signals that a list is to follow
brackets ( )	always come in pairs and go round an aside – a point which is not part of the main flow of a sentence. If you read 'through', missing out what is in the brackets, the sentence should still make sense
dash –	can be used similarly to brackets, but you can use just one to signal a shift to a related point
hyphen -	links words together (as above, in *sub-parts*)
apostrophe '	indicates letters missing (as in *don't*); also indicates belonging to (as in *Philip's*)
inverted commas ' '	used when you quote; speech marks

Question mark **?** and exclamation mark **!** are pretty obvious. You will very rarely need to use an exclamation mark in an essay.

We all make mistakes in punctuation as we write. So it is important to check through the first draft of your essay with this in mind. When in doubt, read the sentence out loud – even in an exaggerated way – and 'listen' to where you make little pauses as you speak it. Often, you need a comma at those points.

7.7.3   Consistency

A common problem with sentences is not making all the parts match up. What is wrong with this sentence of Philip's, for example?

> So therefore <u>woman</u> began to long for the urban or city way of living, if even for a short period so that <u>they</u> could deploy the art of socialising ...

The mistake is that 'woman' should be followed by 'she' not 'they'. 'Woman' is *singular*, whereas the word 'they' is *plural*. (Philip should also put a comma after 'period', and change 'even' to 'only'.) Similarly, in her fourth paragraph Hansa refers to '*a* high ranking wom*en*'. You have to make up your mind whether you are talking about one thing or lots of them.

Another kind of matching up is making the items in a list the same kind of word. Instead of writing 'sociability, amusement and *companions*', Hansa should say 'companion*ship*'. The first two words in the list are abstract nouns, so the third word should be an abstract noun too. Also, some words take partners: 'not only ... but also', for example, and 'either ... or'. When Hansa writes in her conclusion 'women ... were *neither* mainly attracted to the towns' she should add '*nor* escaping from the countryside'.

Another common slip is to have tenses of verbs not matching. Look at this sentence of Philip's:

> The women who <u>lived</u> a fairly comfortable style of life <u>belonged</u> to a class of society where the father or husband <u>would be</u> a land-owner.

'Lived' and 'belonged' are in the past tense. So Philip should use the past tense of the other verb in the sentence; 'would *have been*', rather than 'would be'. (And, incidentally, a 'class of society' is not a place so he shouldn't say 'where'. He should have written '*in which* the father ... '.)

The tense of a verb is its setting in *time*. For example, 'I laugh' is set in the present, 'I laughed' is set in the past, and 'I will laugh' is set in the future. (There are, of course, other tenses too.) The main thing is to be *consistent* in using them. Decide whether you are discussing the past, present or future and then stay there, unless you have a good reason for making a change.

Some of these may seem small points. But I am not nit picking or being critical for the sake of it. Inconsistencies such as these get in the way. They slow your readers down and distract them from taking in the meaning of your sentences. Reading is hard enough without having our attention diverted along the way.

7.7.4 Choosing the right words
Both Philip and Hansa occasionally use words and phrases that don't really do the job they want. We saw, for instance, that Philip uses the word 'resemblance' when actually he means 'contrast'. Here are some other examples from his writing.

	Philip's words	*More accurate words*
Paragraph 1	'portrayal'	portrait, account
	'orientated to'	fitted for
Paragraph 2	'a greater amount of society'	a wider society
Paragraph 3	'variation of'	variety of
Paragraph 4	'amount' of jibes	many jibes

And in Hansa's second paragraph I'd say it is better to refer to the 'exercise' of skills rather than the 'indulgence' of them.

Box 7.9   Choice of words

When you are writing you have to use the words that come to you. You would never get started if you stopped to worry about each one. However, when you are reading over what you have written you should check that you have used words that convey the meaning you intended. The exact meaning of the words you use is more important in writing than in speech.

In the long run your sensitivity to the shades of meaning words carry will increase. But as you study, the best thing to do is just get on with your writing – with a dictionary at your elbow. You may also find a thesaurus useful. A thesaurus lists words in groups of related meanings (MS Word contains one – look under 'tools' and 'language').

Everyday language

Philip uses a phrase from popular speech when he says that these women have 'gone down in history' as experts at organising social events. This is definitely not an academic turn of phrase, since it implies that there is one history we all agree about – a kind of hall of fame for society's all-time 'stars'. Note that Ellis herself does *not* say this; she is very precise. What she says is that women 'sometimes took a leading role' in planning certain social events such as race meetings, balls, theatre performances and concerts.

Phrases like this may seem to give a flourish to your writing, but they are not appropriate in an academic essay. They are not precise enough, and they tend to raise more problems than they are worth. In any case, a flourish is not quite what you are after. What you need is a lively and compelling style that is at the same time simple and direct.

7.7.5   Spelling

Philip and Hansa made very few spelling mistakes. In Philip's essay perhaps you noticed 'wifes' (wives), 'citys' (cities) and 'carreer' (career); in Hansa's 'sparcity' (sparsity).

Do you lose marks for bad spelling? In principle, no. However, your essay marker is bound to be influenced by work with lots of mistakes in it, whether in spelling, grammar or punctuation. They detract from the general effect of your essay as well as making it harder to read. If you want your writing to make its full impact you really need to proof-read your work – take the time to read through it carefully before sending it off to be marked. And of course use your word processor's 'spell check' facility.

If you are very poor at spelling, don't worry that it will hold back your progress. But don't be entirely relaxed about it either. There are websites that offer spelling tests and general advice. And when you are not sure about a word you should look it up in a dictionary. It would also be useful to start making a list of the words you often get wrong, so that you can test yourself from time to time. However, it isn't worth setting out on a major campaign to memorise dozens of words. In general, the more you read and write the more you develop a sense of the broad, though rather idiosyncratic, rules of English spelling.

7.7.6   Presenting your essay

Your university will almost certainly want you to word process your essays rather than write by hand. But however you do it, it is important to present an essay well. Otherwise, it suggests that you don't care enough about your work to read it through and make corrections before handing it to someone else to read. And your tutor is bound to find it harder to make sense of what you are trying to say if there are too many mistakes in it. Tutors usually make allowances for the occasional blunder but, if you want your writing to have its full impact, you must read it through carefully and correct any errors you spot.

See Chapter 8 Section 8.2.8, Reviewing, revising and polishing

We have seen that, although there are good things in Philip's essay, there are quite a number of ways in which his writing could be improved.

Activity 7.3

To test yourself out on the points we have talked about, go back to Philip's second paragraph, starting from 'The country was no place ...', and put in some punctuation and any other alterations that make it read more easily.

Here is my attempt, with the reasons for the changes I made given below.

The country was **now** no place ~~now~~ to exercise these new skills. ~~they had been taught.~~ [**F**or one thing, females outnumbered males. ~~at that time~~] **F**ew chances arose to meet and mingle **in society**. ~~with crowds of people. but~~ **M**ost importantly, the demands of propriety **required that** ~~meant that~~ **women's** ~~their~~ conduct should be impeccable at all times. **A**ny error **could** be seen in such a limited environment. **S**o ~~therefore~~ wom**e**n began to long for the urban ~~or city~~ way of living, if **only** ~~even~~ for a short period, so that they could **put their social skills to use** ~~deploy the art of socialising~~ and mingl**e** ~~ing~~ with a **wider** ~~greater amount of~~ society.

Changes

- 'Now' interrupts the flow of 'no place to exercise these new skills', so I moved it forward.

- When Philip wants to identify which 'new skills' he is referring to he can *either* say 'these new skills', *or* 'the new skills they had been taught' – he doesn't need both.

- Start a new sentence after 'taught'.

- Comma after 'thing' because it's a preparatory bit before the main sentence starts. No need for 'at that time' because he has already said 'now' in the previous sentence. But my square brackets indicate that this sentence should really come out altogether – Ellis does *not* say this.

- New sentence at 'Few'; 'crowds of people' isn't quite right for gatherings of people of this rank – 'in society' or 'socially' captures it better.

- No need for 'but'– just start another sentence at 'Most'.

- What the demands of propriety imposed on women were 'requirements' not 'meanings'. 'Women's' instead of 'their', since readers might be losing track of who 'they' are by now.
- New sentence at 'Any error' – and 'could' is better than 'would', since not every error might be spotted.
- New sentence at 'So'. He doesn't need both 'so' and 'therefore'. Needs the plural 'women'. Doesn't need 'urban' *and* 'city'. Good to put a comma after 'living', *and* after 'period' – since 'if only for a short period' is a side point.

The rest we've already discussed.

How do these compare with the improvements you made? It doesn't matter if yours are different because many of these changes are more a matter of taste and judgement than right and wrong. The main point of the exercise was to focus your attention on the details. Your aim is to achieve directness, simplicity and a nice flow to what you write. You will gradually develop a feel for what works best and when, and your tutor will probably have plenty of suggestions to make.

Key points

The *way* you write is as important as what you say. So when you are writing you must try to:

- use properly formed sentences and mainly simple ones
- punctuate them in a way that makes your meaning clear
- pay attention to grammar, making all parts of sentences consistent
- be precise about the particular words and phrases you use and careful to address your reader appropriately
- present your work with care, reading it through to correct spelling, grammar and any other mistakes.

7.8   Writing style and audience

While it certainly helps to write 'properly', what really counts is being able to write clearly and forcefully. So how did you rate Hansa and Philip on this score?

As I have said, in my view Hansa tends to use whole clusters of words and constructions that are a bit over-formal rather than wrong. She seems to be trying to impress her reader. For example:

> They therefore fled from the country in order to escape the restrictions and consequent boredom placed upon them by the very limited pastimes that a high ranking women in the eighteenth century was permitted to indulge.

Activity 7.4

Hansa's sentence contains 36 words. Can you see ways to reduce it to, say, 20 or so? At the same time, try to make the sentence simpler and more direct.

Normally, we would use a word such as 'allowed' rather than 'permitted to indulge', which sounds rather pompous. And, strictly speaking, we 'indulge *in*' pastimes. Also, 'restrictions' may be 'placed upon' people, but we don't usually say that about 'boredom'. Boredom is something we experience or suffer. It would be altogether simpler and more straightforward to say something like:

> So they fled from the countryside to escape these restrictions, and the boredom that resulted from having so few pastimes. [20 words]

Sometimes Philip, too, seems to be striving to impress by using formal language instead of simple, direct terms. For instance, in paragraph 3 he talks about women being able to meet '... *many more of the female sex*' when he just means 'other women'. And at the end of paragraph 2 he says, '... *so that they could deploy the art of socialising and mingling with a greater amount of society*' – when it would be more direct to say '... so that they could put their social skills to use, and mingle with a wider society.' Similarly, '*This transition was not without a certain amount of jibes from the male population against the women of that time ...*' could simply be put as 'Some men mocked these women for making the transition ...'. Perhaps Hansa and Philip are assuming that they have to sound 'academic' for their tutors.

But who exactly *are* you writing for? How can you develop an appropriate style and tone of voice unless you can picture your reader?

Key points

- Good writing at higher levels of study is primarily to do with the quality of your ideas and arguments. Nevertheless it is important to work at making your written language as technically correct as you can, simply to be able to get your ideas across effectively.

- Improvement takes time, but regular practice and attention to detail will gradually make a difference. As you begin to gain greater control over your use of language, you will also get more pleasure out of writing.

7.8.1 'Speaking' to your reader

Writing is a very special form of 'conversation'. As you write, you are talking to someone you cannot see and who does not reply. You just have to assume that he or she is 'listening' and reacting to what you say. Furthermore, *you* have to take all the responsibility for deciding what is to be said and how, and for sustaining this other person's interest. And you are responsible for establishing the *relationship* between you and your listener.

This is one of the trickiest things about writing. You have to convey a sense of who you assume your *reader* to be, and in what frame of mind he or she will be approaching your words. This is known as a 'sense of audience'. You also have to convey a sense of who *you* are claiming to be and from what *position* you are speaking. Are you speaking as an expert on the subject, as a witty entertainer, a friend, or what? This is known as your 'writing voice'.

So there are two issues here. You have to develop a sense of your audience and of the right tone of voice in which to write.

Sense of audience

Who, then, do you assume your audience is when you write an essay? Is it someone who is very learned and critical, or someone who knows nothing? A standard approach is to say, write for the intelligent person in the street. In other words, assume that your reader has not read the books you have been studying, but that she or he is interested in the question posed by the title of the essay and is capable of picking up your arguments quickly provided you spell them out clearly. This is helpful, but slightly puzzling. The average person in the street is unlikely to want to know about Ellis's views on eighteenth-century women, or to be interested in an academic style of debate. Or people say that you should write for your tutor. But this is a bit puzzling too. You know perfectly well that your tutor already knows about almost everything you are likely to say. So perhaps write for another beginner in your subject is a more realistic formulation – someone who needs things explained fully, but who is basically interested and ready for a well-argued case. However, as we saw earlier, you can assume that this person is familiar with the primary texts you discuss, such as novels and poems, so you certainly don't need to 'tell them the story' in your essay.

Your writing voice

Who are you to present yourself as? Basically, you are a calm detached observer, pointing out to an equal (who happens not to be informed on the subject) some arguments that are relevant to a question you are both interested in (i.e. the question in the essay title). It is not easy to find a comfortable writing voice. It may take several essays before you can settle satisfactorily into one. One of the main reasons you get stuck at the start of an essay is the difficulty of trying to work out where you are 'coming from'. Sometimes you have to take several shots at your opening before you can find a voice in which you can proceed.

Key points

- To write good essays aim for a clear, direct, unfussy style and simple sentences.
- Check that your words say what you want them to.
- One of the key challenges of writing is to develop a sense of your audience and also a voice in which to speak to your reader. Both take time and practice, but as they develop, you become much more confident in your writing.

7.8.2   The significance of writing in your own words

Finding your own writing voice implies that, from the start of your studies, you must *write in your own words* when making notes and preparing essays – even if your writing is weak at the outset. This is a big challenge. You are trying to write in a subject area in which the terms are unfamiliar and your ideas are still forming. If it is also the case that you don't do much writing in your everyday life (true of most people) and you are unused to writing about ideas (true of almost everyone returning to study after a break), it is hard to know where to begin. That is why it feels safer to stay close to the wording of academic books and articles; it seems less likely that you will embarrass yourself by writing nonsense. Yet you are just as likely to write weakly if you rely too closely on the course material – and, as we saw, you run the risk of being accused of plagiarism. Worse still, though, your writing will not improve. Just as you don't make progress in learning to swim while you still have a foot on the bottom of the pool, *you don't begin to develop as a thinker and writer in your subject area if you rely on the words in the study texts*.

The main purpose of writing essays is to practice *using* the ideas you have been reading about in the course. This comes across very clearly from the students talking about the nature of the learning process in Chapter 3.

See Chapter 3 Section 3.2.3, What do you have to do to learn something?

> Often the things I learn most about are essay topics, because the process of structuring and writing an essay helps me to understand the main points of the argument.

This means you have to write about ideas in words that make sense to *you*. They may come out badly to begin with, but like a learner in any field you have to be prepared to make mistakes. It is through exposing your weaknesses that you learn how to do something about them. Also, by using your own words, you show your teacher the progress you are making so that you can get due credit for it. And, having seen where you have reached in your understanding, your teacher can enter into fruitful dialogue with you to help move your ideas and writing along.

A further reason to write in your own words is that you will get more satisfaction out of it. There may be embarrassing moments, but with practice you will build up respect for yourself and your own ideas. This is the most powerful of incentives to carry on studying. If essays feel like a chore, because you are simply making a selection from other people's words and rearranging them on the page, then you are much more likely to give up your studies. You need to allow yourself to experience the deep satisfaction of expressing your own arguments and seeing your writing powers develop.

Key points

There are four reasons why it is important to write in your own words.

- It enables you to learn the ideas in the course in depth, by using them to say things for yourself.

- It enables your teacher to give you credit for your learning.
- It makes possible a genuine dialogue with your teacher about your progress.
- It makes studying much more stimulating and develops your powers of self-expression.

7.9   What is a good essay?

In this chapter we have given a lot of detailed attention to two very short essays, using them as a springboard for discussing what is expected in academic essays generally. However, we shouldn't leave the essays without commenting on their overall quality.

7.9.1   How good are the essays we reviewed?
The significance of context
'How good' depends enormously on the context. In one sense, any essay is excellent if it is genuinely the best you can write at that particular point in your understanding of the subject matter and given your level of experience of essay writing. It's like asking 'How well has my day's walk gone, now that I've reached Bradford Town Hall?' It very much depends whether you started from Low Moor on the outskirts of Bradford, from Halifax eight miles away, or from Manchester nearly sixty miles away over the Pennines. We all have to start writing from where we are, and one measure of the quality of our work is the progress we make from that starting point.

In this case we have two people returning to study after a long gap and not having thrived in their previous studies at school. I was not their teacher but, by arrangement, I asked them to read the Ellis article as an extra item alongside their regular course work. It is on a topic completely new to them and presents some quite subtle arguments. There was no classroom discussion of the article. Nor were they given guidance on how to tackle the essay title, or opportunity to share ideas about how to approach it. In short, they faced a tough challenge. To produce an essay at all was a considerable achievement.

Levels of performance
On the other hand, it would be misleading to say that we can't make comparisons between these essays, or judge them against any general standards.

Near the start of this chapter I asked you to make lists of the strengths and weaknesses of both the essays. Have a look at your notes now, and see how they compare with my judgements.

Philip's essay
Strengths

- a reasonable understanding of the issues Ellis deals with
- a good basic structure

- some good sequences of argument
- a promising feel for language
- fluency of expression

Weaknesses

- the wrong title and consequently a lack of focus
- argument is loose-knit in places – some points are not relevant
- occasionally misrepresents Ellis
- uncertainty regarding the overall argument, so arrives at a weak conclusion
- poor punctuation
- the language is artificial at times – striving for stylishness rather than clarity.

Philip's essay strikes me as a fair piece of work at this level. There are plenty of points that need working on, but also some promising features. He develops some strong argument and has the makings of an effective writing style.

Hansa's essay
Strengths

- subtle understanding of Ellis's argument
- good focus on the question in the title
- generally sound structure
- some very fluent writing in places
- plenty of attack in the opening – strong first paragraph
- good sense of how to draw a conclusion

Weaknesses

- one weak point is her use of paragraphs
- in places, her language is over-formal and sentences too densely packed
- needs to clarify her line of argument (i.e. reorganise a little)
- could pay even more attention to signalling how the argument is developing
- doesn't quite set up the frame of reference within which she is arguing.

Hansa's essay is clearly more accomplished than Philip's. It would attract a higher grade – above the middle range I'd say. That is mainly because she addresses herself to the essay question she was set, and puts together a reasonably well-connected argument that leads to an answer to it. Along the way, she shows that she has a good grasp of the ideas contained in her source material. On the whole, her work is careful and technically correct, and she presents it well.

Feedback
Essay writing is the nub of the teaching–learning relationship between students and their teachers. It is where the teacher gets to see how ideas are developing in the student's mind and the students get feedback on the

progress they are making. The dialogue that develops, in the form of the teacher's comments on the essay and the student's response to those comments in writing the next essay, is of critical significance.

So what did I say to Philip? Here is the note I wrote.

Dear Philip

Well done for getting yourself over the hurdle of sending in your first essay, especially as it's such a long time since you last did this kind of writing. The essay shows a lot of promise. You obviously worked hard on the Ellis article and you have done a good sound job of getting your thoughts together for this essay. The structure of the essay is very solid and, what is more, you have a nice fluency to your writing which gives you a good base to build on.

Where you have come a bit adrift is in not working with the exact title you were set. This made it hard for you to come to a strong conclusion at the end. Also, as you will see from my notes on your script, there are some places where your line of argument could be strengthened. And you will need to spend a bit of time working on your punctuation, as well as a few other points of grammar. None of these should present a major difficulty – they will gradually come right with practice. Just make a habit of looking over my markings and notes carefully and then work out how you can make things read more easily.

Broadly, you are doing exactly the right thing – which is to pitch in and work as best you can with the ideas you have been reading about. As you keep doing this you will find your style getting sharper and your grasp of your subject more secure. Keep up the good work.

I wrote to Hansa in congratulatory and encouraging terms. Hers is a very creditable job of getting to grips with quite a subtle article and an essay title which demands some careful thought. Her all-round performance was good.

We have looked at two very different pieces of writing in response to the same essay title. Each shows a student's mind at work, grappling with challenging new ideas, and each shows particular strengths and weaknesses in both approach and writing style. From all this we have drawn out many important pointers to what you are trying to achieve when you write your own essays.

7.10   Review

See Chapter 8 Section 8.6, Summaries

Let me highlight a few key messages for you to take from this chapter. One is that there is no great mystery about *what* good writing is. You were able to spot it yourself, just by reading the sample essays. The mystery is how to produce it. On the other hand, it is not so easy to judge the quality of your own writing as you progress through your studies, so you will find it useful to return to the *Criteria for writing a good essay* at the end of Chapter 8 when you are about to submit an essay. And, after you get the essay back with comments on it, check through the list and see what progress you are making. Of all the chapters in the book this and the next are the most likely to be worth revisiting over your years of study.

You might also like to think over the fact that as you read the essays in this chapter, you briefly took on your tutor's role. This will have given you insight into what teachers look for as they mark your essays. As you saw, it isn't easy to read and make sense of other people's writing. Nor is it easy to pinpoint strengths and weaknesses and work out how to give appropriate advice. So:

- Be sympathetic to your teacher and present your work as well as you can.
- Don't be too upset if your teachers miss your point or offer advice you think is inappropriate or unfair. It is almost impossible to get these things right all the time.

Finally, be reassured that *you don't have to worry about getting your writing 'perfect' before submitting* it. The essays you have been looking at were not perfect, but one of them, at least, was a good early essay. These students were doing exactly the right thing in getting stuck in and having a go. Just assume that your first attempts will not be particularly wonderful and crack on. A good learner in any field is prepared to make mistakes. The task of the next chapter is to look at how to develop your skills as a writer.

CHAPTER 8
Managing the writing process

This chapter is the second of a pair concerned with essay writing. While Chapter 7 explores *what* it is that you are trying to produce when you write an essay, this chapter looks at *how* to set about the task of writing.

8.1   The challenge of writing

Managing the process of writing assignments is critically important to your progress as a student. It is, potentially, a deeply satisfying activity, but also a very challenging one. Writing is never a simple or straightforward process. You can't expect to sit down at a keyboard and just type out a good piece of work. Writing essays is a multilayered activity; it interweaves your studies of the course, your emerging understanding of the subject matter and your developing powers of self-expression. You need to approach it with intelligence, insight and a strategic understanding of the writing process. You have to be able to manage setbacks, changes to your plans and sharp mood swings. Good writing emerges out of a resourceful response to constraints and challenges (many of which you impose on yourself). It is an intense experience.

As an essay deadline approaches, many students find it all-consuming.

> I take ages to write an essay. And I can't get it out of my head until I finally send it off. Do you find it gets easier? I don't! I keep thinking I'll get faster but I don't.

> It's funny how each essay is dreadful and the next topic always looks so much more interesting than the current one. That is until you're on the next topic and the essay is due and then it suddenly becomes really dull and the hardest one yet.

> I panic because I have read it over so much and I know it off by heart. Then I start thinking I've picked the wrong option ... What madness! Then I finally get the courage to send it off – and the whole thing starts again.

To gain a measure of control over essay writing you need a basic strategy. Section 8.2, 'Stages in the writing process', sketches out an approach which breaks writing into stages so that you can tackle it one step at a time. However, writing is a highly individual activity and people succeed in very different ways. So the stages outlined are not meant as a 'recipe' to be followed slavishly. Take what suits you and develop a strategy of your own. Then keep developing it. Your approach to writing will evolve as you become more skilled at some aspects and switch your focus to others. If ever the Kolb reflective cycle is relevant to studying, writing has to be the prime instance (see Chapter 1 Figure 1.2). It is essential to plan your approach, write, reflect, and plan again for next time.

> I find I'm thinking loads about how I do the writing – what I should do when and what to leave to later – and I get incredibly useful ideas from ... online chatting.

Perhaps the most challenging aspect of writing is to turn ideas in your head into eloquent and purposeful sentences, rather than dry aimless ones. Section 8.3, 'Expressing ideas in writing', outlines some suggestions for tapping into the flow of your thoughts and trying to reproduce the flow of the spoken word in writing.

You can learn a great deal about writing from other students. But what can you learn from *experienced* writers? Having looked in Chapter 7 at short essays by students starting out on their studies, we switch to the other end of the spectrum in Section 8.4, 'Making your essay flow', by taking a close look at how a published author achieves this. Again we use the article by Joyce Ellis at the back of the book. Then finally we review the *experience* of writing – exploring why it is so intense, how to survive its challenges and how to focus on its pleasurable and satisfying aspects.

8.2   Stages in the writing process

Writing an essay does not simply 'happen' on a particular day. Effectively, you begin the process as soon as you begin to study the topic of your next essay. Imagine if you had an essay due in two or three weeks' time: how would you set about it? Here are my eight stages of the writing process:

1   thinking about the essay title
2   planning the writing process
3   studying the course content
4   taking stock before you start writing
5   getting ideas written down
6   organising your material
7   drafting an answer
8   reviewing, revising and polishing.

8.2.1   Thinking about the essay title

You could study the course first, *then* turn your attention to the essay. But does this make sense?

> I have the essay in the back of my mind when I'm reading. That gives me time to think what it's about from all angles. Also I can highlight anything I want to use as I go along.

Reading the essay title (or titles, if there are options) before you study a topic helps to integrate the *learning* and *writing* processes.

- **Learning** Knowing the essay title gives an edge to your thinking as you read, listen and make notes. It helps you to learn in a more focused way.

- **Writing** Knowing the essay title helps you to feed your studies directly into your essay, through (1) picking out material you can use and (2) thinking about different ways of approaching the question.

See Chapter 3 Section 3.2.3, What do you have to do to learn something?

In other words, having the essay title floating around in your mind makes the study process more of a 'dialogue' with the subject matter. As you read you are not just *receiving* ideas but also thinking about what you might *say* in your essay using those ideas.

Teasing out the meaning of the title

Essay titles have hidden depths, otherwise you would be able to answer them in a few lines. So you need to dig down and explore what is in there. One way to do this is to highlight or underline key words, then think about what pointers they give you.

Activity 8.1

Here is the essay title from Chapter 7.

Did higher-ranking women in the eighteenth century migrate to towns mainly because of the attractions of the towns, or mainly to escape from life in the countryside? Discuss in the light of Joyce Ellis's article.

1   Highlight the words or phrases you think are particularly important in this title and add any annotations.

2   Write your highlighted words/annotations as a list. Then against each make a note of what you think it tells you about what should be in the essay.

Here are my markings.

Did higher ranking <u>women</u> in the eighteenth century <u>migrate to</u> <u>towns</u> // (a) <u>mainly</u> because of the <u>attractions of the towns, or</u> (b) <u>mainly to escape</u> from life in the <u>countryside?</u> <u>Discuss</u> in the light of Joyce <u>Ellis's article.</u>

And here are my reasons for these markings.

- The segment before the dividing mark // is the 'stem' of the question: the whole question is about *why* these women migrated.

- The annotations (a) and (b) make clear that I am given *two* possible answers to the question – both of which are underlined – and remind me that I must discuss *both*.

- The word 'or' suggests that these answers are *alternatives* – either (a) or (b).

- The word 'mainly' occurs twice and implies that, even though these are alternative answers, both may be true to some extent. My task is to say whether one or the other was *more* important. (This means that I don't *necessarily* have to come down on one side or the other in the end – I may want to give a rather different answer.)

- The word 'Discuss' suggests that there are arguments *for* and *against*. Again, this indicates that I must examine *both* answers. If I want to propose a different answer, it must not *take the place* of discussion of (a) and (b) but come out of that discussion.

- 'Ellis's article' reminds me that I am not asked to discuss my own views on the matter: I am to pay particular attention to the arguments Ellis explores.

The word 'discuss' in this list is a particularly important one. It is a *process* word; it tells you what your essay has to *do*. Not every essay title includes a process word, but many do. 'Discuss' implies that you should write about arguments *for* and *against* whatever is in the title. Other common process words include: analyse, compare, contrast, describe, evaluate, explain, illustrate, outline, summarise. It is important to identify process words when you are reading an essay title so that you don't go off on the wrong tack.

If your essay *doesn't do* what the process word asks for, *you will lose marks*. You can't afford to pursue your own pet themes, and you can't answer the question you would *like* to have been asked. Instead, you have to focus your mind on the task set. In our case the process word is *discuss*, so you could jot down a few ideas about how someone might arrive at a 'mainly, yes' answer to parts (a) and (b) of the question, and how they might arrive at a 'mainly, no'. This will set your thoughts rolling.

Highlighting or underlining words and jotting down a few notes is a significant stride forward in engaging with the essay title. Instead of looking at it in vague bewilderment, your mind gets to work on how to tackle it.

Key points

- Taking a close look at the title is a vital part of producing a good essay.
- It is very important to look carefully at each of the main words or phrases in turn, otherwise you can waste a lot of time writing about things for which you will not get marks.
- Writing down a few notes helps to set your thoughts rolling, so when you come back to the title later you will have begun to develop ideas about how to tackle it.

8.2.2 Planning the writing process

An essay is a major commitment within your study schedule. It represents a substantial investment of your study time and energy, and from it you can reap significant benefits. If you handle the process effectively, writing the essay will deepen your understanding of the subject matter and advance your writing skills. So it is important to think ahead a bit and plan how you will tackle it.

Planning your study of the topic

First make a list of the set reading and any other studies relevant to the essay topic. What will you need to cover in order to answer the question effectively? You may not have time for all that is recommended, so plan to cover enough to write a well-rounded answer. If you have been asked, for example, to compare two points of view, don't spend so long studying one that you don't have time for the other. Or if you have been asked to focus on DVD-based material, make sure to give it a prominent place in your study schedule. And if you need to spend time tracking down online information, or consulting specific library resources, put this on your list. Use the essay task to think strategically about how you will use your time.

Planning time

Review your commitments over the coming days and work out how you will make time for studying the essay topic. What date is the essay due by? Do you have other work to submit during the period – even perhaps an essay for another course? What commitments do you have in your non-study life? Will you be able to spread the writing over two or three days? How much time will you allow for studying the topic before you switch to writing? Set yourself a target date for starting work on the essay itself. With your writing timetable sketched and your notes on the essay title, you can now set these to one side and move on with your studies.

Key point

■ Producing an essay is too time-consuming and too valuable to leave your preparations and timing to chance. You need to plan strategically, so that you stay in control.

8.2.3   Studying the course content

As we've seen, it is helpful to think ahead about a forthcoming essay before pitching into reading, researching, attending seminars and other study activities relevant to the topic. But it would be a great shame to let the essay dominate your agenda. Different course elements will generate their own themes and you should feel free to pursue what interests you. There are bound to be intriguing and important aspects of any topic that happen not to be linked to essay titles. You would end up with a very narrow and lopsided view of your subject if your whole attention were focused on essays.

On the other hand, if you keep a separate note-pad handy, you can jot down useful points for your essay whenever you come across them. Write the essay title at the top of the page, then note down authors' names, sources, references – whatever seems likely to help. And if a thought strikes about a possible line of argument for the essay, sketch it out. Untidy scraps of notes, which look like nothing much, can turn out to be your best ideas.

You can use highlighter pens and stickies to mark relevant places in course texts (perhaps reserving one highlighter colour for essay material). And, of course, keep an eye on progress with your plan for covering the ground required for the essay. Indeed, as the target date for writing nears, you may need to adjust your plans to ensure that you cover the essentials.

Key points

- Keep a note-pad, highlighters and stickies handy as you study so that you can accumulate information and ideas as they arise, but don't let essays dominate and distort your studies.

- Adjust your reading plans if necessary as the time for essay writing approaches.

8.2.4 Taking stock before you start writing

When you arrive at your target day for starting the essay, you need to take stock and get yourself organised.

Reviewing your strategy

You will need to revisit your plans, review your progress and make adjustments.

- What studying have you managed to complete? If you haven't covered all that you had intended, don't be tempted to carry on reading. It is better to go with what you have done than use up vital writing time. It is always tempting to put off writing. Don't. Get started in good time, so that you can give the essay your best shot.

- Do you still have the time available that you had intended for writing? If not, adjust your writing plans. Keep in mind that writing is a long, drawn-out process. Don't assume that the later stages will be quick and easy.

> I take a long time to do my essays. I like to keep going back as I think about the content and make changes.

Another thing you might take stock of is whether you have any specific goals for this essay. Be sure to read through your tutor's comments on your previous work. Is there a particular aspect of your writing skills that you have been advised to work at?

> Before I start I read my tutor's remarks on my last essay, so I can try to make sure I am applying what has been suggested to improve my writing.

Organising your sources

You also need to gather around you all the relevant books, articles and notes. Then sort it all into piles or folders. This organising can be time consuming, but it is a vital process of 'loading up' into your head a picture of all the resources you have accumulated and where everything is. Your work space may look a mess for some days.

> I usually have all the course material surrounding me as I'm going through – open at various pages to make sure I'm keeping the essay relevant.

Identifying material for the essay

With all your source material gathered together and organised, you now need to work through it reminding yourself of what is relevant to the essay. Again keep a pad handy, so that you can make a list of your sources with notes alongside about what you might use them for.

Look out for relevant arguments, concepts, authors, theories, evidence. A lot should already be marked up from when you did your reading. The point of this run through is to give yourself an overview of what you have gathered together, and to add a few notes reminding yourself how ideas link to each other.

> I read the question, break down the points I am going to write about, then go through my notes to identify which bits relate to the points I am writing about. By the time I start writing, my books have yellow stickies poking out everywhere.

Key points

As you are about to start writing an essay, take stock as follows:

- Review your overall writing strategy in the light of the time now available for writing the essay.
- Assemble all your source material and organise it so that you can find things.
- Skim through your sources marking up what you hope to use in your essay.

8.2.5   Getting ideas written down

You have already begun the process of writing ideas down, in the notes you have made. However, so far the emphasis has been on grasping what *other* writers have to say. Now you need to focus on what *you* are going to say. You don't want your essay to be just a rehash of what you have read. That would be boring for you and would not get you a good mark. And it wouldn't help you to understand the subject, or develop your writing skills. So, put your notes and books to one side and work at developing your *own* thoughts on how to approach the essay title.

> After a few days I usually write down all the things I think should be included in my essay, usually far too much, but I prefer this as I spend a lot of time editing it.

Revisiting the title

Having had the title in your head for a while, your ideas will have moved on. Look again at the words you highlighted and your notes about them. Do you want to highlight other words now, or revise your thinking about their implications? Try sketching some notes in answer to the title question without stopping to think about what you have read. Or try breaking down the question into sub-questions. Then just *write lots of thoughts relating to the title*, without worrying about what comes out. Write down points *for* and *against* – perhaps a whole sentence if one comes to you – and any *extra questions* that the essay title throws up.

My notes in Figure 8.1 are a sample of 'off the cuff' questions and ideas I might want to explore in writing the essay on Ellis. I just wrote them down as they came to me. They may not make much sense to you but no matter; I would only use them for a day or so, then throw them out.

> First I write down key words or phrases that spring to mind when reading the question. These include theories, example texts, ideas, etc. Then I elaborate on them and write paragraphs based on a rough plan of what topic should be where.

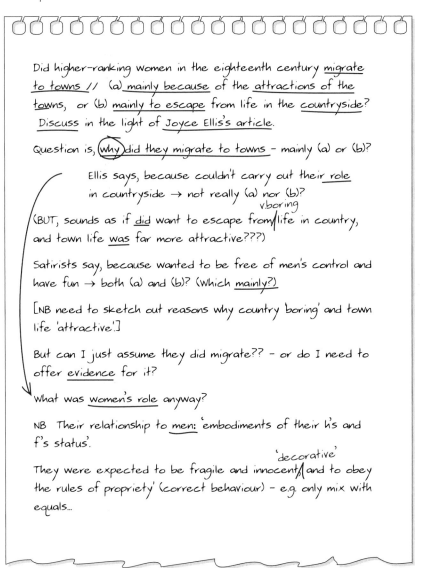

Figure 8.1 Sample of jottings related to the essay title

Pen and pad or computer?

As you can see, I made these notes by hand. I could have organised them as a mind map (see Chapter 5, Figure 5.6). Some people prefer to use the word processor's outliner instead. I tend to use both, note-pad and computer. Sometimes ideas seem to flow more creatively on paper. But the advantage of the outliner is being able to get the ideas down as you think of them and then move them around. Also, it forces you to organise points into a linear sequence, which is how you are going to have to write in the end. In fact, I often type a messy page of handwritten notes into the outliner so that I can sort out the mess before starting to write. It is extra work but it is much less time consuming than getting completely stuck later on or setting off in the wrong direction.

Brainstorming

Sketching out ideas quickly is known as brainstorming. You write fragments of thoughts as fast as you can, flitting from point to point, trying to avoid losing new thoughts while you are writing other ones out. The aim is to create a store of possible ideas.

> At the beginning of an essay I do brainstorming on the title of the essay to come up with ideas of what to write about. Then I do a sort of structural plan, of what, why and how – trying to answer all these questions. Don't know if it's the correct way but it works for me.

> After I've finished my reading I find that certain things tend to stick in my mind. I then have a brainstorming session where I write down absolutely every thing that I can.

By working fast and uncritically you get access to ideas you would perhaps never reach through more logical thinking. Your studies of the course texts will have set all kinds of thoughts churning away half-formed in your mind. Brainstorming aims to *trap* some of these ideas and fix them in writing, *outside* your head. There you can examine them, move them around, tidy them up and improve wording. But get plenty of words on paper before you start the tidying up. Thinking analytically and critically may dry up the flow of ideas. You want to start out with more ideas than you actually need, so that you can throw some away and be left with just the best.

> I try looking at things completely differently, taking the essay question and breaking it into as tiny bits as possible, and writing sentences and paragraphs relevant to them. Once I have all this down on paper I can sort out what I need in the essay and what I don't need.

The point of jotting notes before starting on the writing is to avoid the depressing experience of sitting in front of a blank screen with nothing to say.

> Why is it that I do all the reading, study the other materials, join in the online chat and when it comes to putting fingers to keyboard NOTHING happens?

Most of us, if we sit down and try to start typing an opening paragraph, soon run out of words. It is best not to begin with whole sentences. By busying yourself with jotting down notes you can get your thoughts flowing; then sometimes you will find that whole sentences come out fully formed, perhaps even running on into a paragraph that you can set aside to use later. So concentrate on getting down notes. Once you have some ideas in note form it is much easier to develop them into good sentences.

> I write it all in note form then change it round, I do this sometimes days apart as I seem to be able to keep it in my head and think about it when I am gardening or even when I am relaxing ... I don't think I will ever be able to sit down and write an essay just like that, but you seem to learn more doing it in stages, well I do ...

Box 8.1 Do your essays tend to be too short?

If you keep finding yourself falling short of the word requirements for essays, focus more effort on this note-jotting stage. Just keep writing ideas down, trying to come at the essay title from different angles and making links to different authors, theories or arguments. Remember that you have to *explain* your points fully, so that your reader understands you. You probably need to include more examples and show more carefully how your points connect with each other and to the essay title. Write down ideas for this too.

Key points

- If it helps, 'brainstorm' in a free and uninhibited way to get together some ideas you can work up. Generate more than you need, then throw some away.
- The quality of the essay you eventually produce will reflect the richness of the informal, scrappy notes you make at this preliminary stage.

8.2.6 Organising your material

Now you are ready to start thinking about *structure*. As you saw with the essays written by Philip and Hansa in Chapter 7, structure makes a big difference. Basically it involves:

See Chapter 7 Section 7.4, Essay structure

- going over your notes and grouping ideas together in clusters, then
- working out a sequence for those clusters.

Any kind of crude dividing up is useful to begin with. For example, you might start by separating your notes into points *for* the proposition in the title and points *against*. Next you decide which of these to take first in your essay and which second. Then you could break each of these two clusters into two or three sub-sections, and again decide in what order to take them.

See Chapter 5
Section 5.2.1, Notes
from reading

Using an outliner

This is where working onscreen with an outline view comes into its own. Outliners are designed specifically for creating plans for your writing. They give you complete freedom to move points around into different clusters. You can drag your points up or down the page to cluster them with other points. And you can 'promote' points by dragging them to the left, or 'demote' them under other points by dragging them to the right. For example, look at the notes I made in Chapter 5, Figure 5.2; at this stage, I would select the points that are relevant to the essay title.

This flexibility is a tremendous asset in trying out different ways of structuring your points. And you can keep saving your outline with a new name, then printing it off, so that you can compare different structures without worrying that you are messing up what is already done.

Working on paper

If, on the other hand, you prefer to work on paper, you could cut your notes into strips and sort these into clusters. Then you can look at each of the clusters and work out a sequence for the points within it – perhaps separating them into sub-clusters. You will then be in a position to sketch a rough outline plan. Number the headings and subheadings to help you keep track as you work on the essay. Alternatively, you can colour code your notes, or use index cards and group them together.

Simple but purposeful

Simpler is generally better when it comes to essay plans. Your essay will be easier to *write* if it has a simple structure and, equally important, your reader will find it easier to *read*.

> For a 1,500 word essay I aim for a 100–150 word introduction, then six paragraphs of similar lengths, then a final conclusion of approx 100 words.

The period when you are trying to forge a workable essay plan can be unsettling. The shape may take quite a time to emerge, as your thoughts slowly resolve themselves. When it does, it may be so simple that you wonder why it took you so long. However, simplicity is a sign that your thoughts have resolved themselves. Everything seems simple after you have thought of it.

Marking up your notes

Once you have sketched out a plan, you go back through your notes, labelling points according to where in the plan you think they fit.

> I try to plan my essay into paragraphs and next to every idea I write which para I think it should go into. I then have to leave it for a day to think it over in my head.

Leaving things out

As you plan your essay, you have to make hard choices. Which points will you put at the centre of your argument and which ones will you chop? You make your essay worse, not better, if you try to cram everything in. It is not a matter of how *much* you say, but how well the essay reads *as an argument*.

So if points don't fit, let them go. Don't worry about showing that you have read everything. You are simply presenting a sample of what you can do. In fact, however far you progress with your writing, you will *never* be able to include *everything* you want to say. All readers have limited time and patience. One of the greatest skills of writing lies in choosing what to say and what to leave out.

> ❝ Well, I was surprised last time to find I got a very good result by restricting myself to one area and exploring it thoroughly. ❞

Box 8.2   Do your essays tend to be over-long?

If you always write too many words, you need to be more ruthless in scaling down your ambitions at the planning stage. If your plans are too broad and complicated, your essay becomes very difficult to follow. And if you hurry through your points because of the word constraints, you don't provide enough explanation and evidence for what you say and your writing becomes cramped and impenetrable. Generally, a measured, well delivered explanation of a limited range of points makes for a better essay and is more enjoyable to write.

On the other hand, writing too much and then editing down can also produce good results. By trimming away all the excess, you can end up with a nice taut line of argument – as long as you don't grieve too much over all those butchered words.

Key points

- The planning stage is essential. It is at this point that your essay begins to acquire some coherence and force.
- Planning means sorting your points into clusters and then into a satisfying sequence.
- Your plan should lead you to a point where you can draw a conclusion which addresses the task in the essay title.

8.2.7   Drafting an answer

With your notes sorted and labelled according to your sketched plan, you are ready to start turning notes into sentences. You have decided *what* to try to say. Now you have to concentrate on *how* to say it so that a reader will be able to follow you.

Where to start?

You might start straight into your introduction to the essay, but sometimes it is better to start somewhere else. The introduction can be easier to write when you have seen what you're actually going to say.

> ❝ I used to get completely lost trying to start my essays with my introduction because I didn't know what to put in it. So I often start by writing the middle bits and expand it from there — finally organising it all into the right place and adding an introduction and a conclusion. ❞

However, it can be useful to write a quick sketch of an introduction just to get yourself into the right frame of mind for the first main section. Then you can come back later and work it up properly. Try out different approaches to see what works best for you.

A fluid approach

Try to work in a fluid, open-ended way, turning your notes into more fully explained points, then fleshing out a point a bit more if it seems to need it, or adding a word or two of explanation leading up to it to show where it's coming from. If you plod forward in a rigid, 'linear' fashion, progress tends to be slow and you easily get stuck. You need to be able to see beyond the sentence, to where it is leading.

> ❝ I expand my ideas into sentences, then split them into paragraphs if the ideas get complicated. I worry later about what it's doing to the essay structure. Once I have some ideas in sentences, I can look at whether I've answered the question. ❞

Build up from what you have already sketched out in your notes. Most people find it difficult to compose sentences straight out of their heads.

Reviewing as you go

You may prefer to work to the end of your essay before stopping, so that you don't get bogged down with the first few paragraphs. Or you may find it helpful to stop at the end of a section, print off what you have done and see how it's going. This helps you to switch to the role of your reader; to see whether you have said what you meant to say and whether your writing flows along reasonably well and the tone seems right. Could you make a few tweaks to improve things? Have you done enough explaining to get your points across? Would an example help? Are you remembering to make your points relevant to the essay title? Stopping regularly to review progress can be a good way to develop your writing style, allowing you to 'craft' your line of argument. However, if it discourages you, or slows you down too much because you keep refining the same few sentences, then get to the end before stopping to review.

Shut yourself away

Expressing newly learned ideas to your reader requires full concentration. You have to get yourself into the right frame of thinking. Then once you are into a flow of argument, you want to be able to push along until it runs out. If you keep having to stop and start you can end up doing a lot of mental work without having much to show for it. Do your best to cut yourself off from distractions whenever you are drafting an essay. And try not to make up distractions of your own.

> It's amazing how tidy my house suddenly gets when the essay deadline is closing in.

Taking breaks

On the other hand, do allow yourself breaks. It is very hard to stay productively focused for long spells. You need time to clear your mind, then re-gather your thoughts. Just make sure you achieve a reasonable amount between breaks. It is also good to spread the writing over several sessions. You can usually arrive at a more balanced perspective.

> I go to the pub, gym, a friend's house or just downstairs for a cup of tea or something ... just to relax my mind and reflect on the point I am trying to put across.

Key points

- Start drafting by working from your essay plan and turning your notes into sentences.
- Don't start with the introduction if you find it easier or more productive to start elsewhere.
- Work fluidly, going back over what you have written and reshaping as you go. But also keep moving on. Don't work obsessively on the early sections.
- Cut yourself off from distractions, but take breaks from time to time.

8.2.8   Reviewing, revising and polishing

When you finally reach the end of your draft essay, print it off, put it to one side and take a break. Then, when you are ready for another session – on another day if possible – come back to it and read it through. Then you can look at your essay from a greater distance and more as your reader will see it. Even if you were reviewing and editing as you went along, you need to take a look at the whole essay and check that the essentials are there.

Reviewing

It is generally easier to work on a printed copy of the essay, marking up changes in pen. As you read through, check for the following.

- Do your sentences work? Does the 'sense' move along reasonably smoothly? A good check is to read it out loud. If you find you stumble, or have to pause over the meaning, then probably you have a sentence that is too long or has something important missing (such as a verb, or a link to the previous sentence).

> I always look at the drafts of my essays to see where points can be clarified by use of more concise or appropriate language.

- Do your divisions into paragraphs work? Do the breaks seem to come at the right places, where the focus of the discussion shifts?
- Have you given enough explanation and illustration to enable your reader to understand what your argument is all about?
- Have you provided enough evidence of the claims you make in argument?
- Does your argument make sense as you move from point to point? Have you signalled the main moves clearly to your reader? Is it obvious, as you start each new paragraph, why it is relevant to the question?
- Does your introduction set things rolling effectively? Does it lead your reader from the title to the next paragraph?
- And, most important of all, does your conclusion answer the question in the title? Look back at the words you highlighted in the title. Have you addressed the implications of each of them?

As you read through and mark up changes, think about whether you want to reorganise parts of the essay. Reviewing can be a highly creative process, through which you come to understand your own argument more clearly and get new insights into how to make your writing work better. You learn a lot about the way ideas work in your discipline as you think about different ways to say things.

Activity 8.2

You can practise reviewing your work by digging out a past essay. Review it by asking all the questions listed above. Are there changes you would make to the essay now? Can you see how to reorganise any of your points or paragraphs?

Revising and polishing

Now you need to go through the essay making all the changes you have marked up. It is a good idea to save a back-up copy, so that you can make changes freely without worrying that you will mess things up. You can then go back to your earlier version if you don't feel happy with a change. And be sure to run your word processor's spelling and grammar checks.

Entering all your marked up changes can be surprisingly time consuming, especially if you think of new improvements as you go along. But it is also very satisfying to work your writing up into a more polished form. It is an excellent learning process that helps your long-term writing development.

Referencing

Since one of the purposes of an essay is to show your grasp of the course you are studying, you are bound to draw heavily on the ideas of academic writers. But as well as introducing a selection of relevant ideas, you have to give details of where they come from. You should always provide a reference for every document or article you work from. Then, if they want to, your readers can go and find it to check whether you have represented the author's views fairly and accurately, or just to read it because it sounds interesting.

At the points in your essay when you discuss an author's work or ideas, you must include a reference to it. Sometimes this is called a citation: e.g. '(Ellis, 1995)'; sometimes a reference is made in a footnote. When you quote an author's words or refer to a particular part of the text − a table, for example − or paraphrase an author's argument quite closely, you must include page numbers as well: e.g. '(Ellis, 1995, p. 23)'.

You must also compile a list of all the references you make in your writing, or a bibliography, and include it at the end of the essay − giving full details of each of the sources. You have seen this reference many times in the book, for example:

> Ellis, J. (1995) 'On the Town: Women in Augustan England', *History Today*, vol. 45, no. 12, pp. 20−7.

As I've said, there are different ways of presenting references. The rules vary from one subject area to another and from one institution to another. You must make sure to present them in the way required. So check your university website, or ask your department or the student support services. It is worth doing this early on, because once you get into the habit of referencing it becomes quite routine. But remember, however you set the references out, you should always include as *much* information as possible since the point is to help your reader find the article, book or website easily.

At this stage, then, when your essay is written, you must go through it checking that you have included a reference whenever one is needed. As you come to each reference, make sure there is a corresponding entry in your list of References, or your Bibliography, at the end of the essay, which gives the full details of each source. It can be a finicky business checking all your references and getting them right, but it improves the presentation of your essay a lot. And you will gain credit for a well-referenced essay.

Key points

- In an essay you have to work with other people's ideas. However, you are expected to *acknowledge* where the ideas come from − to say 'as Ellis argues', giving a citation in the text, '(Ellis, 1995, p. 23)', or reference in a footnote.

- You must also provide the full details of your sources in a References list or Bibliography at the end of the essay. When your essay in is draft form, you must check through all your references.

Layout

Take a look at how your essay is laid out on the page. Is it clear and easy to read? Your university or department almost certainly issues guidelines on layout. But in the absence of other guidance it is best to go for plain, simple and clear. Don't use fancy fonts. Use a font size of 11 or 12 point for the main text, unless you have a reason to do otherwise. Stick to black print on a white background. Only use italics where useful, or required, and use bold formatting very sparingly. You may be expected to double space the lines.

Make sure the title is written at the top of the first page, and that it is the same, word for word, as the one you were given. Put your name and the course title or code in a header, so that they appear on every page. You could also put the date in a footer. Number the pages and set generous margins. If you have to submit the essay on paper, print on just one side of the sheet.

Proof read the essay, submit it, and move on

Print the essay off one more time and take a last look through, proof reading it. Make any required tweaks. Then hand your essay in or send it off electronically. There comes a point when you need to get on with the rest of the course and the rest of your life. If you have given an essay a decent shot in the time you have available that is all that's required. Now give yourself a treat.

 I always panic after sending off my essay, wishing I had gone over it one more time. I just have to remember that it's the same for everybody else. You could go on forever.

> ### Key points
>
> - The final stage of reviewing and revising your essay makes a vital contribution to producing a readable, coherent, well-argued and well-presented piece of work.
> - You also need to check your spelling and grammar, the references and page layout to make your essay look as good as it really is.
> - Although time consuming, this is an important part of the learning process because you really get to grips with working out how to express an argument in your subject area.
> - Don't keep revising for too long. Do a reasonable job, then move on.

8.2.9   An overview of the eight stages

Having considered this eight-stage approach to writing in such detail, you can get an overview of the whole sequence in Table 8.1. The second column summarises what you do to complete each stage; the third outlines the mental processes involved and indicates how these contribute towards producing a high-quality essay. So the table both reminds you what to do and explains how the writing process works.

Table 8.1   The eight stages of essay writing

Stage		What you do	What it contributes
1	Thinking about the essay title	Highlight key words and make notes about them.	Focuses your attention on what you are being asked to do.
2	Planning the writing process	Plan how you will cover the reading and make the time.	Keeps you in control of the writing process, so you cover all aspects.

Stage		What you do	What it contributes
3	Studying the course content	Highlight and make notes of essay-relevant material.	Gives your studies a creative edge, as you make links between the essay title and your course.
4	Taking stock before you start writing	Update plans, gather together essay material and get an overview of it all.	Gets your mind sharply task focused and loaded up with all the relevant ideas.
5	Getting ideas written down	Refocus on the title, then 'brainstorm' to get lots of ideas in writing.	Gets ideas out of your head and onto the page where you can examine them and work them up.
6	Organising your material	Group your notes, then sequence them to create an essay plan.	Helps you to arrive at a structured line of argument for your essay.
7	Drafting an answer	Turn your notes into sentences and paragraphs: a dialogue with your reader.	Translates your notes from 'private' into 'public' language, and from vague links to explicit argument.
8	Reviewing and polishing	Read through, revise, proof read and add finishing touches.	Turns raw potential into an attractive read.

The value of breaking writing down into stages

As everyone who has tried writing knows, it is easy to get stuck. You sit and wonder what you are trying to say and how to get yourself moving again. So, it is enormously helpful to think of the challenge of writing as a set of smaller, more manageable tasks, which you can tackle one at a time. Writing becomes less of a mystery and more of an ordinary activity in which you make a finished product by following a sequence of practical steps. Approaching writing in stages also helps you to think about it more *strategically*, because the process has a clearer shape. You can *plan* each stage and try to make sensible use of your time. And should you become stuck, you can switch to a different stage then come back later.

Overlap between the stages

Although it is helpful to be able to think about the stages of writing separately, it is important to recognise that they are not completely separate or rigidly sequenced. Indeed, they overlap and are best tackled flexibly.

- As you plan, you may suddenly think of another source to look at, or some notes you made that you could use after all.

- When you are writing the first draft, you may become aware that your essay plan needs to be altered.
- When you are reviewing your draft essay, you may remember a question you jotted in your notes which could be worked up to use in the introduction.

Since the stages of writing impact on each other, you need to move back and forth between them. No stage is entirely complete until the whole is complete.

Becoming a more powerful writer

If you are to fulfil your potential as a writer you need to give careful thought to each of these stages of writing. You should experiment with different approaches to them, reflect on your successes and failures and refine your strategy. Your writing becomes more powerful as you learn how to blend this sequence of activities together – how much time to give to each stage, which ones you are particularly good at and where you need to work at developing your skills. You don't worry about whether you have flair or genius. You simply think of writing in practical workaday terms and get stuck in, gradually building up your control over the whole process. Powerful and original writing is achieved not through inspiration but by working to a realistic plan within well-defined constraints. Originality is something you happen upon, rather than achieve by seeking it out. What you need is a framework within which you can see a way to take the next step forward. The control this gives enables your writing powers to develop.

Key points

- Being aware of distinct stages of essay writing greatly increases the options open to you and gives you more control over the writing process.
- Treat essay writing as a practical task, not a mysterious search for inspiration.
- It is not a one-session job. Ideally it should be spread over several days.
- Don't simply sit at your keyboard and begin to type; do a lot of your work before you start the writing proper.
- Break essay writing into stages, so that you can tackle it a bit at a time rather than face the whole task at once.
- Work flexibly, moving back and forth between the stages as necessary and moving on if you get stuck.
- Build up your writing ability by developing your strategies and skills within each of the stages.

8.3 Expressing ideas in writing

If you have already made notes of what you want to say, it might seem that writing ought to be straightforward. Not so. You have to take the scraps of ideas in your notes and turn them into whole sentences and paragraphs. You have to give examples, to illustrate to your reader what you are talking about, and also include supporting evidence. And you have to lead your reader carefully step by step from the question in the title through the points you want to make, showing how they follow on from one another. So writing is quite a formal, task-driven form of communication, but it is also one in which meaning has to flow, otherwise your reader will be lost.

Yet so much is undefined at the outset. Where are you going to start from? What will your opening words be? They set the tone for what follows, but you don't yet know what follows. It is a tough challenge. In this short section I outline some approaches I have found helpful in turning half-formed ideas into readable sentences.

8.3.1 Finding your voice

It is hard to get meanings across to an absent reader with the clarity and force you can achieve in conversation with people you know. You sense what you *want* to say but when the words come out on paper and you read them through you can see that you haven't conveyed what you intended. The words are there to be read, but they come across as lifeless and dull. There seems to be no 'voice' speaking them.

One approach to developing a writing voice is simply to make yourself write on a regular basis in order to build up practice at occupying the role of writer. Peter Elbow, who has led writing programmes at a number of American universities and colleges, advocates a technique he calls 'freewriting'.

Box 8.3   Freewriting

'To do a freewriting exercise, simply force yourself to write without stopping for ten minutes. Sometimes you will produce good writing, but that's not the goal. Sometimes you will produce garbage, but that's not the goal either. You may stay on one topic, you may flip repeatedly from one to another: it doesn't matter ... Speed is not the goal, though sometimes the process revs you up. If you can't think of anything to write, write about how that feels or repeat over and over 'I have nothing to write' ... if you get stuck in the middle of a sentence or thought, just repeat the last word or phrase till something comes along. The only point is to keep writing ... There are lots of goals of freewriting, but they are best served if, while you are doing it, you accept this single, simple, mechanical goal of simply not stopping.' (Elbow, 1998, p. 13)

Elbow's idea is that you write continuously for a short burst, about *anything* that comes into your head, without concern for quality or being read by others (a bit like brainstorming except that you concentrate on keeping a flow of words going rather than on producing ideas). When you have finished the writing you put it away, and on subsequent days you do some more. Then a few days later you come back and read over what you wrote looking for places where you feel that your voice breaks through – where your writing achieves some force – possibly a phrase, a sentence, or a whole paragraph. (You might exchange samples of freewriting with another student, so that you can search for each other's voice.) Over a period of time, says Elbow, a number of changes will come about.

■ Sheer accumulation of practice at 'being in the writing situation' will make you feel more comfortable about writing to an audience and will take the awkwardness and formality out of your writing style.

■ The freedom to write 'anything' will release you from the constraints which normally cramp your style, and make your writing more open and creative.

■ The repeated searching through your words to find your 'voice' sharpens your perception of when you are writing powerfully and when you are not.

■ You become more aware of how to set yourself up to break through to an authentic writing voice.

8.3.2   Recognising the openness of writing

Sometimes it feels as though you are searching for the 'right' way to say something. But, actually, there is no perfect way to make your points. Every piece you compose could be written in many other ways – some, perhaps, more interesting and clearer than others. Yet, at the moment you start to write, your imagination tends to be restricted to seeing only one way ahead. So it can help to sketch different outline plans, or to try out two or more versions of a particular paragraph, or several ways of opening or closing your essay. Don't feel you are looking for the 'right' way to say things. Work in an open, experimental way, trying out different approaches. And be content that whichever you choose to go with it is just one of many approaches, none of which is the 'correct' one. Thinking this way helps you to feel less imprisoned inside a particular style of writing. It emphasises your powers of expression and the wealth of possibilities that lie in front of you when you write.

What you need is an open attitude to your writing, which allows you to be *critical* in judging what has worked and what has not, but also *comfortable* in knowing, after you have made your choices, that though there are other ways you could have said things, it is not worth tinkering for too long. Don't hover in anguish over what you might possibly write better. There are so many other interesting things to write about. Just play around with some possibilities, make your choices and move on.

8.3.3   Finding fluency

If, at the beginning of your essay, you try to compose formal sentences one after another, you are asking a lot of yourself. You will find yourself struggling to get started and, when you do, your words may seem ungainly. And though you go back over and over, changing your words, each new version may seem no better. To avoid such frustrating and morale-crushing experiences, and also to find a less stilted style, you need to take the pressure off yourself. You need a more free-flowing way to sketch out some dialogue with your reader. Box 8.4 describes what I do.

Box 8.4   Generating a flow

When I get stuck I leave my keyboard, go and sit in my 'reading and ideas' armchair, with a board to rest on, and sketch scraps of ideas on paper. I write freely, knowing that I'm going to revise later and I don't bother at all how it looks. I write quickly and restlessly – starting on different ideas, switching things around, moving on – until something starts to flow. Then I go with the flow, though I'm always ready to branch off when another thought strikes. I just draw a line out from wherever I am to a space on the page and carry on sketching out the new idea. Then I go back and see whether I want to carry on from where I was. In a way, it is more like the loose-knit, unpredictable process of having an informal conversation. And it's a bit like freewriting, but more focused and task-oriented.

When I feel I have enough ideas to work with, or just feel ready for a change, I go back to the keyboard and switch into my more formal 'composing' mode, working up the scraps, pulling them into shape and making them flow in an orderly and controlled way.

Trying to write polished prose straight off cranks up the pressure, stifles your creativity and blocks the flow of your words. Those mental blocks use up time far less productively than giving yourself time to play around with ideas and forms of words. You need to create space to think and get a written dialogue going.

8.3.4   Reading aloud

It can be very helpful to hear what your words sound like when you read them out loud. You get a new angle on how well the sense flows through your sentences. In fact, if you know someone (another student, a friend or family member) who is prepared to listen, reading to another person can help you develop your *sense of audience* and your writing *voice*. It doesn't necessarily matter whether the listener fully understands or is able to comment on what you have written. In the process of speaking the words to someone else you will *hear for yourself* which passages work best and which don't come across as you intended. And you may also spot typos or expressive flaws that can be easily corrected.

We all tend to feel reticent about exposing our writing to other people, particularly when we are writing about a subject that is new to us. However, you are writing to be read by somebody, somewhere. If you can summon up the nerve to 'be there' as your message is received by someone, you gain fresh insight into the nature of communicating through writing.

8.3.5   Onscreen or on paper?

I find that writing on a pad and composing on a computer work in quite different ways, so I do both. For more routine writing I find word processing fine on its own. But if the writing is challenging and creative, I need to switch to more informal sketching on a pad. After a while I go back to the word processor and use the outliner to tidy up my jottings. I make a lot of use of the outliner in the early stages of writing, but later I stick mainly to the print layout view. For longer pieces with subheadings, I always have the 'document map' open at the left of the screen so that I can see the whole structure and go straight to specific sections when I need to check something. However, having asked others, I know that people work differently. We all have to find out what works for us. The point is to experiment. If you want your writing to develop, you have to take a reflective, creative approach. Try using the facilities your word processor offers, but also try different ways of working with pen and paper.

8.3.6   Separating note making from writing

To be able to write fluently and convincingly you need to be able to give all your attention to 'talking' to your reader. That is why you need to have made notes of what you want to say before you start drafting whole sentences and paragraphs. If you are thinking up *content* at the same time as trying to *address your reader*, you will almost certainly do one or the other badly. Either your points will be weak and disconnected, or your language will be insufficiently clear and expressive. Worst of all, you will grind to a halt. Separating the stage of generating ideas from that of composing sentences is a key way of avoiding these problems.

Key points

- As you work to develop your writing voice it can be helpful to make yourself write regularly, using a technique such as 'freewriting'.
- It is important to relax about trying to say things the 'right' way – and to recognise, instead, that you can say things well in a number of ways.
- You need to develop ways of getting your ideas and words flowing together, by working informally and creatively, rather than trying to compose high-quality sentences straight off.
- You can help to hear for yourself what works, and develop your sense of audience, by reading your work aloud.
- Work flexibly. Try out different places and different writing aids to keep your writing flowing.
- Addressing your audience in writing takes all your powers of concentration. You need to have worked out the main ideas for the essay before you tackle this challenge.

8.4   Making your essay flow

In Chapter 7 we looked at how two students made a very brief essay flow. We saw how they used 'link words' and phrases to carry the meaning forward from paragraph to paragraph and sentence to sentence. Now we will look for further tricks of the writing trade by examining how Joyce Ellis, an experienced writer, carries a more complex argument through a longer piece of writing. Again we return to her article, but this time focusing on her writing technique rather than the content.

8.4.1   Link words

The first thing I want to look at is how Ellis makes her argument flow.

Activity 8.3

Turn to the Ellis article again for a few minutes (pp. 312–15) and look at the way she makes links between paragraphs 3–8. How does the sense get carried along from one paragraph to the next? Pick out the words that you think are significant in achieving this.

I underlined the following words.

Paragraph 4:   '*This* ...'

Paragraph 5:   '*With*', '*however*', '*these* tasks'

Paragraph 6:   No link word at the start; 'Women, *however* ...' (beginning of second sentence).

Paragraph 7:   '*Even if* ...'

Paragraph 8:   'Towns, *in contrast,* ...'

Ellis begins paragraph 4 with the word 'This', which refers back directly to what she has just said at the end of the previous paragraph (i.e. 'female behaviour was ... dysfunctional in a rural setting'). She goes on to say, 'This [dysfunction] was perhaps most obvious in the case of women from the higher ranks of society ...'. So the meaning flows from paragraph 3 to 4 as Ellis takes up the story of these women's changing role, which in fact continues up to the end of paragraph 5. (Check this for yourself.) The connections between paragraphs 4 and 5, in the middle of this account, are more complicated. Paragraph 5 begins, 'With an increasing wealth and sophistication of society, however, many of these tasks were taken over by professionals ...'. '*With* ...' suggests a continuing story (or, history, flowing on from paragraph 4), but the '*however*' that follows this opening phrase signals a significant *change* in these women's role. '*These*' tasks (another reference back to what was explained in paragraph 4) were now carried out by other people. This is a very artful and economical series of links I'd say, which imply processes of both continuity and change.

There is no link word or phrase between paragraphs 5 and 6 at all. However, Ellis doesn't need one because she simply repeats the last word of paragraph 5 at the start of the next. Notice that a change of topic is indicated part-way through, though, with 'Women, *however* ...'. So in the space of some five lines Ellis has managed to change the subject from women to men and back again without ever leaving us confused.

'*Even if* a carriage was available ...' at the start of paragraph 7 suggests a *qualification* to the claim made at the end of the previous paragraph, about women's lack of mobility. And it also takes Ellis neatly on to another aspect of the same topic (the dangers involved in travel). She begins a new paragraph at that point precisely because it is a *different* aspect of the topic.

Finally, at the start of paragraph 8, 'Towns, *in contrast* ...' signals a complete change of subject.

In this way, Ellis manages to introduce and discuss different aspects of her subject while sustaining a thread of meaning throughout, which the reader is able to follow. She uses many words that show how what she is saying follows on from a previous point; whether it adds something, qualifies it, or contrasts with it. She links *analysis* in paragraph 3 with a developing (explanatory) *narrative* in paragraphs 4 and 5, to *further analysis* in paragraph 6 and *description* and *illustration* in paragraph 7 – and so on. As a result, reading her article seems fairly effortless (from the second page at least). That's because *she* is doing the work of 'steering' us, her readers, through the meaning of her text.

Box 8.5   Breaking rules?

It used to be a 'rule' never to start a sentence with 'and' or 'but'. So is Ellis breaking the rules in her second sentence in paragraph 3? The rule can actually be a useful one when you are not very confident about sentence structures. You may be tempted to leave half-formed sentences lying around, hoping that an 'and' or a 'but' will connect them up to something.

In formal terms these two words are conjunctions, which are placed between equal items within a sentence to link them together. Strictly, they should not be used at the boundaries of a sentence. On the other hand, they are so useful as economical devices for carrying meaning over from one sentence to another that it is often worth breaking the formal rule, provided you know what you are doing. 'But' is particularly useful because it is such a quick way of saying 'I am now going to balance something against what I have just been saying'.

'Link words' are the words you use to show the *relationship* between what you have just said and what you are going on to say. Here are some examples.

Table 8.2   Link words

Link words	What they signify
'and', 'also', 'as well as'	you are adding something of a similar kind to what you have just said
'but', 'however', 'although', 'on the other hand	you are about to say something different
'because', 'since'	you are going to explain what you have just said
'for example', 'for instance'	you are about to illustrate the point made
'so', 'therefore'	you are going to conclude an argument and draw out its significance.

Of course, there are many more words of these kinds (including that 'of course', which suggests 'I don't think I need to explain any further because no doubt you get the idea').

Your readers cannot see into your mind. They may not be able to see connections between points that seem perfectly obvious to you. An argument weaves a sequence of points together in an intricate set of relationships. Words like these show how the relationships are meant to work. They show how your readers are meant to understand what you say – they help your readers 'follow' your meaning *as they read*. So you should use them often.

Key point

A writer carries a *thread of meaning* through a piece of writing by using link words and phrases that take you on from sentence to sentence and one paragraph to the next. These words show you how to approach each stage of the argument, given what has been said previously.

8.4.2   Signposting

Some of the links words we have just looked at serve a signposting function as well. For example, 'This' at the start of paragraph 4 connects up with what Ellis has just been talking about (the reason for women's migration) and at the same time launches the argument off in a different direction (an account of women's changing role). 'Towns, in contrast ...' clearly signposts another stage of the argument. At other times, Ellis uses a signposting phrase to pull points together: 'All the evidence indicates that ...' in paragraph 1, for instance. And in the last two paragraphs of the article she signals a summary of what she has been saying with 'Although ..., on the whole ...'. This is followed by the suggestion of a final reckoning in the 'And yet ...' of the concluding paragraph.

Box 8.6 The need for signposts

In an essay you are talking your reader through an argument. In order to follow your train of thought the reader has to know what direction you are headed in and why, and what questions and issues to hold in mind. Readers have their *own* trains of thought, which they are likely to follow in preference to yours unless you keep them in close touch with what you are doing. To maintain the thread of argument for the reader you have to keep signalling what is going on.

As we have seen, one way of doing that is to use link words and phrases to pass meaning from one sentence to another. Another is to use *signposting phrases* which indicate where you have reached in the development of your argument: 'Before discussing X we must ask question Y', or 'having considered the arguments against, we should now ...', or 'a final set of issues we must take into account is ...'.

Some phrases perform both these functions at the same time. An important essay-writing skill is to have a good repertoire of words and phrases you can call on to do these jobs for you.

But you don't have to place a dutiful signpost on *everything* you do. It can be overdone and become boring to read. In the end, you have to make judgements about how much signposting your reader will find helpful. But remember that it is seldom as obvious to your reader as it is to you where your argument is leading.

Key point

Signposting is reminding your reader from time to time where you have reached in the argument and indicating the direction you are taking next.

8.4.3 Sentence and paragraph lengths

A further device writers can use to signal the unfolding of their argument is to play around with the way their words are grouped together in sentences and the sentences grouped into paragraphs.

When we examined students' essays in Chapter 7, I pointed out the advantages of aiming at short sentences whenever possible. However, there are also advantages in *varying* the lengths of sentences in order to shift the rhythm of the essay in places and maintain the reader's interest. Ellis, for example, writes fairly long sentences on the whole, so the occasional short ones have a rather dramatic effect: 'What women sought in the towns, the satirists argued, was freedom from male control' in paragraph 3, for instance; or, in paragraph 6, 'Unfortunately, well-born women were much less mobile than men'. Short, punchy sentences such as these can be used particularly effectively in the introductory and concluding sections of your essay. But you will probably need to use longer sentences when you are explaining or illustrating the main points of your argument.

Similarly, you can vary the *number* of sentences in your paragraphs to alter the texture of the writing. If you look at paragraphs 5 and 6 of the Ellis article, you'll see that they are quite a bit shorter than the surrounding paragraphs. It is significant that they contain the two underlying planks of Ellis's argument about the 'dysfunctional' role of women in the countryside; respectively, the way their role became reduced, and the demands that 'propriety' made on these women. Just as with the short sentences, they stand out from their surroundings and pack more punch.

Paragraphs are clusters of sentences in which you normally discuss *a single* aspect of the topic, or one main theme. In other words, paragraphs often mark those points in your argument when the focus of your attention shifts. Each one should have its own job of work to do for your essay. And you should avoid making them *very* long. Because paragraphing is also a means of signposting the direction your argument is taking, readers will get lost if the signs are too far apart or are confused by a mixture of themes.

Activity 8.4

Having looked closely at Ellis's writing, you could now look at one or two of your own past essays to find patterns in your use of link words, signposting, sentence and paragraph lengths. Do you use links and signposts often enough? How long are most of your sentences? Do they, and your paragraphs, vary much in length?

Key point

Developing an effective writing style is partly a matter of playing around with the effects you can achieve by using sentences and paragraphs of varying length and structure. By changing the tempo you can keep the focus of your reader's attention right where you want it.

In this section we have been looking at how to guide your reader through your essay. You pick them up in your introduction, by getting hold of their attention and starting a train of thought. Then, in the main body of the essay, you divide what you want to say into segments and lead your reader from section to section. Finally, you draw together the ideas you have been presenting and try to show the reader what has been accomplished.

8.5   The experience of writing

Few people feel blasé about writing. Producing a carefully composed piece tends to be an intense experience that not everyone can talk about comfortably. Why should writing evoke strong feelings? And why is it sometimes difficult to discuss those feelings with others who also experience them?

8.5.1 Revealing yourself

As skills go, writing is a special case. Communicating with others is fundamental to our lives – unlike skills such as juggling or ice dancing. What's more, an ability to communicate well tends to be associated with perceptions of how intelligent you are. Revealing in public a lack of talent at juggling is not too much of a threat, whereas revealing lack of ability to express yourself in writing is a much more 'personal' thing. But how would you know whether you have the ability to learn to write well? How much practice do you get? Have you had any training in it? And how much honest, helpful feedback have you had?

8.5.2 By what standards do you judge yourself?

In modern life we are surrounded by the printed word. The impression is created of a world full of people who find writing easy. It seems almost shameful to be weak at it. It's a bit like those first driving lessons when you are surrounded by drivers speeding confidently about, breezing through roundabouts, parking with inches to spare. Unskilled driving is such a 'public' display of incompetence, as you crunch through the gears in the middle of the road with a queue of people behind you. It's almost impossible to imagine that all those other people went through the same humiliation themselves once. Similarly, in your studies you can't imagine that others around you have been through the same struggle to find adequate words and string them together coherently.

With writing the situation is made worse by the fact that what you see in print is generally *published* writing. In other words, most of what you read is written by *experienced* writers, *selected* for their skill at writing. You seldom read the words of ordinary writers who muddle along as best they can. You see mainly the output of writers who are the equivalent of rally drivers. So when, as an inexperienced writer, you read back over your own words, what are you comparing them with? Almost inevitably your writing looks weak in the light of the comparisons you are in a position to make. This is one reason for feeling shy about your writing and for doubting that you have talent. If you compare yourself only with professionals, you are bound to feel inadequate.

8.5.3 Writing: private or public?

Although writing can feel like a very private activity, it is also, paradoxically, intrinsically public. It is private in that you do it alone, locked in your own thoughts, guided by your own rituals and with very little idea of how other people cope with its challenges; yet it is public in that you write to be read by others, perhaps strangers. Indeed, pieces of writing can become a kind of public property, discussed by all and sundry with very little reference back to the writer. There is a wide gulf between the very private world in which writing is done and the public world of reading and discussing. So *is* writing private or public?

It may seem almost indecent to hand over your words to the gaze of others, who know nothing of what went into writing them. The thoughts that floated in your mind brimmed with potential. Their possibilities lay ahead. Then the act of putting them on paper 'fixed' a particular formulation and destroyed all other possibilities. Putting ideas in print is a fateful act. Can words on a page ever live up to your hopes for them? And what of the brazen act of showing them to others, who know nothing of the great intentions behind them, only what they see?

And yet you *do* want the words to be read. What would be the point otherwise? With writing, that is the great tension. You *want* the world to read what you write – but at the same time you don't want *anyone* to read it *yet* because it is so personal and might not be understood as you meant it.

Obviously, you don't write an *essay* with 'the world' in mind as your audience. Yet these contradictory impulses arise: an impulse to express your thoughts, accompanied by a desire to keep them to yourself; a feeling of vulnerability and yet an urge to go on. Writing is a process that gives rise to intensely ambivalent feelings – surges of enthusiasm and feelings of satisfaction one minute, waves of doubt and self-criticism the next.

8.5.4   Coping with criticism

One particularly ambivalent moment is when you get your essay back with comments from your teacher. Many students take a quick look at the *grade*, then shut the essay away in a drawer to 'look at later'. Some find it difficult *ever* to get round to taking the essay out again to see what the teacher wrote. Comments patiently thought out and written down are left unread – too personal and discomforting to face. This rare and costly feedback waits for a future day when it will have lost all relevance. Why?

It is easy to take comments on your writing personally, as though you are being told you are stupid, ill informed or inarticulate. It is difficult to stand back and see essay writing as a process of skill development, in which you benefit from doing tightly defined exercises followed by some detailed commentary on your performance. Each piece you write may feel like a personal statement on an issue of importance – not just a process of going through your paces in front of a 'coach'. Your teachers, rather than seeking enlightenment on the subject of the essay, will be looking out for quite specific signs of the extent of your progress, so as to assist your development. They will focus on what you have *written*, not you as a person. And, furthermore, they are likely to be charitable, doing their best to follow your argument and see the best in it.

But the relationship between you and your tutor breaks the usual conventions of politeness between adults. By sidestepping convention and entering into very direct communications, a teacher gives you the chance to try out new ideas and new techniques and find out whether they work. Teachers may sometimes sound very critical in the frankness of their comments, but that is simply the way this special kind of relationship works. It allows them to 'tell you straight' when your point doesn't come across, when your sequencing of ideas is confusing or when your argument is unconvincing. You are then in a position to work out how to overcome these weaknesses.

Receiving direct and detailed comments on your writing is a privilege, but not an easy one to appreciate. Intensely personal feelings about your writing and the unusually direct nature of your relationship with your teacher make this a sensitive matter. However, it is important to put the relationship into perspective: to learn to live with the irritation caused by criticisms which seem to miss your point, to be glad of the detailed crossing out of your words and substitution of others, and to be able to pay close attention to subtle nuances in the alterations suggested. Would you want a teacher who is like an indulgent parent, admiring everything you write? (Well, you might – but would it do you much good?) To learn how to cope with the academic world you have to brace yourself for whatever comes from teachers, recognising the special nature of the relationship. Most do their best to be civilised and considerate in their remarks, but that will not prevent you from feeling annoyed and misunderstood at times. These are feelings you have to come to terms with in teaching–learning relationships.

Why not leave your tutor's comments aside for a few days and then come back to them in a constructive frame of mind?

Activity 8.5

Look again at one or two of your past essays, this time focusing on your tutor's comments. Think hard about them. What was your tutor suggesting might improve your future writing?

8.5.5   Routine hardships

The other key reason why writing is an intense experience is that it is just plain difficult.

Open-endedness

For one thing, the outcome you are aiming for is *ill defined*. When you paint a door, you know pretty well what you want to achieve and how to set about it. But when you write an essay, perhaps the only thing you can be certain of is that the end product will be different from what you had in mind. Because of this open-endedness, it takes hard thinking at the outset to establish a 'frame of reference' within which to tackle the question. Then you have to continue thinking hard as you develop a line of argument within that frame. This continuing struggle to forge a way ahead gives rise to feelings of frustration and exhaustion at one end of the scale, and satisfaction and elation at the other. So your mood can swing quite sharply as you write.

Then there is the general feeling of uncertainty – an absence of solid meanings to hold on to. Since we all depend on being able to make sense of our surroundings, it is intensely uncomfortable to be faced with sustained uncertainty. That is why the writing experience has a restless quality. You keep wanting to get up and do something else – something more solid and routine. In fact, it may help to switch back and forth between writing and routine chores, to give yourself a break from the pressures of uncertainty.

Being too close to see

When you are in the thick of wrestling with a line of argument and trying to construct intelligible sentences, your attention is so focused that it is very difficult to judge what your words will convey to someone approaching them fresh and without emotional involvement. All you can do is press on and hope for the best. It is, perhaps, only after weeks or even months that you can come back and read your work from sufficient 'distance' to experience it from the point of view of others.

Nausea

According to Peter Elbow (1998, pp. 173–5), 'nausea' will always hit you at some point – a feeling of revulsion as you read your own words. It may come right at the start as the words leave your finger tips, or some time later when you come back to re-read your work, or at any time in between. He says it is a reaction endemic to the process of writing. If you escape it earlier, expect it later.

Keeping going

Finally, essay writing is a long, drawn-out process. With so many stages to it, you have to develop a certain stamina to write regularly. It is tedious at some times and disappointing at others. Consequently it draws on your inner resources of will power and determination, as well as the courage to face possible disappointment. Writing is great when it 'comes right', but that moment can be a long time coming.

Putting the whole picture together it is clear that writing essays is a particularly challenging experience. In the course of it you may feel:

- frustrated when stuck
- uncertain when you can't see where you are heading
- bored when it goes on and on
- despairing when you never seem to have enough time
- repelled when you read what you have written
- disheartened when you come up against the limitations of your abilities
- irritated when you read your tutor's comments.

But don't let me put you off! These feelings *will* come to you at some time or other and, since writing is so private, *you need to know* that you are not alone in experiencing them. If you are ready to cope then you will still be around for the good times.

Why, you may ask, do sane people write essays at all? For the same reason they willingly choose to do other fairly gruelling things – because it is also *intensely rewarding*. No other experience in your studies is likely to be more satisfying than having completed an essay and handed it in, nor more elating than finding that you have done better than you expected when your essay is returned.

8.6   Summaries

In this final section, I include two summaries: a comprehensive checklist of the *Criteria for writing a good essay*, which draws mainly on Chapter 7 of the book; a summary of the principles and practices of essay writing drawing on both Chapters 7 and 8. You can come back to these summaries again and again during your years of study. And there is more about the nature of academic writing in Chapter 3, when you want to read it.

Criteria for writing a good essay

As your tutors read and mark your essays they will be asking the following questions.

- Have you answered the question in the title?
- Have you drawn on the relevant parts of the course for the main content of your essay?
- Do you show a good grasp of the ideas and texts you have been studying in the course?
- Have you given a reference for each of your sources in the main body of your essay and provided a Reference list or Bibliography at the end?
- Have you written in your own words?
- Have you presented a coherent argument?
- Is the essay written in an objective, analytical way, with appropriate use of illustration and evidence?
- Is the essay well written and well presented?

Box 8.7   Some basic principles of essay writing

Your ability to express yourself is fundamental to being a member of society. Developing that ability is one of the most profoundly worthwhile activities you can undertake.

You won't become a good writer by learning a set of formal rules. Essentially, you are learning to communicate ideas and your style will develop through practice at explaining things to a reader in your own words.

Think of writing as a craft in which you are an apprentice. You learn by practising a range of different skills. You get this practice by regularly turning out one piece after another and getting feedback from a skilled reader.

Don't worry about writing well straight away. Just pitch in and write. You have to risk writing badly in order to learn how to write well.

Remember that most of what you read is written by professionals. If you are a beginner, then compare yourself with other beginners.

You cannot judge your own writing until some time after the event.

You have to learn to 'let go' and allow others to see your writing, however far it may fall short of your ideals.

Think of your tutor as a 'coach' who is working on your technique. You won't agree with everything your tutor says, but you will make much more progress with the coaching than without.

Read your work aloud to yourself (or to someone else, if you can) so that you can 'listen' for sentences or passages that don't work.

Always read your tutors' comments on your essays, and try to follow their advice.

Keep practising. Write short pieces regularly (get comments from other students if you can't get them from a teacher). This will:

— help you to establish a sense of audience and a writing voice

— help you to adapt to the critical-analytical academic style of writing

— extend your repertoire of ways of making your writing flow

— increase your sensitivity to the processes of structuring an argument and signposting its development.

Reference

Elbow, P. (1998) *Writing with Power: Techniques for Mastering the Writing Process*, New York, Galaxy Books, Oxford University Press.

CHAPTER 9
Processes of study in the arts and humanities

9.1   The arts and humanities

This chapter is different from the others in the book. So far we have been thinking about ways of approaching a range of different study tasks: reading and making sense of *secondary* source material in textbooks, articles and teaching texts; getting the most out of other ways of studying, for example from lectures, seminars, sound and vision; and learning by 'doing' – using a computer, making presentations and visits and, especially, writing essays. In this chapter we turn to the nature of the arts and humanities themselves and look at the main processes involved in studying them, with a focus on *primary* sources.

Broadly, when you study the arts and humanities you study aspects of our *culture*. You explore people's ideas and beliefs, their cultural practices and the objects they have made, over time. Human history is criss-crossed with the traces of thousands of people who did, said and made things, and these people were to some extent aware of what they were doing. So all these things *mean* something. Your task is to look carefully at people's ideas, practices and products to try to *understand* what they mean. You achieve this understanding by:

- *analysing* the various 'objects' of your study (for example, plays, music, paintings, historical or legal documents, philosophical treatises, maps, buildings, religious ceremonies)

- *interpreting the meanings* of these objects

- *making judgements* of their value

- *communicating* your analyses, interpretations and judgements.

When you study a painting, for instance, you take it apart to see how it works as a painting. You *analyse* it 'as it is in itself', because this gives you many clues to what it might mean. But that analysis is complicated by the fact that the way we understand a painting itself changes over time. For instance, what a religious painting might have meant to the artist and his contemporaries in sixteenth-century Italy cannot be the same as it means to us now. We do not share their way of life. And the painting does not 'appear' the same to us either. We study it close-up in a modern art gallery, or (much reduced in size) as an illustration in a book. Look at the *Madonna and Child* in Figure 9.1 on page 234 Imagine how different the painting would seem to its original audience – perhaps contemplating it during a religious service, high up on the wall of a church, lit by flickering candle-light. What might it have meant to them?

To make an *interpretation* of what the painting means, then, you not only have to study it 'as it is in itself' – you also need to learn as much as you can about the circumstances in which it was made and viewed (who painted it, what it was 'for' and, more generally, about the values, beliefs and way of life of those people at that time). This, too, presents certain challenges. Obviously, we cannot transport ourselves to sixteenth-century Italy. We live *here* and *now*. In the end, we interpret things in the context of our own ideas and beliefs.

So it is as if the painting (novel, vase, song, idea, document, event) has a kind of 'double life' – as it was to people in the past *and* as it is now, to us in the present. You have to try to understand why it means something now, and just what it means. Ultimately, you have to make *judgements* about its *value*.

These inter-linked processes of *analysis–interpretation–evaluation* are what we will explore in this chapter. But it doesn't end there. You also have to *communicate* the interpretations and judgements you make to other people. To explain what you mean, you have to learn to speak and write in the appropriate language. That way, you make your own contribution to an on-going 'conversation' about our culture – a conversation that enables us to understand ourselves, and our purposes and values, as human beings who continue to live in society with each other.

Key points

- Studying the arts and humanities involves coming to *understand* aspects of human *culture*, past and present.
- You study the *meanings* of people's ideas, beliefs, cultural practices and products.
- And, by *communicating* your ideas, you make a *contribution* to our culture.

9.1.1 Different arts and humanities subjects

If studying the arts and humanities helps us understand our culture so that we can live together more meaningfully, why do we study particular subjects or 'disciplines' in our universities? You may be studying a single discipline: a language (ancient or modern), history, art, music, literature, film, religion, law, philosophy – and so forth; or *some* subjects combined, in multi- or inter-disciplinary studies. Why not the arts and humanities in general?

It is partly because our cultural experience is very broad. If we want to *study* a culture, we have to make it manageable. We have to analyse it, or break it down into parts, making distinctions between the different *kinds* of experience we have – such as reading an account of the Roman Empire, watching a play, listening to music on the radio. By isolating these things, and naming them (History, Literature, Music) we can see more clearly just what it is we are dealing with and come to understand it better. We also make these distinctions because cultural experiences such as these are *different*. At bottom, if you can't tell the difference between a song, a painting and a poem, then there is nothing much you can say about any of them. However, such discrimination depends on recognising *similarities* as well as differences between things – for instance, recognising that a great variety of visual images are all examples of what we call 'paintings'. But once you have learned the concept 'painting', and can distinguish between a painting and a song – which we all learn to do as children – then in a sense you 'know' what art and music are. (Incidentally, that means you already know a lot about arts and humanities subjects even if you have not studied them as subjects before. None of us is a true beginner in them.) This kind of analysis enables us to divide up our very wide experience of the world and organise it in our minds.

A main difference between the subjects that make up the arts and humanities, then, is that they have different *objects* of study – plays, poems and novels in Literature; documents, records and diaries in History; paintings, sculptures and buildings in Art History; and so on. Having identified such similarities and differences between the objects of our study, we can go on to look at them more closely. And so, over time, we have been able to make even finer distinctions. Within poetry, for example, we come to recognise different types of poem (such as narrative, epic, lyric, satirical). That is the way we impose some *meaningful order* on our very broad cultural experience and 'discipline' our thinking about it.

Box 9.1   'Living' disciplines

The subjects we study in the arts and humanities are not set in concrete. We make changes to them over time that reflect significant changes in our culture and the way we view it. For obvious reasons, *new* subjects such as Communications, Film and Media Studies have come into being quite recently. This has involved some shifting of boundaries in existing subjects such as Literature, Art History and Philosophy. And even within these older disciplines the focus of attention tends to *shift* over time. For instance, in recent decades feminist writers have drawn our attention to the roles of women as writers and artists, as characters in novels and as depicted in paintings, and as readers and viewers. Also, what was always called English Literature is now often referred to as Literatures in English. That extends the scope of our studies to include English-language writing from Africa, the Americas, Australia, India and the West Indies.

These changes are sometimes dismissed as simply 'fashionable' or 'politically correct'. But that is a mistake. The rise of interest in Gender Studies since the 1960s is partly a result of an increase in the number of women working in universities – which itself reflects women's changing place in our society. And study of Literatures in English has arisen out of a deeper understanding of Britain's past role as an imperial power and the profound cultural effects this has had on its former colonies. As academics become aware that aspects of our cultural experience remain to be explored, their curiosity draws them towards those fresh fields. For a while 'gender' or 'post-colonial' issues seem to be on everyone's lips. Eventually, they may become established as fields of enquiry and be drawn into the mainstream of a range of existing subjects – which are themselves *changed* in the process. Then other issues come to our attention, and so on. This process is what makes even 'traditional' academic disciplines *living* traditions of thought and practice.

It is by imposing order on our experience in this way that, together, we are able to examine the *substance* of our culture in great detail – not only the different ways in which we communicate with each other, but also the very 'stuff' of our ideas, history, literature, art, music, and religious and other practices.

Key points

- We distinguish between *different subjects*, or disciplines, in the arts and humanities.
- The distinctions we make impose *order* on our very wide cultural experience, enabling us to study it closely and understand it better.

9.1.2   Studying the arts and humanities

Having seen how and why distinctions are made between different arts and humanities subjects, does that mean we cannot think of these subjects 'as a whole'? The general label 'arts and humanities' suggests that there *is* something that unites them, at the same time distinguishing them from other subject groupings (such as 'the sciences' or 'social sciences'). Broadly, what unites these subjects is that they focus on:

- cultural 'traditions'
- 'texts'.

Cultural traditions

Just now I said quite confidently that you already know a lot about the subjects that make up the arts and humanities even if you have not studied them before. But how can I be so sure? What makes me certain is that, like everyone else, you were born into a human culture. As you were growing up within that culture you were hearing and seeing all the things the people around you were busy saying, doing and making. And you were learning to think and understand, do, say and make similar kinds of thing. You were probably taught some things directly: by your parents, other adults and children, at school, and through the media. As soon as you could read you also learned from comics and books. But no doubt you just 'picked up' a lot of these customs along the way, as a member of the culture alongside other people.

In the process of growing up you learned to make sense of the world around you, to organise and represent it to yourself in your mind. You learned to recognise similarities and differences between things and formed the ideas or concepts that enable us to think. Among these concepts are the sort we are particularly interested in here – 'story', 'picture', 'song', 'the past'. Even before you could read you were no doubt told stories and listened to them on the radio or on CD; you drew pictures and looked at them in books and on TV; you sang nursery rhymes and heard all kinds of music; and you learned to distinguish between 'yesterday' and 'today'. Even if you were not taught directly about these things you *experienced* them all, over and over again. And when you compare your experiences with those of your friends, you probably find that you sang similar songs, heard similar stories and (if you are around the same age) watched the same TV programmes. That is because you grew up in the same culture.

But we do not only have similar experiences. The very ways in which we think, the meanings we make, the way we speak, our values and beliefs, and what we do, have all 'taken shape' *within* our cultures.

Box 9.2   What is a 'culture'?

A *culture* is the collection of meanings, values, morals, ways of thinking, patterns of behaviour and speech, and ways of life that a group of people *share*. And all modern cultures have histories – they are linked to the *past*. So, through our culture, what we have is shared knowledge and experience of certain customs or cultural *traditions*.

But this does not mean that we all end up like clones. You are, of course, recognisably yourself. You experience things in your own *particular* ways too. And we know that not everyone brought up in the same culture believes exactly the same things or behaves in identical ways. You are quite possibly also a member of a thriving 'sub-culture', which shares a certain kind of (perhaps, religious or moral) belief that is different from the mainstream. In any case, I hardly need to emphasise this point since the idea that we are all individuals, responsible for ourselves and in charge of our own destinies, is one of the fundamental beliefs in British culture. For us, it is more difficult to get our heads round the idea that, in a sense, we are none of us truly individual – because inevitably we live in, and through, our shared culture. Indeed, that is why we can communicate with each other. Perhaps we are more similar than we like to think.

What all arts and humanities subjects aim to explore, then, are aspects of human cultures, past and present. In fact, in the West, many of our values can be traced as far back as Ancient Greece (and beyond), so it is more accurate to say that we explore certain *cultural traditions*. It is because those traditions have been passed on through our culture, and are still alive today, that we can hope to make some sense of the past and of ideas and art of the past. If the culture in which we were reared and live had no 'links' to that past at all, the traces that have come down to us (ideas, values, written texts, pictures, buildings, artefacts) would be alien to us. It would be almost impossible to understand them.

But, equally, our culture is constantly changing – perhaps particularly fast in this age of electronic revolution. As we have seen, the way we 'slice it up' into subject areas, in order to make sense of it, changes too. What we study are *living* traditions.

Texts
We can think of all the 'objects' that we study in the arts and humanities as, broadly speaking, *texts*. They may be literary, historical, legal or philosophical *written* texts; *visual* texts such as paintings, buildings, artefacts,

plays-in-performance and films; *aural* texts, as in the performance of music and in spoken languages; or *symbolic* texts, for example religious ceremonies, maps, architectural plans and music scores. These things are all 'texts' in the sense that they 'stand for' or represent the conditions of time and place in which they were created, and all the knowledge, ideas and activity that went into their making. We cannot re-create those conditions. And we can seldom study the actual knowledge, thoughts or intentions of their makers and doers, past or present. What we study are the results or *outcomes* of all these things – the written accounts, paintings, pieces of music, plays, maps, Acts of Parliament, buildings, and so on – that were and are produced.

When we analyse and interpret these texts in appropriate ways, we can often get 'back' to some of the knowledge, ideas and activity that went into their making. But even when an author tells us how she wrote a particular novel and what she was meaning to say in it, or a painter records what was in his mind, those accounts are not the simple 'truth' of the matter. They are yet more *texts* which we have to scrutinise. *All* these texts are open to our interpretation of what they *mean*.

For instance, we know that the Battle of Waterloo was fought in June 1815. And if we know quite a lot about what happened then, that is because people made written, visual and symbolic records of it that have come down to us: official documents, records of speeches in parliament, journals, diaries, letters, sketches, maps, and so on. These are what we study (not the battle itself, of course). If you were to compare different accounts of the battle – from the French or British side, or by men from different ranks of the armies – then you would probably find that, because they had different 'points of view', their versions of the event are different. They may even conflict. An historian has to study *all* these texts with a *critical* eye, weighing up the evidence for and against particular interpretations of what happened and why, before reaching conclusions. If Wellington himself had left an account of why he made certain decisions during the battle that would, of course, be very interesting. It would be important as 'evidence' which could not have come in a direct way from anyone else. But it would need to be seen as 'what Wellington *thought* he was doing', and be weighed in the balance along with the rest.

Key points

The different arts and humanities subjects are *living* traditions of thought and practice. When you study them, you learn:

- how to *analyse* a range of different texts; *interpret* their meanings and *evaluate* them
- to think *critically* and independently
- how to *communicate* your ideas to others in speech and writing.

The meanings and significance of human activities are never just 'in' the texts you study, ready to jump out at you. You have to question those texts and interpret their meanings for yourself. How to do this is what we will explore in the next few sections of the chapter.

9.2 Becoming familiar with the text

Before you begin your interrogation of a text, you have to get to know it in a general way. In a sense, you can 'see' *visual* texts (such as paintings, sculptures and buildings) all at once; there they are before you. You can look at them from different angles or move around them. But with *written*, *aural* and *moving image* texts – in which words, sounds or images follow on from one another – you cannot become familiar with the whole thing until you have read, heard or seen it right through. If it is quite short there is no problem about this; before you begin your analysis you will do so several times probably. But what if it is a lengthy text, such as a novel or a symphony? How should you approach it?

9.2.1 Reading

There are many different *kinds* of written text, and you need to approach and read them *differently*.

In the case of a *novel*, it is best first to read through the way you normally do – and enjoy yourself. Some people read very quickly. That's fine, because when you get down to analysing the novel you are anyway forced to re-read its various sections much more slowly and study some parts of it especially carefully. Part of the process of analysing anything as long as a novel (a play, film, symphony) is finding a way of dividing it up into manageable 'episodes' – combining certain chapters, scenes or passages together to form groups. Then you can study each episode in detail while keeping a grasp on the whole thing in your mind. So, as you read, you might just be thinking about some suitable way of doing that.

However, if you are reading a *philosophical* text you need to approach it in quite a different way. It is a mistake even to try reading it quickly because you will very soon lose the gist. If you keep going regardless, there's a danger that you will blame yourself for failing to understand what you read, decide you are no good at philosophy and give up. In fact you are not even giving yourself a chance. *Nobody* can read a philosophical text at the speed they read a novel and *understand* what they read. You have to take it very slowly, trying to make some sense of it as you go along, a bit at a time. That is because these texts take the form of an *argument* about certain *ideas*. Unless you understand the first stage of the argument reasonably well you will not be able to make sense of the next stage, and so on. And, often, the argument is dense. Abstract ideas just *are* hard to understand, so every sentence may take a while to sort out.

> ### Box 9.3   Your reactions to the text
>
> A few moments ago I said you should read through a novel and just enjoy it. But what if you are *not* enjoying it? What if you don't *like* a piece of music you will have to spend a lot of time thinking about? Or perhaps you feel thoroughly bewildered by a philosophical argument and at first you can't make head or tail of it.
>
> Obviously, you cannot force yourself to find such a text enjoyable or interesting. But what you *can* do is give it a chance. At this stage you've hardly even been introduced. It may be that you are trying to read it too quickly or expecting it to be something it's not. In any case, when you get down to studying it, looking more closely at this part and that, it will almost certainly make more sense to you. You may even come to enjoy it.
>
> Having said that, you may not. We all have to study some things because they are important 'landmarks' in the subject, regardless of whether we enjoy the experience. So you need to be aware that, from time to time, you may have to just grit your teeth and press on.
>
> However, it is always a good idea to talk things over with other people. See what fellow-students make of the text. What they say may help you to 'come at it' from a different angle and see new possibilities in it.

Reading an *historical document* is different again. Much of it may be easy enough to follow, but there will probably be a number of terms that are 'of the period' or references to unfamiliar people and events that you need to look up. So reading it may be a stop-start process. In any case, you will be reading with certain questions in mind, such as:

- who wrote the document – what do we know about this person's background and particular interest in the matter?
- when was it written – how soon after the events it refers to?
- why was it written – who or what was it written 'for'?
- what was the author in a position to know; is it likely to provide sound information?

Then you can judge whether the document is a *reliable* source for your purposes, and just what it might mean.

So when you read philosophical texts and historical documents even for the first time, you will be beginning your interrogation. This is true of *symbolic* texts too, such as maps and music scores – you have to start 'deciphering' them straight away to make much sense of them.

9.2.2   Listening and viewing

If you are studying music, a foreign language, plays-in-performance, film or the media, you have to do a lot of listening and viewing. Again, you need to be aware that there are different *ways* of doing this.

For example, when you listen to some music for the first few times just to get a 'feel' for the piece as a whole, you don't have to do it in a studious way. You can listen in the car, or at home as you do some chores. But when you come to *study* the music, you need to listen carefully and in an 'active' way – *thinking* about the way the piece is put together or the contribution different instruments make. You need to get organised for this kind of listening[1].

1 *Try to make sure there are no other sounds or noises in the room.* Don't listen in the kitchen when there is a washing machine on, for instance.

2 *Find out where it's best to sit in relation to the source of sound and adjust the volume and tone controls accordingly.*

3 *Concentrate on the silence before you start listening.* Sounds exist in what is otherwise silence. If you stop to appreciate that background, the textures and 'colours' of the music will be more vivid.

4 *Just listen and think – don't do anything else at the same time.* Get used to concentrating on what you hear. Shut your eyes if it helps.

5 *Try to listen without being interrupted.* If you are interrupted it is probably worth starting the piece again from the beginning.

Similar 'rules' apply if you are studying a language and perhaps listening to a tape of native speakers in conversation. You can listen through a few times in a less studious way, just to get the gist. But then, when you get down to work on it, you have to have quiet conditions in which to listen to the various parts of it carefully. And the same with poetry or a novel on tape, and a play on video.

When you are trying to become familiar with texts it helps a lot if you can *surround* yourself with them. You can pin the maps you are studying on your walls, and also illustrations of paintings, buildings and artefacts. And you can get into the habit of tuning in to a music or foreign language radio station, perhaps having it going in the background as you get up each morning.

Key points

- The *texts* you study in the arts and humanities are of *different kinds* (written, visual, aural, symbolic).
- There is also a *range* of texts within each of these categories.
- It is important to recognise the *differences* between texts, so that you can *approach* them with the right *expectations*.
- You need to read, look or listen to the text in the way that is *appropriate* to it, and also suits your study *purposes*.

---

[1] I am grateful to Professor Trevor Herbert of the Arts Faculty at The Open University for his 'active listening' guidelines.

9.3   Approaching analysis

9.3.1   Why analyse?

Whatever kind of text you study, one of your main tasks is to try to understand it 'as it is in itself'. That means *analysing* it. You have to examine it *in detail* so that you can see what it is made up of and how it 'works'.

Just as you read, view or listen to different kinds of text in different ways, so you approach your analysis of them differently. In each case, you ask particular *types of question* using a specialised analytical *language*. We have just seen the sorts of question you will have in mind when approaching an historical document. Let's take another example.

Look at Raphael's *Madonna and Child* (Figure 9.1)[2] To understand how it is 'put together' you need to ask the following kinds of question about it, using some of the terms that appear in italics here.

1   How much of the *picture space* is taken up by the three *figures* and how much by the *background*?

2   Where are the figures *positioned* on the canvas and what are their *poses*?

3   What is 'in' the background and how is this related to the figures in the *foreground*?

4   Which parts of the painting are in *light* and which in *shade*, and where is the *source of light* – where is the light supposed to be coming from?

5   What is the painting's *tonal range*; are there any striking uses of *colour* in it?

6   How is the *two-dimensional* (flat) painted surface made to look as if it has a third dimension, of *depth*, so that the figures appear life-like?

7   What is the relationship of the figures to you, the *viewer* – at your *eye-level*, 'looking' down, away, or what?

In the process of analysing the painting you study as many aspects of it as you can – not only the picture surface itself (the first four questions), but also your (the viewer's) relationship to it. All this gives you important clues to how the painting works. When you then combine the results of this analysis with what you have discovered about both the type of painting you are dealing with and the conditions in which it was painted and viewed, you are able to reach some informed and appropriate interpretation of its meanings and values, and to communicate your judgements to other people.

---

[2] We have only been able to reproduce the painting in black and white, so, among other things, you wouldn't be able to analyse the artist's use of colour. This is only one reason why you should always try to examine original paintings when you can. It is also difficult to get a sense of the scale and texture of a painting from a reproduction, however good it is. Of course, you will often have to use reproductions. When you do you should always read the captions, which give you important information about a painting, including its size.

Figure 9.1 Raphael, *The Madonna and Child with the Infant Baptist* (*The Garvagh Madonna*), probably *C.* 1509–10, oil on wood, 39 x 33cm. Bought, 1865. © The National Gallery, London

Key points

When you analyse a text you *break it down* into parts and *examine* each part in detail, so that you can see how the text 'works' as a whole. According to the *type* of text you are analysing, you:

- ask particular *kinds* of question
- use the appropriate *language* of analysis.

Let's see how these processes of analysis–interpretation–evaluation and communication actually work in practice. To do this we will *separate* them out and *illustrate* each one, taking a short poem as a working example. As we discuss the poem, I hope you will be able to see how to *apply* what we are doing to *other kinds of text* you may be particularly interested in. From time to time I will draw out some of these implications.

9.3.2   Carrying out an analysis[3]

Here, then, is a four-stanza poem we will focus on in the next few sections of the chapter. As you will see, I have left out a word at the end of each line in the third and fourth stanzas. So it presents you with a kind of 'puzzle'. (But I have included the punctuation, and added line numbers for ease of reference.)

1	Whose woods these are I think I know.
2	His house is in the village though;
3	He will not see me stopping here
4	To watch his woods fill up with snow.

1	My little horse must think it queer
2	To stop without a farmhouse near
3	Between the woods and frozen lake
4	The darkest evening of the year.

1	He gives his harness bells a _____
2	To ask if there is some _____.
3	The only other sound's the _____
4	Of easy wind and downy _____.

1	The woods are lovely, dark, and _____,
2	But I have promises to_____,
3	And miles to go before I_____,
4	And miles to go before I _____.

[3] Grateful thanks to Jessica Davies, Associate Lecturer in Literature at The Open University, for analysis of the poem in this section and Sections 9.5 and 9.6 of the chapter.

Activity 9.1

Read the poem three or four times. Then turn poet and try to fill in the missing words in the third and fourth stanzas before you read on. (Don't cheat!)

A clue

Speak the first two stanzas out loud, and notice which of the end words in the lines have similar sounds (that is, which lines rhyme). Notice that the sound at the end of line 3 in the first stanza ('here') matches those in lines 1, 2 and 4 of the second stanza ('queer', 'near', 'year'). If the same pattern is repeated, then you might be able to hazard a guess as to what the sound at the end of lines 1, 2 and 4 in stanza 3 will be. But I should tell you that the fourth stanza has a slightly different rhyming pattern.

A warning

Anxiety can Damage your Health – so do not get anxious about this. It's supposed to be *fun*! (But it will be even more fun if a group of you can get together to do it.)

I have no way of knowing what you wrote of course. But I should reveal that I have played this game before. And I am prepared to bet that, whether you got the words right or not, the ones you wrote were almost all words of one syllable. (Syllables are based on vowel sounds. So 'speed' ('ee') and 'loud' ('ow') are words of one syllable (even though they contain two vowels), and 'fiery' has two syllables because the 'fie' produces the sound 'i' and the 'y' is sounded 'ee' – 'fi/ree'.)

The poem is by Robert Frost and was published in the early 1920s. Here it is in full.

1	Whose woods these are I think I know.
2	His house is in the village though;
3	He will not see me stopping here
4	To watch his woods fill up with snow.

1	My little horse must think it queer
2	To stop without a farmhouse near
3	Between the woods and frozen lake
4	The darkest evening of the year.

1	He gives his harness bells a shake
2	To ask if there is some mistake.
3	The only other sound's the sweep
4	Of easy wind and downy flake.

1	The woods are lovely, dark, and deep,
2	But I have promises to keep,
3	And miles to go before I sleep,
4	And miles to go before I sleep.

Activity 9.2

Now read the poem out loud a few more times.

Note

It will help if you type or write the poem out accurately on a sheet of paper (including the punctuation). Then you can keep it in front of you alongside the book, as we look more closely.

The reason I am so confident that you wrote words of one syllable is that a lot of the words in the entire poem are of that kind, and all but one of the words that end the lines in stanzas 3 and 4 ('mistake'). (Just check that for yourself.) As you were reading through the poem several times your ear will have picked that up. So, if at first you wrote in two-syllable words, they would have 'sounded wrong' – unless, perhaps, English is not your first language or you happen to have very little experience of poetry. This is why I asked you to read the poem aloud. What your ear detects is a certain pattern of sounds – in this case a pretty simple pattern of mainly single sounds. And that is what a poem is, a particular *pattern* of words and sounds. That is why you should try to read poems out loud. Your *ear* tells you what you already 'know' about poetry, so you should always listen to it and put your faith in it, so to speak.

You may have noticed other *patterns of sound* that 'knit' these particular words together: each stanza has four lines, and in each the end-words are matched in rhyming sounds in lines 1, 2 and 4, with the exception of the final stanza, in which all the end-words rhyme. The end-sound of line 3 in each stanza is picked up in lines 1, 2 and 4 of the following stanza. (The rhyme scheme – a shorthand way of noting this kind of pattern – is as follows: *aaba*; *bbcb*; *ccdc*; *dddd*.)

If you picked up my 'clue', you probably worked out from the first two stanzas which of the end-words in the third stanza would need to rhyme. But working out the rhyming sounds in stanza 4 is not so easy; the patterning here takes us by surprise because it is a bit different from each of the other three. We'll discuss this again later. Another thing you may have 'heard' is how long and drawn-out the vowel sounds of the end-words in the final stanza are compared to those of the other stanzas: 'deep', 'keep', 'sleep'. The end-word in the third line in stanza 3, 'sweep', starts this patterning of longer vowel sounds. If you then look at the words *within* these lines you'll find more that sound similar in this respect ('easy wind', 'downy', 'lovely, dark', 'miles to go'). And, generally, the consonants are soft-sounding. If you find it hard to hear these things, read the words out loud in an exaggerated way.

There is another type of pattern here too, in the *kind of words* the poet uses. A lot of these words appeal to our *senses*: of sight (the woods that 'fill up with snow', the frozen surface of the lake in the 'darkest evening of the year'); of hearing (the sound of the horse's 'harness bells', the swooshing 'Of easy wind'); of touch ('downy flake') and sensation ('watch his woods'). The poem evokes a particular kind of scene and a mood that suggests quiet and solitude.

Box 9.4 Finding 'ways into' a text

The hardest part of analysing a text is *getting started*. Here, the game of writing end-words for the poem forced you to start by thinking about sounds. But there are many possible ways into any text. So if you feel a bit bewildered at first, don't despair.

Generally, it is best to begin by thinking about some aspect of the text that seems to *stand out*, striking you forcefully in some way. In a written text, you may be struck by a particular *image* (or comparison) or by repetition of particular images or words, and begin thinking about what they bring to mind. (In Frost's poem for instance, consider the way the snowy landscape is described. The word 'woods' is repeated four times, 'darkest evening' in the second stanza is echoed by 'dark and deep' in the final stanza, and 'sleep' is repeated in the last two lines. What do these words suggest to you? What do you associate with them?) Or it may be the way the words are *laid out* on the page that attracts your attention: a pattern in the dialogue of a play or novel (such as very long speeches regularly assigned to one character and short utterances to another); in poetry, an unusual arrangement of the verses with some lines much shorter than others. In a piece of music it might be a sudden change of *rhythm*, or in *dynamics* (from soft to very loud perhaps). Or you may hear a particularly pleasing *melody* repeated in a slightly different way at different points in the piece. You may see a certain *shape* repeated in a painting (lots of curves for instance), or notice a splash of vivid *colour* on one part of the canvas.

Wherever you begin, as soon as you notice a particular feature of the text and start thinking about it – or start to see or hear some sort of pattern – you will find yourself moving on from one observation to another (as we are doing here with the poem).

Once you think you have detected *any* kind of pattern you should look to see whether it runs right through the text. (Remember, from Section 9.1.1, that analysis involves recognising similarities *and* differences.)

Activity 9.3

Read the poem out loud again. Do any lines sound *different* – breaking the pattern of vowel sounds and soft consonants we noticed?

I'd say there is a different pattern of sound in the third stanza. The first two lines are different from the fairly regular movement of the lines in the first and second stanzas, and the slower, almost hypnotic movement of the final stanza. In the first two lines of the third stanza, you have to pronounce the words clearly because of the sibilants (harness bells) and the harder, dental consonants: 'k', 't', and 'st'. And there are a number of short vowel sounds too ('gives', 'bells', 'ask') which, because they are short, make you speed up as you read. The spaciousness and quiet of the rest of the third stanza – indeed, the poem as a whole – is heightened by the 'shake' of the bells. But 'to ask' (humorously taking the horse's point of view) tells us that the narrator is awake and alert. The sounds then attended to so closely are very like silence ('the sweep/Of easy wind and downy flake'), images of regular movement and softness of touch. But why the earlier disruption, and why this further shift in the movement of the verse? What's the point of this?

Once you ask that kind of question you are thinking about what the poem is *about* – that is, you are moving towards some *interpretation* of its *meanings*. In fact, you will have been asking yourself that kind of question all along. It is impossible to read and analyse something without trying to make some sense of it as you go. However, we began by putting these 'why?', 'what does this mean?' questions to one side. The point of suspending them – while you look closely at patterns of sound, movement, and so on – is that *meaning* in a poem is closely bound up in the *way it is written*. Indeed, the poem *is* the way it is written – these particular words on the page, in this order. (So, too, the painting *is* the marks on the canvas, the music *is* the particular arrangement of 'sounds in time'.) Discovering how the poem *works* is precisely the point of analysing it in detail. If you jump to conclusions about what it means too quickly, you will tend to shut off some other possibilities that may be thrown up by a more thorough analysis of it.

Key points

- Analysing a text shows you how it *works* and gives you many clues to what it might *mean*.
- First, examine a feature of the text that is particularly *striking*, and look out for *patterns* in it.
- Then go on to analyse the text as *fully* as you can before trying to reach any firm conclusions about its meanings.

So, although in reality analysing a text and interpreting its meanings are not separate 'stages' we go through, but are overlapping processes, I will keep them separate for the time being so that you can see more clearly what each involves.

9.4 Interpreting meanings

After you had read the poem a few times, you no doubt pieced together that the 'I' of the first line of the poem, the speaker, has stopped on horseback by some woods, to watch them 'fill up with snow' on the 'darkest evening of the year', and lingers so long that the 'little horse' shakes his harness bells 'to ask if there is some mistake'. The narrator is put in mind of promises to be kept and of the miles still to be travelled. But the attraction of the woods, which are 'lovely' as well as 'dark and deep', is such that the speaker and his horse have not actually moved on at the poem's end. In fact, the title of the poem is 'Stopping by Woods on a Snowy Evening'.

But as far as I can see, we can't be sure about anything else. We don't know *where* this place is. We know the action happens in the evening, because of the repetition of 'dark' and 'darkest' (and the title). And we don't know *who* the speaker is, or *why* she or he watches but is careful not to be seen – by 'he' whose woods they are, whoever he is. So there seems to be plenty of scope for interpretation here.

9.4.1   Knowledge of context and author

Starting with the 'central character' (the traveller-speaker), I would guess that most of us just *assumed* he is male. If someone is doing something as potentially hazardous as riding about alone in the woods through snow on 'The darkest evening of the year', we tend to expect that person to be a man. More to the point, what is known about 1920s American culture – the *conditions* within which this poem was written and first read – suggests that Frost's original readers would almost certainly have made that assumption. Furthermore, we know that this poem belongs to a collection called *New Hampshire* (1923), where Frost himself lived. So we might think that the speaker of the poem is perhaps Frost himself, not just an unidentifiable narrator-traveller.

However, I am speculating here. Is it right to do that? The answer is 'yes' (see Box 9.5) and 'no' (the discussion below Box 9.5).

Box 9.5   Interpreting texts from other times and places

Yes. Like everyone else, artists rely on communicating with their contemporary 'audience' on the basis of the understandings they *share*, as members of the same culture. So when you are studying a text that has come down from the past, or from a culture that is different from your own, it is important to find out as much as you can about the context and practices of the writer, and about that time and place – including the way of life, values and beliefs of the people for whom the text was written. Some knowledge of the *conditions* in which the text was written and received will guide you towards making *appropriate* interpretations of its meanings.

However, you need to be aware that acquiring that kind of knowledge is not a straightforward business. If your subject is philosophy or history, you will be particularly interested in such questions as: what is 'true'? in what sense can we 'know' what happened in the past? and how can we find out? In that connection, notice that what I have just said is carefully worded. I have said that our knowledge of this period 'suggests that ...'; that we are 'perhaps' right to make certain assumptions about the poem on that basis.

You have to be *cautious* in what you say about conditions in the past, and especially so when you are interpreting a text's meanings on the basis of your understanding of the past.

No. You have to be careful *not* to speculate on the basis of some kinds of knowledge, such as what you know about the artist. For instance, I know that Frost lived in New Hampshire both as a child and an adult, and that while he lived there he wrote many poems which describe scenes similar to the one depicted here – of journeys taken and natural landscapes evoked – which are often thought to reflect internal states of mind. In view of this, I might be tempted to interpret the poem not just as the story of a traveller's moment of solitary contemplation, but of the kind of personal journey undertaken by the poet himself. Indeed, many writers and academics who study Frost's poems take this autobiographical approach, stressing the resonance of personal themes in his poems. Some have argued that this poem marked some especially dark passage in the poet's life, and that it expresses a desire for self-destruction. When this was put to Frost, he remarked:

> [John] Ciardi of the Saturday Review ... makes my 'Stopping by Woods' out a death poem. Well, it would be like this if it were. I'd say, 'This is all very lovely, but I must be getting on to heaven.' There'd be no absurdity in that. That's all right, but it's hardly a death poem. Just as if I should say here tonight, 'This is all very well, but I must be getting on to Phoenix, Arizona, to lecture there.'

(Mertins, Louis, *Robert Frost: Life and Talks-Walking* (Norman: University of Omaha Press, 1965), p. 371; quoted in Richardson, 1997, p. 190)

Frost's humorous response makes us aware that, even if we did know all there is to know about a writer's life, we *still* couldn't be sure that he was writing about something he had actually experienced or about himself.

You should not make connections between what you know about artists' lives or times and their 'works of art' in a direct, *unqualified* way. We cannot get inside other people's minds, so we can never know for sure what artists feel or know or *intend* to do in their work. And we can't just take what they themselves say at face value either because, like all of us, they may not be fully aware of what they feel or do. Also, works of art are only ever *partly* 'true to life'. They always contain imaginary elements – even when they are portraits of real people or of actual landscapes. Artists create their work; what they are concerned with is its *composition*. A landscape painter rendering a real scene may, for example, 'move' a tree in order to make a more pleasing pattern on the canvas, or add a figure to the landscape for the sake of visual interest. And these imaginary elements may so transform what was 'there' that it is pretty well impossible to disentangle the one from the other. So, even when there seems to be an obvious connection between 'real life' and 'work', you need to *argue your case* for that relationship rather than just assume it.

For all these reasons, you cannot just assume that the 'speaker' of the poem we are looking at *is* Frost. You cannot make assumptions about what the poet *feels* or *intends*, or what he *means* by the poem. You can only talk in terms of what 'the speaker' says and does; what Frost 'seems' to be doing in the poem; and what *the poem* might mean. The same applies when you are talking about the 'meanings' of a painting or a piece of music.

Key points

When you are interpreting the meanings of a text you should:

■ try to *find out* as much as you can about the *conditions* in which the text was created and received (read, viewed or heard); but

■ try *not to make assumptions* about relationships between 'real life' and 'the work', or about the artist's beliefs, feelings and *intentions*.

9.4.2 Meaning and 'form'

The question remains, what is this poem 'about'? Or, rather, we should ask, 'what *kind* of poem is it?' Poems (paintings, ideas, music, buildings, historical documents) are not all 'one kind of thing'. As we become familiar with poetry we learn to distinguish between different *kinds* of poem, or between different *poetic forms*.

Epic poems, for example, are extremely long stories about the doings of a noble warrior, voyager, or similar 'hero'. Other characters are involved too. They are always described in detail when they are introduced into the story and usually make a dignified 'set' speech which reveals their 'character'. Great battles take place, involving descriptions of the hero's appearance and weapons as well as the action. The style of writing is high-flown and elaborate, in keeping with the epic's lofty themes. These are the literary devices – or, *conventions* – traditionally associated with epic poetry. We interpret the meanings of an epic poem within that framework of understanding. So when a character makes a set speech we do not *expect* it to sound like 'real' speech. And it would be *inappropriate* to criticise the poem for not being 'true to life'. An epic is not supposed to be true to life; it is supposed to be far grander than that.

To say that the meaning of a poem is closely bound up in the way it is written, then, is to say that 'its *meaning* is bound up in its *form*'. When you analyse a poem you come to understand the elements of its 'formal' patterning. This gives you clues to the meanings it is *appropriate* to make.

Box 9.6 'Conventions'

When you sit among rows of people to watch a play, first the curtain goes up – to reveal, say, a living room. We 'accept' this as an artificial device that indicates the start of the play, because of course curtains do not go up to reveal living rooms in real life. Then what you see is a 'room' with three walls. You simply ignore the fact that the fourth wall is missing. (Indeed, it would be odd to complain about this because, otherwise, you wouldn't be able to see the action.) These 'walls' are in fact flat, painted canvases, but you ignore that too. The furniture in the room is all turned to face the audience and people weave around it, wearing costumes, speaking very loudly and making exaggerated gestures, generally also facing the audience. And they perhaps even speak to each other in verse. *None* of these things is natural or 'true to life' (even sitting in rows in the 'audience'). They are all *conventions*: artificial devices that are 'generally accepted' as necessary to the business of presenting and viewing a play. Indeed, they are bound up in what it *means* to stage a play. If you, watching, do not 'accept' these things, then you will misunderstand what you see in a big way. As with the play, so with the epic poem.

Certain conventional 'rules' also govern the way a landscape painting is composed. (Look at the landscape in Figure 9.2). As here, the scene is usually constructed in horizontal 'layers' that seem to recede into the distance – rather as scenery is positioned at the sides of a stage, with one 'flat' behind another – giving the illusion of depth on the two-dimensional canvas. This is another reason why a painting of a real landscape is never a faithful representation of that scene. It is not only that the painter may have added imaginary details to what she or he actually saw. It is that the landscape *form* will make its own 'demands'. In order to give the *illusion* of depth (light, and so on), painters *represent* what they see according to the conventions governing the painting's composition and uses of line and colour. A painting is always an '*imagined* reality'.

Some painters (composers, poets, playwrights) play around with these conventions, and so with our *expectations* of the painting, music, poem or play. A play may be presented 'in the round', for example, with no curtain, stage, or scenery. But they can only do that, and we can only *understand* what they are doing, if we all know what the (normally accepted) conventions are. It is only when we know what the 'rules' are that we can break them, or tell when someone else is breaking them.

Frost's poem is a *lyric*. When you analyse the particular patterns of words and sounds that make it up you are exploring the various *elements* of its lyric *form*. By convention, this type of poem is very short and usually expresses the feelings of a single speaker. Originally, lyrics were poems written to be sung. They are rhythmic and rhyming, and they appeal to the reader's emotions and senses. (Indeed, we have already identified some of these features in the poem.) When you can place Frost's poem as 'a lyric', you approach it with these kinds of expectation. Unlike the grandeur of epic themes, you expect it to engage with some aspect of a world that we know, and to appeal to your feelings as an 'ordinary' human being. So, in recognising its form you are also accepting some *limits* on the kind of interpretation you can make of it – or on the range of its *appropriate* meanings.

Key points

When you are interpreting the meanings of a text you should be *guided* by:

- your knowledge of the *type* of text it is (of its *form*)

- your understanding of the *conventions* that 'govern' the subject matter, purposes, and (formal) elements of the text.

This enables you to make some *appropriate* interpretation of its meanings.

Figure 9.2 Nicolas Poussin, *Landscape with a Man Killed by a Snake*, probably 1648, oil on canvas, 118 x 198 cm. Bought, 1947. © The National Gallery, London

9.4.3   Analysis and interpretation

We have got to the point of recognising that this is a lyric poem, and of thinking that it records a particular moment in time. But you cannot reach firmer conclusions about a text's meanings until you have looked at as many aspects of it as you can. I think we need to go back again to the detail of the poem, because the analysis is not full enough yet.

For one thing, there is something distinctive about the *point of view* being presented. If you look at the first stanza the point of view given is that of the speaker: 'I think I know'. This pattern continues into the first line of the second stanza. But instead of the action or thoughts of the speaker being recorded, now it is the point of view of his horse that is presented. Or rather, it is the *imagined* perspective of the horse, being given by the speaker. This continues into the third stanza, where we learn that the horse gives 'his harness bells a shake/*To ask* if there is some mistake' (my italics).

Activity 9.4

Just stop for a moment to confirm the change in *point of view* for yourself. What are the implications of it; what do you think it might 'mean'?

Well, I think the change in point of view serves to heighten the sense that this event represents a break in the usual pattern of things; the 'little horse' wants to be about his errand, and thinks it 'queer' that they are lingering so long with seemingly no reason for doing so; after all, there is no 'farmhouse near'. His asking whether 'there is some mistake' registers the unusualness of the situation, and in so doing, invites us to ask the same question. Notice that the word 'Between' is used at the start of the third line of the second stanza, and that the line seems to signal to us more precisely where the speaker and his horse have stopped: 'Between the woods and frozen lake'. But does this really help to locate the speaker and his horse more precisely? 'Between' seems to me to suggest a less than certain position. This *uncertainty* is all of a piece with the shifting of perspective from the speaker to the horse, whose puzzlement at the 'stopping' implies that this apparently simple journey may not be quite as straightforward as it seems?

Box 9.7   Making meaning: 'anything goes'?

'Making meaning' is a process that goes on in our minds when we come up against something in the world, or ideas in a text, that we try to make sense of. But it is clear from talking to other people that we do not always make the same meanings, even of the same events and texts. We may respond to and interpret them differently. Indeed, on that basis, some people think you can just say what you like about a poem, painting or piece of music; there is no 'right' or 'wrong' about it because we all 'respond' to it differently, emotionally and in our imaginations. So it *means* different things to us. In the realm of interpretation, 'anything goes'. But this is a big mistake.

In the first place, just because we sometimes interpret things differently does not mean that we always or even usually do. In fact, I'd say that very often we make similar meanings to others in our culture. That's why we can understand each other, often in subtle ways, and laugh at the same jokes. But in any case, we *cannot* say just what we like about a poem, painting or any of the other objects we study. If we think we can that is because we are only thinking about *ourselves*, about our feelings and fancies. We are forgetting about the other half of the equation – the *text* we are studying and trying to interpret the meaning of. That text imposes some *limits* on the interpretations we may make. We are limited by our understanding of the *kind* of text we are dealing with – by its conventional *form* – and by our knowledge of the *conditions* in which it was created, and read, seen or heard. In view of those limitations, what we should say is that there is a certain *range* of *appropriate meanings* we may make.

It is *within that range* that we may well disagree because of the differences there are between us. In some texts the range is wide, so there may be much to disagree about. But this is far from saying that 'anything' goes. Rather, it suggests that we *can* be 'more' or 'less' right in our interpretations.

Continuing to think about 'place' and 'time' in the poem, take a good look at Frost's use of syntax. A pattern emerges here too. Almost all the verbs are either in the present tense ('I think I know', 'house is', 'he gives', 'woods are', 'I have', 'I sleep') or are infinitives ('To watch', 'To stop', 'To ask', 'to keep'). Using the present tense helps the poet achieve a strong sense of immediacy, I think, capturing a particular time and a place (which is what helps us identify this as a lyric poem). But the verbs in the infinitive give a more indefinite feel: Frost simultaneously suggests a moment 'out of time', in which the speaker is not in any one place in particular. Here then is a tension between two different 'states' of being. What could it mean? Are there perhaps other tensions in the poem (might there be a pattern here)?

I think a tension can also be seen in the overall movement of the poem, from stanzas 1–3 (stopping 'between the woods and frozen lake') to stanza 4 (moving on). The first line of the fourth stanza affirms the speaker's love of the woods – the words evoke a sensuous enjoyment of their depth and darkness – and this is followed by the word 'But': 'But' the speaker has 'promises to keep' and 'miles to go'. Where we might expect closure at the end of the poem – and, as we've seen, this is suggested in the rhyming pattern of stanza 4 (*dddd*) – we seem to get open-endedness. We do not know to whom promises have been made, about what, or where the speaker is going or what he will do when he gets there. However, what we can say is that the movement of the poem is from contemplation and enjoyment of the natural world to consideration of the claims of another 'world': the social world of promises and obligations. (Incidentally, you may have noticed that this is the world in which the poem opens – 'Whose woods', 'his house', 'the village' – so perhaps we have really come full circle?) The word 'But' turns the poem around. It heightens the sense of the speaker being tugged in these two different directions. And what about the significance of 'before I sleep'? While this may seem little more than a reference to the journey that must be completed (and so a way of telling himself to continue on down the road), the repetition gives it particular resonance. This might, after all, be a metaphorical journey. For example, can we think of the tension as between the place of 'contemplation' and 'action' in human life? Or, does the repeated word 'sleep' evoke the end of life's journey?

But perhaps you are protesting at this point. Isn't that going much too far – reading things 'into' the poem? Wouldn't that interpretation go against the grain of what the poet himself said about the meaning of the poem? Actually, I don't see why. Frost may have dismissed the idea that the poem is about death, but some kind of death-urge or suicide mission is not the only possible way of interpreting it. I am suggesting here that the poem is about two kinds of journey, with an outward journey symbolic of an inner journey.

However, having said all that, this is an example of the kind of interpretation we might *not* agree about – *within* our understanding of the poem's 'range of meaning'. We can at least agree that it is unlikely to have some other range of meaning altogether. That is because, in carrying out a fairly full analysis of the 'formal elements' of this 'lyric' poem, *everything* we have discovered chimes with the interpretation of it as a journey characterised by conflicting desires and obligations and *nothing* about it seems to suggest otherwise.

Key points

When you are *interpreting* a text, you should try to reach an understanding of the 'range of meaning' you may make by combining:

- your knowledge of the text's *form* (the *conventions* that govern its composition); and
- your understanding of the *conditions* in which the text was created and received.

When you also take account of

- the outcomes of your analysis of its formal *elements*

you are able to make some *appropriate* interpretation of the text's meanings.

Now, we will try to make some judgements about the text.

9.5   Evaluation

As we have seen, you are fully *immersed* in the text while you try to discover how it works and what it is about. But in order to make some *judgements* of it you have to shift your stance a bit. You have to 'stand back', as it were, and ask yourself: 'What do I think about these things I have discovered?'

Basically, you need to ask two *kinds* of question about the text's 'value':

1   *What values* are represented in the text (emotional/ social/ moral/ intellectual ...)? Are they *good* values (for us, here and now), or not?

2   Is the text *of value*; is this text a good one of its kind?

Returning to the poem, we'll look at each of these questions in turn.

9.5.1   The values represented by the text

The first question here is *what values* does the poem stand for? If the poem is about the experience of conflicting worlds – the world of the woods and the world of social obligation – what is it 'saying' to us about that?

Activity 9.5

Stop and think about this question of what values the poem 'stands for'. Jot down a few of the thoughts that occur to you – and also make a note of what their opposites might be.

For instance, the first things that occurred to me were:

(for) solitude	(against) demands of society
(for) wonder/awe	(against) cynicism

How did you get on? Other things I wrote down are:

For	*Against*
freedom	*duty/obligation*
simplicity	*confusion*
quiet	*hustle and bustle*
uncertainty	*unreflective self-assurance*

The point of thinking about the opposite of whatever the text seems to stand for is that, whenever we *affirm* one thing we also (by implication) *deny* its opposite. So looking at what the text seems to be 'denying' can help you get clear what values it *does* represent.

Take the first pair of terms I thought of, 'solitude' versus 'demands of society'. Thinking about how the pull of the 'real world' enters into the poem (it does so in the very first line with 'Whose woods', which tells us that these woods are owned by someone, and 'his woods' emphasises this), reminds us of how much this is a special moment. The poem's evocation of quiet and a sense of removal from everyday realities is what we note most immediately, but its opposite is always implied, and ever more powerfully as the poem moves towards its end. This world which offers peace, beauty and solitude exists side by side with the realisation that there is also another world, a world of people and obligations. The artfulness of the poem is in the way the two worlds are established and balanced, and the way in which that which is denied makes itself felt. The speaker is aware that the woods by which he is stopping belong to someone in the village; they are owned by the world of men. But at the same time they *are his*, the speaker's woods, too, by virtue of what they mean to him in terms of emotion and private significance.

Looking further down my list, it is not as if the poem 'says' anything as crude as 'abandon the world of duty and obligation and retreat to the freedom of the woods'. But we can see that in evoking and *beautifying* this state of hushed communion with the natural world – the readiness to wonder at such stillness, the fascination of the empty wastes of black and white, and the heightening of the senses involved – the poem *celebrates* all these things. And, in doing so, does it seem to 'recommend' these *as values* over their opposites?

Box 9.8   Making assumptions

You might think that, having examined the text carefully and reached some interpretation of its meanings, there should be no difficulty about deciding what values it represents. But this is not always the case – they may not be *obvious* to you at all. That is because values are often *assumed by* the text (simply taken to be true), and so hidden from view. It is as if the text speaks to us 'out of' certain *underlying* beliefs. So, at this stage, you may have to dig around the text a bit more to be clear about them (as we are doing here). As readers, we all make certain assumptions too – we are not conscious of everything *we* 'take to be true'. And some of the things we know we believe, we possibly haven't given much thought to.

For instance, you may have assumed from the start that this poem was recording the literal journey of a man who steals a moment to reflect on the beauty and quiet of the snow-filled woods. And there is nothing unreasonable about this. However, we are now interpreting the poem as more complex: a contemplation of conflicting demands; an internal journey.

Texts of all kinds, especially philosophical texts, challenge us to *explore* our assumptions, and really *think* about what we believe and why.

So, having identified some of the values the poem seems to stand for, are they 'good' values – for us, here and now – or not? What do *you* think?

You might take one of a number of positions on this. For example, you could argue along something like the following lines.

1   The poem evokes, beautifies and celebrates the simplicity of the natural world. In doing so, it draws our attention to the imaginative possibilities of human insight – its intensity, our willingness to empathise, and the heightening of our senses involved. And so, it espouses values that are freedom-enhancing.

At this point there are at least a couple of different directions your argument might take:

(a) At a time when we seem to be obsessed with practical concerns of various kinds (with technology, the economy, material comfort), it suggests that what we are, and may be in relationship to the natural world, is at least as valuable as our duty to others and to society. The poem makes us question some of our modern assumptions; to think again about what it means, as human beings, to be fully alive.

(b) But this view of things is actually far from freedom-enhancing. The values the poem represents are anti-social values. As the poem idealises the natural world, so it devalues the public realm and the obligations and responsibilities that belong to it.

On the other hand, leaving the first sentence of argument 1 above as it is, you might go on to argue:

2   The romantic, almost unreal setting of the poem and the hypnotic beauty of the verse are seductive. What we have here is a slight poem that celebrates a highly subjective experience, a fantasy about the daring of

'breaking free' from the bounds of society. As such, it bears no relationship to reality and tells us nothing of value.

The point to note here is that there is no reason why you should *accept* the values the text seems to represent. We have seen that you certainly need to try to understand *what* those values are, and *why* they might have been held – otherwise you are not in a position to make informed and appropriate judgements at all. But that is not the same thing as 'accepting' them.

Sometimes, you may find a text a good example of its kind *technically*, yet judge its values abhorrent – a painting that seems to 'celebrate' a bloody massacre, for instance, through the way the brush strokes are lovingly executed. This is why it is helpful to keep your assessment of the values the text stands for *separate* in your mind from your critical assessment of that text, as a painting, poem, or whatever. However, notice that *all* the 'arguments' I have just set out about the values that the poem stands for depend heavily on critical assessment of it – which we are about to look at. Even argument 2 refers to, and recognises, the 'sensuous beauty' of the verse.

This is just another way of saying that the processes of analysing a text and interpreting its meanings are fundamental to making judgements about it. The more thoroughly you analyse the text, the better you will understand it and the surer your judgements will be.

Key points

When you are *assessing* the *values* a text represents, you should:

- *question* those values (whether they are assumed by the text or are more obvious)
- try to *examine* your own values, and the assumptions you may be making
- firm up your judgements only when you have analysed and interpreted the meanings of the text as *fully* as you can.

9.5.2   The value of the text

We now turn to a *critical assessment* of the poem *as a poem*; the question is, is it a 'good' poem? To that we should add 'of its kind'. As we saw, we must judge it as a *lyric* poem – it would be inappropriate to think of it in the same terms as, say, an epic, because the conventions that govern the epic's form (its subject matter, purposes and formal elements) are very different. It is always important to understand what *kind* of text you are dealing with not only because that knowledge guides you towards some appropriate interpretation of its meanings, but also because it places limits on the judgements you can make of it.

As we have seen, by convention the lyric poem:

- takes as its *subject matter* some aspect of a human experience we recognise
- has the *purposes* of appealing to our senses and engaging our feelings
- is in lyric *form*: short and song-like (rhythmic, rhyming).

These, then, are the *criteria* against which we make our judgements. I think it is safe to say that we have seen all these things in the poem during the last few sections of the chapter. The question is, how *well* does it do them?

As regards the poem's subject matter, we might ask 'does it "talk" to us about some aspect of the human world we recognise, *in a meaningful and illuminating way?*' Looking at the series of 'arguments' I sketched out a couple of pages back, clearly the world of the poem is recognizable to us, and it is possible to make several different kinds of connection between what the poem 'says' and some of our current social, moral and intellectual concerns. These are meaningful connections and, I would say, potentially illuminating. But what do *you* think?

Turning to the poem's 'purposes', *how well* does it engage our feelings and appeal to our senses? Again, we have discussed the way the poem *evokes* feelings of empathy with the speaker's wonder and awe at the natural world. It achieves this through: the natural setting (of a snowy landscape at evening); the increasingly languorous movement and sounds of the verse, interspersed with the more excited agitation of the first two lines of stanza 3; the imagery ('*downy* flake'); the syntax (the present and infinitive verb forms), and the shifting point of view. We have also seen that the poem appeals *directly* to our senses of sight, hearing and touch.

Here we have also impinged on our last criterion, the poem's song-like *formal elements* (especially its movement and rhyming, but also syntax, imagery, and so on). In short, in Section 9.3.2 we saw how the whole is 'knitted' closely together by interwoven patterns of sound, movement and imagery – that not a word of it is carelessly placed. Indeed, the verse is rich beyond what seems possible at first sight.

What is striking is how a poem so short and apparently simple can carry such a weight of analysis, interpretation and evaluation. But we must remind ourselves that this is, after all, a short lyric poem. We should not expect it to bear *too* much weight.

Box 9.9   Personal response

Do you think I like this poem? Perhaps it's obvious that I do. If you have 'picked up' my enjoyment of it, it must be something about the way I have written because it is the *poem* we have been concentrating on *all the time*. In fact, I know it off by heart (which is perhaps not too surprising by now). But, anyway, I am only telling you so in this box.

That's because if I say to you, 'I love this music; it reminds me of lambs in springtime', what I am telling you is something about *myself*. If you find me a fascinating person you will no doubt be interested to know how I feel. But if it's the *music* you are interested in, then you are no closer to understanding it at all. Emotional or imaginative responses to a text are *not the same thing* as critical assessment of it and judgement of its values – arrived at through processes of analysis and interpretation. And it is the *texts* we study that are our main focus, not ourselves.

But that doesn't mean your personal responses are unimportant. Far from it. If you are moved by a novel, a passage of music, a sculpture or an idea, it is not only interesting but also a pleasure to work out why: what it is about the text that affects you in that way. Very often the text becomes more interesting and affects you more deeply the more you think and learn about it. Your feelings and intuitions are also very helpful guides to your analysis of it – showing you 'ways in', what to look out for. In any case, the very powerful effects that art and ideas can have are perhaps why you are keen to study the arts and humanities in the first place. Even so, sometimes what you study may seem dull and uninspiring. Or, in extreme cases, you may find certain ideas and representations totally unacceptable or even shocking. In every case, the point is to understand *why* – what it is about *the text* – whether it is something you love or loathe.

However, if it seems to you that analysing texts simply 'spoils' your enjoyment of them, then perhaps you shouldn't be *studying* these subjects. Why not just continue to enjoy your experiences?

In making a critical assessment of this poem it helps to be familiar with a range of other lyric poems, so that you have something to compare it with. And this is true generally. You become surer in your judgements as you become more familiar with the *kind* of poem, painting, piece of music, argument, or historical document you are faced with.

We should note here that the criteria for evaluating historical documents and philosophical arguments are different, both from each other and from the kinds of criteria we have been looking at. As we have seen, the analytical questions you ask about a document are to do with the type of source it is, who its author was, when and why it was written; and therefore *what* it is actually telling you and how *reliably*. These are the criteria against which you judge it. A 'good' document is a reliable source that is useful for your purposes.

Philosophical texts argue through 'problems' – such as an ethical dilemma, the question of free will, of what exists, and so forth. In evaluating this kind of text, you are concerned with the *logic* and '*truth*' of that argument. A 'good' argument is logically sound and also illuminating.

Key points

When you are making a critical assessment of the *values* of a text, you should:

- recognise that the *text* is your focus; be guided but not bound by your personal responses to it
- evaluate the text according to the *criteria* that are appropriate to its *form* (its subject matter, purposes and formal elements).

9.5.3   A 'circle' of understanding

It may seem as if analysing, interpreting and evaluating a text are 'stages' we go through, one after the other. But it's nothing like as mechanical as that. You do not analyse a text into separate parts, then 'add up' those parts to produce some interpretation of the whole, and then evaluate it. Rather, analysis, interpretation and evaluation are *overlapping processes*. They are different *kinds* of activity, as we have seen by looking at them separately. But when you try to understand a text you are unfamiliar with, what you actually do is 'circle around' it in the following sort of way.

- As you read, listen to or look at the text for the first few times, you form some impressions of what kind of text it is and what it is 'about'. And of course you respond to it, emotionally, in your imagination and intellectually.

- These perceptions help you find 'ways into' the text, and you start to analyse parts of it carefully.

- Then you draw back and have a think about how the whole thing looks now.

- Guided by that, you go back into the detail of another part of the text – draw back again, and see how that further analysis affects your view of the text's meanings as a whole.

- Meanwhile, you are beginning to make judgements about the text, which you also revise as you go along.

And so on, back and forth between the *parts* of the text and your conception of it *as a whole*, shifting your attention and revising your interpretations and judgements as you go. What we did in Section 9.4.3 ('Analysis and interpretation') comes closest to this process.

You do this circling around as you *engage actively* with the text and *make meaning* of it in your mind. 'Meaning' is not a thing; it is not just 'inside' the text, waiting to be 'uncovered' when you apply certain analytical techniques to it. Making meaning is a *process*. What you do is more like 'communicating' with the text – looking at and 'listening' to it, as it were, and 'talking back' to it. The *last* things you firm up are your judgements: of the values the text represents, and its value as the kind of text it is. After all that, you are ready to communicate your interpretations and judgements to other people.

9.6   Communicating your ideas

If you were talking to a friend about a picture hanging on your living-room wall, you might say: 'I really like that portrait because the figure looks so lifelike'. That is, you'd make some kind of *judgement* about the painting. (I've never heard anyone say 'I really like that portrait because of the little white brush stroke in the top right-hand corner'.) So, in effect, you turn the process we have just been through on its head. When you are communicating your ideas to other people, you *start* with what were the *conclusions* of that process – and you go on to present an *argument* in support of your judgements that draws on the detail you discovered in the text. Having previously taken the roles of investigator and judge (or 'critic') of the text, you now have to take on the role of *advocate* for your interpretation of it. As an advocate, you try to *make a case* for your view of the text's meanings and value that will *convince* other people.

9.6.1   Making a convincing case

Let's suppose you wanted to argue in support of the 'stem' of the first argument in Section 9.5. Here it is again, broken down into its component parts.

(a) The poem (i) evokes, (ii) beautifies and (iii) celebrates the simplicity of the natural world.

(b) In doing so, it draws our attention to the imaginative possibilities of human insight – (i) its intensity, (ii) our willingness to empathise, and (iii) the heightening of our senses involved.

(c) And so, it espouses values that are freedom-enhancing.

This is an outline sketch of the *argument* for, say, an essay. There are three main points (a, b, c), the first two of which contain several different claims (i, ii, iii.). *All* these claims have to be *demonstrated* in order to make both main points in a convincing way. In the process you will have demonstrated point (c), your conclusion, so at that stage you would just need to sum up the argument.

But how do you 'demonstrate' a claim convincingly? If you look back to what we did in Section 9.3.2 you will see how. You have to *explain* what you mean, using examples from the text to *illustrate* your meaning; and you have to provide some *evidence* from the text that shows you are right to say what you do about it.

Let's take the first claim in point (a), that the poem 'evokes' the beauty and simplicity of the natural world. We saw that this depends on the poem's success in engaging our feelings and appealing to our senses. So you could demonstrate the claim by referring to:

- the natural setting, of woods, a dark, snowy landscape – offering textual detail as *illustration*

- the regular, then more jagged, then languorous movement of the verse – quoting some of the words of the poem to *illustrate* this, the long and short vowel sounds and soft-sounding and harsher consonants

- the syntax – quoting a word or phrase that appeals to each of our senses, as *illustration*; *explaining* and *illustrating* the significance of the verb forms

- the imagery ('easy wind', 'downy flake') – offering textual detail as *illustration* and *explanation*.

In each case you are also providing *evidence* in support of the claim, by referring to *precise* details of the text and/or *quoting* relevant words and phrases directly from it. As a result, your reader should both understand what you are saying and find your argument convincing.

As you actually write the essay, the main difficulty you face is keeping this argument *going forward* while also including as much detailed reference as you need to explain, illustrate and justify what you say at each stage. So, at the points when you 'interrupt' the onward flow of the argument in order to provide this textual detail, you need to *remind* your readers where they have got to and where they are headed next, before you set off again. That is because, when you present a case in writing, you can't 'check' with your readers to make sure they are following your meaning. You need to keep 'signposting' the direction your argument is taking.

Box 9.10   Why communicate?

Studying arts and humanities subjects involves learning particular ways of expressing ideas and of 'arguing a case' that is illustrated and is supported by appropriate kinds of 'evidence'. That is, we learn to think, speak and write in the *ways* and *terms* that are appropriate to the subject we are studying. Those are the ways and terms in which *everyone* who has studied the subject speaks, so that we can understand each other and learn from each other. In short, we learn how to *join in* that ongoing discourse.

Indeed, each subject in the arts and humanities is itself a different kind of discourse (a way of using language and other symbolic forms (such as pictures and music) communicatively, so as to *produce meaning* and *understanding*). Poetry is one way in which human beings communicate with each other and art is another, different, way; so is music; so is a legal document or an Act of Parliament; and so is a philosophical argument. When we are actively reading and thinking about these texts, then, we engage in a kind of 'communication' with them.

Similarly, when you discuss your interpretations and judgements of these texts or write an essay, you become a participant in the academic discourses that are related to them – that produce meaning and understanding *about* the different subjects we study. You are making your own enquiries and producing your own 'texts'. The essays you write are judged according to how close you come to 'speaking' appropriately, within the terms of the academic discourse concerned.

The upshot is that, in the arts and humanities, the *knowledge* we have is what we have made and continue making through our *discourse*, past and present. Whichever way you turn, communication is the name of the game.

See Chapter 8, Section 8.4.2, Signposting

So, as an advocate for your interpretations and judgements of the text, you have to present a clear and consistent line of argument that is well explained and illustrated and also supported by appropriate kinds of evidence. And you have to try to write simply and directly to your readers in order to *engage* their minds.

Key points

When you are *communicating* your interpretations and judgements of a text you have to make a *convincing case* in support of them.

At each stage of a written argument, you should:

- *explain* yourself clearly and give *examples* of what you mean by what you say (illustrations drawn from the text)
- provide appropriate *evidence* from the text
- use the appropriate *language* of communication
- 'signpost' the *direction* your argument is taking.

But what exactly is 'appropriate' evidence? And how do you know what terms are the appropriate ones to use?

9.6.2   Different kinds of 'evidence'

The *terms* you use and the *ways* in which you support your argument depend on the subject you are studying and what *kind of text* you are talking or writing about.

Quoting from written texts

We have seen that when you are discussing a poem, you talk about its 'rhythms' or movement, its patterns of sound such as 'rhyme', and its 'imagery' and 'syntax', *quoting* words, phrases and lines from the poem as evidence of the points you want to make about it. And this applies to play-texts and novels, too. As you discuss the 'characters' involved, you quote parts of their 'dialogue' or passages from the 'narrator's' descriptions of them. You also *quote* from relevant parts of historical documents when you discuss their 'purposes', their 'reliability' as 'sources' of information and the 'evidence' they provide. You also quote from a philosophical text when you discuss the 'premises' and 'logic' of an argument. However, in philosophical writing, part of the process of showing that you understand the ideas you have been grappling with is being able to *invent* examples of your own to illustrate the points you make. What matters most is how carefully you handle the details of the argument and how clearly you *explain* yourself.

Box 9.11   Presenting quotations

Some general points about quoting from secondary sources are discussed in Chapter 7, Section 7.6.1 (using quotation marks and three dots – an ellipsis – to indicate that some words have been left out, for example). Those conventions apply when you quote from *any* prose passage such as an historical document, novel or philosophical argument. But when you quote more than a few words you should *indent* the quotation rather than trying to incorporate it in the flow of a sentence, as follows:

Ellis concludes that:

> The steady migration of women into the towns was the logical consequence of conventional perceptions of femininity and of correct female behaviour ...

In this case, you do *not* use quotation marks because you are indicating that it is a quotation by indenting it.

However, when you quote from poetry you have to show where lines end. If you quote only a few words you can incorporate them into a sentence, separating the lines with a slash (/):

In 'gives his harness bells a shake/ To ask if there is some mistake' the consonants are sibilant or dental and the vowel sounds shorter, in keeping with the horse's impatience and the tinkling sound that the words evoke.

If you want to quote more than one line of the poem in full, you should indent the quotation:

Here, though, the consonants are sibilant or dental and the vowel sounds short:

> He gives his harness bells a shake
> To ask if there is some mistake.

Notice that all punctuation marks must be included in the quotation too. Indeed, *whenever* you use quotation you must quote *accurately*.

Representing visual and symbolic texts

We saw that when you discuss your judgements of a visual text such as the landscape painting or the *Madonna and Child*, you talk about its 'composition': the way the 'picture space' is organised; the relationships between 'foreground' and 'background', and between 'figures'. You discuss the way 'perspective' is used in the painting to show 'depth'; the painting's 'tonal range', and its uses of 'colour', 'shape', 'line', 'light' and 'shade', and 'light source'. This kind of description is based on detailed observation of the painting. But here – and when you discuss a sculpture or building, and symbolic texts such as maps, plans and music scores – you may also want to include your own *sketches*, *diagrams* or *notation* to demonstrate these relationships, and show precisely which elements of the text you are drawing attention to.

Precise reference to 'linear' texts

You may find it more difficult to provide evidence from texts in which sounds, words or images follow on from one another over time (such as music and videos, plays and novels). Music is perhaps particularly hard to pin down. Sounds weave in and out of each other so that at first you may experience the music as seamless. But there are different 'movements' or 'passages' in music; moments at which a 'melody' is first introduced and later passages when it is repeated, for example. You can distinguish between these and other, different passages in the music by locating them within a description of the music's 'development', making precise reference to its *structure*. A certain 'chord' sounds just *after* the 'first repetition' of the melody, for instance; or just *before* the trumpet 'fanfare'. You can also identify and *describe* the patterning and effects of different elements of the music, such as its 'harmony', 'rhythm', and 'timbre' (the quality of sound associated with different instruments or voices).

Although novels, play-texts and film-scripts are written rather than aural texts, they are similar in the way that they unfold bit by bit, in a linear way. Here, too, you can identify particular developments or moments by locating them within the overall *structure* – in this case, of the 'plot' – and again by reference to *time* and *event* (after the scene at the ball, when the characters first meet, before the picnic, during the thunder storm). And, as with music, you can *describe* and discuss formal elements, such as 'character', 'tone of voice', 'dialogue', 'point of view'. However, in these cases, you can *also* quote relevant words, sentences and short 'speeches' from the text.

When you are discussing the performance of a play or moving images, you again think in terms of 'plot' and structure, identifying particular moments in the ways we have just seen. Here again, you can include your own sketches or diagrams to provide evidence of the visual relationships you are discussing.

Multiple texts

Very often you will be studying 'the art' or 'the literature' of a particular period and therefore a *number* of texts rather than just one. Or perhaps you will be using a range of *different* documents as the basis of your interpretation of an historical event. And what if your subject is interdisciplinary (Religious or Classical studies, say) and you study many different *kinds* of text (written, visual and symbolic), 'bringing together' your judgements of them to explain certain beliefs, practices or ways of living?

In all these cases, the processes of analysis, interpretation and judgement we have discussed still apply to *each* particular work of art, building, document, ceremony and so forth that you study. And the kinds of evidence you use to justify your judgements of these different texts are also just as we have seen. However, the *danger* here is that you may be tempted to analyse and interpret these many texts less carefully than you might when dealing with only one or two – moving too quickly towards your judgements, and then too quickly again towards their implications for the times, beliefs or ways of life you are discussing. This is known as 'reading off the text' (that is, off its surface), and you should try not to do it.

For example, if your subject is Religious Studies and you are discussing the beliefs of, say, late nineteenth-century British society, there will be many different sources you might study – hymns, paintings, poetry, scientific theories, church buildings, accounts of religious ceremonies. In this situation, it is better to select a few representative texts and talk about them in some detail rather than opting for thin coverage of a large number of them. In the end, precise and detailed reference to fewer texts makes for a more convincing case.

Evidence 'from authority'

When you present evidence for your judgements in an essay, you don't *only* draw that evidence from primary sources. You also often call on the 'authority' of other writers on the subject (critics, academics), drawing on their judgements. You can see in Chapters 4 and 5 how to read and 'make sense' of other people's ideas in books, articles, TV programmes, and so on; and how to weigh up these ideas and use them to help you form your own. As regards your writing, you have to learn how to use this kind of 'evidence from authority' – how to work other people's ideas into your argument, and also how to acknowledge your sources.

Key points

You should present *evidence* for your interpretations and judgements of a text in order to *justify* them (showing your reader why you are right to say what you do).

According to the *type* of text you are discussing, you should:

- use appropriate *kinds* of evidence
- 'speak' in the appropriate *terms*.

See Chapter 7, Section 7.6.2, Providing evidence

9.7 Beliefs and theories

'Authorities' (critics, historians, philosophers and so forth) of course argue from *their* interpretations of what a work of art, an event or an idea means. And their judgements are based on certain *beliefs* – about the nature of the objects they study and about what they themselves do as readers and interpreters of them. From our discussion of 'Stopping by Woods on a Snowy Evening', you have seen what my beliefs are: that people can reach some understanding of a text through the processes of analysing its formal elements and acquiring some knowledge of the conditions in which it was created and received. Because I was talking about these very processes, I said all that explicitly. But, very often, what writers believe about these things is 'assumed by' rather than 'stated in' their argument. For example, look again at these judgements about the poem:

> The romantic, almost unreal setting of the poem and the hypnotic beauty of the verse are seductive. What we have here is a slight poem that celebrates a highly subjective experience, a fantasy about the daring of 'breaking free' from the bounds of society. As such, it bears no relationship to reality and tells us nothing of value.

Activity 9.6

Stop for a few minutes and think about what *beliefs* lie 'underneath' these judgements.

It seems to me that beneath the judgements lie the beliefs that there is quite a strong relationship between a poem and the 'real world', and that if a poem has no relationship to 'reality' then it does not tell us anything worthwhile.

And the moral judgement here – that it is improper to celebrate what might devalue the social world – also implies that a poem should say something of *moral* value to us.

Now that we have unearthed these beliefs we can take a good look at them. We can see more clearly what is involved in agreeing with the argument (again asking, what does it 'deny'?). Then we can decide whether we do agree or, if not, what exactly we disagree with. So, do you agree with these beliefs or not? For instance, do you think that there is quite a strong relationship between a poem and 'real life'?

Of course I don't know what you think about that. But you have seen that I think there is a strong relationship. The poem's form is conventional (agreed, as it were, *by people*). It was created and received within certain conditions, and it is received now within different sorts of condition. I believe it does communicate something to us about both those worlds. However, as we saw in Section 9.4.1, I do not think this relationship between 'art' and 'reality' is either a simple or a direct one. What I was trying to say there is that *none* of the texts you study simply *reflects* the world of human experience 'as it really is'. As created objects, they are *artificial*. ('Artificial' *means* 'made by art, not natural'. That is, *people* made them, with different purposes in mind.) They are not simply 'true to life' and they do not 'tell' us things in the direct way this speaker suggests. Remember the painting of the 'real' landscape, with its imaginary additions and conventional form? But think, too, about an historical document, such as an Act of Parliament. We have to interpret the meanings of all these texts.

In my understanding of 'reality', human invention and imagining is as much a part of our world as anything else. So I would not agree that fantasy is necessarily worthless. And I think that works of art can communicate all kinds of things, not just about our moral values. In saying all this, I am disagreeing with what the speaker appears to understand by both 'art' and 'reality' – which in both cases seems far too narrow – and about the relationship between the two, which seems too direct.

However, not everyone would agree with my beliefs (perhaps you don't). For instance, some people believe that texts of all kinds have no relationship to the 'real world' because there is no such thing; what 'really' exists are the ideas and beliefs that we human beings have – that we *construct* in our minds and *represent* in our texts. So a text can only be related to the constructions – or, other 'texts' – that have come before it.

These are just a few of the ideas people have about what a work of art *is* and what *relationship* it has to the worlds of its makers and receivers. When such ideas are connected together in a thorough-going way we say we have a *theory* about these things.

Box 9.12 Theories

A theory is a 'system of ideas' through which we *explain* something. In the arts and humanities we try to explain such things as the role of the artist, the nature of the text, the way the text is received and interpreted, and the relationships between these things. However, people have not developed a single, 'universal' theory that attempts to explain *all* these things, at all times and in all places. Rather, a number of theories guide us towards looking closely at different aspects of this 'complex' of issues and relationships. Some theories draw attention to the artist's role; some focus on the text and its 'context'; and others explain readers' 'reception' of the text, in their contexts.

In the course of your studies you will no doubt come across many different theories (indeed, it may seem there is a bewildering array of them). You will be asked to *apply* them to the texts you study. That is because theories suggest *different* ways in which you can view the text. As you approach a text from this or that 'point of view', you come to understand and *value* it differently. And, in the process, you become clearer about your own beliefs and ideas.

Using theories prompts you to ask different *kinds of question* about the text, from a range of points of view. For instance, can you see what kinds of question this speaker was asking when making judgements about the poem?

> The values the poem represents are anti-social values. As the poem idealises the natural world, so it devalues the public realm and the obligations and responsibilities that belong to it.

The speaker has approached the poem from the point of view of the way the words in it relate to ideas about the material world. The approach draws on cultural-materialist theory, broadly speaking. As a result of adopting this stance, the speaker 'comes at' the poem from a different angle from the other speakers, 'sees' different things in it and makes very different kinds of judgement from them. If you had not thought about the poem in cultural-materialist terms yourself, you may have found this interpretation and the associated judgements surprising and interesting. And does this prompt you to wonder *why* you hadn't?

Whether you are aware of it or not, your interpretations and judgements of the texts you study are based on certain beliefs: about the world, about the nature of those objects, and about your role as 'critic' of them. If you are *not* aware of it, then these beliefs lie beneath what you say, as *assumptions*. We can't be aware of all the assumptions we make, all the time. But, as you study, you should be thinking about at least some of these things. Our beliefs change, and our thinking becomes richer, as we assess other people's ideas and try applying their theories.

Key points

Examining other people's beliefs, and applying their theories to the texts you study helps you:

- recognise the *assumptions* that academics and critics make in their writing
- look at texts from different *points of view*, asking different kinds of question about them, and so
- become clearer about your *own* assumptions and beliefs.

Leaving the poem behind, we turn in the next chapter to one of the main ways in which you can become a *participant* in the subject(s) you study. It is when you do some research of your own that you understand more deeply how all the processes we have been looking at actually work in practice.

References

Frost, R. (2001 [1923]) 'Stopping by Woods on a Snowy Evening' in Lathem, Edward Connery (ed.), *The Poetry of Robert Frost*, London, Vintage.

Richardson, M. (1997) *The Ordeal of Robert Frost: The Poet and his Poetics*, Chicago, IL., University of Illinois Press.

CHAPTER 10
Online research and project work

10.1   A world of information at your fingertips

With a computer connected to the internet, you have access to information and resources undreamt of by earlier generations. Moreover, these resources are available on demand, for twenty-four hours every day. Whether you are setting out on a sizeable research project or just checking train times, the internet will help you find what you need. There is a whole world of information out there if you have the skills to find your way around it.

10.1.1   Information literacy
People with skill in accessing and using information are said to be 'information literate'. According to the UK Higher Education Funding Council:

> Information literacy is increasingly important in this 'information age', not just for study purposes but in all aspects of life. ... In the modern world, people increasingly need skills of evaluating and managing information, in both their personal and working lives.

> (HEFCE, 2004)

Finding up-to-date, accurate and relevant information means knowing how to search for it *online*. And managing this information means knowing how to *file* it effectively on your computer.

As a student, however, you need more than purely technical web-searching and filing skills. You need to know how to access *online libraries* and *academic databases*. You need to be able to weigh up the *academic credibility* of what you find. And you need to know how to make *appropriate use* of it within your studies. So, whether you are new to online searching or relatively experienced, you probably need to invest time in developing your information literacy.

10.1.2   Developing your information skills
One of the most remarkable features of online research is how easy it is to get started. Yet, your skills will develop indefinitely as the internet grows and changes, with new resources appearing and search tools becoming ever more sophisticated. The aim of this chapter is to help you with the first steps. The rest you can learn through experience or by seeking further advice.

In Sections 10.2 and 10.3 'Finding information' and 'Finding academic material' I describe some searches and show what I found. Bear in mind that if your computer is set up differently from mine, the search I describe won't work in exactly the same way for you. The details will also date quickly as the internet develops. However, the important thing is to understand the general principles. To follow equivalent steps you may need to use your software's

Help facility, or perhaps ask someone with more online experience. Section 10.3 also looks at how to check the academic credibility of what you find online.

Section 10.4 'Misuse of online data' draws attention to some of the pitfalls of using the internet indiscriminately or unethically. And finally, in Section 10.5, we discuss how to find images online and use them in independent project work.

Key points

- Information literacy is a basic life-skill for modern living. It involves recognising when you need information or resources and knowing where and how to search for it.
- All students need to develop skill in finding the key pathways to resources in their field of study.

10.2 Finding information

10.2.1 A quick search

Searching online can be a serious and thoughtfully planned activity, but it can also be a quick hunt for some information without which you may be held up. For example, in Chapter 4 we looked at Hansa's attempt to read the Ellis article. Instead of being anxious about the meaning of a key term like 'dysfunctional' she could have used the internet to help her. Here's how I looked up this term.

1 My computer was on, so I opened a browser window. Then I opened a search engine and typed 'dictionary' in the search box. I was offered several dictionaries to choose from, so I clicked to open one and typed 'dysfunctional' in the search box. In an instant the text shown in Figure 10.1 appeared on the screen.

2 After reading this (and notice that you can click to hear how words are pronounced) I tried another dictionary, which offered me the text shown in Figure 10.2.

3 These two definitions give a pretty clear idea of what 'dysfunctional' means, so I printed them out in case I might want to think about them again later.

Don't be surprised if you follow the same steps as me but get different results. The internet is constantly changing.

What did I need to know to be able to carry out this search?

See Chapter 1 Section 1.8.1, What equipment and skills do you need?

- I knew how to open a web browser.
- I also knew about search engines. I used Google (actually, GoogleUK (www.google.co.uk) because it has a helpful option to search just UK pages). But I could have used Alta Vista, Yahoo, Excite, or others. Your browser may list some search engines in the 'Favorites' or 'Bookmarks' menu.

Figure 10.1   Search results (Source: *The American Heritage Dictionary of the English Language* (2000), available at htttp//:www.bartleby.com/61/, accessed 31 August 2007)

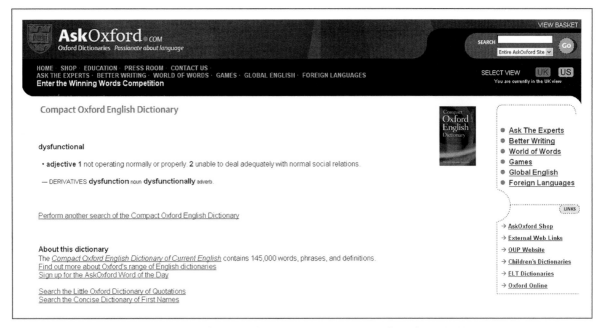

Figure 10.2   Search results (Source: *Compact Oxford English Dictionary* (2005), available at http://www.askoxford.com, accessed 31 August 2007)

- I set up my browser's home page so that when I open it I am taken directly to my favourite search engine (look up 'home page' in your browser's Help to see how to do this).

- I had the experience to guess that typing 'dictionary' would be enough for the search engine to find me some useful results. I also guessed that by typing an unusual word like 'dysfunctional' directly into the search engine I might find what I wanted to know.

- I also knew about using 'links' (hyperlinks) to move from one web page to others. I knew that when the mouse pointer changes to a 'pointing finger' icon then I am over a link. And, in my browser, if I click on words that are blue and underlined I am taken to a new web page.

Perhaps some of this is new to you and you need advice from someone with more experience. Once you have done a few searches, however, it all seems very simple.

10.2.2   Filing web addresses

As soon as I found the dictionaries I saved their web addresses in case I wanted to visit them again. This is very easy: when I opened a dictionary's website, I went to my browser's menu toolbar and clicked on 'Favorites', then 'Add to Favorites'. (I was using Internet Explorer as my browser; in Netscape the equivalent menu is 'Bookmarks'.) Before you save a web address check that you are on the website's homepage so that your saved link takes you back to the right place.

You can, if you choose, accumulate an extremely long list of web addresses. However, it then becomes difficult to find an address you want. Because I use the web a lot and want to be able to find addresses quickly, I set up a filing system in Favorites. Figure 10.3 shows an example of a filing system.

Figure 10.3   Example of a filing system using Favorites

See Chapter 2 Section 2.4.3, Maintaining a filing system

When I click on the Favorites menu a list of folders drops down. In Figure 10.3 you can see that I have opened the Study folder, revealing three more folders inside it: two for course topics and one for study skills. It is a hierarchical filing system. I decided to store some dictionary site addresses in the main Study folder; you can see that two are listed. This enables me to click on any one of the links and be taken straight to that online dictionary.

I created the folders by clicking on 'Organize Favorites' (see Figure 10.3, under 'Add to Favorites') and using the buttons available. To store a website's address, all I had to do was click on 'Add to Favorites' and then on the folder ('Study') that I wanted to add it to.

Saving useful web addresses in a well-organised filing system is a key strategy for effective web searching. The World Wide Web is a huge, unstructured and potentially confusing environment to work in. But if you take the time to set up your own customised system of links to the sites you visit regularly, it soon becomes familiar and extremely convenient.

Key points

- For a quick information search, just type a well-chosen word or two into a search engine. If you don't find what you want, try different words or other search engines.

- Make a shortcut to your favourite search engine(s), so that you can use it whenever the need strikes. Save the address in your Favorites folder or set it as your home page.

- Set up a web-address filing system, so that you can keep track of all the useful web addresses you save.

10.3   Finding academic material[1]

In Section 10.2.1 I described carrying out a quick, informal search to see if anything useful showed up. But what if you were doing some project work for your course which meant that you had to carry out your own research? Let's say I am interested in the Augustan period of English Literature and I am intending to do a project on one of its main authors. This would involve searching for specifically *academic* information and resources. It is not best to use an ordinary search engine for that. When I tried to, using Google to search for 'Augustan', Figure 10.4 shows what I found.

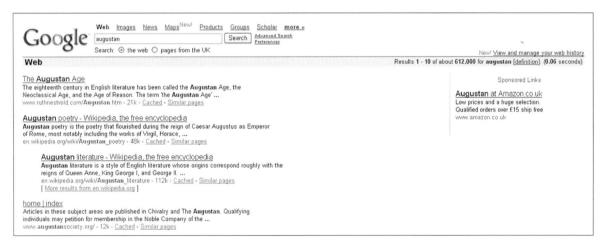

Figure 10.4   An ordinary search (Source: http://www.google.co.uk/, accessed 31 August 2007)

[1] My thanks to Open University colleagues Simon Rae (Institute of Educational Technology) and Derek Sheills (Arts Faculty) for their help with this section.

This is not very helpful. Mainly I am directed to a general encyclopaedia, which might be useful, but what I want at this stage is some ideas about good source material on the subject – articles and books I might consult to get me started.

10.3.1   Advanced searches

For this I will need to do an advanced search. Figure 10.5 shows what a search on Google Scholar came up with.

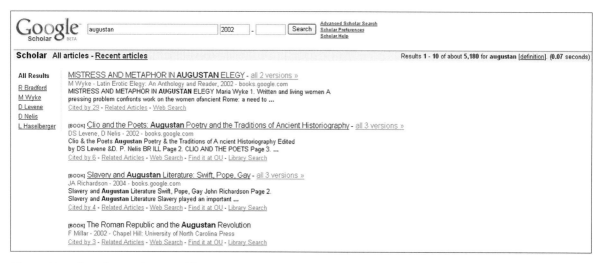

Figure 10.5   An advanced search (Source: http://scholar.google.com/, accessed 31 August 2007)

This is a bit more like it. The third entry, Slavery and Augustan Literature, is a more specific topic than I really want but at least it identifies some of the major writers of the period. Armed with this knowledge, I could use 'Swift' or 'Pope' as my search terms on this or another search engine.

Your university library will be able to give you advice about making advanced searches in your subject, and may offer some training in it.

10.3.2   Gateways and portals in the arts

The best way of searching for academic resources is to consult a subject-specific gateway, such as Intute (www.intute.ac.uk) shown in Figure 10.6. This gateway includes an area designed specifically for arts and humanities scholars. It is so called because it is precisely a 'gateway' to a host of other subject-specific websites and resources on the internet, available at the click of your mouse. What the site presents is a catalogue of resources for us to browse and choose from.

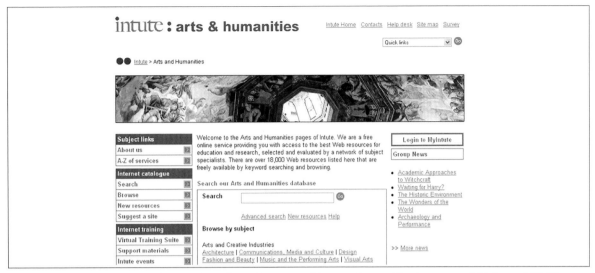

Figure 10.6   Intute gateway (Source: http://www.intute.ac.uk/artsandhumanities/, accessed 31 August 2007)

As you can see, the guardians of Intute have had their resources vetted by specialists so you can be pretty sure that they are, as claimed here, among 'the best Web resources for education and research' in your subject. And these materials are also up to date – see the 'New resources' button on the left of the screen, under 'Internet catalogue'. Gateways such as these are invaluable. Intute would certainly provide all the resources and information I might want for my project work, and much more.

Key points

- Invest some time exploring the sources in your field. Practise finding relevant articles and journals, so that when you are under pressure with assignment deadlines you can find what you need quickly.

- Find out from your university library how its catalogue works and what access it offers to wider information sources. Take advantage of any training offered on information searching; it will pay big dividends.

- When you need to do a serious search for literature, start by finding the major gateways and databases in your field.

- Take a flexible approach to searching. Start from different points and pursue different avenues of enquiry. Gradually you will begin to recognise the main features of the network of knowledge in your field.

10.3.3   Evaluating text-based websites and materials

When you have found an article or other material on the internet – especially if its value is not attested to by gateway guardians – you need to assess

See Chapter 4
Section 4.6, Reading
critically

269

whether it is actually the kind of thing you could use. How reliable is the source website likely to be? How useful will the material be for your purposes?

The Open University Library's SAFARI website offers a checklist, called PROMPT, for evaluating sites and written material found on the web (The Open University Library, 2001). Academically respectable websites and materials are seen to have certain characteristics which you can assess by asking a series of questions, as shown in Box 10.1 (based on PROMPT).

Box 10.1   Evaluation checklist

Presentation – does the website specialise in academic writing and research (probably quite formal and sober in appearance), as distinct from a popular site (rather flashy, aiming to persuade or sell things)?

Relevance – is the website relevant to your interests? (You must go online knowing what you are looking for.) Is the material pitched at the right level for your course?

Objectivity – does the material in the website try to be detached, fair and balanced, leaving you to draw your own conclusions?

Method – does the material offer evidence of the claims made in it, refer to other writers' work, and provide lists of references (including to other websites)?

Provenance – who provides the website, and can you trust them? (e.g. university sites and the BBC are generally regarded as reliable)

Timeliness – when was the material produced? When was the site last updated? (Non-academic sites often do not provide this information.)

You will find it helpful to remind yourself of this checklist when searching the web.

10.4   Misuse of online data

Having stressed the immense benefits of searching the internet, it is important to conclude on a note of caution.

10.4.1   The myth of infinite access to knowledge

See Chapter 3, Understanding how you learn

Access to the internet will not turn you into a wise and knowledgeable person. A mountain of data does not amount to *knowledge*. Ideas and information are of value only if they are put into a context. It is the *understanding* within which what you find on the web is framed that constitutes knowledge; and developing understanding takes time and thought.

Websites that are carefully structured and lead you through a well-organised sequence of ideas will help you to acquire knowledge – always provided that you start out with a well-formed idea of what it is you are looking for. The internet is invaluable when your thoughts have reached a point at which you need more resources, but meandering across cyberspace at the whim of a search engine will leave your knowledge untouched.

10.4.2   Substituting a search engine for your brain

It is easy to produce dreadful assignments by using a search engine to do a quick, undiscriminating trawl. Searching for a few words from your assignment task, copying from websites you come across and then pasting together disconnected bits and pieces to present as your assignment will get you a very low grade. And you could be accused of plagiarism.

It is *not* the purpose of assignments to show that you can use a search engine, or that you can copy and paste text. Anyone can do those things. It is an insult to your teachers' intelligence to expect them to waste time looking at a 'what I found on the web' scrapbook.

It is an excellent use of the internet to conduct a careful search, using relevant portals and databases, evaluate what you find using the PROMPT criteria, then work carefully selected elements of it into your line of argument. But using your search engine as a substitute for your brain is simply a waste of everyone's time, including your own.

10.4.3   Plagiarising assignments

A variation on this theme is to substitute a search engine plus someone else's brain for your own. If you hunt for other people's assignments online, then submit them as your own work, wholly or in part, this is plagiarism. Together, word processing and the internet have opened up huge opportunities for cheating. However, not all the technology is on the cheats' side. Plagiarism detectors are increasingly sophisticated, making it quite likely that students will be caught if they substitute the words of others for their own. Just as it takes moments for a search engine to trawl the internet, it takes very little time to scan an assignment looking for matches with other work. Universities come down hard on plagiarism because it threatens the integrity of assessment and awards systems. Plagiarising other people's assignments is not an intelligent risk to take.

10.4.4   Theft of intellectual property

The ICT age has placed new emphasis on the concept of intellectual property. Now that most texts are produced in electronic form and many are accessible on the internet it is extremely easy to 'capture' other people's words and images and reuse them. You might easily do this without ill will. You see a well-expressed idea and grab it for your electronic files, so that you can think about it some more. So far so good. You are allowed to take a copy for private study purposes, and it is fine to quote from these sources provided you make clear which words are quoted and include a reference. However, when you are writing something of your own, if you incorporate borrowed words without any acknowledgement it is of course plagiarism. If you then publish what you write, whether conventionally or on the internet, it also becomes theft of intellectual property and an infringement of copyright law.

Box 10.2   Government advice on intellectual property

A number of exceptions allow limited use of copyright works without the permission of the copyright owner. These uses are known as fair dealing [...] It is allowed to make single copies or take short extracts of works when [they are] used for research that you do not make any money from or [for] private studying, [or for an] educational course [...] If your use is for non-commercial research and/or private study you must ensure that the work you reproduce is supported by a sufficient acknowledgement.

(UK Intellectual Property Office, 2006a)

Copyright applies to computing and the internet in the same way as material in other media. [...] If you download, distribute or put material on the internet that belongs to others you should ensure that you have the owner's permission, unless any of the exceptions apply.

(UK Intellectual Property Office, 2006b)

Key points

The accessibility of online information is open to a number of abuses.

- It is easy to be seduced into a kind of 'beachcombing' on the web. Confusing information with knowledge, you can wander from website to website collecting disconnected snippets instead of working seriously and coherently with new ideas.

- It can be tempting to duck the challenge of essay writing by assembling your accumulated bits and pieces and presenting it as your finished assignment. This leads to very poor academic work.

- A further temptation is to plagiarise – to trawl the web for an assignment on the same topic to present as your own. This is increasingly risky and brings harsh penalties.

- The texts you find online are the intellectual property of the person who published them. It is important to be aware of intellectual property rights and to avoid breaking copyright law.

10.5   Using research in project work

To explore how to search online, evaluate the results and use them in a research project, let's take a case. We will assume that you are studying a course in Art History and trying to find images to illustrate and explore the representation of intellectuals in portraits in the twentieth-century inter-war period.

In fact, at the click of a mouse you can access thousands of images on the web. This is exhilarating, and also overwhelming – and it raises a number of questions. Where do you start? How do you know if you are seeing whole images or doctored versions of them? And how can you be sure that any accompanying information about the images is accurate and reliable?

10.5.1 Online searches for images [2]
Your method of finding an image will of course depend upon your reason for searching for it in the first place. There is a variety of different *types* of website that you might visit, depending on your needs.

Google Image Search
If you know the title of an image or the creator's name, and you just want to see what it looks like, it is quick and easy to use Google Image Search (part of the Google search engine). You can also do a subject search (e.g. for portraits). Simply type in the title of the work or the artist's name and click on search. (I typed in *Mona Lisa* and got 56,800 hits in 0.10 seconds!) A number of large thumbnails will appear on your screen. By clicking on each thumbnail you will see a larger version of the picture, and also a link to its host website which may give you some useful information about it.

However, it can be time consuming to work your way through the thumbnails, sometimes the links to host websites don't work, and sometimes these sites are not very helpful after all. You can speed up the process by trying to assess the addresses of the host websites that appear under each thumbnail, getting a sense of the host's main interest. For instance, in the case of well-known paintings, host websites can range from commercial greeting-card or table-mat manufacturers to the gallery that currently owns the work. Obviously, the gallery's site will be the most reliable for your purposes. Try this kind of search right now if you like.

Picture agency sites
Google Images will not normally include images from commercial picture libraries. If you want to find out what images are available on your subject, then picture agencies are a good source. They exist mainly to supply the media and publishing industries. Some will ask you to register before you start searching, but don't be deterred by this basic form filling because it is designed to protect their livelihood. These sites have simple search facilities – you just type in the keywords that relate to your subject (in this case, portraits of intellectuals). The trick is to find the *right* keywords, so be persistent and try every variation you can think of: perhaps 'portrait' and 'author' and the inter-war period dates, as a start. If that doesn't work, you could try 'writer' or 'novelist' instead of author.

Picture agencies divide into general and specialist suppliers. The giants of the general agency world are Corbis (http://pro.corbis.com) and Getty Images (http://editorial.gettyimages.com). Between them they represent thousands of contemporary artists and photographers, historical collections and institutions.

[2] Grateful thanks to Audrey Linkman of the Arts Faculty at The Open University for providing the first draft of this and the next section.

Their sites are easy to use, require no registration and offer an excellent starting point for searches on most subjects.

Gallery, library and museum sites

Once an image has been digitised it is capable of seamless manipulation. Unless you can see the original artefact you have no way of knowing whether the digital version has been enhanced, manipulated, or cropped. For educational and research purposes you need to be reassured that the digital file replicates the original as faithfully as the technology allows. You are dependent for this on the reputation of the institution hosting the site, and on the level of documentation it provides about itself, its digitised collections and the technical specifications of the digital images. So the most reliable sites are the galleries, libraries and museums that own the original works. They are primarily concerned with scholarship and research so their websites should provide accurate contextual information about images, their provenance (or origins) and date, details about their creation and medium, links to related items in the same collection and references to articles or publications in which the image has been cited. But some institutional websites are better than others.

As a model of excellence against which you can judge other institutions, pay a visit to the website of the Library of Congress Prints & Photographs Online Catalog (http://www.loc.gov/rr/print/catalog.html).

Difficulties of accessing good images

The technology of the web can affect your access to images. If you don't have a broadband connection, you will appreciate the time it can take to download them. Furthermore, most host sites can afford to place only a proportion of their holdings online, so sometimes you will not find what you are looking for. And sometimes the host's website is unreliable. Some sites can be revised to such an extent that the images you want are removed or existing links don't work; other sites can become outdated or disappear altogether. Using image databases offers a way round these difficulties.

A database provider defines the subject content, selects the images and, equally important, decides how much contextual information to provide about them and determines their quality. Academic librarians normally subscribe to image databases and they are then made available to the university's staff and students. (The Open University, for example, currently subscribes to SCRAN, the Scottish Cultural Resources Access Network.) These sites have been vetted, and you can depend on them being reliable. Find out what your university's library gives you access to.

The technology also affects the appearance of images. Colour is particularly problematic. You can be reasonably sure that the colours you see on your computer screen will *not* be the same as the colours in the original image. This is a problem for students of Art History, in which accurate reproduction of colour and tone is important for a full understanding of a painting.

In short, image databases should be quick and easy to access, and they should provide high-quality images and metadata, but they do not, and cannot, represent all that is available to you on the web.

10.5.2 Evaluating images

Once you have found some pictures, you have to evaluate them as images and decide how useful they will be to you. Let's assume that your project is entitled 'The representation of intellectual life in Britain in the interwar period, 1920–1936'. One of the things you want to do is find portraits of a number of writers of the period to see what they tell you about how these people wanted to project themselves and also how the artists saw them. So you search the National Portrait Gallery site (http://www.npg.org.uk) and find a formal portrait of the writer Sylvia Townsend Warner, a photograph taken by the society photographer Howard Coster in 1934 – see Figure 10.7.[3]

At first sight, you may be tempted to think that a photograph such as this is accurate and objective because it is produced by a machine – the camera merely reacts to the light that falls on the subject – and so this is a 'true' representation of the sitter. But in fact all photographs are created by the person behind the camera, who makes choices about when to take the picture, what to include in it and what lighting to use. Lighting is particularly important because it helps define mood; sunny highlights can be cheerful, shadows may convey sombreness or gloom. And these choices influence the ways in which the viewer responds to the subject. So a photograph doesn't represent the subject 'as it was' but, rather, as the photographer *chose* to represent it.

In your research you might find out that Coster and some of his contemporaries shared a number of ideas about the purpose and functions of the portrait, and they adopted working methods that expressed those ideas. Their underlying belief was that the purpose of a portrait is to convey the sitter's character as well as appearance. And the dominant idea was the need to *idealise* the sitter – to convey a positive rather than negative impression – which they achieved by manipulating the portrait's four constituent elements: expression, pose, backdrop and lighting. These ideas and practices, then, worked together to produce the image we see. But they are not apparent in the photograph. They work like scaffolding, vital in the construction phase but not visible in the finished product. If we want to analyse what an image has to say, we really need to understand how it was made.

[3] The National Portrait Gallery site lists a number of images of Sylvia Townsend Warner, including this one (which is currently not available to view online). This image is discussed by Penny Tinkler in her book *Smoke Signals* (2006).

Figure 10.7 Howard Coster, *Sylvia Townsend Warner*, 1934, photograph from an original 10 x 8 inch film negative. Photo: National Portrait Gallery, London

Activity 10.1

So, armed with this knowledge of Coster's beliefs, what impression do you have of Sylvia Townsend Warner? Look in turn at the four elements of the portrait: expression, pose, backdrop and lighting. What does the image suggest about her? Jot down your ideas.

Here are my thoughts. First, her *expression*. She is serious; she is not smiling and she is not looking at the viewer. She seems to be lost in her own thoughts. Also, she has her glasses on her nose. Some women might have felt a bit self-conscious about that. Perhaps the glasses convey the idea of reading and close study – the intellectual activities of the writer. They could be taken to indicate an intelligent woman. Her expression might suggest, then, that she is a serious, self-contained, intellectual person.

Does her *pose* reinforce this initial impression? She is sitting facing forward – as though we might be going to have a conversation. But it seems to me there is a contradiction here. It isn't just that her head is turned away from us, but that her left hand, palm inwards, is placed firmly on her knee and seems to act as a barrier that marks out her private space. The pose works to reinforce the notion of self-containment and independence. And the chin resting on the right hand has come to be recognised as the pose of the thinker. So the idea of an intelligent, intellectual woman gains support too. But the sitter has also used her pose – or the photographer has – to project an image of an unconventional woman. She is sitting with her legs crossed, a harmless enough position to us today but long regarded as a pose a lady would never adopt in her portrait. And she has boldly agreed to be photographed holding a lighted cigarette. To be photographed smoking in the interwar period was a radical departure for a woman and signalled her successful entry into the public domain on 'equal terms' with men (Tinkler, 2006, pp. 172–3). Notice too how the cigarette has nearly burned down to the end, emphasising the idea of a woman taken up with and distracted by her thoughts.

However, a comparison between the sitter and the *backdrop* exposes another contradiction. She is wearing a skirt and a pretty blouse that suggest conventional femininity, as does her jewellery. But the backdrop is stark. A chair is the only prop permitted in the portrait. And its arms enclose the sitter, thereby emphasising her self-containment? The dark, empty background concentrates attention on the sitter while adding weight and seriousness to the picture. Finally, as regards *lighting*, high side-lighting falls on her head and upper body – perhaps suggesting a woman with brains *and* heart?

We may surmise that Sylvia Townsend Warner collaborated with the photographer in projecting this image, certainly of a woman, but one who is serious and independent, a self-contained intellectual, and who is also unconventional while holding her own in society. All this was not apparent at first sight, which is why it is so important that we learn to analyse and understand the ideas that are presented in images. But how far this reflects any kind of reality is another question. To make this kind of judgement, in the context of our research project, we would need to call on sources other than visual ones.

10.6   Doing project work

Many courses in the arts and humanities include a substantial project-work component involving research, even if of a limited and guided kind. This is an opportunity for you to study a topic of your own choice in depth, working independently and extending interests and ideas of your own. It involves:

- setting your own targets
- posing central questions to explore
- seeking out the primary and secondary source material you need
- analysing and interpreting your material, and assessing its value
- producing a substantial text of your own.

Doing this kind of work gives you an idea of how knowledge is *created* in your field. When all goes well, it increases your enthusiasm for your subject, brings a great sense of achievement and produces a deep kind of understanding. But it is demanding. It can be very interesting and satisfying, but it can also go badly wrong.

The biggest pitfall is that almost everyone is *too ambitious* to begin with. Things always turn out to be more complicated than they seem and every aspect of project work is deceptively time-consuming. There are several stages involved, each of which takes time and effort. One of the keys to success is recognising the importance of each stage and spreading your time and energies across all of them. These *stages* are:

1   Formulating a question to explore
2   Planning the enquiry
3   Carrying out the research
4   Writing a project report.

The third stage looks like the bulk of the work. But deciding on the question to investigate, narrowing it down sufficiently, and designing and planning the project always take a lot of thought. You can easily let these early stages eat too far into the time you have for the project as a whole. Then the third stage almost always throws up plenty of unexpected problems. However, the writing phase is the one that really catches people unawares. You have to present your research in the wider context of the subject from which it arises, and also work out how to structure the report so that your line of argument is clear and leads to your conclusions. And you have to keep the forward momentum of that argument going while also introducing what you have discovered – of which there is plenty. All this takes several draft stages and a lot of time.

10.6.1   Formulating a question

See Chapter 3 Section 3.4.1, Reading

When you make your own enquiries you draw on your existing knowledge of a discipline or subject area and decide on a *specific* question to explore; a question that is relevant to some aspect of the subject and which interests you. That means you must have some understanding of what the important questions and issues are in your subject, and why they are important. In other words, you must have acquired appropriate 'frameworks for thinking' within your discipline.

It is very important to be clear about what you are setting out to do, and not to be too ambitious. If you start from an interest in a broad issue such as 'portraiture in the twentieth-century inter-war period', you need to make this a more focused and precise enquiry that is manageable within the *time* and *word limits* set for the project. For instance, you might come up with 'Representations of Intellectual Life in Britain, 1926–36'. You have narrowed the scope of the enquiry in terms of both your emphasis and the time period concerned.

But it is most helpful if you actually put the enquiry to yourself *as a question* rather than a 'topic heading'; as, for instance, 'How was intellectual life in Britain represented by artists ...?' The *question* focuses and channels your enquiries by forcing you to seek out some 'answers' to it. You must analyse the factors involved and explain and justify your conclusions. Working from the topic heading, it is all too easy to meander around the issues in a rather aimless way and, ultimately, find yourself on the receiving end of the project marker's most common complaints: 'Failed to relate project work to the wider context'; 'Didn't use the information: too descriptive, not enough analysis and explanation.'

While you are reading around the subject, and the question you will explore is taking shape, you need to make *preliminary enquiries* into what *resources* are available to you. If you cannot easily get hold of the main primary sources you need then you will have to re-define the enquiry and make changes to your research question. In the case of representations of intellectual life during this period, we have seen that many such images are available on the web; it looks as if primary source material will not be a problem. You will also need secondary sources, such as general histories of the period and more specialised intellectual histories. Again, it is likely that these are fairly readily available. If you also wanted to track down newspaper reviews or articles on foremost intellectuals, you would need to look for these on the web or use the reference section of your university library. The library may also be able to get material for you through inter-library loan schemes. But if any of this source material turned out to be too difficult or impossible to access, then you would have to alter your plans. Making these enquiries *early on* enables you to change the direction of your work before you have invested too much time in it.

10.6.2   Planning your enquiry

At this stage, you will be deciding what *methods* of enquiry to use and the *scale* of investigation to attempt. Will examining images, histories and newspapers provide enough of the right kinds of information? Or is it possible to seek first-hand information by interviewing some artists of the period? (But bear in mind that the survivors would be well into their nineties by now.)

Whatever decisions you make about method and scope, you will certainly need to use as primary source material portraits of a number of intellectuals of the period, such as Sylvia Townsend Warner. As regards secondary sources, you might start with a *specialist encyclopaedia* on your subject. These provide a general overview of the field and usually contain extensive bibliographies, so they are a good place to begin. But you will also want to read up-to-date work. For that you must refer to the *academic journals* that regularly publish scholarly articles and the results of recent research in your field, many of which are available electronically. There are specialist journals that cater for all arts and humanities subjects and any good library will have lists of them. And of course you can do a 'literature search' online (see Section 10.3, above). You may well find that other people have carried out fairly similar enquiries, and you will want to learn from the methods they used as well as refer to their discoveries in your work.

Having identified the material you need, you have to get access to as much as you can before the start of the next stage of the project. At this point you also have to decide what *deadlines* you need to meet at every stage of the project and draw up an appropriate timetable for your work, perhaps week by week. And you may well be asked to submit a *project outline* for discussion with your tutor. Your tutor's advice will undoubtedly save you time and effort later on, so do not miss this or any other opportunity for guidance and help.

10.6.3   Carrying out research

See Chapter 4, Reading, and Chapter 5, Making notes

During this stage you get down to the business of analysing and interpreting the meanings of your primary source material – portraits – just as we did with the photograph of Sylvia Townsend Warner in Section 10.5.2. You will also need to explore the beliefs and techniques of the artists concerned. And you will analyse your secondary source material (newspaper reviews, books and articles) in the ways outlined in earlier chapters of this book. As you do all this you will be making notes towards your project report. In this connection, it is very important to write down full *references* for all the material you use *as you read each item*. Then you can easily find particular parts of it again when you need to. And you will also be building up your References list or Bibliography *as you go along*. It is much better to build this kind of list up gradually rather than leaving yourself with a lot of fiddly work to do at the end.

See Chapter 8 Section 8.2.8, Reviewing, revising and polishing

Whatever style of referencing you use, what matters is that you always make the references in the *same* way throughout You should also keep your references together in one place as you work (on cards, in a notebook or online) so that you don't lose anything. You have to keep your source material and notes well organised too, or you will waste a lot of precious time hunting around for things.

Towards the end of the research phase you should be starting to make an *outline plan* for your project report and even to draft sections of it as they begin to take shape in your mind. And, as the deadline for the writing stage approaches, you may simply have to call a halt to your investigations.

Whatever your topic, there is always more material than you can handle in the time available. You must be ruthless about keeping to your schedule.

10.6.4   Writing the project report

Finally, you write up your project report. It is important to recognise that this will go through several *drafts*. You can't just sit down and write a report on this sort of scale quickly or easily. You will have gathered far too much material for that. And it may take you a little while really to get into the writing. Towards the end of the research phase, as you face up to writing proper, many people reach a kind of plateau where nothing much seems to be going on. The excitement of the planning and discovery stages is behind you. You may have become so familiar with your topic that it seems trivial, and your findings insignificant. But push on. Once you are fully engaged in writing you will re-discover your enthusiasm in the intensity of the experience. Talking about your work with other students and friends helps at every stage, and especially now when you are really having to sort things out in your mind.

See Chapter 8 Section 8.6, Summaries

Try to achieve *different* things at each draft stage. For the first full draft, aim to just get everything down on paper, even if you are dissatisfied with parts of it as you write. Writing a research project report involves a lot more than producing a description of your work. You have to:

- explain the *rationale* for what you have done, outlining the background from which your question arose so that your readers can see its significance
- explain your choice of research *methods*
- plot a coherent line of *argument* for your report that takes you towards your conclusions and, as you analyse your material, explain yourself clearly and justify your judgements.

So it is quite enough just to get things down somehow at first-draft stage.

As you work towards the second draft you can go back over the unsatisfactory parts of the report. Concentrate on the *structure* of your argument, making sure that ideas are adequately linked and sections follow on one from the other towards your conclusions. Then re-organise and prune your writing until it is closer to the required length. As we saw in Chapter 9, the difficulty with writing on this kind of scale is keeping the forward momentum of argument going while at each stage adequately explaining your ideas and introducing appropriate illustrative material and evidence. So, to enable the reader to follow you, you must keep 'signposting' the direction your argument is taking. Finally, for the third draft, you will need to check that the meaning of each sentence is clear and polish up the report. Your writing is the means through which your ideas exist, so care lavished on expression is not an optional extra.

See Chapter 8 Section 8.2.6, Organising your material

It is very likely that you will be using a word processor so the draft stages will not be as distinct as this account suggests. But it is very important *not* to try to do everything at once. It is still worth behaving as if you were producing

See Chapter 8 Section 8.2.8, Reviewing, revising and polishing several separate drafts; at particular points going through your writing with these *different* aims in mind.

10.6.5   Research skills

This kind of independent work teaches some very valuable skills:

- how to set about an enquiry
- how and where to find source material and information
- how to make your own investigations
- strategic planning
- time management
- cutting corners and being pragmatic
- analysing and interpreting primary and secondary source material
- forming your own conclusions
- writing clearly and concisely when you have a lot of very varied material to present
- making a convincing case.

You need to approach a project with care and allow yourself time to develop these skills. And you will need all the help you can get. So start your project work early, seek your tutor's advice at every stage and study carefully any 'project guidance' material that is offered. Above all, be *modest* in your aims and take very seriously all *deadlines* for different stages of your work, for project outlines and draft reports.

Key points

When you undertake your own enquiries:

- don't be too ambitious at the outset; define a narrowly focused *question* which you can investigate fully in the time available
- make a *timetable* for your work and stick to all deadlines; start early and allow plenty of time for each project stage (especially writing the project report)
- in your report show why your investigation matters and what it contributes to your discipline or subject area; include analysis and explanation as well as description in the report
- try to achieve different things at each draft stage of the report
- if in doubt about source material, ask your tutor or a librarian
- if in despair, don't suffer in silence; get in touch with your tutor and other students, or anyone who is prepared to listen.

When it is successful, this kind of work is a great opportunity to explore your own particular interests. In spite of the time it takes, it is all-absorbing and very rewarding. It helps you really get 'inside' the subject you are studying.

References

HEFCE (2004) 'Enhancing excellence in learning and teaching', *HEFCE Strategic Plan 2003–08*, available at http://www.hefce.ac.uk/Pubs/hefce/2004/04_17/ (accessed 31 August 2007).

The Open University Library (2001) 'Section 5 Evaluating Information', *SAFARI*, http://ltssolweb1.open.ac.uk/safari_guests/contentsframe.htm (accessed 31 August 2007).

Tinkler, P. (2006) *Smoke Signals: Women, Smoking and Visual Culture in Britain*, Oxford and New York, Berg.

UK Intellectual Property Office (2006a) 'Exceptions to Copyright', available at http://www.ipo.gov.uk/copy/c-manage/c-useenforce/c-useenforce-use/c-useenforce-use-exception.htm (accessed 31 August 2007).

UK Intellectual Property Office (2006b) 'Copyright applies to...computing and the internet', available at http://www.ipo.gov.uk/copy/c-applies/c-compute.htm (accessed 31 August 2007).

CHAPTER 11
Preparing for examinations

11.1   The positive side of exams

Are you looking forward to your exams? I guess not. An exam is not most people's favourite part of a course. Yet it isn't simply an unpleasant ordeal *en route* to getting a qualification. In spite of the stress and the disruption to your life, exams can make an extremely valuable contribution to your learning. In fact, *because* of the stress an exam can help you find the will-power and energy to take matters in hand and finally pull your understanding of a course together into the best shape you are capable of. During the rest of your studies there is always something new to get on with, and you keep moving from one topic or text to the next. When an exam approaches you can take stock, asking yourself 'What is this course all about? How can I bring all my new knowledge under control?'

An exam brings a *performance* element into your studies. With an essay you can work for as long as you choose before submitting it, but in an exam you have to perform at a specified time and place. You have to 'think on your feet' and try to get things as right as you can first time. This puts pressure on you, but the pressure can be a creative force. The exam is a kind of ritual that helps you to draw a peak performance out of yourself. If you can channel all your nervous energy into sensible preparations for it, you will come to understand the course far better than you ever would otherwise; revisiting topics studied some time earlier often leads to a fuller, much richer understanding of them. Similarly, once you are in the exam, the pressure to write off the top of your head can help you take command of your new knowledge, saying things as they come to you in ways that make sense to *you*. You are no longer reliant on what is said in the books. You present the knowledge as your own.

The stress exams create is a powerful fuel – very useful but quite volatile. It can help you to achieve a great deal, but you need techniques for *managing* and *using* it. These techniques are what this chapter aims to provide.

- Section 11.2 helps keep your anxiety levels down by poking holes in some common myths about exams.
- Section 11.3 switches from myth to reality by outlining some common pitfalls you should avoid.

Then there are three sections looking at how you can take a positive approach to exams.

- Section 11.4 explores strategies for tackling exam revision.
- Section 11.5 discusses how to make final preparations prior to the exam.
- Section 11.6 considers how to manage your performance during the exam itself.

If you use these sections to plan a strategy of your own you will be able to approach exams confident of doing the best you are capable of. You sign up for courses because you want to learn. If you approach exams properly, they can help you to achieve that goal.

Box 11.1   The exam model assumed here

Exams vary in the time allowed and the number of questions you have to answer. Traditionally, exams in the arts and humanities are of three hours, allowing one hour for each of three essay answers. However, some exams are now only two hours long, and some involve a range of question types – for instance, you may be asked to analyse a text, such as an historical document (a 'gobbet'), or a painting, or complete multiple choice questions. And some exam papers are divided into sections, each of which attracts different marks.

In what follows I shall talk in terms of a three-hour exam in which you have to answer four essay questions, each of which carries 25% of the marks, because this is quite difficult to handle. When you have found out about the details of your exam you will have to make appropriate adjustments to what is said here.

Key points

- Exams may be challenging experiences but they can make a major contribution to your learning.
- You can use the stress created by exams as a positive force if you harness it to help you pull the course together and understand the issues better.

To control and channel this stress:

- you need to keep your anxieties in perspective
- make sure you know what is expected of you
- work out sensible plans for preparing for the exam.

11.2   Myths about exams

The tensions around exams create warped perceptions. And the effect of generations of students sharing their warped perceptions has given rise to some unhelpful myths. If you want to take a constructive approach to exams, a good first step is to take these myths apart, then cast them aside.

11.2.1   To fail would ruin your life

The stress of having to 'perform' in an exam can help you to focus a lot of energy on the effort to do well. But the other side of that coin is becoming preoccupied by fears of failure. You begin to feel that a bad result is the worst thing that could happen to you. And, of course, it *is* disappointing not to do well when you have put a lot of time and energy into something. But exams are *not* a life-or-death matter. Most people get results similar to their marks during the course, but if you don't pass it is not the end of everything. Life goes on. Taking a course of study is a worthwhile undertaking, and you will gain a great deal from it whether or not you do well in the exam. If you want to you can usually resit. Recognise that you will survive the worst the exam can throw at you – failure – shrug your shoulders and do your best.

11.2.2   The exam will expose you as a fool and a fraud

❝ I'm having restless nights. I just can't get the exam out of my head. ❞

It is quite common to dream of being in an exam unable to answer a single question. Exams seem to bring out lurking fears of being revealed as an imposter – as though you have only been pretending to understand the course and now the exam will expose the awful truth. Dreams of abject inadequacy show the intensity of our hopes and fears. Our fantasy examiners sternly probe for any signs of weakness and mercilessly reject anyone with less than comprehensive knowledge of the course. Yet real exams are not at all like that. Examiners are delighted when students pass and usually go out of their way to find what is good in the answers they read. And nobody will think you stupid if you don't do well. Nobody will accuse you of wasting their time. People will just be sorry and hope that you do better next time.

11.2.3   You have to know the whole course in detail

Many students (especially part-time students) will have to miss out some sections of a course. Even the best students tend to specialise in those areas that interest them. You have done well to make it as far as the exam. It is no use at this stage worrying about what you have left out. It is far better to consolidate what you *have* done than attempt any desperate catching up on what you haven't. It is too late now for studying from first principles.

Box 11.2   Cutting exams down to size

To put things in perspective, think about the practical constraints of exams. How much can you write in a three-hour exam? Not a whole lot. So you don't need to know 'everything'. If you have to answer four questions you need to know enough to write about three sides on each (depending on your handwriting). And bear in mind that your marker is not going to examine your script in fine detail to see whether it's worth publishing. Markers spend between five and ten minutes on an answer, seeing whether the general gist seems right, whether a reasonable number of key points are there and whether the argument flows tolerably well. That is how exams are. Your essays during the course are your opportunity to put together detailed and carefully thought-out arguments for close reading by your tutor. Exams are much more rough and ready exercises, both in the writing and the marking.

So *don't* worry about having left out parts of the course. You just need to be able to pull enough together from what you *have* studied to write for around 40 minutes on your chosen topics.

11.2.4   If you haven't understood everything it isn't worth taking the exam

If you fully understand everything then you are studying a course that is too easy for you. It is normal to feel confused by new knowledge. Any decent course sets all kinds of ideas turning over in your mind, some of which you will still be sorting out months later. If you have *tried* to make sense as you studied, you have probably made more progress with understanding than you realise. But on any challenging course you can't expect to achieve a full grasp of every issue by the time of the exam. The point is to use your preparation for the exam to pull things together, to make *the best sense you can*.

11.2.5   Exam questions are impossible to understand

Your first look at a past exam paper for your course may give you a bit of a fright. Exam questions often look very broad and demanding at first sight. They may look abstract in form and seem oblique in their wording. However, the obliqueness is not malicious – noone is trying to trick you or trip you up. Rather, the examiners are usually trying to point you towards a *specific topic* in the course without answering the question *for* you, or they want to give you some *choice* about which texts you will discuss in your answers (plays, paintings, documents, etc.). In other words, they are trying to be helpful.

Always keep in mind that the exam is a test of your understanding of the *course* you have been studying, not your general knowledge. The answer to each question on the paper lies somewhere within what you have studied. So don't panic. Instead, carefully match what you know of the *course* against what the *questions* seem to be asking. There is no mystery; the examiners want you to display knowledge of specific parts of the course. It is a question of working out which parts.

11.2.6   An exam shows up the gaps in your education

Some people worry that their whole educational background makes them somehow inadequate to the task ahead; that failings and omissions in the past will come home to roost in the exam. This is a misleading trick that anxiety plays. An exam is *not* a test of general knowledge (it would be impossible to mark in a standardised way if it were). In fact, it is a big mistake to try to answer an exam question using only your general knowledge – your script marker is unlikely to be impressed. The marking guide will list some quite specific points from the course for which marks can be given. Going off on your own tack, however well informed you may be, is a high-risk strategy. If general educational background does show through, it is in the roundedness of answers and the refinements of writing style that might push a good answer up to excellent. In other words, educational background may help with the finishing gloss, but it is not part of the basics of getting the job done.

11.2.7   Exams are for people with a good memory

Most university-level exams are *not* memory tests. The point of studying arts and humanities subjects at higher levels is to develop the *skills* of textual analysis and interpretation and your *understanding* of ideas. The purpose of the exam is to give you an opportunity to show how well you have understood the texts and the concepts explored in the course. You will be asked to *use* your knowledge and ideas to *argue a case*. If you revise constructively before the exam, the role of pure memory will be quite small. Concentrate on *organising* your notes and your thoughts during the revision period (see Section 11.4). On the basis of your revision, you will find it fairly easy to remember as much textual detail as you need to illustrate and support your arguments.

11.2.8   Exams are for quick thinkers and writers

See Section 11.5.1, Get your thinking in before the exam

Can you think quickly enough and write quickly enough to pass an exam? Probably. You should, in any case, do most of your thinking in advance of the exam itself, so sheer speed of thought is not a key factor. What *does* matter is how well you *organise* your ideas and how well you *plan* your exam strategy. Working to a good plan, you can use time in an exam extremely efficiently.

On the other hand, speed of handwriting may be a significant factor if it seriously restricts the amount you can get down. If you can write 500–700 words in 40 minutes, that should be sufficient to get a high mark, although it is impossible to give hard and fast rules about this. Some students write short pithy answers that are very good while others write pages without saying much. The fact that you have a lot of adrenalin pumping in an exam will help you to write much more quickly than usual, but if you have doubts, give yourself some practice in writing at speed beforehand – especially if you normally use a word processor and are not in the habit of writing by hand. If you are seriously worried about being a slow writer, talk to your tutor, an educational adviser or a counsellor. They may be able to arrange for you to have extra time for the exam. (Most universities will make special exam arrangements for students who have real difficulties of any kind.) In general, though, it is far more important to focus on the quality of your answer rather than the speed at which you can write.

11.2.9   You have to revise until you drop

Exam folklore abounds with stories of heroic last-ditch orgies of work, deep into the night. There may be some truth in them; we *are* capable of extraordinary feats when the pressure is on. But the telling of these stories is more do with the intensity of people's hopes and fears than with reality. It is *not* true that all preparations can be effectively accomplished at the very last moment, especially if you are studying part-time and have to keep another life going at the same time.

Box 11.3   How your mind works under pressure

Your mind works differently under pressure, and you need to understand those differences in order to 'manage' yourself in the build-up to the exam. In the days just before the exam the tension builds up, providing you with lots of nervous energy. You can get a lot done, but it is harder to keep yourself under control and channel your energy in helpful directions. Being highly charged makes you good at focusing attention on concrete matters in hand, but less good at thinking through broad, abstract issues. Do your broad planning well in advance, so that as the exam approaches you have clear-cut strategies already worked out: for tackling revision, for allocating time in the exam, for taking the exam questions apart, for structuring your answers. If you have well-developed plans, you will find you can think surprisingly clearly once the exam has started. But if you leave all thought about the exam to the last couple of days you will just be in a flap.

Key points

- Failing an exam is not the end of the world; keep your anxieties in perspective.
- Everyone wants you to pass, including the examiner.
- Don't worry about what you haven't done during the course. Work out how to make the best use of what you have done.
- You are not expected to understand 'everything'. There are bound to be areas of the course about which you feel confused and under-prepared.
- Don't panic when you look at past papers. Exam questions usually link directly to things you have covered in the course.
- Don't worry about what you didn't know when you started the course. Build on what you have learned during the course.
- University exams are more about what you understand than your memory for details. Getting your course notes organised will sort your memory out.
- Speed in an exam is mainly to do with having very clear plans and sticking to them.
- Don't turn your life into a complete misery by working all hours just before an exam. You probably will work intensively in the last few days. But do it in a planned way. Use your time efficiently, conserve your energies and keep yourself calm.

In the realm of myth, exams are monstrous ordeals survived only by superhuman effort. They are devised by sadists to expose the weaknesses of ordinary mortals. They bring life-shattering consequences. And so on – the stuff of nightmares. The reality is much more mundane. Exams do bring stress, but they are just another part of the education process which countless people cope with, mostly successfully. To experience the least pain and achieve the results you deserve take a practical approach. Be *realistic* about *yourself* and about *what the exam requires of you*. Prepare yourself carefully and sensibly to build up to a 'peak performance'. *Don't* waste your energies dithering about in a panic.

11.3   What to avoid

Having disposed of some myths, what about the reality? What mistakes might you actually make? We can get an idea of this from what boards of examiners say in reports on exams. While their reports frequently stress how *well* many students tackle exams, they also identify some common faults.

11.3.1   Not answering the question

It isn't just *what* you know but *how* you say it. You are expected to *use* what you know to *argue a case* in answer to the *specific question* that has been set. If you don't, your script marker sighs, writes 'Doesn't answer the question' below your answer and marks you down accordingly. Examiners point to several ways you can fail to answer the question.

- Not recognising what one of the *key terms* in the question means. (For instance, answering a question on 'primitive' art thinking that the term means 'uncultured'.) You have to think carefully about what each of the words in the question might mean, and also pay attention to the dates given for any period you are asked to discuss. If there is a term you don't know, avoid the question. Your marks will be badly affected if you guess and get it wrong.

- Not recognising which *issues* from the course are being raised. Every question tries to point you towards specific texts, concepts or issues covered in the course. You have to spot which.

- Not offering *critical analysis* and *argument*. However the question is posed, it is generally expected that you will be presenting arguments for and against a point of view (or points of view) implied in the question. Your first job, as you read a question closely, is to identify the point of view it presents. Your next job is to remind yourself of some other point(s) of view from which you can criticise that position. Your answer can then be constructed as an argument between two (or more) positions.

- Not taking an *objective stance*. You are not supposed to harangue your reader with personal opinions and flamboyant rhetoric. You should observe the same principles of objectivity in an exam as in your essays. That means you must provide evidence from the texts you discuss to support the points you make in argument.

- Not arriving at any *conclusions* regarding the question. Your answer looks much more purposeful and relevant if you refer back to the exam question at the end of your answer and briefly explain how what you have said helps to answer it.

See Chapter 8
Section 8.6,
Summaries

These are all familiar requirements. They apply equally to writing essays. You simply need to note that although exam answers are much shorter and scrappier than coursework essays, they are judged in roughly the same way – although at lower levels of expectation in recognition of the constraints.

11.3.2   Not using material from the course

Examiners complain that with some scripts it is hard to tell whether the student has actually studied the course. In other words, these students overlook a basic principle of any end-of-course exam: namely, that it is set up for you to *demonstrate* that you have worked on and thought about the content of the course. You should treat each question as an opportunity to discuss the *objects* and *ideas,* and use the *terms*, presented in the course. When you are arguing a case you must *illustrate* and *support* your points by *detailed reference* to some of the texts you have studied. You will also need to draw on other people's ideas and theories about those texts, that is, on the judgements made by some of the authorities in your field.

> I found that, looking at a question, names and dates would spring to mind. As the exam is all about showing you have studied the course, the examiner only knows this if you put in details from the course.

In order to make good use of both the primary and secondary source material in the course, you have to prepare yourself well for the exam.

11.3.3   Stuffing answers full of facts, dates, names

You also have to use the course material discriminatingly. You are *never* asked to 'Write all you know about ...'. Exam markers are not interested in whether you can memorise a section of a text and repeat it. They want to know whether you can put your knowledge and ideas to work: whether you can *select* material appropriately from all that you have studied in the course, *using* it to answer the *particular question* you are asked. That includes making selections from among the primary texts you might discuss in relation to the question – part of the test is being able to make appropriate choices. If you cram an answer full of facts, dates, references to texts and quotations, without placing them in the context of an *argument* and without selecting them for their *relevance* to that argument, it looks as if you don't understand the subject and are hoping that sheer memory will get you by. It won't.

11.3.4   Using time badly

A *very* common mistake is to produce a long first answer but write just a few sentences and some scrappy notes for the last. This is a shame, since marking schemes are usually very straightforward. Each question carries a certain number of marks and good work on one answer cannot be taken into account when marking another. It is very difficult to push a high mark up even higher by spending more time on an answer. Let's say that you are taking a four-answer exam, with all answers equally weighted, and you manage to get a 90% score on your first answer but follow up with 45%, 30% and 15% because you had not left enough time to complete the later answers. Your overall score would be 45%. Whereas, if you spent less time on the first answer and got only 75%, but used the time gained to pull your other answers up, you might end up with 60%, 55% and 50%. This would give you an overall score of 60% – a much better result. It is far easier to pick up marks at the lower end of the scale than at the upper end, so in this kind of exam it *always* makes sense to spend *roughly the same amount of time on each question*, however weak you feel on some of them.

11.3.5   Violating the rubric

The instructions that are given in an exam paper are called 'the rubric'. For example, the exam-paper rubric may instruct you to answer 4 questions. If you answer only 3 you will lose 25% of the possible marks straight away. The rubric of an exam question may tell you to focus on a particular part of the course in your answer. If you ignore this instruction you will not attract marks. Similarly, if you are asked to base an answer on 'at least three' novels of the period and you refer to only two, you will lose roughly a third of the marks for that question. You must do *exactly* what the rubric of the exam paper and of each question tells you to do.

11.3.6   Poor presentation

Finally, examiners also complain about answers that are:

- unstructured (have no sense of a beginning, a middle and an end)
- lacking any division into paragraphs
- written in note form, rather than sentences
- in unreadable handwriting.

These requirements should be familiar from your essay writing. It is obviously harder to pay attention to presentation under exam conditions. But, equally, the job of markers is harder than your teacher's, as they grapple with a mountain of scripts. With the best will in the world, it is difficult to do justice to judging an answer that is very hard to read and follow. You can't help the relative scrappiness and untidiness of your exam answers when compared to your essays. But neither can the exam marker help being influenced to some extent by excessive difficulty in working out what you are trying to say.

These, then, are the things examiners complain about in their examiners' reports, alongside the very pleasant and encouraging things they also say. We turn now to what you can do to make sure they say nice things about *your* answers.

Key points

- Read the exam-paper rubric and the questions carefully, and make sure you follow all the instructions given.
- Always be sure to include ideas, terms, references to texts, quotations, dates, examples/cases, and names from the course.
- Don't try to cram in everything that might possibly be relevant. Select what is appropriate to your argument.
- Always spread your time fairly evenly across questions that carry equal weighting.
- Try to present your answers in a way that doesn't require a cryptographer to read them.

11.4   Revising for exams

11.4.1   What is the point of revision?

The primary purpose of revision is to pull together all that you have learned during the course. Grappling with new knowledge will have thrown your ideas into disarray. Revision is the process of tidying up the mess, and getting your thoughts into useable order. Without a revision period the content of a course tends to drift away from you, incoherent and unresolved. Revising provides an opportunity to *reconstruct* the course, so that the knowledge you have encountered becomes more securely your own. Consequently, revision is *not* a mammoth memorising task but a much more *constructive* activity. It should not be a dull process of scanning endlessly through pages of notes, hoping something will stick. It is purposeful, creative, thought provoking and potentially very satisfying.

11.4.2   When should you start revising?

There is no 'right' answer to this question. Some students make a start two or three months before an exam, others leave it to the last fortnight. The right time for *you* depends on:

- the amount of time you can spare for revision outside other study and life commitments
- your personal style of studying – whether you are better at short intensive bursts of effort or longer sustained periods
- the kind of course it is and what you are trying to get out of it.

It would be a shame to panic too early and spoil the later parts of a course by being obsessed with revision. On the other hand, we saw that it is a serious mistake to avoid thinking about the exam until the very last moment. You won't do yourself justice if you leave too little time for revision.

Don't think of exam preparation as a single, huge task, or you will find it hard to get started. There are various activities which make an important contribution, as you will see from the rest of this section. Some of these activities, such as drawing up a timetable, can be done fairly quickly. Start early on with some of the smaller tasks, just to get yourself going and so that your focus gradually shifts towards the exam.

What you should definitely do a couple of months before the exam is to start thinking about your strategy, even if you don't actually begin revising until later. The final weeks of a course are often busy, with essays to hand in and other coursework still continuing. Your personal life will also make its demands. Finding time for revision isn't easy. You need to start making estimates of how much time you hope to find and thinking about how you will find it, otherwise you will be overtaken by events.

11.4.3   Get hold of past exam papers

One task to undertake well before the end of the course is to get a clear picture of what is expected of you in the exam. The best way to do this is to look at papers from previous years. If past papers are not available, then be sure to use the specimen paper – in any case, this will be all that is available when a course is new. There may also be printed notes about the exam. Look on the course website or ask staff in your department. And be sure to check with your tutor that the format of the exam is unchanged from previous years.

Get hold of whatever information you can, then take the time to go very carefully over the exam papers and notes. Until you have done some serious revision, the questions may make you gulp. But it is better to get the fright over with well ahead of the exam, while you still have time to do something about it. (You certainly don't want the experience of seeing a paper for the first time in the exam itself.) Read the instructions on the paper and make sure you understand them. Take careful note of the way the paper is organised.

- How many questions are there?
- How many do you have to answer?
- Is the paper divided into sections?
- Do you have to select questions from different sections?
- Do all the sections carry the same marks?

Then explore how the paper connects to the course content.

- Is it obvious which questions match up with particular parts of the course/ texts?
- Is there a question on each major section of the course?
- Can you tell which topics are likely to come up in particular parts of the paper?

If you can, compare papers from different years.

- Do you get a sense of the kinds of question you can expect?
- Is there a pattern? If so, is it predictable enough to allow you to focus your revision on certain selected course topics/texts? (But be wary of restricting what you revise too much.)

When you have found out all you can by examining the papers, talk with other students and compare your conclusions. Ask how they plan to tackle the paper. Get what advice you can from your tutors, and make sure there is nothing about the paper that puzzles you. You need to have a very clear understanding of the exam paper before working out your revision strategy. And it helps you think about which aspects of the course you will select for revision.

11.4.4   Gather together your notes and books

One of your key tasks is to get yourself organised. Unless you have a superbly efficient filing system, you will have accumulated mounds of assorted bits of paper, annotated texts, notes, handouts, photocopies of articles and half-read books. Set aside a session simply to sort everything out. This is more than just housekeeping; the act of tidying everything into neat piles reminds you of what material you have and pushes you into thinking about the overall shape of the course. When you can look around and see *what* you have got and *where*, you are in a much better position to get a clear perspective on the revision process. Imposing some order on your material, and your surroundings, also has a generally calming effect.

11.4.5 Work out a revision strategy

Having studied the structure of the exam paper and gathered together and organised your course materials, you are ready to think about how to manage your revision.

- Draw up a list of the main topics or themes of the course and decide which of them you are going to revise for the exam.
- Look at your piles of course material and think about which items will be the most important to focus on in your revision.

In choosing what to focus on, don't assume that you are going to do any new reading. By revision time it is too late for learning from first principles; you need to consolidate what you have already learned. Play to your strengths and interests.

> I chose parts of the course because a) I enjoyed them most, so it wasn't a big chore to revise them, and b) I got my best essay marks for them.

- Make a list of your chosen themes or topics, with the relevant sources alongside (texts, articles, notes, essays).
- Think about priorities. If time runs short, which are the items you will definitely revise? What might you leave out? Mark the priorities on a list.
- Read the rest of this chapter, or just look through the subheadings, to get an idea of activities you might want to include in your revision strategy.

All this will take quite a lot of thought, but go ahead and write something down even if you are undecided. Making a first attempt at a strategy will set you thinking. You can modify it later as you have further thoughts and talk with other students. Once you get into the thick of revision and run into life's complications, you are likely to have to modify your strategy several times. The point is, having sketched a plan, you can keep reviewing your situation and making intelligent adjustments.

11.4.6 Make a revision timetable

Having sketched a strategy, you need to work out how you are going to fit it into your busy life. Drawing up a revision timetable is essential. It is the only way to make life manageable in the run-up to the exam. It will also make you feel better and more in control of events.

- Get a blank calendar for the weeks ahead (you could use your computer's calendar feature to print off a couple of months). Write in the date of the exam or exams, and due dates of your remaining coursework. Then write in all your major work and social commitments.
- Highlight the main places on the calendar where you might be able to make time for revision.
- Tot up a rough estimate of the total time you think you can set aside. Then think about how to share it out between the items in your revision plan. Jot down estimates of hours against each item – this will start to bring

a flavour of reality to your strategy. You will see just how limited your time is for each, and how important it is to be practical in your ambitions and know where to cut corners.

- Finally, starting with your highest priority revision activities, write them into your timetable.

> I've been revising the first part of the course this week. I'm averaging about 2 hrs a day about 5 days a week. I tend to do most on Wednesday which is my day off.

Remember to allow time for studying the last part of the course, and set aside some time for the final stage of pulling things together and practising writing out exam answers. Divide the remaining revision time into equal parts for each aspect or section of the course you have decided to revise. It is tempting to allow more time for your 'best' topics and to try to squeeze the others in at the end. However, it is much safer to assume equal time for each revision area if all questions carry the same number of marks. You don't want to end up with too little time for the topics which most need sorting out, or to leave no time at all to brush up the very areas in which you hoped to do especially well.

If you are sitting a number of exams over a period of a week or two, a timetable is an absolute necessity. You will have to plan very carefully in order to achieve a certain amount of revision for each exam before the exam period proper starts. *All* your exams are important, so don't revise for one very thoroughly and another not at all. Divide up your time roughly equally amongst them. During the exam period, you will also need to work out what last-minute revision is possible, for which exams, and when.

Don't worry about getting your whole timetable worked out straight away. Just sketch a general picture and write down some specific tasks to start on in your first couple of sessions. Fill out the rest of the timetable as you get properly into the swing of revision, and modify it as events change your plans.

11.4.7   Don't try to re-read the course

Revision is not a rerun through the whole course. You haven't the time and your mind would switch off in protest. You need to take a much more active and more selective approach. Many exams are designed to allow you to be selective in your preparation. Assuming you have studied the logic of the exam paper carefully and understand the choices open to you, you can be ruthless in ignoring whole sections of the course. It is not worth just dipping into course topics, doing a bit here and a bit there, because you won't end up with enough knowledge to write a good exam answer. You need to spend long enough to pull together the big picture for the themes you have chosen to revise, so that you can answer questions from whatever angle they come and however they are worded. Your review of these topics needs to be systematic.

11.4.8   Don't try to memorise your course notes

Don't be tempted to gather up your course notes and read through them all trying to memorise them. You need to be able to *think* in the exam, not recite back your notes. You need ideas in your head, not strings of words. To do something more constructive, try to work out what questions you might be asked and highlight key points. Always work with a pen in your hand, *creating* something as you go – your mind will stay in gear for much longer. Any memorising should come in the last day or two and be based on 'summary' notes (see Section 11.4.10, below).

11.4.9   Identify key questions

This is a very powerful strategy. Try to identify two or three core questions in each section of the course you are revising, then try to write notes that answer those questions. Sometimes your tutor or an author will have identified key questions for you. At other times you have to tease them out for yourself. The process of seeking out key questions and answers to them gets your mind working in the way it needs to work in the exam. It will alert you to the kinds of question that *could* be asked about the course content you have been studying (in effect, you are making up your own exam questions). And it helps you to think in terms of pulling together ideas in the way that's needed to answer exam questions.

11.4.10   Make summary notes

Having identified a key (exam-type) question for the part of the course you are revising, you might go on to do something like the following.

1   Plan a full answer to it in note form, under headings and subheadings, drawing on the various articles, lecture notes, course books, essays, etc., you have gathered together for that particular topic or aspect of the course. This should *include* detailed reference to the particular texts you would discuss in relation to the question (paintings, poems, music, documents, or whatever). In other words, plan the *argument* and also the *substance* of your answer.

2   After you have done that, extract the main points from these notes to produce a single *summary sheet* of headings for that question, plus the key points of the argument and, alongside them, your textual references and quotations or other evidence. Your notes are now very portable; you can keep them in your handbag or pocket and read them over and over in odd moments.

Now set yourself another possible exam question for this same part of the course and repeat the procedure; plan the answer in note form and go on to produce your one-page summary sheet. You'll find that a slightly differently focused or worded question, even covering pretty much the same territory as before, means you must put together a rather different argument and foreground different texts and evidence. You should keep doing this, trying to anticipate every possible question you might be asked on this section or aspect of the course. As you proceed, you will no doubt find yourself repeating some of the material you put together before (both argument and substance). You will find that some ideas and some textual detail, dates, etc., are already in your memory, and that you don't need to refer back as frequently to the texts and your other course material. Then, always mindful of your revision timetable, go on to apply the same strategy to the other parts of the course you have chosen to revise.

The effort to 'boil down' your course material in this way is extremely valuable because it converts both the broad themes and ideas of the course, and your detailed analyses of texts, into a form that is much more manageable for the purposes of answering questions in exams. As you know, there is not much time to think in an exam, or to write at tremendous length, so you don't want to be sifting through masses of material in your mind towards an answer. These *condensed* versions of arguments and main points, along with appropriate textual detail, are much closer to what you will have time to think through and write about. You can scan mentally through the main items on your summary sheets and select whichever are relevant to the question you are asked. This then leads your mind back to the fuller notes that 'lie behind' them. The general principle is to create a systematic *overview and retrieval system*.

See Chapter 5 Section 5.3.2, How memory works

This strategy also gets you into the habit of thinking in terms of *questions* and *answers to them* right from the start of the revision process. It gives you a well-focused and absorbing task to be getting on with, rather than the kind of aimless scanning back over old material that dulls your spirits and sends you to sleep. And condensed notes supply you with just the kind of 'pulled together' versions of the course that will be invaluable in the future, when you want to remind yourself of what the course was about.

There are various ways of putting a summary notes strategy into practice. Some people find mind maps very helpful (see Chapter 5, Figure 5.6).

> I worked from my highlighting in the course books – picking out the key points. I wrote all these into notes – then made mind maps. It was time consuming, but the repeated writing of the key words and ideas etc. made them stick. Then I spent 2–3 weeks reading them over and over again. The mind maps helped me focus. As soon as I went into the exam I was able to recall the points relevant to each exam question and draw the mind map onto the exam paper as my plan.

Other people value the discipline of getting ideas down to index-card brevity (see Chapter 5, Figure 5.1).

> I'm trying to condense as much information as possible onto index cards – one or two for each topic. I have brief notes on the main figures, relevant facts and dates, pros and cons for key issues. I take the cards wherever I go (read them on the bus, at work, etc.) in the hope the info will sink in.

And you can of course take full advantage of any electronic notes you have made using the outliner function – cutting and pasting from different sets of notes to create 'master documents' for each revision topic; moving sections of notes around very easily, reorganising them under new headings; printing off, with different levels of headings showing. Or you can create tables with headings to help organise your knowledge.

This 'summary notes' strategy is a substantial time investment, but it pays off.

See Chapter 5 Section 5.4.1, Pulling your knowledge together

11.4.11   Try answering past exam questions

Towards the end of the revision period the most useful activity of all is to attempt past exam questions. You don't need to write out a full answer every time, though occasional practice at that may be useful. A quick exercise you can do frequently is to rehearse the vital first few minutes of working on a question; in other words, those minutes when you examine what the question means and sketch out rough notes for an answer.

> I bought past exam papers and wrote the questions onto index cards along with the course essay questions. The cards I carried with me ALWAYS. When I had 10 mins spare, I shuffled the index cards, pulled a question out at random and did a quick mind map of an answer to it. It meant I didn't panic when I turned over the real paper – and I got a good pass.

Give yourself ten minutes to produce an outline answer to a question you haven't seen before, then look back at the course material to see what you have left out. Ask yourself:

- What is this question getting at? (Underline the key words in the same way as for essays.)
- Which section of the course/topic does the question relate to?
- What main points of argument will I make, and in what order? (Sketch an outline plan.)
- What texts shall I refer to/what examples and evidence can I draw from the course? (Add to the plan.)

See Chapter 8 Section 8.2.1, Thinking about the essay title

This is worth doing many times, because it helps you develop the intellectual agility to get to the heart of questions quickly and answer precisely, drawing on relevant parts of the course and set texts. It helps you to organise your knowledge in the right sort of way for the job in hand. You will soon get used to

- **sifting** through what you know of the course material
- **selecting** the most relevant items for the question, and
- **arranging** them in a suitable order for a coherent answer.

Practising writing out answers in full is not quite so urgent because, once you have an outline, the writing process is fairly similar to writing an essay (though with less time), which is a skill you have practised during the course. What you have not practised is 'thinking on your feet'. The way you think about an essay question is too reflective and lumbering for an exam. You need to develop a nimbler style.

11.4.12   Try writing against the clock

If you haven't taken exams for a long time, it is obviously useful to get in some practice at working against the clock. You may not find the time and energy for a full-length practice, but it could be useful to write a single timed answer now and then. However, two notes of caution: first, you will have the benefit of a lot more nervous energy on the exam day, so your informal try-out may underestimate your true capabilities; second, don't be discouraged if your answers look unimpressive compared with your essays. Timed answers will never reach the same standards as your course work.

11.4.13   Keep in touch with other students

Make time to stay in touch with other students (whether in the classroom, by phone, or online). It is very easy to develop a warped perspective on exams during the stress of revision. You begin to think your problems are much worse than they really are, or you bias your revision too sharply in one particular direction. The best way to keep a sense of proportion is to talk to other people about what you and they are doing. This is a time when attending classes, or dropping into online chatrooms, is particularly useful. Sharing ideas makes revision a lot easier and more pleasant. Don't think of time spent talking as simply time lost from revising. Also, group revision can be extremely efficient. It throws up all sorts of insights into hidden problems and misunderstandings. It helps you to knock your ideas into shape and gives you many valuable clues and tips.

> We did a lot of essay plans, brainstorming topics and questions. I felt reassured that I could do it. It's amazing how much you retain that appears again under pressure.

Key points

Elements of exam revision strategy.

- Study *past exam papers* and *specimen papers* thoroughly.
- *Organise* all your course materials, so that you know what you have and where.
- Carefully *select* the parts of the course you intend to revise.
- Make a *timetable* for your revision.
- Seek out the central *issues* in each of the parts of the course you have chosen to revise and think up exam questions you might be asked.
- Prepare answers to these questions in full, in note form, and then condense your notes into one-page *summary* sheets.
- Make use of whatever *techniques* appeal to you – mind maps, index cards, grids, or outliner notes.
- Practise jotting down *outlines* for answers to past exam questions.
- Practise *writing* one or two answers in full against the clock.
- *Keep in touch* with other students and with your teacher to maintain your grip on reality.

11.5 Getting 'geared-up' just before the exam

Of course you should relax sometimes, get plenty of sleep and take some outdoor exercise in the final days before an exam. But this is also when you should be building yourself up to a peak of preparation towards the exam performance. You can concentrate remarkably well when it is too late to worry about the frills. You forget your plans for re-reading this book, or making sense of that theory you never really understood. You leave those possibilities behind and concentrate all your energies on marshalling what you know. Relaxed is the last thing you want to be when you enter the exam. Calm and unruffled possibly (if you can manage it), but you should be keyed-up like a tennis star at a tournament or a stage performer on the first night, ready to give your big performance of the year, transcending your normal limits by force of all that nervous energy and single-minded concentration.

11.5.1 Get your thinking in before the exam

How will you do justice to everything you've learned, when you have only three hours in the exam? How long do you spend on a coursework essay: six hours, ten hours, or more? How can you condense that writing process into four 45-minute bursts? Clearly you can't. As a result, exam answers don't look like your regular essays. They are shorter, more disjointed, and much less polished. Yet, it is surprising how much you *can* get into an exam answer in spite of the time constraints. Although you can't work out a carefully considered response, as you do for coursework essays, you can get pretty close *provided you get a lot of your thinking done before the exam itself.* During the revision period you will have decided which parts of the course you are going to concentrate on. You will have identified some key questions and issues and rehearsed them in your mind. And you will have practised working up arguments, illustration and evidence in response to such questions. Then, in the exam, what remains is to:

- pick your questions
- quickly settle on plans for using what you know to answer them, and
- stick to your plans, for better or worse.

You need to be in a highly organised, efficient and pragmatic frame of mind for the exam. Having stopped worrying and wondering, you can focus intently on doing your best with the immediate tasks in hand, cutting corners and generally exercising cunning.

11.5.2 Draw up a time plan for the exam

Using time effectively is one of the most important factors in doing justice to yourself in an exam. You cannot afford to leave this to chance, and you certainly don't want to take up precious time working out a time plan *in* the exam. So you need to think carefully about how you can get the best out of yourself. It is very worthwhile drawing up a plan of how, ideally, you might use your time in the exam. Figure 11.1 shows one possible version.

See this chapter Section 11.6, Working out your tactics for the exam

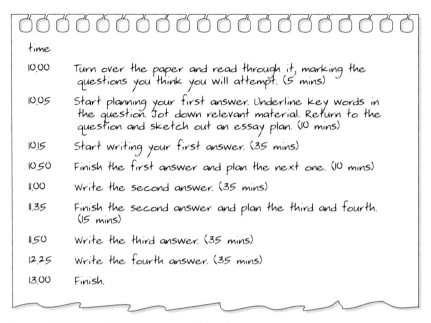

time	
10.00	Turn over the paper and read through it, marking the questions you think you will attempt. (5 mins)
10.05	Start planning your first answer. Underline key words in the question. Jot down relevant material. Return to the question and sketch out an essay plan. (10 mins)
10.15	Start writing your first answer. (35 mins)
10.50	Finish the first answer and plan the next one. (10 mins)
11.00	Write the second answer. (35 mins)
11.35	Finish the second answer and plan the third and fourth. (15 mins)
11.50	Write the third answer. (35 mins)
12.25	Write the fourth answer. (35 mins)
13.00	Finish.

Figure 11.1 Sample time plan for a three-hour exam

You won't be able to stick to your plan exactly, but it will serve as a guide. (Read Section 11.6 'Working out your tactics for the exam' before drawing up your plan.)

11.5.3   Changes to your mental powers
During the last couple of days before the exam, load your plans and strategies into your head, keep going back over your summary note sheets and generally wind yourself up for action. Because the pressure builds up in these final days, your mental powers will change. You will be *less good* at *deep thinking* tasks, such as sorting out the underlying meaning of a difficult course text. But you will be *better* at working at more *routine* things like checking over your notes, practising answering questions, or reminding yourself of your strategy for the exam. Because of this, you should not leave *basic revision* to the last few days; you will only depress yourself and get into a panic. Deliberately switch your work mode and use these days as your polishing-up period. Like an actor at a dress rehearsal, it is too late now to learn new lines or decide on a different interpretation. You just have to 'go with it' the way it is, and keep running over your lines in your head to make sure everything is in place.

11.5.4   Anxiety
As the exam draws closer, you may find the tension starts to get on top of you. There are several types of anxiety that can develop at exam time. You may experience a general uneasiness that builds up gradually over a long period, until (very usefully) it provides the spur to a really intensive burst of

work. This is a normal precursor to any kind of performance. You need to make sure you *use* the tension productively. Set yourself practical tasks that keep you busy. Remind yourself that this is *your* exam; you are doing it because *you* have chosen to. Remind yourself too that the tension you are feeling can be a very *productive* force, helping you to achieve some difficult learning. Ideally, you learn to live with exam stress and use it to achieve things.

Your anxiety may however develop into a pall of gloom which spoils the last part of the course. You may find all your thoughts becoming centred on the exam. In this case, keep talking to other students and to your tutor about your doubts and fears and your plans for tackling them. Talking releases tension, helping you to keep things in perspective.

You may, though, be one of the few students for whom this is not enough. In the period immediately before the exam your anxiety may build up to a point where you can't sleep and your health begins to suffer, or where work, or family and friends begin to be affected. If you find this happening, then go to your doctor for advice. Some people find breathing exercises helpful, or meditation, or some other way of focusing intensively on reducing the physical manifestations of anxiety. If you feel bad, don't suffer in isolation. Look for help. You will find plenty of suggestions and advice about this on your university website.

11.5.5   Checking the arrangements

Because you get so 'geared up' in the last day or two, you can become quite inattentive to the ordinary details of life. People sometimes make peculiar mistakes, like turning up for the exam on the wrong day or at the wrong place. So it is a good idea to get all the details of the exam sorted out well in advance. You don't want to be worrying about anything trivial on the day. Mark the exam time very clearly on your calendar. You might even consider making a practice journey to the exam centre and finding the room, then you won't have a last-minute panic about which bus to catch, where you left the address of the exam centre or where the entrance to the building is.

> I was dreaming that I got to the exam centre and had forgotten my ID and had to go all the way back home to get it.

11.5.6   On the day

On exam day, try to be calm. Go about your normal business of getting up and starting the day. Take a short stroll perhaps, or do a few exercises to get yourself tuned up and functioning properly. Do not attempt any last-minute revision. Don't even glance over your notes; it will only disturb your carefully stored ideas. Get to the exam centre in good time and keep walking around if you have to wait to get in. Don't let the other candidates disturb you; remain apart if you need to. When you are in the exam room find your desk and calmly settle yourself in your seat. Set out your favourite pens on the desk and check that you have everything you need – insert your wax earplugs if they help. The exam room always seems a strange place, full of people (whom you may not know) all locked obsessively in their own thoughts. Don't let the strangeness distract you. Just keep your mind ticking over in neutral, ready to slip into gear when the lights change. If you have prepared yourself sensibly there is no point in worrying. In fact, once the exam has started you may find it surprisingly exhilarating and challenging. It's astonishing how much you can do in only three hours when you have keyed yourself up to a peak of mental fitness.

After the exam it is *not* a good idea to engage in a post-mortem, either with other students or by scouring your notes to see what you might have done. It will just make you feel bad. And, in any case, there is no point. It's over.

Key points

- In the last day or so, stop trying to revise and concentrate on pulling together what you've already done.
- Get your thinking in before the exam. Work out exactly how you intend to tackle all aspects of the paper, and sketch a plan of how you will use your time in the exam.
- Talk with others if you are getting overstressed.
- Check the practical arrangements for the exam, including travel.
- Try to keep calm on the exam day. Stop thinking about revision. Don't let yourself be distracted by the conditions of the exam or the other candidates.

11.6   Working out your tactics for the exam

It is important to work out in detail what you are going to do in the exam itself. You can't afford to leave anything to chance. You need to work out exactly what has to be done and exactly how you think you will tackle it. If you do this you will improve your performance enormously.

11.6.1   The nature of the task ahead of you

When you enter the exam you have to be ready to work at peak efficiency. You have three hours to make the best showing you can of all the work you have done during the course and during the revision stage. You can't afford to waste time dithering, moping, or staring at the ceiling. You have to have a clear plan of attack. You may not be able to stick to it, and in the end that may not matter. What is important is that you are clear at all times about what you intend to do next.

In order to give a very practical slant to this discussion I will assume (as in Box 11.1) a three-hour exam in which you are asked to answer four questions. I will also assume that you can take the questions in any order you like, and that you can write any notes and jottings in the exam book (as long as you cross them out afterwards). If your exam is different, you need to find out *how* it differs, and make the necessary adjustments to what follows.

Box 11.4   Open book exams

Some exams allow you to take in course texts and even notes. This is a doubtful privilege. It isn't really consistent with the high-speed writing you do in an exam to be thumbing through books and notes. It may be reassuring to know that you can look up the odd quotation if you want to. But in essay-type exams you need the ideas in your head, so you can think with them, not scattered around you in books. Moreover, if you tend to be anxious you may spend far too much time desperately trying to find things, to be sure that you have them right. Far better to take the plunge and say to yourself, 'This is it! I'll press on with what is in my head and hope for the best. Arguing a good case of my own is more important than details from books.'

11.6.2   Reading the question paper

The exam starts when the invigilator tells you to turn the exam paper over. If you have done your work on past papers, the general appearance of the paper should not be a surprise. However, you may find it difficult at first to take in the words because you are so keyed up. So, although it might seem sensible to read carefully through the whole paper first, you may not be capable of doing that effectively. It may be better to do something more active to get yourself moving.

Certainly it is no bad idea to scan quickly through the questions, putting ticks against 'possibles' and crosses against 'definitely nots'. This will give you a first impression of what is on offer. But don't ponder over every question in detail. Search out the questions you have prepared for. It is desperately risky to let yourself be deflected from a prepared subject onto an unprepared one because of the wording of the question. Your prepared topic may look more difficult to you *because* you know so much about it. Other questions may look easier *because* you are not clued-up enough to realise their full implications. Don't attempt to flannel your way through an unrevised area. You are much more likely to produce a solid answer on a prepared theme, even if you feel unhappy with the actual question.

11.6.3   How soon to start writing

It may be a good idea to find a question you *know* you are going to attempt and pitch straight in. If you are inclined to freeze under pressure, or if your mind tends to go blank, then starting to write can be a good way to get yourself past the opening tensions and into action. There is no reason to worry about starting your first question before reading the rest of the paper if you are confident that it is on a topic you have revised. Some people prefer to scan through the whole paper first, but if it suits you better to jump straight in, do it. However, you *do* need to plan your answer – think about the wording of the question and jot down some notes before starting to write.

11.6.4   The order in which to take the questions

If you are allowed to tackle questions in any order you like, you may as well follow your own best interests. Some people recommend starting on your very best question to build up your confidence. Others say take your best question second, when you are nicely warmed up and not so likely to be tempted to run wildly over your time allowance. In any case, it is a good idea to take your best questions earlier rather than later, to make sure that you have enough time to score well, to give you confidence and allow you to get nicely into your stride.

11.6.5   Examining the question

See Chapter 8 Section 8.2.1, Thinking about the essay title

As with essays, make a point of underlining the key words in the questions you intend to answer. This makes you take a positive approach from the outset, and it focuses your attention on answering the precise question set. The words you underline are the ones you will have to think about carefully in deciding what material you can use and how to organise it. If you rush into the question and make mistakes about the issues it addresses you will seriously damage your chances.

11.6.6   Drawing together material to include in your answer

As soon as you have underlined the key words in the question, jot down very quickly the material you think you will use in answering it. Don't worry at first about *how* to use it. Just write down arguments, concepts, theories, texts, etc., to reassure yourself that you have plenty of material to work with. (This is where you think back to the summary sheets you produced.) When you have a preliminary list – it may be just five to ten words – you can begin to sort out what to use and what to leave out. Keep in mind that exam questions *always* ask for material from the course. Note plenty down at this stage, because once you start to construct an answer to the question, you will be fully occupied and you may then find that an important part of your argument has completely slipped from your mind. A single word is usually enough to trigger your memory, enabling you to retrieve the main points of argument and relevant textual detail. Work fast, and don't hesitate to make a mess of your exam booklet. You can cross out all your jottings later.

11.6.7   Balancing what you know and what the question asks for

As you answer a question, you have to steer a course between two equally dangerous traps. One is that you become so mesmerised by the question that you lose confidence in your ability to answer it. You may stop believing that if you search properly you will find the material you need amongst all that you have stored in your head. If that happens you may be tempted to bluster your way through, trying to answer off the top of your head. The opposite trap is that your mind becomes so fixed on all the material you have recently stored in it that you spill your knowledge all over the pages of the exam booklet, regardless of its relevance to the question you are answering. Both are very easy traps to fall into. The approach I recommend below sets out to play these two temptations off against each other.

My suggestion is that you move quickly back and forth between the question and the knowledge stored in your mind. In this way you can make sure that each has due influence. Choose the question and do a quick 'first take' on what it is about. Then leave the question and go to your knowledge of the course to jot down some possible content. Return to the question to get it more sharply in focus. Then go back to your list of material to knock it into the shape you need. Finally, with a quick look back at the question, you start answering it in a way which brings question and knowledge together.

11.6.8 Taking time to plan your answer

However, will you have time to spare for all these preparations? It takes a lot of nerve to spend precious exam time planning your answers. But, bearing in mind the comments of examiners about 'undisciplined' answers, it is time well spent. The question is, how long should you spend? You will have to judge that for yourself, but between five and ten minutes is a reasonable target. If you don't sketch out a plan, you will run the risk of 'going blank' in the middle of an answer. Writing tends to absorb the whole of your attention, so when you get to the end of a paragraph you can find that the next point has flown. Your argument jerks to a halt and you are too keyed up to re-think your plan. At this point you will waste far more time than it would have taken to write a plan. And your answer will be poorer into the bargain.

> After my last exam I realised how important sketching answer plans is. ... Much better first essay, passable second, third fair too. Just wish I'd practised handwriting. I'm so used to cutting and pasting text on the computer.

But don't let planning become a 'displacement activity'. Even a truly beautiful plan is no substitute for the actual essay answer. So don't spend any longer than 10 minutes on it.

11.6.9 Sticking to the point

In your enthusiasm to show your knowledge of the course, don't forget to keep to the question. Exam markers are searching for points that relate directly to the question; they are not pleased by having to wade through paragraphs of uncensored and unsorted material. You will not gain any marks for uncritically throwing course material before the examiners' eyes in the hope of fooling them into thinking you know what you are talking about. Of course, you must be sure to draw in plenty of material from the course, but you must always do it with a clear purpose, so that you don't appear to be padding out your answers or busking to conceal your ignorance. Anything you write that is not relevant to the question is just a waste of your time.

11.6.10 Sticking to your plan

Keep the time plan you prepared before the exam (see Figure 11.1) in front of you at all times, and keep checking your watch. You can afford to slip five or even ten minutes off schedule, but be very wary of getting further out of line. If you find yourself falling behind time with an answer, draw it to a close as quickly as you can. Don't leave the question half finished in the hope that you will have time to come back to it. Most likely you won't, since you are running late, but more importantly by then you will have lost your train of thought. Make the best of what you've achieved thus far and write out whatever conclusions you can manage to draw while the question is still hot in your mind.

11.6.11   When to plan your later questions

> In the past I've got panicky and while I'm answering one question, I'm wondering what I can write for the next, which ISN'T GOOD. So I cover up the other questions.

When you have your first two questions under your belt, it is a good idea to rough out plans for the other two in turn, *before* writing the third. The reason for this is that you need time on your side when you are planning. It is very hard to think straight in the final stages of an exam, as you become mesmerised by the approaching deadline. All too often the last answer represents the desperate casting about of a mind that has long passed beyond the stage of thinking coherently. You will probably be able to write at your *fastest* during the last hour of the exam *provided you have planned what to say*. So do the thinking that requires calm analysis at the half-way point, when you have passed through the initial tension and have settled into a steady working mode. Then you will be ready to take advantage of your manic energy in the final stages, when you may be able to get down reams of useful material.

11.6.12   What to do if your time runs out

If, in spite of all your plans, you do end up with too little time for your last question, it helps to write out notes showing how your answer would have developed if you'd had the time. If you present an answer *entirely* in note form, you are unlikely to scrape a pass. But if you have *part* of an answer already written out, some clear notes for the rest of your answer might convince the marker that it is worth a reasonable mark. However, it would scarcely be fair on the other candidates to allow you the benefit of the extra time you spent on the earlier questions *and* a generous benefit of the doubt on an uncompleted question. The marker will probably give you *some* credit for good notes, but basically you need to write out an answer in full to be in the running for a good mark. So take steps to make sure you *don't* run out of time!

11.6.13   Presentation

Most people write less tidily and legibly than their best in exams. But do *try* to make your work legible. Start each question on a new page and number the questions clearly. Draw a line across the page between your jottings and the essay itself, and remember to score through your jottings when you have completed the answer. If your handwriting or your written English is shaky, it is too late to worry; you can only work to improve them gradually over your years of study. In any case, try to remember your script marker a little as you write, and avoid being so overwhelmed by the need for speed that your writing descends to a desperate scrawl.

> **Key points**
>
> - Scan through the paper finding the questions you have prepared for.
> - Start writing soon, if it helps to 'unfreeze' you.
> - Take your best question first or second.
> - As you tackle a question:
>   - examine the wording carefully
>   - very quickly list some relevant points from the course
>   - take the time to plan your answer before you start writing
>   - move back and forth between the question and your list as you sketch an outline plan for your answer
>   - remember that everything you write should be relevant to the specific question asked.
> - Consider planning the last two questions mid-way through the exam.
> - Stick to your time plan for the exam; don't run wildly over your deadlines.
> - Do your best to write legibly.

11.7   Will you do yourself justice in the exam?

Of course you ought to pass the exam, assuming you have been getting on all right with the course itself. Really, you should do about as well in the exam as you have been doing in the course. In principle, the exam is just another way of confirming what your coursework has already shown. But although this is more or less how things turn out for most people, it is not so in every case. There are at least four possibilities.

1   Some people do better in exams than in their coursework. Exams actually bring out the best in them. Perhaps you are one of these – or could become one with a good exam technique.

2   Many people do just about as well in the exam as in their coursework. Obviously, this is fine and as it should be.

3   Some people tend to perform rather less well than in their coursework (scoring say 10 to 20 per cent lower). They pass, but don't do as well as they had reasonably hoped. If you are one of these people then this chapter is especially for you. Every time you have an exam, read it to remind yourself of all the practical ways in which you can get a better performance out of yourself.

4   A few people have a tendency to come crashing down, way below their potential. If you are one of them, then I hope this chapter has been helpful, but I strongly recommend that you also seek support and advice. There is no point in struggling away on your own if you persistently ruin your good work when it comes to exams.

Whichever of these categories you think you fall into, you have nothing to lose by thinking positively. *Of course* you deserve to pass. You will forget important things in the exam, but so will everybody else. Your exam answers won't look as impressive as your essays but the same is true for everyone else. Be realistic about the exam. Yes, it may be a chore. Yes, you will have to focus a lot of attention and energy on it. But you will also learn a lot in the process. And if you follow all the suggestions in this chapter, you *can* make yourself into a well-tuned exam 'performer', achieving feats way beyond your normal, everyday powers. So don't let exams intimidate you. You are *likely* to pass.

POSTSCRIPT

You have now reached the end of the book. But of course you haven't reached the end of becoming a better student of the arts and humanities. That process never ends. Just when you think your note-making technique is honed to a smoothly functioning routine you find it has become too mechanical, or you make too many notes, or the wrong notes, or you come across a book that defeats your routine. Just when you begin to think you have cracked it with writing, you come to an essay that just won't go right or a tutor who criticises the very things you thought you were good at. At times like these, when your studies take an unexpected turn and knock you back, you will find it useful to return to this book and revisit basic study principles. Also, as you become a more experienced student, many of the ideas you took in at an earlier stage acquire a different significance. Coming back to the book afresh, you will find you make another range of meanings built upon those extra layers of experience. So don't set the book aside for ever. Keep it where you will be able to find it. Learning to study is a life-long process.

APPENDIX

'On the Town': Women in Augustan England

By Joyce Ellis

Extracts from Ellis, Joyce (1995) '"On the Town": Women in Augustan England', *History Today*, vol. 45, no. 12, pp. 20–7.

para. 1

Modern demographic research suggests that in what is known as the 'long eighteenth century' the female population of England's larger towns expanded dramatically, producing what one demographer has called 'a remarkable predominance of women' in contrast with the more balanced or emphatically male-dominated populations of smaller settlements. [...] All the evidence indicates that urban populations were unbalanced principally by a net inflow of female migrants.

para. 2

Hours of rigorous, computer-aided academic research has, therefore, vindicated to some extent the standard cliché of Restoration and eighteenth-century literature about women's enthusiasm for urban life. Women were consistently portrayed in plays and poetry of the period as being ready to adopt any stratagem, however underhand, to escape from the boredom and restrictions of the countryside. The young heroine of Etherege's *The Man of Mode* (1676), for instance, was so much in love with London that she 'can scarce endure the country in landscapes and in hangings'. In contrast, contemporary satirists represented towns in this period as 'female territory', meccas of unbridled consumption and frivolity to which women were irresistibly drawn.

para. 3

Of course it was not only women who expressed a preference for urban life: many men would have agreed with the north-eastern landowner who contemptuously refused his mother's pleas for his return from London in 1720 with the rhetorical question 'Surely you don't think me such a fool as to prefer the charms of a stupid, dull, country life to the pleasures of the Town?' But these pleasures were thought to be especially attractive to women, not simply because women were by nature self-indulgent and superficial, but because urban life allowed them to gain the upper hand in their age-old struggle to escape their natural subordination. What women sought in the towns, the satirists argued, was freedom from male control. Such claims, however, reflected long-standing literary conventions and equally long-standing male anxieties rather than contemporary reality. It is much more plausible to argue that urban life attracted a disproportionate number of women not because they were trying to escape from or to subvert accepted gender roles but because 'correct' female behaviour was all too often dysfunctional in a rural setting.

para. 4

This was perhaps most obvious in the case of women from the higher ranks of society, the main targets of male satirists, whose lives in the country were increasingly circumscribed by conventional expectations of female fragility and propriety. Women from wealthy families were seen as the embodiments of their husbands' and fathers' status. It was, therefore, vital that they conformed to contemporary norms which had shifted decisively in the seventeenth century towards an ideal of delicate, innocent and essentially decorative womanhood. Women's physical and mental inferiority had, of course, long been an accepted fact, but at the same time the wives and daughters of wealthy farmers and landowners had been expected to play an active part in managing their households or even their husband's land: thus girls were trained in the many practical and supervisory skills they would need as adults.

para. 5

With an increasing wealth and sophistication of society, however, many of these tasks were taken over by professionals, allowing well-born women much greater leisure, but in the process creating a vacuum which the expensive 'accomplishments' that such women acquired from smart boarding schools or private tutors could not readily fill in a rural setting. Most of these new feminine skills were essentially designed to be shown off in public, and yet the demands of status and propriety meant that women's sociability was far more strictly controlled than that of men.

para. 6

Men could to some degree socialise with those both above and below them in the hierarchy without losing face: a great landowner, for example, could dine with his tenant farmers and local tradesmen as a gesture of neighbourliness and courtesy. Women, however, could only mix with their equals, so that a woman's opportunities for sociability outside her immediate family were confined to those of her own social standing who lived within travelling distance. Unfortunately, well-born women were much less mobile than men. Relatively few women were able or willing to ride and were thus dependent on the availability of the family carriage unless, like Elizabeth Bennett in *Pride and Prejudice*, they were prepared to walk.

para. 7

Even if a carriage was available, travel along unlit, unpaved country roads carried its own dangers: Elizabeth Montagu and her family were overturned so often on their way to visit friends that she 'began to think ... a bone-setter a necessary part of equipage for country visiting'. 'Fear', she declared in 1737, 'is never so powerful with me, as to make me stay at home' but floods, snow or mud sometimes made travel completely impossible. Lady Jane Coke, for example, was marooned in her house ten miles outside Derby for four months in the winter of 1748–49 by the 'continual rains' which made the roads impassable for a carriage. Of course, to some extent, her husband was marooned too, but men in this situation had many more resources to fall back on. The education given to men from the social elite was almost expressly designed for a rural setting. They were all, in effect, trained to be country gentlemen, able not only to manage their estates but also take an active pleasure from them through riding, hunting, shooting and fishing. Their womenfolk, meanwhile, had no outlet for most of their particular social skills: instead they had to make do with recreational needlework, writing letters and reading whatever books could be found in the house, with frequent walks in the grounds between downpours as their only exercise. [...]

para. 8

Towns, in contrast, offered such women a variety of respectable occupations, amusements and companions, all of which they could enjoy in a degree of physical comfort. Young single women and widows were particularly prone to boredom in the countryside and had a greater incentive to settle permanently in town, but even married women felt the need for regular visits 'to brush off the rust a little'. The greater concentrations of both people and wealth found even in provincial centres meant that women could socialize on a much wider scale without sacrificing their status and respectability by mingling with those too far beneath them. The relatively compact built-up area of most towns was also an advantage, putting this wider circle of acceptable acquaintances within easy reach, especially as improvements in the urban environment, including better pavements and more efficient street lighting, and in public transport, such as sedan chairs and hackney carriages, meant that women were much more mobile in the town than in the country. [...]

para. 9

The urban environment also offered so many more places to go. The delights of Bath or London were obviously exceptional but even in much more modest towns the social calendar was enlivened at least once a year by a regular season of balls, assemblies, race meetings, theatre performances and concerts. Women sometimes took a leading role in planning and running these events. [...]

para. 10

The effects of maintaining these [social] distinctions meant that, in smaller towns, there were sometimes too few male partners for ladies anxious to dance, but at least they could (and did) dance with each other while their menfolk retreated to the card room. Moreover, whereas in earlier periods 'country ladies were stewed up in their father's old mansion houses and seldom saw company, but at an assize, a horse race or a fair', towns gradually developed a wide range of amenities such as landscaped walks, circulating libraries, and tea, confectionery or pastry shops where women could meet without the stigma attached to taverns or coffee houses.

para. 11

Above all there were the shops, which in the course of this period were transformed into 'perfect gilded theatres' providing 'as agreeable an amusement as any lady can pass away three or four hours in'. Sophie von La Roche, a German visitor to England in the 1780s, was impressed by the shopping facilities even in provincial towns, noting in particular the wide pavements which allowed well-dressed women 'to pursue their way safe from the carriages, horses and dirt', and the combined effects of street- and shop-lighting which meant that window shopping could continue well into the evening.

[*Owing to the length of the original article, a section on poorer women and the town has been omitted.*]

para. 12

Although a few contemporaries seem to have been sympathetic to women's attraction to what one character in *The Country Wife* (1675) termed 'the innocent liberty of the town', on the whole the opinion-makers of Augustan England seem to have seen every woman as a potential 'naughty town-woman', attracted to the urban environment by expectations of a liberty that was likely to be very far from innocent.

para. 13

And yet in holding up the image of health, wholesome and rosy-cheeked countrywomen as the epitome of innocence and domestic virtue, such critics were ignoring the reality of rural life. The steady migration of women into the towns was the logical consequence of conventional perceptions of femininity and of correct female behaviour, perceptions which inflicted on country gentlewomen nothing worse than boredom but which made the lives of poor women a constant struggle for survival against the odds. In the towns, in contrast, these odds were tilted slightly in women's favour.

INDEX

abbreviations in note taking
   98–100, 105
abstract learning 46
abstractness in writing 53
academic
   disciplines 53, 54
   journals 280
   knowledge, access to 53–4, 255
   values 54
   voice 63, 64, 122
academic discourse 53, 54–8, 255
academic style of writing 52–8,
   79–81, 153, 180
   detached stance 80–1
   see also writing
accommodation for studying 38–9
active engagement in reading 69, 71,
   86–90
age and memory 110–11
alternative schools of thought 91–2
amenities, making use of 40
analysis
   in studying 45
   of texts 233, 235–9, 244–7, 253
   in writing 57, 58, 79
anxiety before examinations 42, 302–3
arguments
   getting the gist of 59, 76,
     83, 100
   setting up 56, 58
   structure of 91
arguments in essays
   arguing to a conclusion 165–6
   explaining 171
   frames of reference 167
   illustrating 171–2
   introducing your own ideas 168–9
   link words 213–15
   linking points together 164–5
   making a case for 254–6
   presenting 163–71
   providing evidence 172, 174–5
   signposting 215–16
arts and humanities
   conventions in the arts 242–3

cultural traditions 227–8
different subjects in 225–7
studying 224–5, 227–30
text analysis 233, 235–9
assignments *see* coursework; essays
assumptions
   academic disciplines 53
   academic writing 53
   evaluating texts and 248–9
asynchronous conferencing 131
audience
   addressing an 138, 142–3
   sense of 184, 211
audio 21, 149–50
authors, confidence in 90

balance, importance in life 33
beginnings
   of essays 159–60
   of presentations 142
beliefs, influencing judgement
   259–62
belonging in a group 43, 134–5
bibliographies 55, 205, 279, 280
books 88–9, 305
bookshops 40
brainstorming 198–9
breaks, taking 203

calendar, course 35–6
card indexes 74–5, 96, 298
case studies 148, 150
charts, study week 33–4, 35–6
collective thinking 122
communicating your ideas from texts
   253–9
computers
   communications 19
   equipment needs 17–18
   getting started 18–19
   taking precautions 19, 20
   uses of 16–17, 20, 23
   see also Information and
     Communications Technology;
     software

concentration
  essay writing and 202–3
  keeping up 37
  lack of 7–9
  listening and 62
  span when reading 85
concept cards, index system 74–5
conceptualising 15, 46
conclusions of essays 165–6
conferencing, online *see* online
  conferencing
connections between points 122, 164–5
consistency, grammatical 178–9
context
  essays and 186
  for reading 91
controlled learners 14
conventions in the arts 242–3
Cornell notes system 102–4
course calendar 35–6
course materials
  drawing on for essays 185, 193–5
  failure to use in examinations
    290–1
  revising *see* revision
coursework
  breadth of 28
  management of 29–32
  planning ahead 35–6
  see also essays
creative writing 153
creativity, support for 115–16
credits, system of 32
crises while studying 28–9, 42
criticism
  evaluating texts 250–2
  judging writing 156, 218–19
  in reading 90–3
  from tutors 219–20
  in writing 57, 58
culture
  cultural traditions 227–8
  definition 228
  interpreting texts from other
    cultures 240

databases *see* online information;
  websites

debate, in writing 55, 58
deep learning 14, 152
delivery of presentations 143
dialogue 63, 119
diary, study 16
dictionaries 74, 180, 264–6
difficulties
  with group discussion 126–8
  with reading 69, 70–1, 72–3,
    75–9, 89–90
disciplines, academic 53, 54
discussion
  after presentations 143
  classroom 125–8
  momentum in 63
distractions 8, 9, 27, 36–7
  avoidance of 202–3
drafts of essays 201–6
dyslexia 93, 104

editing essays 200–1, 202
educational gaps, and
  examinations 287
eLearning 20–2, 23
electronic notes *see* outliners
Ellis, Joyce, ' "On the Town":
  Women in Augustan England'
  6, 312–15
  academic style of writing 52,
    53, 55–7
  making notes from 95–100,
    113–14
  memorisation and 106–7
  reading of 69–73, 75–8, 79–81,
    82–3, 86–7, 90–2
  students' essays about 155–73,
    174–83, 186–8
  writing techniques 213–17
email 17, 19
employers, role in lifelong
  learning 6
encyclopaedias, specialist 279
endings
  of essays 160
  of presentations 142
environment for study 38,
  39, 81–2
equipment for study 38–9, 82

essays
    answering the question 159–60,
        165, 174–5
    arguments, presenting *see*
        arguments in essays
    basic principles of essay writing
        222–3
    criticism 219–20
    definition 153
    drafts 201–6
    editing 200–1, 202
    eight stages of writing 191, 206–8
    explanation in 171–3, 192–3
    fluency in 210–11, 213–17
    getting organised for writing
        193–4, 195–6
    good essay, criteria for
        writing 222
    good qualities 186–8
    ideas 168–9, 185–6, 196–9, 254–6
    involvement of course materials
        in 185, 193–5
    language in 175–82, 213–16
    learning, role in 64
    length of 199, 201
    plagiarism 173–4, 185, 271
    presenting 181–2
    'speaking' to your reader 183–4
    structure of 160–3, 199–201
    style of 182–6
    titles of 159–60, 191–3, 196–8
    what is required 155–9
    word-processing of 181
    words used in 64, 179–80, 185–6
    writing of 153–4
    see also writing
eTuition 22
European Computer Driving Licence
    (ECDL) 20
evaluation
    of images 275–7, 280
    of texts 247–53
    of websites 269–70
evidence
    communicating, from
        texts 256–9
    in essays 172, 174–5
    in writing 57, 58, 91

examination questions
    how to tackle 305–9
    identify key questions 297
    not answering 290
    understanding 287
    using course materials 290–1
examinations
    bad use of time 291
    using course materials 305
    doing yourself justice 309–10
    failing 285–6
    myths about 285–9
    positive side of 284–5
    preparation for 301–4
    presentation of answers 292
    revision for 114, 293–300
    rubric 292
    stress 42, 284, 285, 288–9, 302–3
    tactics for 304–9
    using past papers 293–4, 299
experimental approach to writing 210
experts, learning from 61
explanation in essays 171–3, 192–3

facts
    memorisation 107
    overuse in examination
        answers 291
failure in examinations 285–6
feedback
    from assignments 64, 219–20
    from discussions 63
    from tutors 154, 155, 181, 187–8,
        189, 219–20
fellow students
    different kinds of 123
    in group learning 22, 125–30
    group visits and 144–5
    keeping in touch with 300
    morale boosted by 43, 123
    social support 10–11, 13,
        123, 300
figures, memorising 107
filing systems 39
    electronic 17, 23
    importance of 12
    for notes 117, 280
    web addresses 266–7

first sentences, skimming 82–3
fluency in essays 210–11, 213–17
frames of reference
    of arguments in essays 167
    when reading 60
    when speaking 61
freewriting 209–10

galleries, image resources of 274, 275
gateways, internet 268–9
gist
    of argument 59, 76, 83, 100
    of text in reading 108
Google 264, 267, 268, 273
grammar
    in essays 175–82, 214
    grammar checking 18, 177
    role of eLearning 21–2
grids, organising information
    in 111–13, 114
'group chemistry' 124
group learning 120–38
    advantages of 62–3, 65
    collective progress 122, 124
    difficult experiences 125–6
    doubts and fears 126–8
    good experiences 125
    how it works 121–3
    maximising gain from 133–7
    online 19, 22, 130–4
    students' expectations 128–30
    types of 120–1
    variability of 123–4
    see also presentations
group presentations 143–4
group visits 144–5
grouping information, for
    memorisation 109, 111–13

handouts in lectures 102, 105
handwriting, speed in
    examinations 288
help with studies 28–9, 137–8, 154
highlighting words
    in essay titles 192–3, 194
    in examinations 306
    whilst note taking 71, 73, 83,
        86–8, 89

hints and tips
    lecture notes 104–6
    for studying 4, 5–6
holist learners 13–14
humanities see arts and humanities

ideas
    brainstorming 198–9
    communicating, from texts
        253–9
    engaging with new 58, 61–2
    essays, introducing into 168–9,
        185–6, 254–6
    essays, planning 196–9
    expressing in writing 209–12
    in group discussion 121, 122
    from learning 46–7, 49, 50
    from listening 61–2
    from note taking 115–16
    from talking 119, 121
identity, sense of 64
images
    evaluating 275–7, 280
    searching for 273–5
impulsive learners 14
incentives 45
independent learning 13, 28
index cards 74–5, 96, 298
information
    developing information skills
        263–4
    information literacy 263, 264
    versus knowledge 270–1
    overload 41
    sources of 47
    structuring of 109–10
    see also online information
Information and Communications
    Technology (ICT) 16–23
    accreditation 20
    equipment needs 17–18
    intellectual property, theft
        of 271–2
    skills needed 18–20
    see also software
intellectual property, theft
    of 271–2
internet access 17, 23

interpreting meanings of texts
    239–47, 253, 255
introduction to essays 201–2
investment
    of time 85
    in yourself 3–7, 24

journals, academic 280
judgement
    beliefs and theories influencing
        259–62
    evaluation of texts 247–53
    judging writing 156, 218–19
    in essay arguments 169–71

key concepts in note taking 96, 100,
    102, 103, 105
key skills 7
    ICT skills 16, 20
knowledge
    accessing academic 53–4, 255
    becoming knowledgeable 65–6
    capturing 95–106
    versus information 270–1
    from learning 48–9
    organisation of 111–14
    using 43
    see also learning
Kolb's reflective learning cycle 14, 15,
    16, 45, 69

language
    everyday in essays 180
    link words in writing 213–15
    'proper' English 175–82
    signposting in essays 215–16
    of subject areas 122
layout of essays 205–6
learning
    aspects of 50–2
    assignments, role of 64
    audiovisual media and 148–51
    definition 50
    eLearning 20–2, 23
    gaining of knowledge 48–9
    independently 13, 28
    in lectures 146, 147
    lifelong 6, 24

from listening 61–2, 65
managing the work 29–32
new ideas 46–7, 49, 50, 58, 61–2
from reading 59, 65, 83–4, 92–3
reflective 14–16, 45
speaking and 62–3, 65, 119
from study 49–50
taking responsibility for 12, 26–9
types of learner 13–14
writing and 63–4, 65, 152, 191–2
see also group learning;
    knowledge; studying
lecture notes
    Cornell system 102–4
    tips on making 104–6, 147
lectures 104–5, 146–7
libraries 40
    online resources 16–17, 270, 274
lifelong learning 6, 24
link words in writing 213–15
listening
    challenges of 62, 65
    in group discussion 135
    ideas from 61–2
    learning by 61–2, 65
    to lectures 104–5, 146–7
    to music 231–2
lists
    of references 55, 173, 204–5, 280
    To Do 30–2, 44–5
literature searching 55
    see also online searching
'living' disciplines 226
lyric poems 243, 244, 246, 250, 252

management
    abbreviations in note taking
        98–100, 105
    of group discussion 120, 123–4
    of morale 9, 12, 41–4, 45
    self-management 44–5
    of tasks 28, 29–32, 37
    of time 3, 9, 28, 32–8
meaning
    explaining in essays 171–3, 192–3
    interpreting, of texts 239–47, 253,
        255
    link words clarifying 213–15

'making meaning' from texts
245–6
memorisation
of course notes 297
facts, names and figures 107
grouping information 109, 111–13
spelling 180–1
techniques 108–10
of text 106–7
memory
and examinations 287–8
how it works 108–10
important points 106–7
worries about 110–11
mental powers, before examinations
302
mind mapping 104, 113–14, 198, 298
mistakes
grammatical 176–7, 178–9
spelling 180–1
mnemonics in memorisation 110
morale
lifting of 42–4, 65, 123
lowering of 41–2, 101
management of 9, 12, 41–4, 45
museums, image resources of 274
music, listening to 231–2
myths about examinations 285–9

names, using 107, 291
'nausea' when writing 221
'nesting' of information 109
netiquette 133
note taking 94–118
capturing knowledge 95–106
for essays 194–5, 196–9, 212
highlighting words 71, 73, 83,
86–8, 89
ideas from 115–16
key concepts 96, 100, 102, 103, 105
and learning 51, 62
memory and 106–11
organising knowledge 111–14
when reading 70, 71
notes
for capturing ideas 115
comprehensive 98–9
detailed 100–1

in examinations 306
lecture notes 102–6, 147
in the margins 88–9
outliners 96–8, 116, 198–9, 200
for project work 280
from reading 95–102
revision and 297
strategies for 106, 117, 118
summary notes 297–9

objectivity 57, 58, 270
obstacles when reading 73–82
'"On the Town": Women in
Augustan England' see Ellis, Joyce
online conferencing 19, 131–4
online dictionaries 74, 264–6
online information
eLearning materials 21
evaluating 267–70
finding 40, 264–9
image resources 273–5
libraries 16–17, 270, 274
misuse of 270–2
online searching
advanced searches 268
developing skills 263–4
finding academic material
267–70
project work and 272–7, 280
quick search 264–6, 267–8
see also search engines
open-endedness
in discussion groups 120
in writing 210, 220
Open University PROMPT evaluation
270
openings of essays 159–60
organisation
of essays 193–4, 195–6, 199–201
of knowledge 111–14
of papers for revision 294–5
of self 12–13
of work 29–32
outliners 96–8, 116, 198–9, 200, 298–9
overhead projectors 140

paragraphs in essays 161–3, 216–17
paraphrasing 75–6, 90

participation in group discussion 125–8
performance
    in essay writing 186–7
    in examinations 284
personal development 43
picture agencies 273–4
plagiarism 56, 98, 173–4, 185, 271
planning
    the course weeks 35–6
    essay process 193–4, 199–201
    of presentations 140
    project work 279–80
    sticking to plans 36–7
    for study 14–15, 26–8
    time in examinations 301–2, 307, 308
    the workload 29–30
    see also strategies
poetry
    analysis of 233, 235–9, 244–7
    evaluating 247–52
    interpreting meanings of 239–47
portals, internet 268–9
Poussin, Nicolas, Landscape with a Man Killed by a Snake 243, 244
PowerPoint software 140–1
practical learning 46, 121
precision, in writing 57, 58
preparation
    answers in exams 306–7
    for exams 301–4
    for group discussion 135
    of presentations 139–42
presentation
    of answers in exams 292, 308
    of essays 181–2
    of information 270
presentations
    by students 138–9
    on the day 142–3
    group 143–4
    practising 142
    preparation for 139–42
primary sources 47, 144, 224
printers 17
private-public conundrum in writing 218–19

process words 193
progress, collective 122, 124
project work
    carrying out 277–82
    formulating a question 278–9
    online groups and 133
    planning 279–80
    research skills 281–2
    using online research in 272–7, 280
    writing the report 280–1
PROMPT evaluation checklist 270
provenance of websites 270
publishers, quality of 90
punctuation 21, 22, 176, 177–8

Qualification and Curriculum Authority (QCA) 7, 20
questions
    answering in essays 159–60, 165, 174–5
    critical, on text 90–2
    in examinations see examination questions
    formulating for project 278–9
    identification in revision 297
    setting your own 77, 89
    spotting the underlying question 76–7
quotations 172–3, 256–7

Raphael, The Madonna and Child with the Infant Baptist 233, 234, 257
readers, writing for 183–4, 215–16
reading
    academic level versus everyday 59–60, 69, 79
    actively 69, 71, 86–90
    around lectures 146–7
    challenges of 59–60, 65
    critically 90–3
    difficulties with 69, 70–1, 72–3, 75–9, 89–90
    examination questions 305
    experience of 69–73
    getting stuck 89–90
    learning through 59, 65, 83–4, 92–3

notes, making from 95–102
obstacles to 73–82
process of 59–60, 69
speed of 82–6
texts 230–1
this book 3–4, 5, 6
time for 85–6
reading aloud 211, 236
references
automating 18–19
to 'linear' texts 257–8
listing 55, 173, 204–5, 280
in websites 270
reflective learning 14–16, 45
relevance of websites 270
responsibility for your studies 12,
26–9
revision
excess before exams 288
fellow students and 300
identify key questions 297
mind mapping 114, 298
organisation of papers 294–5
past exam questions 293–4,
299
point of 293
selectivity 296–7
strategy 295
summary sheets 297–9
timetable 295–6
when to start 293
rubric, examination 292
rules
of grammar, breaking 214
in group discussion 126–7,
129–30
for listening 232
in presentations 139

SAFARI website 270
scholarship, in writing 55–6, 58
search engines 264–6, 268, 271
searching see online searching
secondary sources 47, 144, 224, 256
for project work 279–80
self-development 6–7, 43
self-help groups 137–8
self-management, successful 44–5

sentences 175–7
consistency in 178–9
first, skimming 82–3
length of in essays 216–17
serialist learners 13–14
signposting in essays 215–16
skills see key skills; study skills
skimming when reading 82–3, 89
slides for presentations 140–2, 143
social arrangements while studying
40–1
social support 43–4
fellow students 10–11, 13, 123, 300
online conferencing 131–2,
133–4
software
index cards 75
learning use of 19, 20
for presentations 140–1
for references 18–19
types needed 18
web browsing 264–6
see also word processing
speaking see talking
special needs 93, 104
specialist terms 74
speed of reading 82–6
spelling 180–1
spoken word 58, 62–3, 119
see also talking
spontaneity, speaking and 62–3
strategies
essay writing 195
memorisation 108–10
note taking 106, 117, 118
revision 295
self-management 44
using time 34–6
see also planning
stress of examinations 42, 284, 285,
288–9, 302–3
structure
creating 43
of essays 160–3, 199–201
in group discussion 120
of information 109–10
study diary 16
study environment 38, 39, 81–2

'study kit' 38–9
study skills
    acquiring 12–13, 24
    ICT skills 18–20
    investing in 7
    need of 4
    practising 122
    project research 281–2
    reflective learning 14–16, 45
study week charts 33–4, 35–6
studying
    arts and humanities 224–5,
        227–30
    challenge of 7–12, 24
    equipment for 38–9
    learning from 49–50
    managing the work 29–32
    objects of 47
    planning 14–15
    social arrangements 40–1
    taking responsibility for 12, 26–9
    time management 32–8
    ways of 4
    see also learning
style, essay 182–6
    see also academic style of
        writing
subjects, different arts and humanities
    225–7
summarising, when listening 62
summary cards 96
summary notes for revision 297–9
surface learning 14
symbols in note taking 98–9

talking
    challenges of 63, 65
    in group discussion 135–6
    listening to 145–51
    as morale booster 10–11, 43–4
    as part of learning 13, 62–3, 65
    'speaking' to your reader 183–4
    see also presentations
tasks
    breaking down 30
    completion 14–16, 37
    managing 28, 29–32, 37
    scheduling 28

texts 228–30
    analysis of 233, 235–9,
        244–7, 253
    becoming familiar with 230–2
    communicating ideas about 253–9
    evaluating 247–53
    form of 242–3
    interpreting meanings of
        239–47, 253, 255
    'linear' texts 257–8
    personal response to 251–2
    representing visual and symbolic
        257
    studying multiple 258
    understanding 253
    your reaction to 231
theories, influencing judgement
    259–62
thinking
    aloud 13
    collectively 122
    before examinations 301, 302
    on paper 94
    speed in examinations 288
    whilst reading 84, 91–2
    for yourself 92
    see also ideas
time
    bad use in examinations 291
    creating 33–4
    essays and 194
    management 3, 9, 28, 32–8
    planning for exams 301–2, 307
    planning for revision 295–6
    and reading speed 84–6
    running out of, in exams 308
    strategic use of 34–6
    timing presentations 142, 143
timeliness of websites 270
titles of essays 159–60, 191–3
    noting ideas for 196–8
To Do lists 30–2, 44–5
transparencies for presentations
    140–2, 143
tutorials 22, 132
tutors
    comments on essays 154, 155, 181,
        187–8, 189

criticism from 219–20
learning from 13
management of group discussion
    120, 123–4
role in group learning 128–30
support from 43
typing 19, 20

UK Quality Assurance Agency for
    Higher Education 32
underlining words *see* highlighting
    words
understanding
    in examinations 287
    in group discussion 126
    from learning 8–9, 43, 50–2
    when reading 59–60, 76–9, 89–90
    studying texts and 253, 255
unfamiliar words 52–3, 71, 73–5
university, challenges of 26–9

values
    academic 54
    represented by a text 247–50
video 21, 148–9, 150
virtual learning environments 22, 23,
    40
visits, group 144–5
visualisation, in memorisation 109, 110
voice
    academic 63, 64, 122
    essay writing 184, 209–10

websites 16, 40
    evaluating 269–70
    filing web addresses 266–7
    gateways and portals 268–9
    images, searching for 273–4
    student homepage 22–3
    see also online information

word processing
    essay writing 181
    grammar checking 18, 177
    outliners 96–8, 116, 198–9, 200,
        298–9
    tables 112–13
    typing 19, 20
words
    choosing 179–80
    counting 18
    link words 213–15
    looking up 73–4, 76
    unfamiliar 52–3, 71, 73–5
    writing your own 64, 185–6
work habits 33–5
writing
    academic style of *see* academic
        style of writing
    'against the clock' 300
    challenges of 64–5, 79–80,
        190–1
    developing skills 152, 154
    different kinds of 153
    experience of 217–21
    expressing ideas in 209–12
    getting help with 154
    getting to grips with 152–4
    importance of 152–3
    judging 156, 218–19
    learning through 63–4, 65,
        152, 191–2
    open attitude to 210, 220
    private *versus* public 218–19
    for readers 183–4, 215–16
    speed in examinations 288
    style 182–6
    'voice' 184, 209–10
    words, using your own 64,
        185–6
    see also essays